THE ENTERTAINMENT INDUSTRY: AN INTRODUCTION

THE ENTERTAINMENT INDUSTRY: AN INTRODUCTION

Edited by
Stuart Moss

Tourism and Entertainment Subject Group
Leeds Metropolitan University
Leeds
UK

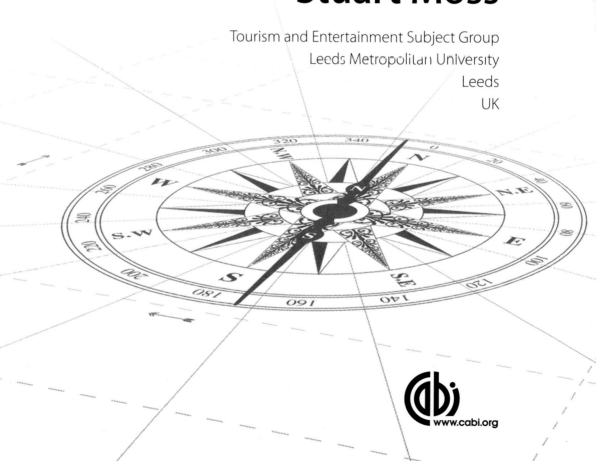

www.cabi.org

CABI is a trading name of CAB International

CABI Head Office
Nosworthy Way
Wallingford
Oxfordshire OX10 8DE
UK

Tel: +44 (0)1491 832111
Fax: +44 (0)1491 833508
E-mail: cabi@cabi.org
Website: www.cabi.org

CABI North American Office
875 Massachusetts Avenue
7th Floor
Cambridge, MA 02139
USA

Tel: +1 617 395 4056
Fax: +1 617 354 6875
E-mail: cabi-nao@cabi.org

A catalogue record for this book is available from the British Library, London, UK.

Library of Congress Cataloging-in-Publication Data

The entertainment industry : an introduction / edited by Stuart Moss.
     p. cm.
 Includes bibliographical references and index.
 ISBN 978-1-84593-551-1 (alk. paper)
1. Amusements. 2. Performing arts. I. Moss, Stuart, 1972-II. Title.

GV1471.E48 2010
790.1068--dc22

                              2009021471

ISBN–13: 978 1 84593 551 1

Typeset by SPi, Pondicherry, India.
Printed and bound in the UK by Cambridge Univresity Press, Cambridge.

The paper used for the text pages in this book is FSC certified. The FSC (Forest Stewardship Council) is an international network to promote responsible management of the world's forests.

CONTENTS

Contents

FOREWORD

One can only guess how, where and when it may have happened, but it was probably a lightning strike upon a tree in Africa around 200,000 years ago that caused the first fire to be seen by the earliest relatives of modern humans. It may have taken thousands more years, but eventually at some point in prehistory, our ancestors began to understand how fire worked so that its power could be harnessed and used for warmth, light, cooking, security…and entertainment. Some anthropologists believe that the mesmeric dance of flames captivated those who would huddle around fires in the darkness, moulding early humans' thinking skills and helping to develop imagination. At some point in prehistory, and fired by imagination the storyteller was born, both verbally in spoken language and song, and visually painted onto the walls of caves. Stories may have been about everyday life and routine occurrences, but the firing of the imagination would certainly have helped to create exaggerations, and from these fictitious accounts, legends were born.

Humans sat around fires for thousands of years, and still do today, especially in parts of the non-industrialized world, where indigenous people still live their lives as their ancestors have done for many generations before. This along with rituals such as singing and dancing is what passes time after a day performing routine tasks such as hunting, gathering firewood, building homes and cooking.

Throughout the centuries, audiences have watched, clapped and cheered various types of performances, from displays of dancing or athleticism, to musicians playing instruments, stories being told, and gladiatorial slaughter. As technologies developed, buildings were constructed in which audiences could be housed in a purpose-built theatre to witness, hear and experience such spectacles.

The development of the written word, followed centuries later by the first books, and rises in literacy meant that audiences could easily mentally escape into another world as their minds processed words into images.

Invention, innovation and commodification in the industrialized world (particularly Europe and North America) have seen the creation of devices that were specifically designed to captivate audiences. Still and moving image projection, recorded sound, cinema, radio, television and the telephone all have their origins over a century ago, and throughout the 20th century flourished due to a continual cycle of reinvention, innovation and creativity. Societal changes, including industrialization, urbanization, rises in disposable income and available leisure time, changing fashions, the rise of the 'experience economy' and a growing consumer demand to be kept entertained have lead to the development of numerous industries with one common goal – to captivate audiences, and to be paid for doing so. By the mid-20th century, the burgeoning availability of home electrical entertainment devices meant that the fireplace was demoted and the television (and later its associated peripherals) was promoted into being the focal point for communal rooms in the home.

Away from the home, visitor attractions began to be developed; these included amusement and theme parks, museums, and restored historical buildings and sites. As time went by, these became more elaborate; theme parks developed rides that were seemingly death-defying, which captivated riders and spectators alike; while other visitor attractions found new methods by which to captivate audiences. Museums moved from static displays in cases to showing interpretive movies, and having interactive exhibits.

As businesses flourished, some with divisions in broadcasting, printed media, cinema and visitor attractions, takeovers occurred and major corporations formed, all sitting comfortably with their captivated audiences happily handing over money for products and services. Then, in 1995, something happened that would transform many of these entertainment organizations forever. Microsoft released an operating system for personal computers (PCs) called Windows 95. This alone did not send ripples around the entertainment industry, but it did offer a view into the looking glass of what was to follow by containing two multimedia music videos: 'Good Times' by Edie Brickell and 'Buddy Holly' by Weezer, both of which played on the operating system's 'Media Player' programme. Something else that Windows 95 contained was a program by the name of 'Internet Explorer', which could browse through the then hundreds of thousands of interlinked pages on the World Wide Web. Internet Explorer was by no means the first Web browser, but it was the first to be mass-produced with a commercially available operating system, which took the Internet out of the domain of scientists and enthusiasts, and into the hands of the general public.

Due to the slowness of dial-up access to the Internet, early web pages were largely text-based, text that is written is copyright of the author. Therefore, when early web pages created by fans and uploaded onto servers contained reproduced scripts from television series such as *Monty Python*, alarm bells should maybe have begun to ring. As technologies developed, fan pages on the Internet went on to include photographs that were scanned in from magazines, another clear breach of copyright. Many organizations were slow to enforce copyright, simply because of the newness of what was happening, and their lateness to catch on to it, many simply did not believe in it.

This early age of Internet innocence all changed around about the turn of the millennium, when affordable broadband sped up Internet access; making it possible to transfer large files quickly. Suddenly the focus of the Internet began to change as people began to actively seek and download content such as music and movies. Peer-to-peer file-sharing programs appeared such as Napster that allowed for files to be shared with other users of the same peer-to-peer network, illegal downloading and piracy burgeoned, making the industry take note of what was going on, as the MP3 became king.

In the 21st century, the pace of change has been even more frenetic, with the convergence of the Internet and other media and communication platforms leading to a truly mobile entertainment experience. This century so far has seen mobile phones become multimedia devices, audiences flocking to (and spending hours upon) online social networking communities such as Facebook, analogue media largely deceasing in favour of digital electronic formats, on-demand television content being made available via the Internet, and high-definition television in our homes.

The entertainment industry is vast, encompassing areas as diverse as hip hop to opera, theme parks to tall towers, and ballet to bird hides. It is moving at a faster pace than ever before, where a continuous cycle of invention and innovation drives once disparate areas together, creating global mega-brands, whose primary goals remain unchanged – to captivate audiences, and to be rewarded for doing so. Influences in the external social, technological, economical, environmental, political, legal and ethical (STEEPLE) environments have largely dictated and transformed how, where and when this occurs, and will continue to do so. How business and organizations within the entertainment industry adapt to these continuous changes, will largely dictate whether or not they survive in this highly charged and increasingly competitive business environment....Welcome to the entertainment industry!

LIST OF FIGURES

LIST OF TABLES

chapter 1

An Introduction to the Entertainment Industry

Stuart Moss

> *Entertainment is something that can engage or captivate an audience through sensory stimulation, which can invoke an emotional response amongst that audience.*

Historically the word 'entertainment' has served a number of definitions going back over 500 years, many of which are now obsolete or rarely used. Current and relevant definitions of entertainment include: 'that which affords interest or amusement' (OED, 2008); 'an activity that is diverting and that holds the attention' (Wordnet, 2008); and 'amusement or diversion provided especially by performers' (*Merriam-Webster*, 2008). Entertainment can be found in a plethora of guises, from that which is intentionally provided for an audience such as a stage show, to one of nature's spectacles such as flocks of migrating birds. The commonality between these two examples of entertainment is that they are both capable of diverting the attention of an audience, i.e. captivating, quite possibly in an amusing or agreeable way. The key difference is that a stage show is put on with the specific intention of captivating or holding the attention of an audience, whereas flocks of birds do not migrate with the intention of captivating an audience, they are just doing what comes naturally to them, but because we do not see this phenomenon regularly, it is novel and it has the ability to be captivating.

AN EMOTIONAL RESPONSE

Entertainment is a humanistic concept; as human beings we are drawn or engaged by sensory inputs to our bodies: sight, sound, touch, taste and smell. Our bodies are capable of processing these inputs mentally into thoughts and emotions, which in turn can generate physiological outputs such as laughter, screams, smiles, raised eyebrows, frowns and flinching. People differ, so the degree to which we are drawn or engaged by sensory inputs can vary greatly from one person to the next, as can the way in which we react to these inputs.

One of the key determinants in deciding whether something should be considered as being entertainment is whether or not it can invoke an emotional response among audience members. An emotion is 'a reaction involving certain physiological changes, such as an accelerated or retarded pulse rate, the diminished or increased activities of certain glands, or a change in body temperature, which stimulate the individual, or some component part of the body, to further activity' (MSN Encarta, 2008). Emotions can be both positive (pleasing) and negative (displeasing) in nature. We feel emotion through external sensory stimuli. Not everything that stimulates our senses is entertainment, but anything that can engage or captivate an audience through sensory stimulation that can invoke an emotional response among an audience very often is entertainment. Figure 1.1 highlights some of the most common emotions that audience members experience while being entertained.

Common emotions associated with entertainment

Positive						Negative
Adoration	Affection	Acceptance	Anticipation	Agitation	Aggravation	Agony
Amazement	Attraction	Amusement	Astonishment	Anxiety	Annoyance	Anger
Bliss	Bonded	Assurance	Awe	Anxious	Bitterness	Disgust
Delight	Confident	Calm	Comprehension	Apprehension	Consternation	Dread
Desire	Courage	Caring	Surprise	Boredom	Contempt	Fright
Ecstasy	Dignity	Cheer	Thoughtful	Dejection	Depression	Fury
Elation	Eager	Compassion		Disappointment	Despair	Hatred
Euphoria	Empowered	Content		Displeasure	Despondent	Horror
Exhilaration	Enjoyment	Elegance		Distress	Disliking	Insulted
Glee	Enthralled	Empathy		Embarrassed	Dissatisfaction	Mortified
Infatuation	Excitement	Eustress		Envy	Disturbed	Outrage
Inspiration	Happiness	Friendship		Exasperation	Fear	Panic
Love	Jolliness	Gladness		Frustration	Greed	Shock
Lust	Joy	Gratified		Grumpiness	Grief	Suffering
Motivation	Liking	Harmonious		Guilt	Hostility	Terror
Victorious	Longing	Honourable		Insecurity	Humiliation	Torment
	Positivity	Hope		Irritation	Loathing	Vengefulness
	Pride	Interest		Jealousy	Misery	
	Relaxation	Nostalgia		Nervousness	Mourning	
	Respect	Optimism		Regret	Remorse	
	Satisfaction	Pleasure		Resentment	Revulsion	
	Security	Relief		Rivalry	Sadness	
	Thankful	Responsible		Troubled	Scorn	
	Thrill	Sentimental		Unease	Shame	
	Wonder	Sympathy		Worry	Woe	

Fig. 1.1. Common emotions associated with entertainment.

There is a popular misconception that entertainment is something that has to be 'funny' or pleasing – this is simply not the case at all, but stems historically from the usage of the word 'entertainment' to describe 'light entertainment', which predominantly covers the stage, comedy, song and variety. In the broadcast media, light entertainment was often a series of short performances that were designed to engage and amuse, without being too 'heavy going', or requiring too much attention. Light entertainment was also generally intended to be non-offensive – therefore, it provoked predominantly positive emotions. Today, most broadcast media providers still have an 'entertainment' department that is responsible for comedy, music and popular culture output; there are also 'news', 'current affairs', 'politics' and 'sports' departments (as well as others). It is the remit of all these departments to provide entertainment for their audiences in that their output is intended to engage or captivate an audience through audio-visual stimulation, which can invoke an emotional response. However, it is typically the remit of the entertainment department to provide output that is intended to invoke predominantly positive emotions among audiences. All of this fuels the theory that entertainment should be 'fun', but there is a great deal of entertainment that provokes negative emotions, including anger, fear and grief.

Not every film that is produced for the big screen is a comedy or a 'feel-good' film, provoking pleasing emotions; many do just the opposite – Steven Spielberg's 1993 film *Schindler's List*, was based upon the true story of Oscar Schindler, a member of the German Nazi party who was also an industrialist and saved the lives of many Jews during the Second World War. The film depicted brutal and realistic footage of what life was like for those in concentration camps. In cinemas, the majority of audiences sat transfixed and in silence at the gruesome scenes unfolding before them. The film was not intended to impart positive emotions upon audience members (although the outcome of the film is positive in that Schindler succeeded in saving many Jewish lives), it was designed to educate using the medium of film to tell a true story that invoked grief, outrage, anger, disgust and dread among audience members with brutal and graphic scenes of murder and suffering. *Schindler's List* was voted the ninth best American film of all time by the American Film Institute (BBC, 1998); this is testimony to how effectively it achieved its aims, and how audiences were engaged and affected emotionally by the film.

The quality of entertainment is often measured by an audience to the degree that it invokes an emotional response among that audience – this leads to opinion. The degree to which we are emotionally affected by entertainment typically influences our opinion of how good or bad we think it is. Dore (2002) in Lieberman and Esgate (2002) states that 'everyone seems to have an opinion…because the (entertainment) industry is open and available for public critique' (p. xv). If after watching a stand-up comedian a member of the audience stated 'that was really funny', it would suggest that the person thought the comedian was good, which contains a suggestion of recommendation. By watching a show that is 'labelled' a comedy, this person expected to feel positive emotions, including happiness, amusement, joy and glee. These emotions are then physically transformed by the audience into laughter and applause; a comedian that doesn't invoke an emotional response among the audience that results in laughter and applause is usually considered as being 'not funny' and therefore a 'poor' comedian – or low quality entertainment in the opinion of that audience.

Entertainment needs an audience, without one entertainment cannot exist. Most people would find horses kicking footballs a novel sight, and therefore quite entertaining, but if nobody was around to witness the phenomenon of football-kicking horses, then no entertainment took place, as no audience was entertained. Novelty is important in the entertainment industry. In other words, something that is not experienced commonly, so that when it does occur it diverts the attention of those who experience it, and thus they become an audience to that novelty. Novelty is the quality of being new, original or unusual, and a great deal of entertainment industry provision is novel; sword swallowers and stilt walkers are not everyday sites to most people, and therefore could prove to be a novel and entertaining spectacle. Novelty is one measure by which the quality of entertainment may be measured by an audience. The challenge is to present something that the audience will find novel so that they are entertained by it. The now defunct 'National Centre for Popular Music' in Sheffield, UK, was a museum that was praised for its novel building design, but slated for its unremarkable and dull exhibits, which led to low visitor numbers and eventually the Centre's closure (BBC, 2004). The buildings are now used by Sheffield Hallam University's Students Union, as an entertainment venue and the base of a radio station.

THE ENTERTAINMENT INDUSTRY

An industry is a 'systematic work or labour; habitual employment in some useful work, now esp. in the productive arts or manufactures' (OED, 2008). The word 'industry' describes a specific group of companies or businesses that work towards a common purpose. Internally an industry involves inputs (finance, raw materials, human capital); processes (production, packaging, marketing); and outputs (primary, secondary and tertiary products that are both tangible and intangible) (Kotler *et al.*, 2008). The collection of bodies that exist globally, which provide products (both tangible and intangible) that have a primary purpose of engaging or captivating an audience is the entertainment industry. Primary purpose is an important concept when defining whether a product or entity is a part of the entertainment industry. Not everything man-made, which we as individuals find entertaining, is within the entertainment industry; in order to highlight this point, the example of railway enthusiasts (train spotters) will be used. Railway enthusiasts are people who have an in-depth interest in railway trains and often gather at stations or by railway lines to watch trains pass by, sometimes keeping a record of the numbers on the side of locomotives and carriages. Railway enthusiasts find trains very entertaining in a way that most people would not. Trains were created with the primary purpose of transporting people or freight from one location to another, and not as an entertainment product; therefore, they are not within the entertainment industry. With that said, if a novel type of train such as a vintage steam locomotive was run, it could have a purpose of engaging an audience of enthusiasts (and interested others) through sensory stimulation (site, sounds and smell) of the train, which would give that type of train the right to claim that it is at least partially within the entertainment industry. Steam locomotives are no longer an everyday sight in the majority of industrialized nations, so when one is run it provides a novelty, the result of which is entertainment to those who are interested in it, and/or captivated by it.

An office block is not primarily an entertainment venue as it has not been created with the primary purpose of captivating an audience through sensory stimulation. If, however, an office was converted into an observation point, with informative and explanative displays that would facilitate an audience of people to experience city views – this would become an entertainment venue and is an example of the commodification of a resource for the purposes of audience appreciation and therefore entertainment. This example highlights the very thin line that exists between what falls within the entertainment industry, and what does not. Figure 1.2 denotes a view that is visually stimulating and quite captivating; however, the location from which it was taken (a footpath) is not a part of the entertainment industry.

The entertainment industry is vast. It encompasses 18 unique sectors, which are as follows: Staged Story and Variety; music; bars, pubs and clubs; cinema and film; broadcast media; audio-visual media; the internet; gaming; printed media; commercial gambling; spectator sports; thrillertainment; edutainment; sellertainment; culturtainment; spiritual entertainment; health entertainment and adult entertainment.

Within each sector of the entertainment industry, there are a plethora of sub-sectors providing thousands of types of entertainment products, running into millions of actually produced tangible and intangible products, worth around US$1 trillion annually (Vogel, 2007). Quite simply, the accumulated worth of all of the sub-sectors of the entertainment industry makes it the largest industry in the world, generating more revenue than any other industry. The entertainment industry is growing exponentially; the world in which we live is becoming increasingly industrialized, and recreation-seekers on the whole have greater amounts of both time and

Fig. 1.2. The view of the harbour from a footpath in Fira on the Greek island of Santorini.

disposable income, to spend on entertainment, which bodes well for the industry. The number of sectors within the entertainment industry will increase by number in future years, as tastes change, technology advances and products diversify, producing new 'specialisms'.

ENTERTAINMENT, CULTURE AND CREATIVITY

Culture can be taken as meaning a representation of a society at a particular time, and in a particular place. From an artistic perspective, the word 'cultural', meaning 'of or relating to intellectual and artistic pursuits' (OED, 2008), first appeared in the English language in the mid- to late nineteenth century. However, the recognition of the socio-economic importance of artists and their markets as a cultural industry was not formally recognized until 1947 by Adorno and Horkheimer (O'Connor, 2007). Cultural products have been created for the commercial market for centuries, but it is only in the last century that the production of cultural commodities has accelerated with the development of technologies of reproduction (O'Connor, 2007).

The creative industries are those that are based on individual creativity, skill and talent. They are also those that have the potential to create wealth and jobs through developing intellectual property (DCMS, 2008). Creative as an adjective comes from the verb 'create' which is 'to make, form, constitute, or bring into legal existence (an institution, condition, action, mental product, or form, not existing before)' (OED, 2008). The definition of 'creative' as an adjective given by the same source is 'having the quality of creating, given to creating; of pertaining to creation; or originative'. Therefore, the creative industries can be thought of as the collective of individuals, companies and businesses that are responsible for the production of original creative output. 'The creative industries are the key new growth sector of the economy, both nationally and globally' (Hesmondhalgh, 2007, p. 145). According to the DCMS (2008), the creative industries include: advertising; architecture; art and antiques markets; computer and video games; crafts; design; designer fashion; film and video; music; performing arts; publishing; software; and television and radio. This view differs slightly from UNESCO's, which states that the creative industries are primarily crafts, design, publishing, cinema and music (UNESCO, 2008). Those who create original creative products are often referred to as 'artists'; so the creative industries are primarily concerned with the production of original artistic output.

The views expressed by both the DCMS and UNESCO are respected globally, even though there are differences between them. Many of the sectors within the entertainment industry are creative in nature, in that they involve the creation of original intellectual property. Applying both the DCMS and UNESCO definitions as the basis as to what constitutes the creative industry to entertainment industry sectors, it can be seen which sectors are creative in their output and which sectors are not; those that are not creative can certainly be considered cultural based upon their propensity to be representative of the societies that they are within. Some entertainment industry sectors are both creative and cultural, in that their sub-sectors are a combination of both original artistic output, and products that are socially representative. This is highlighted in Fig. 1.3.

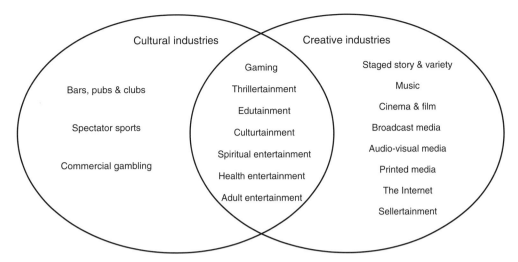

Fig. 1.3. Entertainment industry sectors within the context of the cultural and creative industries.

ENTERTAINMENT AND RECREATION

Entertainment is a recreational concept, relating to phenomena or activity that can hold the attention of those experiencing it. Those who experience entertainment are the audience, and an audience can be as large as a global television audience running into millions of people, or as small as one person having his or her palm read.

In terms of recreation, consider the word 'recreation' as re-creation as in re-making or re-constructing. According to psychologist Abraham Maslow, recreation serves a purpose that is essential to the fulfilment of our cognitive and aesthetic stimulation (Pigram and Jenkins, 1999), and is the process by which the mind and/or body can be rejuvenated through participation in pursuits that are considered as being satisfying or gratifying to self. These activities may include leisure pursuits, sports, hobbies, pastimes, and entertainment. Abraham Maslow created a hierarchy of needs (see Fig. 1.4), and this hierarchy is designed to demonstrate what humans need in order to survive and thrive. The lowest level of the pyramid denotes physical needs that our bodies must have in order to function. The next level denotes safety needs that we desire in order to have a sense of well-being. Above this are love and belonging, which are about our need to be with other people. This is followed by esteem, which is what we desire in order to feel positive within society about our accomplishments and contributions. The very top-level is self-actualization, this is where we can perform the 'extras' in our lives, where we as people can participate in activities for the sheer enjoyment and for no other reason, this is where recreation comes into our lives.

Recreation is often participated in by individuals to rejuvenate themselves outside of work and 'life's daily routine'; historically this free time has been described as 'leisure time' and all pursuits undertaken in this time (including entertainment) have been described as being 'leisure'.

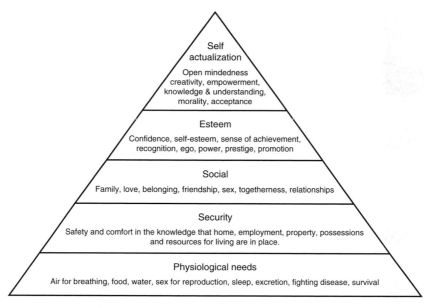

Fig. 1.4. Maslow's hierarchy of needs.

However, a clear distinction needs to be drawn as to what is entertainment and what is leisure; unfortunately, this is easier said than done and there is certainly a 'grey' area between these two modes of recreation. On a basic level, entertainment must have an audience, but this is not true of leisure which requires participants; some recreational pursuits such as 'gaming' require both and can claim to be both leisure and entertainment. This does cause confusion and the terms 'entertainment' and 'leisure' are often used and misused interchangeably, as in Fig. 1.5, where perhaps recreation, sport or leisure would have been a better choice of wording for people who organize volleyball matches for tourists to participate in.

The benefit of recreational participation is often positive mental and/or physical well-being. Recreational activities do not typically include the everyday functions that we perform to survive and live in our accustomed lifestyles. Tasks such as work, study, travel, sleep, eating, domestic chores, family and relationship responsibilities, and hygiene are not typically recreation, although there is an increasing 'blur' between the working and non-working parts of our lives (MINTEL, 2000) and this includes recreation. For many people the majority of hours in the day are taken up by the everyday functions listed above, but the few hours that remain can be used recreationally, including being entertained. This is highlighted in Fig. 1.6.

As a recreational activity, entertainment is enjoyed by people in their own time to satisfy a number of needs that are recreational in nature, for example listening to music or watching television may satisfy the need to relax, and reading a book or surfing the Internet may satisfy a thirst for knowledge. All forms of entertainment may satisfy the need to pass the time or alleviate boredom.

Fig. 1.5. 'Entertainment' misused?

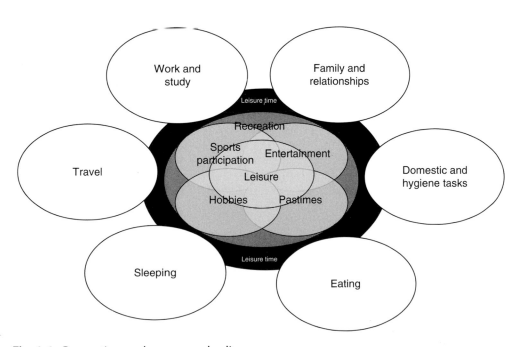

Fig. 1.6. Recreation and our everyday lives.

PENETRATION AND IMPACT

In a highly competitive industry, it is important that entertainment correctly serves its purpose, and is adequately promoted, so that those who are exposed to it, especially the target audience, get what they want, and if they do not, the result is often disappointment, and negative reviews. Entertainment provided by industry is something that we choose to participate in, wherein we are not bound by any law or means of survival to be entertained or to take up any entertainment product. The entertainment industry is one where there is a strong reliance on positive reviews and recommendation, and unfortunately for some organizations, 'getting it wrong' has and will continue to prove costly. Figure 1.7 highlights where entertainment products may be placed, based upon audience penetration, and how strong an emotional response audiences have to this entertainment. It must be highlighted though that people and their opinions of entertainment vary greatly, the matrix is based upon the metaphorical 'bigger picture', and it is entirely plausible that some individuals will disagree with the placement of certain products within the matrix.

A description of each triangle zone within the matrix now follows:

Flash Gun – sure to get an audience's attention, this is entertainment that is brash and readily accessible, but has a low emotional impact due to it being considered 'typical' and not particularly novel. Characteristically flash guns are loud and bright, but can be quite superficial and not intended to promote depth of thought or emotion. Popular music videos, short animations, cartoons in printed media, karaoke and billboard posters can all fit into this category.

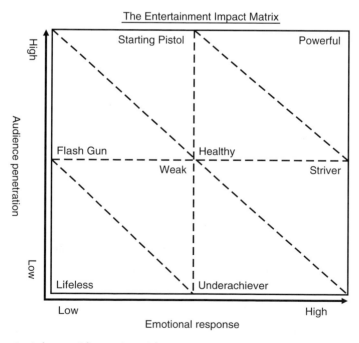

Fig. 1.7. The entertainment impact matrix.

Starting Pistol – very attention grabbing through the use of headlines and often extrovert media, starting pistols are commonplace and have a greater impact upon an audience than flash guns. However, this type of entertainment is not intended to have a significant long-lasting emotional effect. Television adverts, newspapers, magazines, news and current affairs broadcasts, much online entertainment, wrestling shows and some spectator sports events fit into this category.

Healthy – this is mainstream unashamedly commercial entertainment, which reaches the masses, and is well received by audiences, who find it engaging and emotive. Popular music and entertainment related to popular culture, mainstream cinema and film, television soap operas, theme parks, computer gaming, some staged story, many fiction book titles, and popular spectator sports fall into this category.

Powerful – these are the best-sellers, the legends, the biggest and the best. All forms of entertainments that have mass appeal and promote a strong emotive response among audiences. Powerful entertainment of all forms is extremely lucrative, and has a profound effect on audiences leading to strong recommendation to others. The most legendary films of all time, the best-selling books, the most popular television programmes, and the biggest-selling musicians are all within this category.

Lifeless – considered by audiences as the 'worst' kind of entertainment, this is typically not attention grabbing, and fails to have any significant impact upon most audiences, who usually bypass it. Entertainment in this category is rarely experienced, and when it is, the majority of audiences fail to find it entertaining. This could be down to any one or more of the following: a lack of novelty, confusing or repetitive storylines, poor quality, and/or unprofessionalism. Television shopping channels, radio broadcast advertisements, party political broadcasts and a lot of online content fall into this category.

Weak – typically considered as being of a low quality, weak entertainment fails to reach most audiences; those that do find it, tend to use it as a distraction, rather than as something that they can engage with. Repeats of old television programmes, imitations of more popular entertainment, television spin-offs from films, and technologically outdated entertainment such as old video game consoles fall into this category.

Underachiever – this is entertainment that fails to reach out to the majority of potential audiences, but to those who do experience it, there is a significant emotional, impact-provoking deep thought. Underachievers are often not promoted correctly or adequately, are too new to have been heard of, are targeted towards the wrong audiences, or are inaccessible to most audiences. World cinema, new and a great deal of non-popular music, niche entertainment products such as 'freak shows', some cultural and spiritual entertainment and minor television channels often fall into this category.

Striver – highly emotive, strivers have a deep emotive impact but often do not reach mass appeal. Strivers often develop a cult status among audiences, and over time this can develop into wider more commercial gains, an actual example of this being Quentin Tarantino movies, many of which have moved from being strivers to healthy or powerful entertainment. A great deal of science fiction, horror, alternative comedy, alternative music, health entertainment, adult entertainment, gambling entertainment and some staged story falls into this category.

AUDIENCE AND ENTERTAINMENT INDUSTRY INTERACTION

The sectors that make up the entertainment industry interact with audiences in three distinct areas, these are as follows: events, venues and visitor attractions and the media. An entertainment industry event is one where the core product of the event has the primary purpose of providing entertainment to an audience; typical examples include concerts and spectator sports fixtures. Venues and visitor attractions are physical locations that are capable of entertaining an audience through their normal business functions, without necessarily having to stage any additional entertaining events, examples of which include museums and theme parks. The media is any means by which entertainment can be broadcasted, stored or physically distributed, and typical examples include DVDs and books. Mapping the sectors of the entertainment industry against such definitions, it is clear to see that the media is present within the majority of entertainment industry sectors, most of which offer some media-related products as in Fig. 1.8; also see the following chapters and each entertainment industry sector's sub-sectors.

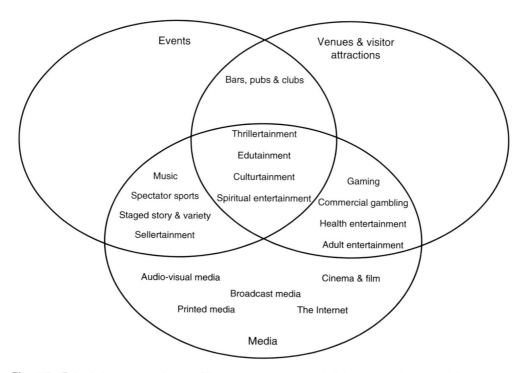

Fig. 1.8. Entertainment sectors within events, venues and visitor attractions, and the media.

THE ENTERTAINMENT ENVIRONMENT

The entertainment environment is the wider location in which audiences interact with entertainment provided by entities with the various entertainment industry sectors and sub-sectors. The entertainment environment surrounds us; after all, the very diverse entertainment offering provided by the entertainment industry can be found almost anywhere. There are nine distinct entertainment environments, which are as follows: the contained resort environment; the coastal environment; the cruise ship environment; the home environment; the mobile environment; the online environment; the rural environment; the transport environment; and the urban environment. These environments are all unique in their nature, through size, make-up or physical/virtual presence (and sometimes a combination of these things). Some types of entertainment are more predominant in particular environments than they are in others, for example nightclubs and theatres are concentrated within the urban environment due to their need to attract custom, and theme parks are more predominantly in the rural environment due to their need for large amounts of land.

Once upon a time, only the privileged were entertained in their homes, while the majority of audiences had to travel by foot or other means of transport to be entertained, and entertainment in the workplace was completely unheard of. Technological advancements, as well as

Table 1.1. The Entertainment Environments.

Environment	Characteristics
Coastal	The coastal environment offers a unique geographical landscape in that the land meets the sea or ocean. In Britain, the term 'seaside' is often used to describe these areas. The sea and particularly beaches attract tourists, and typically in response to this, coastal urban settlements are created to cater for visitors, which often include an array of entertainment facilities and venues. A unique type of coastal entertainment venue or visitor attraction is piers
Contained resort	A contained resort is typically targeted towards tourists, and these are often found in locations where tourists like to visit. Contained resorts can vary in size from relatively small resorts covering less than a square kilometre such as caravan parks, to mega resorts covering vast distances, such as Walt Disney World Resort. Resorts include an array of facilities including accommodation, catering facilities, bars, leisure amenities such as swimming pools, and entertainment venues including theatres and nightclubs. The idea being that once there, visitors do not need to leave the resort

(Continued)

Table 1.1. Continued.

Environment	Characteristics
Cruise ship	Almost like floating contained resorts, cruise ships consist of accommodation, catering facilities, bars, leisure amenities such as swimming pools, and entertainment venues including theatres, nightclubs and casinos. On a cruise, visitors are taken to a variety of destinations and often use the ship as a floating resort, so by day they may be out exploring the port where the ship has harboured, and by night making use of the facilities on board the ship as it travels to its next destination, Consequently much entertainment on board cruise ships takes place during the evening, at night and when the ship is at sea.
Home	The term 'home entertainment' gained popularity in the 1980s when home stereo units, television and video recorders became both commercially available and affordable. The home environment is media based and consists of the entertainment provision that has been purchased for use in the home
Mobile	The mobile environment is media-based and is the entertainment that can comfortably be taken virtually anywhere; this includes MP3 players, portable media players, mobile telephones, books and newspapers. The mobile environment is one of the fastest-growing environments as more and more media formats shrink to make them easily portable
Online	This is the only virtual environment available to date. To interact with entertainment in this environment we do not need to physically travel anywhere, but due to new mobile technologies, we can now access the Internet from almost anywhere. The online environment is classed as an environment in its own right due to the propensity of those accessing it to consider that they 'went' online
Rural	This environment is largely devoid of human habitation with a very low population density. This sensitive environment relies on visitation from outside of its own area, which itself can cause conflict between local residents and those seeking entertainment. The rural environment has the advantage that it offers large open spaces, and therefore can cater for entertainment entities that require large amounts of space. These include music festivals, theme parks, and zoos and safari parks

(Continued)

Table 1.1. Continued.

Environment	Characteristics
Transport	Getting from one point to another using a mode of transport can take time, and often during that time those travelling seek a distraction to occupy or entertain them. In-car entertainment systems, which were once non-existent before the car radio became available, are now elaborate and can include MP3 and DVD players. On some buses and trains, radio and television or movies are available, as is wi-fi Internet access. Commercial passenger jets have an established in-flight entertainment program consisting of films, television programmes, games and radio
Urban	Densely populated towns and cities predominantly make up this environment that feeds off large populations of visitors from close by, as well as incoming visitors. This is the most concentrated entertainment environment in that it contains the widest variety of entertainment industry entities with representation from every sector of the entertainment industry, from cinemas, museums and theatres, to nightclubs, live music venues and casinos

increases in personal disposable income and industrialization throughout the twentieth and twenty-first centuries, have significantly dispersed the settings in which an audience can be entertained from set venues and locations to almost anywhere.

At one time, films could only be viewed at a cinema; now they can be watched in the home, due to DVDs and televisions, as well as while travelling via portable media players or even mobile phones. The view from a moving bus, train or aeroplane used to be considered novel by passengers, who would be entertained by the sight of the passing and changing landscapes. Today this is not so much the case with travel being commonplace, and passengers seeking alternative sources of entertainment to occupy them while being 'captive' onboard their transportation.

The tourism and entertainment industries share both commonalities (predominantly visitor attractions and large-scale entertainment venues) and numerous differences. According to Mathieson and Wall (1982, p. 1) tourism is the 'temporary movement to destinations outside the normal home and workplace, the activities undertaken during the stay and the facilities created to cater for the need of tourists'. Swarbrooke (1995) noted that visitor attractions are the driver of many tourist journeys, for example Las Vegas is a city that has grown and thrived due to revenue brought into the city by tourists that have come to experience the city's numerous casinos and other gambling venues, spectacular stage shows, and the novelty of 'the strip' where hotel and casino buildings and grounds have become tourist attractions in their own right.

People travel from all over the world to visit Las Vegas, and the vast majority of these are tourists. However, the Las Vegas metropolitan area has over two million residents (WorldNow, 2008), and it is highly likely that a proportion of these residents access some of the entertainment facilities 'on their doorstep' within Las Vegas, but this does not necessarily make them tourists – mainly due to the locality of their destination. Residents of all towns and cities make use of local recreational amenities and entertainment facilities, but this does not make them tourists.

The entertainment system model denotes where we connect with the entertainment industry in its various environments. It is based upon the concept of Leiper's Tourism System model (1995), which considers the whole tourism system including traveller generation, transport, accommodation and attractions. Unlike Leiper's system in the entertainment sector, there are both tourist and non-tourist (local) perspectives to consider. The entertainment system (like Leiper's) features three zones: home, transit and destination, and its purpose is to demonstrate the environments in which the entertainment industry interacts with consumers within these zones (see Fig. 1.9).

The salient points to take from this model are the accessibility of the mobile and online environments throughout, which can provide entertainment almost anywhere. The model also highlights the importance of the destination zone in providing numerous environments for entertainment to take place in a live (non-media) setting. Governments and local authorities are aware that with a growing experience economy, the importance of developing a good entertainment infrastructure for the benefit of both tourists and local residents alike is essential in terms of destination development, economic growth and social needs – be that in Las Vegas, Nevada or Leeds, West Yorkshire. The inclusion of the cruise ship environment within the destination zone rather than the transit zone may be contentious, and indeed this environment *could* straddle both environments. However, as the majority of people who go on a cruise actually travel to the cruise ship, and spend an extended amount of time within this environment, it is considered much more than mere transport alone.

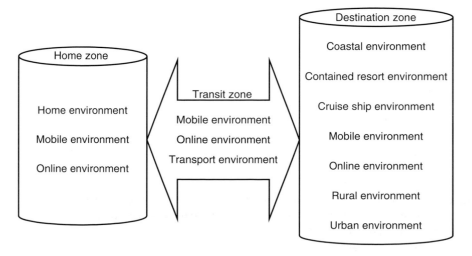

Fig. 1.9. The entertainment system.

The following chapters of this book are designed to give an insight into the 18 identified sectors of the global entertainment industry. Drawing upon examples from countries around the world, each sector and a variety of sub-sectors will be analysed, highlighting products; trends; markets; social, technological, economical, environmental, political, legal and ethical (STEEPLE) impacts; organizational and product case studies; and finally to offer an insight into what the future will hold for each sector.

REFERENCES

British Broadcasting Corporation (BBC). (1998) Citizen Kane tops movie lists. [Internet] London, British Broadcasting Corporation. URL available at: <http://news.bbc.co.uk/1/hi/entertainment/114597.stm>.

British Broadcasting Corporation (BBC). (2004) New life for doomed pop centre. [Internet] London, British Broadcasting Corporation. URL available at: <http://news.bbc.co.uk/1/hi/england/3570533.stm>.

Department for Culture, Media and Sport (DCMS) (2008) Creative industries. [Internet] London, DCMS. URL available at: <http://www.culture.gov.uk/what_we_do/creative_industries/default.aspx>.

Hesmondhalgh, D. (2007) *The Cultural Industries*, 2nd ed. Sage, London.

Kotler, P., Armstrong, G., Wong, V. and Saunders, J. (2008) *Principles of Marketing*, 5th ed. Prentice-Hall, Harlow, UK.

Leiper, N. (1995) *Tourism Management*. RMIT Press, Melbourne.

Lieberman, A. and Esgate, P. (2002) *The Entertainment Marketing Revolution: Bringing the Moguls, the Media, and the Magic to the World. Financial Times*/Prentice-Hall, London.

Mathieson, A. and Wall, G. (1982) *Tourism: Economic and Social Impacts*. Longman, Harlow, UK.

Merriam-Webster (2008) Entertainment. [Internet] Massachusetts, *Merriam-Webster*. URL available at: <http://www.merriam-webster.com/dictionary/entertainment>.

MINTEL (2000) *2020 Vision: Tomorrow's Consumer*. Mintel International Group, London.

MSN Encarta (2008) Searched for emotion. [Internet] Washington, Microsoft Corporation. URL available at: <http://encarta.msn.com/encnet/refpages/search.aspx?q=emotion>.

O'Connor, J. (2007) *The Cultural and Creative Industries: A Review of the Literature*. Creative Partnerships, Leeds, UK.

Oxford English Dictionary (2008) *Oxford English Dictionary*. [Internet] Oxford, Oxford University. URL available at: <http://www.oed.com/>.

Pigram, J. and Jenkins, J. (1999) *Outdoor Recreation Management*. Routledge, Abingdon, UK.

Swarbrooke, J. (1995) *The Development and Management of Visitor Attractions*. Butterworth-Heinemann, Oxford.

UNESCO (2008) Creativity. [Internet] UNESCO, Paris. URL available at: <http://portal.unesco.org/culture/en/ev.php-URL_ID=34326&URL_DO=DO_TOPIC&URL_SECTION=201.html>.

Vogel, H. (2007) *Entertainment Industry Economics: A Guide for Financial Analysis*, 6th ed. Cambridge University Press, Cambridge.

Wordnet (2008) Wordnet search: Entertainment. [Internet] New Jersey, Princeton University. URL available at: <http://wordnet.princeton.edu/perl/webwn?s=entertainment&sub=Search+WordNet&o2=&o0=1&o7=&o5=&o1=1&o6=&o4=&o3=&h=>.

WorldNow (2008) Las Vegas area population reaches 2 million. [Internet] Nevada, KLAS-TV. URL available at: <http://www.lasvegasnow.com/Global/story.asp?s=7453765>.

chapter 2

Staged Story and Variety

Dr Ben Walmsley

Live entertainment that is often set on (or within) a purpose-built area where a pre-determined story and/or routine is recited, acted or performed.

Since the singers of the *Iliad*, human beings have developed an affinity for storytelling because people love imitations and learn from them (Blakley, 2001). In the days of Plato and Aristotle, storytelling was celebrated as never before or since, and the legacy of this period lives on in the mythical tragedies of Sophocles, Aeschylus and Euripides, which are still performed today. Indeed, ancient Greece gave us the very term 'theatre' from the Ancient Greek *theatron*, 'a place for viewing' and the term provides the key to any understanding of live performance, which we can define as a staged story or routine performed in a specific arena.

Today, theatre is both a place and an action: it encompasses not just the venue where staged entertainment takes place, but the act of performance itself. This active notion of theatre harks back to the medieval troubadours and wandering minstrels, who travelled from place to place performing in streets, parks and royal courts, a tradition which lives on today in buskers and street performers and in the myriad touring theatre, dance and opera companies which perform all over the world.

Memorable performances are based on a powerful story or myth – for example Oedipus killing his father and marrying his mother. This is what links the traditional forms of live entertainment such as theatre, opera and ballet. This chapter will review the old and new types of staged story that comprise the diverse performance side of live entertainment, revealing their common ground and exploring their socio-economic impacts.

Socio-technological Factor: Global Audiences

Staged performances have moved on from the theatres of ancient Greece and thanks to technology they can now command a global audience. On 8 August 2008, more than a billion people around the world tuned in to watch the opening ceremony of the Beijing Olympics in the city's Bird's Nest stadium, constituting one of the largest live television audiences ever. This spectacular event showcased China's rich cultural heritage and featured opera, puppetry, dance, performance poetry, acrobatics and tai chi. The overwhelming success of the event showed how powerful a staged performance can be, and how it can succeed in bringing people together on a social level and on a global scale.

Perhaps with this in mind, Jude Kelly, Chair of Culture, Ceremonies and Education for London 2012, has pledged to place culture at the heart of the UK's Olympic celebrations.

Staged story and variety can be divided into five main sub-sectors (or genres), and each of these genres itself comprises many different types of performance, as illustrated in Fig. 2.1.

What is striking here is the diverse range of entertainment offered within staged story and variety; and although some of these classifications are new, and perhaps controversial, they are all based on the traditions of live performance, on a rehearsed routine or story. What is also

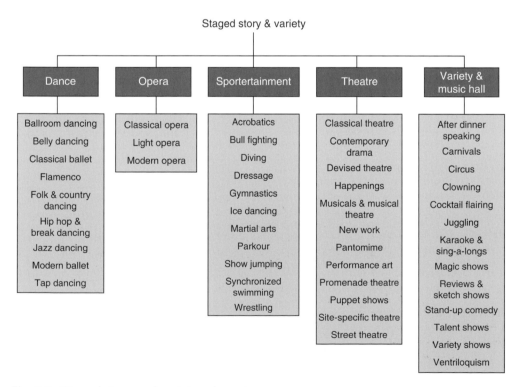

Fig. 2.1. Staged story and variety sub-sectors.

apparent here is the degree to which staged story and variety is being integrated into other sectors of the entertainment industry. This is particularly striking in the crossover between this sector and spectator sports (see Chapter 12, this volume), which has created a new, contemporary 'generation' of sports that incorporate performance and artistic elements.

The benefits of attending live performances are complex, but the main core intrinsic benefits include engagement, distraction, escapism, inspiration, education, wonder, awe and humour. Marketing literature refers to beautiful transformational and transcendent experiences, which take people out of the everyday and create or reinforce a sense of community (Matarasso, 1996; McCarthy *et al.*, 2004; Brown and Novak, 2007). Some people seek nostalgia (adults taking children to the local pantomime, perhaps) while others seek inspiration and truth.

Environmental Factor: The Carbon Cost

The performing arts are slowly waking up to the environmental impact of their industry. In September 2008, the Greater London Authority published its Green Theatre report, which explored the carbon footprint of London's theatres and disseminated best practice in trying to reduce it. The report estimated the annual carbon footprint of the city's theatres at 50,000 t and concluded that the industry could reduce its CO_2 emissions by almost 60% by 2025 and make considerable financial savings if it implemented all the recommended actions (GLA, 2008).

DANCE

This is a movement-based art form, where performers use choreographed or improvised steps and gestures to tell stories and convey emotions. They achieve this by moving in a stylized way in time to music or another rhythmic inspiration. Many diverse forms of dance have developed over the centuries, and Table 2.1 summarizes the main genres that still exist today.

OPERA

Opera is a staged spectacle where highly trained singers perform a story from a text (libretto) set to a musical score. It originated in Italy towards the end of the 16th century and quickly spread throughout Europe in line with the Renaissance. It harks back to the great lyric poets such as Homer and is reminiscent of ancient Greek theatre, whose choruses sang all their lines. Unlike theatre and dance, opera has not diversified enormously over the centuries, but there are three main variations worthy of exploration; these are highlighted in Table 2.2.

Opera often takes place in lavish and classical venues such as that shown in Fig. 2.2.

Table 2.1. Dance sub-genre and characteristics.

Type of dance	Characteristics
Ballroom dancing	Derived from the balls of the Regency era, the term ballroom dancing covers an eclectic range of dances such as waltzes, foxtrots, sambas and tangos, where a leader and follower dance as a connected pair
Belly dancing	Tradition Arab folk dance characterized by circular motions of the hips and chest, shimmies, balancing props and the use of silk and chiffon veils
Classical ballet	Originating from French court life, ballet is a highly technical and choreographed form of dancing, which has developed a vocabulary of its own. Classical ballets such as *Swan Lake* are generally performed to classical music played by a live accompanying orchestra
Flamenco	Originating from Andalusia, Flamenco is a Spanish folk dance performed to flamenco guitar music and characterized by its intricate, audible footwork
Folk and country dancing	Another generic term for traditional popular dances, usually liked to social occasions. Classic examples are Scottish, Irish, Barn and Morris dancing in the UK; and country and western and line dancing in the USA
Hip-hop and break dancing	An acrobatic, street dance style developed amidst the African-American and Hispanic youth culture of 1970s New York. Although hip hop incorporates breaking, popping, locking, krumping and house dance, break dancing remains its hallmark style
Jazz dancing	With African-American origins, jazz dancing is another umbrella term for popular dance styles such as Swing, Jitterbug and Charleston. It is exemplified today in Broadway and West End musicals such as *Chicago* and *Cabaret*
Modern ballet	A hybrid of classical ballet and modern dance, which is less narrow in its choreography and performed to a whole range of music
Tap dancing	Developed in America in the 19th century and immortalized perhaps by Fred Astaire and Ginger Rogers, tap is a lively, rhythmic dance so-called because of the noise of the dancer's shoes tapping on the ground

Table 2.2. Opera sub-genre and characteristics.

Type of opera	Characteristics
Classical opera	By far the most popular genre, classical opera strives to recreate or breathe fresh life into the operas of composers such as Mozart, Puccini, Verdi and Wagner
Light opera	As their names suggest, light or comic operas are more light hearted versions of classical operas, usually with happy endings. In France, Offenbach was the leading practitioner of the *operetta*, while in the UK, Gilbert and Sullivan's light operas are still popular today
Modern opera	Modern (20th and 21st centuries) operas are characterized by features such as atonality (non-classical harmonies) and smaller orchestras. The most famous British proponent is Benjamin Britten, who composed *Peter Grimes* and *Billy Budd*

Fig. 2.2. Frankfurt Opera House, a classic opera and theatre venue.

SPORTERTAINMENT

Unlike spectator sports – which involves participants engaging in sport and spectators being entertained by them – sportertainment refers here to a convergence of sport and artistic performance. It is perhaps most evident in the case of martial arts, where the performance is removed from its sporting context altogether and placed exclusively in an artistic or entertainment context – think of *Crouching Tiger, Hidden Dragon* for example. Table 2.3 highlights some of the best examples of sportertainment, and demonstrates how they are connected to the other types of staged story and variety.

This list is far from exhaustive: other sports such as figure skating, skateboarding and stunt skiing could also be included here, while a whole new generation of spectator sports (particularly X-games and other extreme action sports) is also becoming increasingly theatrical (see Chapter 12, this volume).

Table 2.3. Sportertainment sub-genre and characteristics.

Type of Sportertainment	Characteristics
Acrobatics	A collective term derived from the Greek 'high walking' to describe disciplines such as tumbling, diving, trapeze and aerial work. As a graceful, highly choreographed discipline, acrobatics transect gymnastics and the performing arts and are often incorporated into films (stunts), theatre and variety shows
Bull fighting	Although a classic (if controversial) spectator sport, the setting, costumes, acrobatics, cultural traditions and pageantry behind bull fighting lend it the theatrical air of a death-dance, which make it also a performing art (see Chapter 16 for detailed information about this performance-based cultural spectacle)
Diving	While predominantly a spectator sport, diving again combines gymnastics with dance to create a series of graceful, predetermined movements
Dressage	As a form of ballet and gymnastics for horses and their riders, dressage is an ancient art that merits inclusion here
Gymnastics	Gymnastics evolved from ancient Greek exercises and from circus performance skills. As such, they incorporate a grace, agility, routine and coordination, which align them also with dance
Ice Dancing	As a dance on ice, ice dancing is an excellent example of the merging of sport and the performing arts, combining set rules and competition with beauty, grace and performance
Martial Arts	A collective term for various types of formalized fighting techniques. Like wrestling, gymnastics and acrobatics, martial arts incorporate a series of set manoeuvres and are therefore akin to dance

(Continued)

Table 2.3. Continued.

Type of Sportertainment	Characteristics
Parkour	Parkour typically involves the artistic exploration of obstacles within the built environment. Founded by Frenchman David Belle, the core principles of parkour are to train the mind and body to overcome obstacles in an emergency using efficient movements. Unlike a traditional sport, it has no set rules or competitive element; instead, it is a disciplined art, which trains the body for flight
Show jumping	Although essentially a spectator sport, as an art based on a preset routine, show jumping also displays significant elements of performance and dance
Synchronized Swimming	A combination of swimming, gymnastics and dance, synchronized swimming is essentially a choreographed routine of elaborate movements in water, set to music
Wrestling	A martial art dating back over 4000 years to ancient China and Egypt, wrestling involves an unarmed, hand-to-hand struggle between two contestants. Although essentially a sport, many forms of wrestling comprise a staged (and sometimes preordained) routine and share their stylized choreographed movements with certain types of dance

THEATRE

As discussed earlier, theatre is both an action (the art of writing and producing plays) and a noun (the place where plays are staged). As opposed to other types of performing arts, theatre is generally characterized by storytelling using gestures and the spoken word. Today, there are many different forms of theatre, and the best way to appreciate its many different guises is to explore its different manifestations as highlighted in Table 2.4.

Theatre is most popular among the older demographic and is continually struggling to attract young adults. In response to this, the British Government has announced that over the next 2 years, over half a million free seats will be made available to people under 26 in all the main theatre productions in England. The aim is to break down the barriers preventing young people attending the performing arts and to engender in them a sense of ownership of their theatrical heritage. Only time will tell whether this is a sound investment or a desperate measure.

Fig. 2.3. A musical cabaret performance.

Table 2.4. Theatre sub-genre and characteristics.

Type of Theatre	Characteristics
Classical theatre	Traditional, spoken drama rehearsed and performed by actors from a pre-existing script. Examples are Greek tragedies like *Antigone*, Shakespeare's plays and arguably also modern classics by playwrights such as Ibsen, Chekhov, Arthur Miller and Samuel Beckett
Contemporary drama	Generally refers to plays from recent decades which are relatively traditional in form. Contemporary British playwrights include Harold Pinter, David Hare, Caryl Churchill and David Harrower
Devised theatre	A form of theatre where the script or routine is created collaboratively by an artistic team, usually including actors and often involving a process of improvisation
Happenings	Theatrical events that originated in America in the late 1950s and blossomed in the 1960s. With surrealist origins, they usually took place in artistic environments and involved some element of surprise, spontaneity and audience participation

(Continued)

Table 2.4. Continued.

Type of Theatre	Characteristics
Musicals and musical theatre	Any piece of theatre that is predominantly musical in nature, whether sung or played by an orchestra or band. Classic examples are *Oliver* and *My Fair Lady* (see Fig. 2.3)
New work	This genre includes all new pieces produced for the stage, which may or may not have a script. It includes commissioned plays such as *Black Watch* (see below) and submitted or self-produced work
Pantomime	Inspired by French fairground performers of the early 18th century, pantomime has become a quintessentially English form of burlesque Yuletide entertainment. Many modern pantomimes such as *Dick Whittington* and *Cinderella* stem from the Victorian era and feature stock characters including the ever-popular pantomime dame
Performance art	Performance art grew out of the 'happenings' of the 1960s and is enjoying a renaissance today in the form of multi-art-form installations. Linked closely to conceptual art, performance art is delivered by an actor and involves a relationship with a live audience
Promenade theatre	Promenade theatre takes place in a space with no formal stage (often outdoors). Audience members follow the actors as the action shifts from one area to another. Famous proponents of this genre are the Théâtre du Soleil in Paris
Puppet shows	Puppet theatre uses dolls and similar figures, which traditionally imitate human behaviour in a parodic style. The earliest known examples were the stringed puppets or marionettes used by the ancient Egyptians, Hindus and Greeks (Senelick, 1995). Other popular formats include hand, glove, shadow and rod puppets. The best-known example is *Punch & Judy*; more modern proponents of puppetry-inspired theatre include the leading British theatre company Improbable, the South African Handspring Puppet Company and again the Théâtre du Soleil
Site-specific theatre	Theatre designed specifically for a particular site or space. A good example is the work of Edinburgh-based Grin Iron, who have recently performed in a shop, a tenement flat and an airport
Street theatre	Literally, theatre which takes place in the street. Good examples are mystery plays, *The Sultan's Elephant* and La Machine's mechanical spider (see below)

Ethical Factor: Offence Versus Freedom of Expression

Theatre has traditionally challenged the status quo by staging plays which question the ruling parties and social values of the day. But are there stories which should never be told? In December 2004, Gurpreet Kaur Bhatti's play *Behzti* (Dishonour) was cancelled mid-run by Birmingham Rep following widespread protests from the local Sikh community, which eventually became violent when a breakaway group attacked security guards, broke windows and set off fire alarms inside the theatre. Two days later, Bhatti went into hiding after receiving death threats and the theatre cancelled the production due to fears for the safety of its staff and audiences. The play upset many in the Sikh community because it featured a scene depicting rape in a Sikh temple, which many Sikhs felt publicly degraded their religion. Controversies such as these highlight the ongoing polemic between those who oppose censorship and demand the right to artistic freedom and those who expect their values and identities to be protected from perceptions of insult and blasphemy.

Case Study: National Theatre of Scotland

The National Theatre of Scotland (NTS) grew out of decades of discussion and debate. Despite the country's long and proud theatrical heritage, NTS is, perhaps unbelievably, Scotland's first ever national theatre and it is certainly no coincidence that it followed close on the heels of Scotland's devolution in 1999. NTS was launched to the public in February 2006 with its inaugural production, *Home*, which comprised ten shows in ten locations all over Scotland.

The Mission

As Edward Gordon Craig put it, theatre is not made from stones and bricks but through human bodies and voices (National Theatre of Scotland, 2005). This is a central tenet of the NTS, and it is what makes the company unique, for NTS was the first national theatre in the world established to function without a theatre of its own. Instead, it aims to be truly national by working in close partnership with the existing theatre community to bring the best of Scottish theatre to audiences all over Scotland.

The company's founding business plan contained the following statement of intent:

> Scottish theatre has always been vibrant, demotic and pioneering. With the arrival of the NTS, we now have an opportunity to transform the meaning of national theatre on a global scale by creating a truly innovative structure, free of bricks and mortar institutionalism, which will be alert, flexible and radical. We can lead the world by creating a groundbreaking organisation producing outstanding theatre. (Ibid, p. 3).

(Continued)

Case Study: Continued.

The National Theatre of Scotland's international strategy aims to ensure the company's work is seen in an international context by high-profile touring and international festival appearances; and identify and develop relationships with key international artists and companies, who are invited to create work all over Scotland, influencing and working with existing artists and companies. The company has already exceeded its international ambitions with three successive appearances at both the Edinburgh International Festival and the Edinburgh Fringe; *Black Watch* headlining almost every major international theatre festival in the world; three productions touring to New York; and three international co-productions showcasing in Scotland.

At the same time, it has produced work that is quintessentially Scottish and which goes to heart of and challenges Scotland's history and national identity. *Mary Stuart* brought fresh life to Schiller's classic play, which imagines a meeting between Elizabeth I and Mary Queen of Scots; *Tutti Frutti* reincarnated John Byrne's legendary Scottish 1980s TV hit of the same name; *Venus as a Boy* staged Luke Sutherland's fantastical tale of an Orcadian transvestite who winds his way to Soho; and *Black Watch* told the story of a group of ex-soldiers from Fife who fought and lost in the Iraq War.

The Model

Much of the company's success is due to its strategic business model. Unconstrained by the constant pressure and restriction of programming for specific spaces, NTS can focus its human and physical resources on creating world-class theatre, reacting quickly to local and world events which, in turn, produce the 'urgent stories' it strives to tell. By co-producing with other theatres and theatre companies, it also succeeds in tapping into and supporting the best talent in Scotland, while providing a properly funded infrastructure to maximize the country's artistic potential abroad.

Precisely because it is unencumbered by a venue of its own, the organization is forced into finding creative and appropriate spaces for every new production it produces (see Figs 2.4 and 2.5). Therefore, to date the company has performed in tower blocks, forests, ferries, museums, drill halls, football stadia, shop windows, tenement flats and village halls as well as in the great theatres of Scotland like Glasgow's Citizens', Dundee Rep, the Royal Lyceum, Eden Court, the Traverse Theatre and His Majesty's Theatre in Aberdeen.

This strategic approach ensures that the existing physical infrastructure of Scottish theatre is used to the full without the wastefulness of designing, constructing and maintaining yet another expensive public building. It also means that the company is highly mobile and light on its feet; able to tour the length and breadth of the country (and indeed the world); and to constantly reach new and diverse audiences, many of whom, research suggests, are put off theatre by the strangeness and imposing aspect of theatre buildings themselves.

Fig. 2.4. *Home Caithness*, performed in Caithness Glass Factory. (Image by Dominic Ibbotson, courtesy of National Theatre of Scotland.)

Fig. 2.5. *Home Glasgow*, performed in and around a tower block in Cranhill in Glasgow's East End. (Image by Peter Dibdin, courtesy of National Theatre of Scotland.)

Case Study: Continued.

So the company's unique and flexible model frees it up strategically to achieve its mission to the full.

Finance

In 2007–2008, NTS received public subsidy of £4.3 million, which represented 70% of its turnover. It earned £1.3 million in income and spent £4 million on productions. The company is governed by an independent board of directors who, among other things, are responsible for ensuring its financial efficiency and probity.

Along with Scotland's four other national companies (Scottish Opera, Scottish Ballet, Royal Scottish National Orchestra and Scottish Chamber Orchestra) NTS is directly funded by the Scottish Government. This is a controversial arrangement in the context of arts funding in the UK, most of which is based on the so-called arm's-length principle, whereby government funding is distributed via Arts Councils, who act as quangos (agencies financed by, but independent of, government).

Supporters of the arm's-length principle fear that direct government funding could easily lead to political and artistic interference – if, for example, NTS produced a show that was highly critical of the current administration, this could potentially damage the relationship between the company and its funders. This arrangement also creates an anomaly in that Scotland's biggest theatre company is funded differently, separately and more generously than the rest of the theatre community – a situation that could foster resentment and impede any strategic overview.

Blurring the lines

Until relatively recently, theatre was aimed at the masses. Shakespeare drew upon a wide variety of storytelling genres and techniques to keep his audiences entertained: his plays are eclectic melting pots of comedy and tragedy, poetry and prose, rhetoric and bombast, music and dancing.

With the rise of the middle classes (and in the UK following the Licensing Act of 1737 and the Theatres Act of 1843), staged entertainment became more elitist, with clear battle lines emerging between the spoken word, opera and ballet on one side and more popular forms of theatre on the other. This polarization persisted in the UK until the Second World War, which destroyed many of London's theatres and music halls and brought live entertainment to its knees. However, in the past few decades, directors, writers and performers have started to experiment again with their genres, blurring the lines between high art and low art and fusing the various art forms. They have been inspired and assisted in this endeavour by cultural globalization and technology. Popular forms of theatre can now be found in a variety of locations, as illustrated in Fig. 2.6.

Fig. 2.6. Children's theatre being performed in a shopping mall.

Technological Factor: Special Effects

Radical developments in technology have revolutionized the way in which artists and entertainers tell their stories. From live-streamed transmissions from London's Royal Opera House and the New York Met to the innovative use of sound, film and projection in plays such as the National Theatre's *The Waves*, technology is constantly opening up staged entertainment to new formats and audiences. The British producing company Artichoke are masters of harnessing technology to tell a story: In May 2006 they brought French company Royal de Luxe's *The Sultan's Elephant* to the streets of London, mesmerizing audiences young and old with a 42 t mechanical elephant and a 6 m tall princess, who travelled on a London bus and disappeared in a rocket; and as a centrepiece of Liverpool's European City of Culture 2008 celebrations, they promenaded a 15 m high mechanical spider through the city centre, where it climbed up a tower block before escaping down the Mersey Tunnel.

VARIETY AND MUSIC HALL

Until 1843, London theatres were restricted by the patents of Charles II and the Licensing Act of 1737, which gave certain theatres the exclusive right to use dialogue. This forced the many theatres not privileged by the monopoly into musical forms of entertainment and led to the rise of the music hall.

Music hall as a genre is characterized by rousing popular songs and burlesque comic acts. For many people it is typified by classic Cockney folk songs such as 'Doing the Lambeth Walk', and indeed the Canterbury and the Bower in Lambeth, London were two of the most famous music halls of their day. As a venue, the music hall was distinguished from a theatre by its cafe-style layout, with audiences seated around tables and smoking or enjoying light refreshments.

In 1884, the iconic Empire, Leicester Square opened as a theatre. Buoyed by the Victorian confidence of the Empire, Alhambras, Palaces, Gaietys and indeed Empires began to spring up all over the country, reflecting the wealth, glamour and exoticism of the time. These theatres turned their back on the gaudy brashness of music halls and sought to attract the well-heeled Victorian gentleman and his wife with dazzling architecture and breathtaking acts of Variety.

As its name suggests, Variety generally incorporates a diverse range of acts usually introduced by a compere. It is essentially a populist form of staged entertainment, based on music, comedy and magic, which developed from the music halls of the 19th century, transferring to popular theatres and working men's clubs in the 20th century and then to radio and television. Although certainly past their heyday, variety and music halls live on in certain forms of Saturday night television (e.g. talent shows like 'Britain's Got Talent' and 'the X-Factor') and in special gala performances such as the Royal Variety Show. Table 2.5 illustrates its main surviving genres.

Table 2.5. Variety and music hall sub-genre and characteristics.

Type of variety/ music halls	Characteristics
After-dinner speaking	A private form of public address, where a speaker uses oratory and storytelling techniques to entertain an audience after a meal
Carnivals	Originally the Roman Catholic festive season preceding Lent, the carnival now refers to any large, outdoor popular festival characterized by music, dancing, costumes and floats. Brazil's Carnaval, London's Notting Hill Carnival and the Mardi Gras in New Orleans and Sydney are the best known examples today (see also Chapter 16, this volume)
Circus	A family show performed in an arena or tent by a travelling troupe of performers including any combination of clowns, acrobats, trapeze artists, tightrope walkers, jugglers, stunt artists, unicyclists and trained animals
Clowning	A grotesquely comical form of performance, where actors wearing red noses and brightly coloured wigs and costumes entertain their audiences by their incongruous movements and outrageous behaviour, which often parodies social norms

(Continued)

Table 2.5. Continued.

Type of variety/ music halls	Characteristics
Cocktail flairing	'The act of flipping, spinning, throwing, balancing and catching bottles, drinks and various bar tools while in the process of making cocktails' (Experience Days, 2009). Flairing was popularized by Tom Cruise in the hit film *Cocktail*, and is included here because of its links with juggling and live performance
Juggling	A performance art where objects are thrown or moved in a mesmerizing way
Karaoke and sing-a-longs	Of Japanese origin, Karaoke is essentially an amateur form of entertainment, where participants sing along to pre-recorded backing tracks of popular songs.
	Sing-a-longs represent the growing trend of audiences gathering in a cinema to sing along to the sound track of a musical film
Magic shows	Events involving a mixture of magic tricks, conjury, hypnotism, illusionism and the supernatural designed to perplex, amaze and delight a live audience
Reviews and sketch shows	With origins in vaudeville and music hall, reviews and sketch shows are generally humorous, satirical performances comprising musical and theatrical vignettes
Stand-up comedy	Comedy shows where a single comedian directly addresses the audience and entertains them with a rehearsed or improvised routine
Talent shows	Live performances where participants compete against one another in any of the performing arts
Variety shows	As described above, shows incorporating a variety of music, comedy and magic acts, as illustrated in Fig. 2.7
Ventriloquism	The act of manipulating or throwing the voice to make it appear as if it's coming from elsewhere – usually the mouth of a puppet, which the ventriloquist manipulates in time to his or her speech

GLOBAL ENTERTAINMENT

The work of companies like Artichoke reflects a growing trend for cross-border collaboration and touring. Specific EU funding has encouraged and enabled co-productions between EU member states; and together with cheaper flights, the rise of the international festival has led

Fig. 2.7. An impromptu variety street performance in Covent Garden, London.

to a renaissance in cultural exchange. But with wildly fluctuating currency exchange rates, rising fuel prices and restrictions on visas, it remains to be seen whether the trend will last for very long. These issues have compounded the traditional challenges of international touring, and there is increasing evidence of the industry maturing and consolidating as the smaller companies struggle to survive.

But cultural globalization is still alive and kicking and the many benefits of international touring and collaboration still inspire performing arts companies from all over the world to co-produce and tour to learn more about their craft by telling their stories to a global audience. International arts festivals such as the Edinburgh International Festival, the Festival d'Avignon, the Sydney Festival, the New Zealand International Arts Festival and Toronto's Luminato Festival continue to provide an international platform for the world's elite to show-case their work, while Broadway and London's West End offer a year-round home to some of the world's best theatre. The most successful shows, whether commercial like *Les Misérables* or subsidized like *The History Boys*, can now extend their lives for season after season on the world stage, which makes them attractive to Hollywood film producers and turns them into truly global products (and potential cash cows for the companies behind them).

Economic Factor: the Economics of Culture

Cultural trade is a significant and burgeoning sector of the world's economy. Since 2000, it has seen annual growth of over 7% and now represents over 7% of global GDP (UNESCO, 2005). In the 1990s, cultural trade almost doubled, but exports were dominated by a limited number of rich countries, with developing countries accounting for less than 1% of exports. In the UK, there have been several attempts to assess the economic impact of live entertainment. Shellard (2004) assessed the economic impact of the English theatre industry at £2.6 billion per annum. But this figure included neither touring nor non-building-based theatre, so his estimate is certainly conservative.

This type of research is both complex and controversial because there is no standard methodology or categorization available, and in the past few years, researchers and lobbyists have moved away from economic and social inclusion arguments, focusing instead on exploring the intrinsic benefits of live entertainment. For the main benefits of international collaborations and touring are far from economic. According to UNESCO (2005, p. 84), cultural goods 'convey ideas, symbols, and ways of life. They inform or entertain, contribute to build collective identity and influence cultural practices'.

THE FUTURE

Many of the examples of staged story and variety explored here have been around almost as long as human beings themselves, and it seems therefore that they fulfil in us some kind of primitive need that will not be easily replaced.

Figure 2.8 illustrates the immediate future for this entertainment industry sector. Perhaps the greatest challenge facing this sector of entertainment in the coming years is the rise of home entertainment – cheaper, higher quality and readily available television programmes, films and games as well as the increasing penetration of online entertainment. At the same time, this challenge also presents a fantastic opportunity: As live experiences become more scarce, they become more special, and one of the lasting unique selling points of live performance is that it cannot be replicated digitally. However, with young people spending more time indoors and online, the long-term survival of the sector depends on its ability to adapt to their needs and entice them over its thresholds. It also depends, as ever, on governments' willingness to keep investing in the arts even in difficult times, as many of the art forms in the growth and maturity phases rely on this investment to survive.

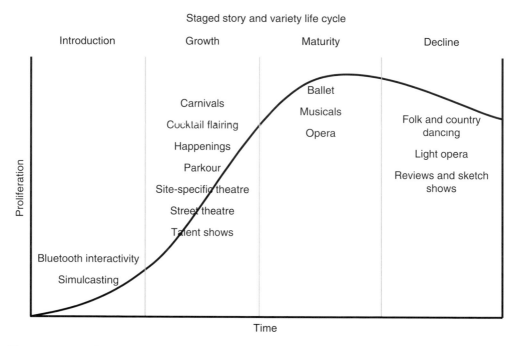

Fig. 2.8. Staged story and variety life cycle.

Introduction

Bluetooth interactivity – traditional theatres will begin to follow the example set by movie theatres by offering images and performance information to mobile phones via Bluetooth to people within the venue. This may include performance and interval times, as well as novelties such as songs and images from performances.

Simulcasting – this involves opera houses and theatres live streaming concerts and performances to outdoor or indoor audiences (New York Met and Royal Opera House have led the way here). However there are interesting copyright and moral rights issues here that will need to be ironed out in the next few years before this new art form can really take off.

Growth

Carnivals – the combination of the 'festival culture', cheaper foreign travel and cultural globalization has seen a steady growth in local, regional, national and international carnivals. (See also Chapter 16.)

Cocktail flairing – although the European pub, bar and cafe trades appear to be suffering from the double blow of the smoking ban and the global recession, high-end hospitality still seems to be booming, and it is likely that consumers will become increasingly demanding of their nightlife in the new 'experience economy' (Pine and Gilmore, 1999). Whether hosting a cocktail party at home or out with a group of friends, tomorrow's consumers are likely to want some added value with their alcohol, and flairing provides just that.

Happenings – the original and professional forms of this art form have seemingly been in a state of decline. However, since 2003 there has been renewed interest in this art form, when *Harper's Magazine* editor Bill Wasik created a 'Flash mob' in Manhattan. The Internet and particularly social networking web sites have been used since by Internauts to create further 'Flash mob' groups, whose purpose is to quickly assemble in a pre-arranged public location, perform an unusual action for a period, and then hastily disband. Recent media exposure has further increased the popularity of flash mobs, including people undressing to expose a T-shirt that read 'Live United', and then standing motionless at Union Station in Washington, DC, in November 2008, and the T-Mobile 'Dance', a choreographed dance routine participated in by 350 people, and filmed live on location at London Liverpool Street Station, this was subsequently made into a television commercial.

Parkour – the success and exponential growth of parkour is set to continue as action films and online gaming keep on prospering. As the art form requires no special equipment or specific place; it is an accessible activity which is open to all classes and cultures around the world. Its particular cult popularity with the younger demographic means that it is likely to survive well into the 21st century at least.

Site-specific theatre – innovative business models such as the National Theatre of Scotland and audience development initiatives into widening access have led to a growth in theatre taking place beyond the walls of a theatre. As an inventive and often irreverent genre, site-specific theatre attracts a young and risk-taking demographic and as audiences become more demanding, participative and creative, it is likely to continue to grow in popularity.

Street theatre – the success of street performances such as *The Sultan's Elephant* has given a new energy to street theatre. Although street theatre is one of the oldest forms of live public entertainment, it is currently enjoying a renaissance thanks to the growth in festivals and to increased investment from governments and public funding bodies.

Talent shows – the continuing success of televised talent shows such as the X-factor has encouraged a new generation of amateur talent contests in bars and holiday resorts and has even led to new business models (again, the X-factor has led the way here with the televised audition–contest–winning single–live tour model).

Maturity

Opera – although opera audiences are remaining strong, the substantial production and set-up costs of opera mean that as public funding becomes more and more squeezed, only the biggest and best will survive. The changing business model of London's Royal Opera House is a case in point: its recent acquisition of the DVD production company Opus Arte marked a significant turning point in the public funding of the arts, and demonstrated that to survive in the digital age, opera companies will have to diversify into multi-platform production and distribution.

Ballet – with a similar history and facing similar challenges to opera, ballet is likely to develop in the same way as opera, with only the biggest and best companies surviving.

Musicals – seemingly at the top of their game, musicals have enjoyed a renaissance in the past few decades. But as with opera and ballet, their prohibitive set-up costs mean that very few musicals are commissioned or produced and only the most popular make it to the stage, where only the very best survive.

Decline

Folk and country dancing – although leisure pursuits such as line dancing boomed in the 1990s, the trend seems to have faded into obscurity and many traditional forms of dancing such as English Morris dancing are now facing extinction as the older generation take to their armchairs.

Light opera – although still popular among older audiences, the genre is now largely restricted to local amateur groups. Its future among younger audiences looks doubtful as its stories, humour and musical style become increasingly forgotten.

Reviews and sketch shows – this particular form of live performance seems to be in irreversible decline as younger audiences stay at home or opt for more modern and sophisticated pastimes.

REFERENCES

Blakley, J. (2001) *Entertainment Goes Global: Mass Culture in a Transforming World.* USC Annenberg, The Norman Lear Center, Los Angeles, California.

Brown, A.S. and Novak, J.L. (2007) *Assessing the Intrinsic Impacts of a Live Performance.* WolfBrown, San Francisco, California.

Greater London Authority (2008) *Green Theater: Taking Action on Climate Change.* Research Report. Greater London Authority, London.

Matarasso, F. (1996) *Defining Values: Evaluating Arts Programmes.* Comedia, Stroud, UK.

McCarthy, K.F., Ondaatje, E.H., Zakaras, L. and Brooks, A. (2004) *Gifts of the Muse: Reframing the Debate about the Benefits of the Arts.* RAND Corporation, Santa Monica, California.

National Theatre of Scotland (2005) Business plan. Glasgow, National Theatre for Scotland – Unpublished company document.

National Theatre of Scotland (2008) National Theatre of Scotland. [Internet] Glasgow, National Theatre for Scotland. URL available at: <http://www.nationaltheatrescotland.com>.

Pine, J. II and Gilmore, J.H. (1999). *The Experience Economy: Work Is Theater and Every Business Is a Stage.* Harvard Business School Press, Boston, Massachusetts.

Senelick, L. (1995) Puppets. In: Banham, M. (ed.) *The Cambridge Guide to Theater.* Cambridge University Press, Cambridge.

Shellard, D. (2004) *Economic Impact Study of UK Theatre.* Research report. Arts Council England, London.

UNESCO (2005) *International Flows of Selected Cultural Goods and Services, 1994–2003.* Research Report. UNESCO Institute for Statistics, Montreal, Canada.

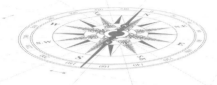

chapter 3

Music

Stuart Moss and Dr Stephen Henderson

Entertainment that involves instrumental and/or vocal sounds that are relayed in an organised, structured and continuous manner.

Up until the late 19th century, it was only possible to listen to live music and songs, as technologies that recorded them had not been invented. Audio recorded on to media formats is largely a 20th-century phenomenon, the development of which is covered in detail in Chapter 7 of this book. This came about when entrepreneurs backed by businesses began to harness the creative talents of composers, musicians and songwriters by recording and commodifying their creative outputs for commercial gain, which made music available to the masses. The first major record labels to carry out this function were Edison, Victor and Columbia at the beginning of the 20th century; these companies were also involved with the manufacturing of the devices that actually played records (phonographs and gramophones). Indeed, Edison's flat disc (record) was the product that kick-started the music recording industry. Edison famously held tone tests having musicians perform live on a darkened stage before playing his disc and challenging the audience to see if they could hear the difference. In this way, he introduced the concept that these were re-creations of a performance and not simply recordings. Of course, nowadays, with all manner of studio technology to hand, the re-creation versus recording debate is redundant as listeners recognize the difference between studio and live recording. Indeed, the emphasis on re-creation has almost reversed to ask the question as to whether live musicians can truly recreate their studio recordings in a live situation.

After the end of the Second World War, music on vinyl records grew rapidly in popularity, particularly from the 1950s onwards. Competition to secure the rights to work created by artists was fierce, and major record labels were formed with the intention of attracting artists and forming exclusive distribution contracts with them. At the same time the number of music genres that were popular (particularly among the youth) began to grow as new emergent artists appeared that would take established music forms in new directions. A modest but steady rise in disposable income meant that people had money available to spend on 'luxuries' such as music and fashions, and alongside this 'youth cultures' emerged (see Chapter 16, this volume), with a demand for music, which meant that record labels were actively 'hunting' new recording artists. A department that arose in most major labels was 'Artists and Repertoire', commonly known as A&R, which has a responsibility for finding new artists, and developing their creative output to suit a particular image or 'scene'. A&R scouts are consultative in nature and highly aware of changing fashions and trends, particularly emergent music scenes. In such a dynamic business environment, the role of A&R has been pivotal in the success of a number of major labels. Some key forms of popular music that were established throughout the 20th century and into the 21st century are highlighted in Table 3.1.

Table 3.1. Popular music development in the 20th and 21st centuries.

Origins	Genre
1900s	Broadway, Ragtime
1910s	Blues, Calypso, Jazz, Scat
1920s	Country and Western
1930s	Swing
1940s	Avant-Garde, Bebop, Experimental Music, Latin Jazz, Rock and Roll, Rhythm and Blues
1950s	Easy Listening, Folk Revival, Rockabilly, Ska, Soul
1960s	Art Rock, Blues Revival, Dub, Experimental Rock, Funk, Garage Rock, Hard Rock, Heavy Metal, Krautrock, New Age, Northern Soul, Power Pop, Prog Rock, Psychedelic Rock, Reggae, Rock, Rocksteady, Salsa
1970s	2 Tone, Dancehall, Disco, Electronica, Glam Metal, Glam Rock, Hardcore Punk, Hip Hop, Industrial, Industrial Metal, Industrial Rock, New Wave, Political Hip Hop, Punk, Soft Rock, Urban
1980s	Acid House, Acid Rap, Alternative Hip Hop, Alternative Rock, Breakbeat, Christian Hip Hop, Death Metal, Drum N Bass, Electro, Electro Hop, Electro-Industrial, Emo, Gangsta Rap, Garage, Ghettotech, Goth, Grunge, Hardcore Hip Hop, Hip House, House, Indie Pop, Indie Rock, Lo-Fi, Melodic Hardcore, Miami Bass, New Romantic, Pornocore, Post-Hardcore, Ragga, Rap Metal, Rap Rock, Rave, Shoegazing, Speed Metal, Swingbeat, Techno, Thrash Metal
1990s	Britpop, Country Rap, Crunk, Hardcore Techno, Horrorcore, Jungle, Nerdcore, Nu Metal, Reggaeton, Speed Garage
2000s	Basslines, Dubstep, Grime, RnB

The traditional key business functions that are performed by record labels are as follows: contracting the services of recording artists, including musicians and singers, as well as their managers; marketing and promoting work by recording and musicians who are signed to them, including creating music videos and web sites; producing work created by artists for the commercial market (commodification); distributing such products to retailers; and enforcing copyright upon work by artists and musicians that are signed to them.

Fig. 3.1. Hip hop is one of the most successful music genres of the late 20th century.

Legal Factor: Intellectual Property Theft

By far the most contentious of intellectual property issues from all creators of audio and visual products is the rise of the Internet, and peer-to-peer (P2P) networks which developed in the 1990s to allow sharing of files, via both upload and download mechanisms making intellectual property in electronic format freely available through the Internet (Michel, 2006). In 2008, 95% of all downloaded music was illegally downloaded rather than legitimately purchased (BBC, 2009). Combined with this, the rise in home computers and particularly recordable CDs and DVDs has led to significantly large operations producing illegal counterfeit copies for sale through street markets and sellers. Both the music and film industries are living the nightmare that they may sell one official CD/DVD which will then be copied and passed around consumers only too willing to get themselves a bargain.

(Continued)

Legal Factor: Continued.

In this area, two contrasting views have emerged with the industry seeing this as threatening sales to such an extent that they will no longer be able to financially support the creation of further entertainment, while a majority of particularly younger audiences often see such file-sharing as a victimless crime. Artists often fall between the two views with some feeling that their royalties on sales have been reduced, while others feel that the copied files go to people who wouldn't have bought in the first place but might be encouraged to buy in the future if they like what they hear or see.

Today there are four major record labels that have a global presence. These are Warner Music Group, EMI, Sony Music and Universal Music Group. Each of these labels also owns numerous subsidiary labels and brands, some of which are affiliated to a particular music genre, e.g. Grand Hustle Records specialize in hip hop and R&B, and are a subsidiary label of Warner Music Group. Apart from the major labels and their subsidiaries, there are also independent labels that are not owned or affiliated with any of the major labels. Independent labels rose to prominence in the 1980s, when the previously non-popular output of these labels became popular through artists such as 'The Smiths' and 'The Fall' who were bands signed to independent label Rough Trade Records. This gave birth to the term 'indie' as a music genre that covered largely white alternative rock and post-punk bands, many of which were signed to independent labels, although the eventual commercial acceptance of such music led to major labels signing many of these once independent bands. Today an independent band or artist can largely be thought of as one who works without the assistance of a record label, and handles the recording of their music using their own computers and specialist software, and the promotion and supply of their music through the Internet.

The modern global music business is estimated to be worth in excess of US$130 billion annually (IFPI, 2009), which is made up mainly of sales of physical and digital music products; licensing of music in other forms of entertainment such as computer games, movies and ringtones; live performance revenue; and performance rights from broadcasters or the owners of venues that play music to customers In the UK, this is monitored by the Performing Rights Society (PRS) (see Fig. 3.2), who collect an annual fee from venue owners where music is played and distribute this to recording artists. Although a proportion of this revenue is now very much under threat with the advent of the Internet and technologies that make illegal distribution and copying of music virtually unstoppable (see Chapters 7 and 8, this volume).

The process by which music has traditionally been commodified and supplied by labels is demonstrated in Fig. 3.3.

Fig. 3.2. Performing Rights Society sticker on a restaurant door.

Fig. 3.3. The traditional music supply chain.

CREATION

Music like any art form is creative by its very nature, it is preconceived, written and arranged by composers, musicians and songwriters and performed by artists such as musicians and vocalists.

Composition

This is the creative process that artists undergo that typically involves piecing together a collection of sounds either from musical instruments or computers into a particular sequence, for songs this involves the addition of lyrics that usually rhyme.

Recording

Traditionally this has taken place in recording studios, and is the formal stage when a music track is performed and recorded. At one time this was on to analogue media; however, now tracks are recorded on to digital multi-track recorders and computers. Advances in computing technology now mean that it is possible for artists to record tracks at home on to their own computers. This has exacerbated the proliferation of independent artists who make music for the love of it, and not for record labels to profit from.

Engineering

This is when recorded sounds may be modified, manipulated, enhanced and altered. This was once the role of professionals who would use sophisticated and expensive consoles, but again technological advancements now make it possible for independent artists to engineer their own tracks, often as they create them.

Remixing

More than mere engineering, remixing involves creating new versions of a particular audio track; some remixes may only contain subtle differences, but more elaborate remixes may sound like a completely different track. Artists working for a record label may have no involvement in this process, and often find their work altered in a way that is far removed from the original artistic direction in which they went. However, record labels may realize that higher sales volumes can be achieved by tapping into different music genre markets through remixes. Modern-day remixing has its roots in (dub) reggae, rocksteady and ska music from the 1960s and 1970s. Remixing is most synonymous with various genres of dance music, although every genre of music today has remixes created, it is extremely common for tracks to be released in several alternative remixes, an example being rock band 'The Killers' whose track *Mr Brightside* was officially released in two different rock versions, and five different dance-/club-style remixes.

REPRODUCTION

The finalized track(s) is mass-produced on to physical formats (predominantly CDs) or hosted upon web sites where it can be purchased in electronic format.

Packaging and formats

Only physical formats require packaging, today CDs are the predominant physical format, these require a case, and within that case an inlay and/or booklet with further information about the artist and the songs is often contained within the CD case. When music was produced on vinyl, packaging took on a greater significance, as albums were 12" in diameter, which

Fig. 3.4. A selection of vinyl LPs and 12" singles with gatefold sleeves, pull out posters and lyric sheets.

meant that the larger art work needed to look eye-catching and impressive. Vinyl albums and singles would sometimes come with accompanying posters, booklets and in special editions (see Fig. 3.4) such as picture discs. This, however, did not translate as easily on to the smaller-sized CDs, which did sometimes come in special editions such as box sets, or with giveaways, but more commonly with additional remixes on the CD, largely due to their higher capacity. Downsizing the physical product meant that packaging was more standardized and simpler, with more emphasis on the music itself rather than the package in which it came. The development of the Internet further exacerbated package downsizing, as previously difficult to access images and information about artists became easily available online, thus further reducing the need for elaborate packaging, to the point where downloadable music content comes without any packaging, although some software such as iTunes and Windows Media Player will download album artwork to accompany MP3 files on computers and media players.

PROMOTION

The competitiveness of this industry sector has already been stressed within this chapter, and in such a dynamic business environment music promotion is key to the success of record labels and their artists.

Live performance

Live performance of music has traditionally been an essential aspect of its promotion, and is typically referred to as a concert or (more informally, and particualrly in relation to popular music) a 'gig'. While, historically, live music and dance were one and the same, with attendees going out to dance halls, they are now quite distinct entertainment forms. Gigs are staged musical performances (see Fig. 3.5), that are usually rehearsed and depending on the size and scale of the performance may incorporate a number of theatrical props, including costumes, special effects, pyrotechnics, dancers, and laser and light displays. Gigs are typified by their size, duration and genres of music being performed; some examples could include an orchestral performance; a rock concert; or something much more large-scale such as a music festival, which may include numerous bands playing across several stages or venues over several days. The majority of live music performances rarely make headlines, although a number of bands and artists incorporate controversial theatre into their live music shows, guaranteeing newspaper headlines and wide exposure, some famous examples include: 'Ozzy Osbourne', who in 1982 bit the head off a bat on stage in Des Moines, Iowa; 'The Beastie Boys', who in the 1980s had topless women dancing in cages, and a large inflatable penis on the stage; 'Public Enemy', who during the 1980s and 1990s had performers on stage dressed in combat fatigues and brandishing 'Uzi' sub-machine guns; and 'Marilyn Manson' who uses fake blood, fire and violent imagery.

Live music events are promoted by music promotion companies (promoters). A promoter will take the responsibility for producing and distributing publicity materials, as well as placing

Fig. 3.5. A indie-rock gig.

adverts in the media. Promoters may work for a set fee, or more commonly a financial cut in profits from ticket sales, which can be useful in motivating them to promote events effectively.

Throughout the 1950s and 1960s, popular music had developed as an art form loved by young people. As these youngsters grew older and more joined the ranks, the audiences for popular music grew from a few hundred to a few thousand. As larger venues were sought and popular music moved slowly from clubs to theatres, it was only a matter of time until large-scale events moved outdoors. In the late 1960s, American audiences became used to the idea of seeing their musical heroes in the outdoor setting of stadiums. Ironically, it was British acts such as 'The Beatles', 'The Rolling Stones' and 'Led Zeppelin' who provided the entertainment as part of what became known as the 'The British Invasion'. The iconic stadium moment came when The Beatles performed at the Shea Stadium in New York where they opened their 1965 tour with a record-breaking crowd of 55,600 at the height of 'Beatlemania'. From there, it was inevitable that other open air venues would be used for enjoying music.

Social Factor: the Development of Music Festivals

If Beatlemania was the spark that ignited the fuse of stadia for music events, it was the hippy counterculture that inspired 'Woodstock'. Billed as 'An Aquarian Exposition – Three Days of Peace and Music', the festival was organized on 600 acres of farmland located south-west of Woodstock in upstate New York. Around 30 of the most popular acts of the time appeared, including 'Jimi Hendrix', 'The Band', 'The Who' and 'Janis Joplin', who played to an audience estimated to be as large as 500,000 people. Though music fans hail this unprecedented gathering of the finest popular music acts of the time, it also flagged the need for the improved organization of such large-scale events. For example, there was a single stage open to the natural elements, which was regularly battered with rain, and access for artists to this area was also fraught with problems. As a consequence, the running times were considerably late with The Who appearing in the middle of the night and Jimi Hendrix's closing set starting as the sun came up. Collier (1969) described the chaos caused by traffic, births, deaths, drug use and shortage of water – all these aspects would be considered priority issues to be managed by today's festival organizer but, at the time, the view of one attendee was simply quoted as 'The whole thing is a gas. I dig it all, the mud, the rain, the music, the hassles'. Though Woodstock couldn't claim to be the first music festival (with others such as 'Newport Folk Festival' and 'Monterey Pop' predating it), it did give a huge push to the idea of a youthful gathering based around the popular music of the time. In the UK, for example, music festivals had occurred on the Isle of Wight in 1968 and 1969, but the 1970 festival attendances were boosted to levels similar to Woodstock and brought with it attendant problems, pushing the abilities of organizers' management skills.

(Continued)

Social Factor: Continued.

Music festivals have grown in number and spread across continents. They range in size and duration from a few hundred (see Fig. 3.6) to many thousand attendees and a single day to a week or longer. However, rarely do any of these festivals reach the crowd numbers seen at Woodstock and the like. Those early music festivals were freewheeling affairs with a hippy counterculture that suggested music should be free for all and, indeed, these festivals often became something of a 'free-for-all'. Yet, music promoters saw the potential for making money and slowly pushed aside the hippy attitudes to create commercially aimed music festivals. Audience expectations increased with the choice and variety available for their enjoyment, meaning that no longer did they 'dig…the hassles'. Often, for example, the mature festival attendee will reject simple camping options in favour of better on-site (or off-site) accommodation (Steinhauser, 2008). Furthermore, the public as consumer has become increasingly protected by law, with festival organizers not only having customer needs to satisfy, but also legal requirements, particularly health and safety which festival organizers and promoters must actively comply with.

Fig. 3.6. An urban city-centre-based music festival.

The expansion of the market for music festivals has resulted in increased competition and a range of options for festivals to position themselves as 'different' in the eyes of

(Continued)

Social Factor: Continued.

potential attendees. In Fig. 3.7, typical positions for festivals are indicated based on dimensions of the range of age in the audience and musical genres in the programme. In this way, relative competitive positions can be seen for different festivals, though, clearly, there are a variety of attendee or festival attributes that might be used as competitive dimensions, e.g. ticket price (from free to expensive) or aims (commercial versus social and cultural). The modern music festival attendees does not limit their choice to one based on the range and quality of the music on offer. Attendees look at the opportunities to generally socialize, have fun and be entertained (Henderson and Wood, 2009). In an ironic twist that takes us back to the original 'feast'-style definition of 'festival', this has seen the emergence of the boutique festival where music is just one part of the entertainment alongside what might best be described as a street theatre approach to the day. As Fig. 3.7 implies, this wider approach opens up a wider market and further opportunity for the festival promoter.

		Range of musical genres	
		Narrow	Wide
Range of audience age	Narrow	Though these might be deemed 'special interest', they might be large or small. For example, indie rock for youth audiences, e.g. V Festival, Reading/Leeds Festivals, Benecassim, punk rock; and opera festivals for older audiences, e.g. Glyndebourne.	Unusual to find festivals of this nature as the wide selection of genres is likely to have less appeal to a narrow age-range audience. Examples can be found that run over an extended period and use multiple venues and have another focus, e.g. Celtic Connections.
	Wide	Typically, festivals that feature long-established music genres where playing music means as much as watching others play such as folk music,e.g. Cambridge Folk Festival.	Typically, these are large, multi-stage and multi-format (including poetry, comedy, etc.) festivals such as Glastonbury and Latitude that have something for a range of audiences.

Fig. 3.7. Festivals positioned on range of audience age and musical genres.

Marketing, publicity and media exposure

Granting the media access to music prior to its official release is essential in its promotion, and 'hype' build-up, so that when music is released, there are buyers ready to make the purchase. Radio stations and disc jockeys (DJs) regularly get advanced promotional copies of new tracks due to their potential to influence the buying public. Today these are as electronic files; however, they used to be provided as 'white labels' which were vinyl records that had a blank white label as their centrepiece and came in a blank white sleeve, so as not to reveal too much information about the track. The rising popularity of television from the 1960s onwards meant that this medium could also be used to promote music. Music was often performed live either on dedicated music programmes such as *The Old Grey Whistle Test* (which ran on the BBC between 1971 and 1987) or upcoming artists were given a performance slot on other types of television programmes such as chat shows. When artists were unavailable to perform, their new songs were sometimes played over montages of pre-recorded footage of the artist, or songs were simply played in the studio while dance troupes performed to the song. 'Pop promos', which were video clips of artists played alongside newly released songs, began to appear in the early 1970s and were distributed to television broadcasters. The rock band 'Queen' released their single *Bohemian Rhapsody* in 1975; prior to its release a lavish and theatrical promotional video of the band performing the song was distributed to broadcasters. This was considered ground-breaking, and was widely played on television, giving the song widespread exposure and contributing to its commercial success (over 2 million copies sold, and 9 weeks spent at number one in the UK singles chart).

In 1981, Music Television (MTV) began broadcasting as a cable television channel in the USA. The channel played back-to-back music videos, hosted by 'video jockeys' (VJs). Its popularity grew rapidly throughout the 1980s, as more and more newly released music tracks came with a music video. Today, MTV is a global brand with regionalized versions of the channel in the UK, Europe, Australia and Asia (among others). It is now standard practice for artists signed to major labels (or subsidiaries) to produce music videos with new single releases, many of which are highly theatrical in nature, incorporating all manner of special effects.

Other methods by which new music is publicized are impromptu live performances in actual retail outlets; interviews with the band/artists in the media; media advertisements, such as television adverts and large billboard-sized posters; online promotional web sites and downloadable materials; written press and media releases with accompanying photographs; and publicity stunts.

In the case of independent musicians, who release their music through the Internet, there is less emphasis (and often none) by them on marketing, publicity and media exposure, as their motivation to create music is often down to the love of their art, rather than for commercial gain, although as more independent artists arise, and with an increased emphasis by record labels on an online and accessible presence for their artists, combined with a less corporate inaccessible image, independent artists may find an increased necessity to compete in the online marketplace, with promotion being a vital tool in this battle.

Reviews

As with virtually all (and particularly commercial) art forms, so-called expert reviewers and critics publicize their opinions of newly released music in the media, this can influence some undecided buyers, although fans who are loyal to a particular artist are less likely to be swayed by the opinions of others. Gaining positive media reviews is particularly seen as a success by labels and artists, as this will boost sales. A phenomenon of the Internet age, and particularly Web 2.0 (see Chapter 8, this volume) is the proliferation of independent and fan-based reviewers who express their opinions in discussion forums, on social networking web sites, and in blogs.

DISTRIBUTION AND RETAIL

With physical media, a distribution network is paramount in order to transfer quantities of recorded products to retailers that can then sell them on. It is common for physical media products such as CDs to be supplied in bulk to retailers, and most record labels have distribution deals with distributors to ensure that sufficient quantities of stock are maintained at retailers.

The migration to online sales means that there is now a reduced need for distribution to retailers as more sales are now taking place online. This has led to the creation of specialist aggregators whose role is to supply digital music to online retailers. Companies such as 'Awal' and 'Tunecore' are aggregators that offer services to place electronic music with online retailers such as 'iTunes', 'Napster', 'Rhapsody', 'AmazonMP3' and 'eMusic' (for digital rights management (DRM) free music largely from independent labels) (Fusiarski, 2008). In this business system, the entire business is undertaken online, this includes the subscription to the aggregator and payment for services; the music files being transferred from artist to aggregator; each music file being assigned a unique universal product code (UPC) (barcode equivalent); the music files being transferred from aggregator to retailer; the retailer receiving payment from the customer; the retailer transferring music file(s) to the customer; the retailer registering the sale; and the retailer paying royalties directly to the artist.

Online sales of music are steadily increasing, as sales of physical formats are steadily decreasing. Current figures suggest that around 25% of all legitimate music sales take place online (BBC, 2009), with an annual increase in online sales of 150% between 2008 and 2009. The first major label signed band to release an album exclusively online was 'They Might Be Giants' who released their album *Long Tall Weekend* in mp3 format in 1999. In 2007, 'Radiohead' released their *In Rainbows* album as a 'free' download, where fans could pay anything from nothing up to £100 for the ten files that make up the album (BBC, 2007). Alongside this, fans were offered the option of buying a physical product that also included extra tracks, a vinyl version of the record and booklet with lyrics. Though Radiohead have been accused of being gimmicky to attract publicity for the release and are cagey about actual figures, this approach was declared a success, although Radiohead band member Thom Yorke has since announced that the band will no longer make any further albums (Baby, 2009). A different approach was adopted by 'The Charlatans' who gave away the album *You Cross My Path* via the XFM Radio web site at the time of its initial release. Though it is hard to speculate without the details, these approaches support a viewpoint that some artists have decided that it is important to get the music in the hands of music fans as this should lead to packed concerts where profit can be made. This is a complete turnaround in the approach to the way that music sector has traditionally done business, where once live performances were used to drive music sales, now the music has become a promotional medium to drive sales of tickets for live music performances, where other products such as artist-related clothing and media products can also be sold. The music supply chain is changing, it is becoming less cluttered as artists can now maintain greater control over their finances, cutting out the 'middlemen' and putting more profits directly into their own pockets, rather than into the record labels.

Record labels have seen their profits from music sales fall, which has drastically affected income; EMI reported losses of £757 million between 2007 and 2008 (Maltby Capital, 2008); this realization has led to the development of the '360 degree deal' (BBC, 2008) where the artist hands over the rights to not only their income from recordings, but also that from both merchandise and touring. EMI tempted Robbie Williams into this type of deal for £80 million in 2002; it also became clear that this sort of deal can also be done by music promoters such as 'Live Nation' who have signed similar deals with 'Madonna', 'Jay-Z' and 'Nickleback' (Lindvall, 2008).

Case Study: Live Nation

Clear Channel Communications (CCC) was founded in 1972, and began to acquire a range of radio stations across the USA. Over time, the US government realized that any domination of this key communication sector gave companies the power to influence public opinion and attitude. To control this, legislation was introduced to restrict the ability of companies to own radio stations and this soon began to limit the ability of CCC to expand. Acquisitions of competitors by CCC were often accompanied by the need to dispose of some of their other radio stations. As the management were concerned about the ability to grow the company, they diversified into other media such as television, advertising and live events, and in doing so became a media group.

Government concerns about excessive power were tested in 2003 when Natalie Maines of 'The Dixie Chicks' indicated from a London stage that she was 'ashamed the president of the United States is from Texas'. However, it was not her comments in relation to the Iraq War and George Bush that caused concern but the reaction from American radio stations (CNN, 2003). CCC were accused of using their power and influence to remove The Dixie Chicks' music from radio airwaves (Krugman, 2003), although others suggested that the main influence was that of listeners reacting in anger at what was said (BBC, 2003). In 2004, a Denver court caused ripples to flow further around the music business world as CCC were accused by a local independent promoter of threatening to remove the airplay of music by artists who preferred the independent promoter over CCC (DBJ, 2009). With monopolistic concerns building, CCC acted to separate their live events business in 2005 with the creation of Live Nation.

Live Nation moved forward as a global live music events business over the following years, promoting world tours by major acts including The Eagles, U2, Coldplay, Jack Johnson and Bryan Adams. In addition, they played a major role in the Live Earth concerts in 2007 where Al Gore and Kevin Wall initiated a programme of concerts to highlight the need to pay attention to the protection of our environment. The decline of recorded music sales caused Live Nation to offer '360-degree deals' to artists, giving them control over all aspects of their musical output including touring, merchandise and music sales.

These moves concerned those involved in music due to the extent of control held by Live Nation, but others highlighted the point that their control only related to a relative handful of major artists and was, in truth, just part of the music industry restructuring being driven by the digital age. The detractors of Live Nation went into overdrive when Live Nation merged with Ticketmaster. Fans of Bruce Springsteen seeking face-value tickets from Ticketmaster were redirected from the Ticketmaster web site to TicketsNow where 'unwanted' tickets were available for resale at premium prices. This led to Bruce Springsteen and his management team posting a note to fans on his web site apologizing and warning of the possible consequences of the Live Nation and Ticketmaster merger. Picked up across the media, including Springsteen's home territory (North Jersey, 2009), the timing of this problem could not have been worse for Live Nation as it raised the profile of issues surrounding merger.

(Continued)

Case Study: Continued.

Despite the concerns that the globalization of the live music industry and the power of its major players present, there needs to be some balance in the argument about monopolistic positions as this is not a problem exclusive to live music. Firat and Shultz (1997) have identified that global markets and increased competition has fragmented markets allowing many organizations to thrive. In the world of live music, while large global players have developed, there are many smaller, local, independent promoters who have successful businesses. Live Nation may well argue that their activities may appear to dominate in some markets but that this is all part of their involvement in the globalizing mass media entertainment industry, and does not detract from live music itself. Quite clearly, this debate will roll on within the live music industry and many other globalizing, fragmenting markets.

CONSUMPTION

The consumption of music takes place at the point whereby an audience hears it. This includes live music attendance, listening to music on a car radio while driving, listening to music on a personal MP3 player, and listening to music on a stereo. The ways by which we consume music have changed in relation to societal developments such as the development of music festivals, fashions and music genres, and technological developments including the creation of new media, and then media-less music (see Chapter 7, this volume).

THE FUTURE

There is an undeniable demand for music that has grown rapidly in the last 60 years, and has seen more artists releasing more music year upon year, how the industry continues to adapt to changes in demand for how music is supplied and consumed will largely dictate which organizations survive, and which ones face demise. The emergent music supply chain featured in Fig. 3.8 indicates how the music business is changing and will continue to change.

Fig. 3.8. The emergent music supply chain.

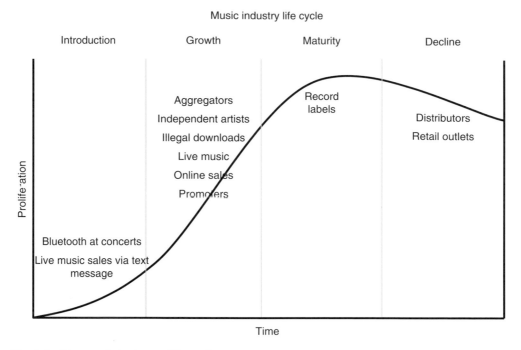

Fig. 3.9. The music industry life cycle.

The future for some aspects of this entertainment industry sector is highlighted in Fig. 3.9.

Introduction

Bluetooth at concerts – the potential for artists to interact with thousands of fans at concerts via mobile technologies and Bluetooth has yet to be fully exploited. Not only can the timings of bands appearing and set lists be easily broadcast to audiences, but promotional images, details of forthcoming releases, snippets of songs and videos, and song and track information can also be sent via Bluetooth to give concerts an element of added value, while at the same time promoting commercial releases.

Live music sales via text message – taking the above notion a step further, live music can now be sold directly to audiences as it happens; screens on stages could advertise that the song being performed live 'right now' can be purchased immediately by sending a SMS text message (charged at a premium rate) to a certain number. As soon as the song being performed ends, those people who text the number would receive a text message with a link to download the track. This could potentially be very lucrative with concerts that have thousands of people in attendance.

Growth

Aggregators – the recognition of increasing online sales will lead to more aggregating companies entering the marketplace, which will undoubtedly be a new business area for many record labels.

Independent artists – the number of artists 'going it alone' without the help of a record label will increase as artists, who may have only been used to receiving small royalties from record labels, take control of their finances in order to reap higher rewards.

Illegal downloads – these will continue to increase unless piracy laws are enforced or incentives are put in place to prevent this.

Live music – recognition of potential income streams from concerts by artists will lead to more live music events taking place, where commercial exploitation of merchandise and other sales can guarantee additional income.

Online sales – these will continue to increase until online sales become dominant.

Promoters – the recognition of the importance of live music will lead to more promoters entering the marketplace. EMI and Live Nation may have formed a business model that other record labels will follow.

Maturity

Record labels – this is now a defunct term, and is often abbreviated to simply 'labels'; recorded losses by EMI mark the beginning of the end for those labels who fail to adapt to the rapidly changing business environment. Unless labels can adapt and in doing so reinvent the ways by which they do business (and in doing so give artists better financial rewards), they will most certainly enter a terminal decline.

Decline

Distributors – as more sales go online, the number of units of physical music items distributed to retailers has and will continue to decrease, for music distributors this is now a terminal decline.

Retail outlets – the record shop that was so popular from the 1950s to the 1990s has entered terminal decline as more sales go online, and more music is downloaded illegally. Record shops have diversified in the face of this into general media outlets also selling DVDs, computer games, posters, books and T-shirts. Even online sales of these have meant that closure for some chains has been inevitable.

REFERENCES

Baby, L. (2009) *Thom Yorke: Making Another Album Would Kill Radiohead*. [Internet] London, InTheNews.co.uk. URL available at: <http://www.inthenews.co.uk/entertainment/music/thom-yorke-making-another-album-would-kill-radiohead-$1318072.htm>.

British Broadcasting Corporation (BBC) (2003) Dixies dropped over Bush remark. [Internet] London, BBC. URL available at: <http://news.bbc.co.uk/1/hi/entertainment/music/2867221.stm>.

British Broadcasting Corporation (BBC) (2007) Radiohead album set free on web. [Internet] London, BBC. URL available at: <http://news.bbc.co.uk/1/hi/entertainment/7037219.stm>.

British Broadcasting Corporation (BBC) (2008) Music firms tune into new deals. [Internet] London, BBC. URL available at: <http://news.bbc.co.uk/1/hi/business/7480183.stm>.

British Broadcasting Corporation (BBC) (2009) Piracy still prevailing. [Internet] London, BBC. URL available at: <http://www.bbc.co.uk/6music/news/20090116_downloading.shtml>.

Cable News Network (CNN) (2003) Dixie Chicks pulled from air after bashing Bush. [Internet] Atlanta, CNN. URL available at: <http://www.cnn.com/2003/SHOWBIZ/Music/03/14/dixie.chicks.reut/>.

Collier, B. (1969) Tired rock fans begin exodus. [Internet] New York, *New York Times*. URL available at: <http://www.nytimes.com/learning/general/onthisday/big/0817.html#article>.

Denver Business Journal (DBJ) (2009) NIPP's case proceeds against Clear Channel. [Internet] Denver, DBJ. URL available at: <http://denver.bizjournals.com/denver/stories/2004/04/05/daily13.html?jst=b_ln_hl>.

Firat, A. F. and Shultz, C.J. (1997) From segmentation to fragmentation: markets and marketing strategy in the postmodern era. *European Journal of Marketing*. 31(3), 183–207.

Fusiarski, A. (2008) How to get your music distributed on iTunes (and keep most of the money). [Internet] Cape Coral, Florida, Musicbizhacks.com. URL available at: <http://musicbizhacks.com/how-to-get-your-music-distributed-on-itunes-and-keep-90-of-the-money>.

Henderson, S. and Wood E.A. (2009) All-rounders or single-trackers - Segmenting the music festival audience. Proceedings of the Academy of Marketing Conference 2009. Leeds Metropolitan University, Leeds, UK.

International Federation of the Phonographic Industry (IFPI) (2009) [Internet] London, IFPI. PDF Document available at: <http://www.ifpi.org/content/library/the-broader-music-industry.pdf>.

Krugman, P. (2003) Channels of influence. [Internet] New York, *New York Times*. URL available at: <http://www.nytimes.com/2003/03/25/opinion/channels-of-influence.html>.

Lindvall, H. (2008) Deal or no deal? [Internet] London, *The Guardian*. URL available at: <http://www.guardian.co.uk/music/musicblog/2008/jul/25/dealornodeal>.

Maltby Capital (2008) Maltby Capital Ltd annual review year ended 31 March 2008. [Internet] London, EMI. URL available at: <http://www.emigroup.com/NR/rdonlyres/0753D5E3-20C6-433E-A616-D1BC4482BB42/1662/MaltbyCapitalLimitedAnnualReviewStatements1.pdf>.

Michel, N.J. (2006) The impact of digital file sharing on the music industry: an empirical analysis. *Topics in Economic Analysis & Policy*. 6(1), Article 18.

North Jersey (2009) Springsteen blasts Ticketmaster: 'We condemn this practice'. [Internet] Hackensack, NJMG. URL available at: <http://www.northjersey.com/breakingnews/Springsteen_i.html>.

Steinhauser, G. (2008) A grown-up's guide to summer rock festivals. [Internet] New York, *The Wall Street Journal*. URL available at: <http://online.wsj.com/public/article/SB121562290292839651.html>.

chapter 4

Bars, Pubs and Clubs

Stuart Moss

Venues (or 'units') of varying sizes, where the sale of alcoholic drinks is typically the core business function, and where entertainment is provided to encourage patronage.

The bars, pubs and clubs sector of the entertainment industry is typified as being a sector that contains entertainment venues, which have a core business function of selling alcoholic beverages, and use entertainment to encourage visitation and patronage in order to increase beverage sales. The type and variety of entertainment on offer vary according to a number of factors including: venue size, day of the week, location, time of the year, physical structure and layout, and legal regulations.

Humans have enjoyed the consumption of alcoholic beverages for thousands of years, particularly as part of social gatherings. Bars, pubs and clubs offer both leisure and entertainment experience in a social environment where customers can relax, while eating, drinking and chatting with friends. The consumption of alcoholic beverages is ingrained into many cultures as an accepted societal norm; this may be as a regular aspect of socialization, or for particular occasions where a specific type of alcohol may be consumed, an example being champagne being drunk as an aspect of celebration. Alcohol can act as both a stimulant and a relaxant, and as such is often utilized by people to alter their mental and emotional state during periods of recreation. The consumption of large quantities of alcoholic beverages can lead to intoxication, the resultant effect upon the individual being the impairment of physical and mental faculties, otherwise known as 'being under the influence of alcohol', or drunkenness.

Drunken behaviour causes individuals to act in a manner which they may not normally be accustomed to, sometimes this may be as harmless as the lowering of personal inhibitions, resulting in singing, dancing and the participation of other largely 'harmless' activities; however, there is also a 'darker' side to drunkenness. Violence and other forms of antisocial behaviour are known to increase at night (particularly late at night) in urban locations with a high concentration of venues that are licensed to serve alcohol. Antisocial behaviour can often take place away from bars, pubs and clubs, in locations such as taxi queues, food takeaways and areas where crowds of people may gather. This can dissuade people from wanting to be in such locations at night-time, which can have a damaging impact upon the night-time economy of such areas. In addition to this, there are financial implications for governments and local authorities who are required to police such areas, and treat casualties of drunkenness in hospitals and medical centres.

Legal Factor: Licensing Laws

As a result of such alcohol-related 'issues', a licensing system and laws exist in many countries that are designed to regulate the sale and consumption of alcohol, reducing the negative impacts associated with alcohol consumption including antisocial behaviour, and health and safety concerns. Licensing systems and laws serve a number of purposes; some typical examples include the following:

- Placing age limits upon those who are allowed to purchase (and sell) alcohol, the most common age limit globally for the consumption of alcohol is 18; however, there are some variations upon this including: Poland and Samoa – 16; Cyprus, Germany and Greece – 17; South Korea – 19; and Fiji and the USA – 21. These are just examples, and this list is by no means exhaustive.
- Prohibiting the sale of alcohol to a person who appears to already be drunk. This can cause problems in some licensed venues, particularly those in city centres, and as such, many licensed venues have trained security (or door-staff) whose presence is designed to deter troublemakers, and remove those persons from premises who are liable to cause or are causing a problem.
- Making it illegal to consume alcohol in particular locations, for example, on sidewalks or pavements outside of licensed venues.
- Prohibiting the sale of alcohol to particular groups of people; in the UK, it is illegal to serve alcohol to a police officer in uniform.
- Restricting the actions of those who have consumed alcohol, e.g. making 'drink-driving' illegal.
- Making it necessary for those who own licences to sell alcohol on their premises to complete a training course, or gain certification of their suitability; in the UK, this is a stringent process that is certified by the British Institute for Innkeepers and Bars (BIIB).

It should be noted that in a number of countries (particularly Islamic countries), alcohol consumption is largely banned, examples of such countries include Brunei, Kuwait, Libya and Saudi Arabia. As such, an alternative 'cafe culture' exists in place of bars and pubs where traditional drinks such as hot and cold teas may be consumed. In some countries, these may be accompanied with the smoking of cigarettes or hookah pipes, which are water-filtered smoking

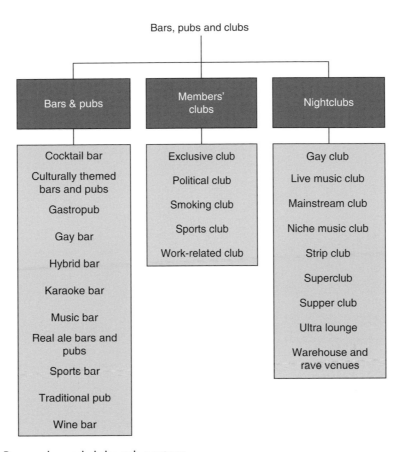

Fig. 4.1. Bars, pubs and clubs sub-sectors.

pipes that are used for the smoking of tobacco, herbs and fruits. These venues may also provide entertainment, such as traditional singers, dancers and musicians, but these are generally geared towards tourists as part of a 'culturtainment' experience (see Chapter 16, this volume). Figure 4.1 highlights the sub-sectors within this sector of the entertainment industry.

BARS AND PUBS

Also known as inns and taverns, bars and pubs are typically small- to medium-sized venues that offer seated areas with tables that allow customers to socialize while consuming drinks, as well as food. The word 'pub' is actually an abbreviation of 'public house', which is a term that is distinctly English in origin, but is now also used in other countries, particularly those with a British Commonwealth influence. Globally the word 'bar' is now more commonly used to describe this type of venue. In mainland Europe, bars and pubs may also be referred to as 'cafes' and in warmer climates often feature outside seating areas. Table 4.1 gives a breakdown of the most common types of bar and pub.

Fig. 4.2. Customers dancing inside a hybrid bar.

Fig. 4.3. A traditional Northern Irish pub.

Table 4.1. Bars and pubs and their characteristics.

Type of bar or pub	Characteristics
Cocktail bar	As the name suggests, these bars specialize in providing cocktails, often from a cocktail menu. The actual cocktail creation process has been turned into a performing art form (flaring), and is used to 'wow' audiences
Culturally themed bar	See 'Cultural Gastronomy' in Chapter 16 (this volume)
Gastropub	A pub that specializes in the serving of high-quality food from extensive menus. In gastropubs, the sale of food rather than drinks is usually the core business function
Gay bar	This is a bar targeted towards and frequented predominantly by homosexuals, with gay iconographic theming
Hybrid bar	A late-opening bar with a DJ and a dance floor (see Fig. 4.2) that can function as a combination of both a bar and a club; it can be difficult to distinguish the difference between some of the larger hybrid bars and nightclubs
Karaoke bar	A bar that offers either an automated or DJ-controlled karaoke facility, so that patrons can sing along on stage with a microphone, often very badly and creating a comedic spectacle for audiences. Karaoke was developed in Japan, but became popular globally in the late 1980s
Music bar	A bar that offers regular live music entertainment. This may be through having bands playing, such as 'Jazz Bars' or through a musician providing background music such as a 'Piano Bar'
Sports bar	Typically themed around several sports, with sporting memorabilia and decor, sports bars usually screen sporting fixtures, and feature table sports such as pool and football for customer use
Real ale bars and pubs	Bars and pubs that focus on the provision of specialist beers, particularly local beers, and unusual beers from around the world, such as fruit beers. Real ale bars and pubs often feature very little musical or televised entertainment

(Continued)

Table 4.1. Continued.

Type of bar or pub	Characteristics
Traditional pub	These are considered 'old-fashioned' by many younger patrons. Traditional pubs are based on the model of having two rooms: a 'tap room' (or bar) and a 'lounge'. The tap room has traditionally had very basic or plain decor, and has been a very 'male' environment, often featuring a pool table and slot machines. The lounge is perceived to be the 'best' room, and usually has more plush furniture than the tap room. Traditional pubs are losing popularity in the face of more contemporary competition. A traditional pub is featured in Fig. 4.3
Wine bar	A bar that specializes in the sale of wine (still, sparkling and champagne), usually from extensive wine lists. These are often located in urban centres, and are considered as expensive 'high-end' venues

Bars and pubs feature a number of forms of entertainment that are used to increase custom, these are highlighted below.

Competitions and quizzes including bingo – these are played in some bars and pubs on a midweek night in order to boost custom.

DJs – they are a regular feature on Friday and Saturday nights in many pubs; DJs are used to create a 'party' atmosphere.

Gaming machines – these are common in bars and pubs, particularly gambling 'slot' machines (outside of most of the USA), as well as quiz machines and arcade-style gaming machines.

Karaoke – these are typically mobile karaoke machines, hired for special occasions, parties, and sometimes on regular nights, often hosted by a professional karaoke singer or DJ.

Live music – this is a regular feature in bars and pubs with bands and singers often playing on particular nights during the week, or at weekends in order to beat the competition.

Stand-up comedy – while stand-up comedians are still relatively rare in bars and pubs, they are becoming more commonplace, particularly during midweek nights, when they can bring in additional custom.

Televised sports – in Europe, Africa, Asia and South America, this is most commonly live soccer games, while in North America televised games in bars and pubs are more commonly American football, basketball and ice hockey, and in Australia and New Zealand the most popular televised sports in pubs and bars are cricket and rugby. Numerous other sports may

Fig. 4.4. Televised sports attract customers to bars and pubs.

also feature, but those broadcast in pubs and bars are typically the most high-profile games, which cost a premium, and require equipment and a subscription, which may make them inaccessible for some viewers to have at home. Freely available premium sports games in pubs and bars, brings visitors in (see Fig. 4.4). While there is usually a high subscription cost for pub or bar owners to broadcast televised sports games, the increased sales of particularly drinks usually more than pays for this.

Social Factor: the Feminization of Bars and Pubs

A post-millennium trend among governments and authorities particularly in northern Europe and North America has been to introduce smoking bans in public places including bars, pubs and clubs. This has resulted in many such venues being revamped and redecorated, leading to a phenomenon referred to as the 'feminization' of bars and pubs. Once a very male domain, bars and pubs are actively working to shed themselves of this outdated image in a number of ways including: redecorating in bright modern colours; providing drinks that are popular with women, particularly bottled (and draught) wine and ciders, as well as having cocktail menus; removing dart boards and pool tables; having more comfortable seated areas within pubs; providing more extensive menus; and providing outside social space (where smoking may take place) and in doing so creating heated outside drinking areas, and better maintained 'beer gardens'.

(Continued)

Social Factor: Continued.

The feminization of bars and pubs has also led to a greater opportunity for them to be utilized as more generic entertainment spaces, particularly with staged story and variety performances. Comedy clubs in bars and pubs (often on a particular night each week) have grown in number over the past 10 years, and the increasing popularity of stand-up comedy means that this trend will most likely continue. What is only just beginning to appear is the use of bars and pubs for the purposes of theatrical performances, either on a stage or utilizing the layout of venues to provide entertainment such as: storytelling, poetry recitals, dance shows and small-scale plays.

MEMBERS' CLUBS

The domain of wealthy, gentlemen only, members' clubs have been in existence for just over 200 years. As their name suggests, these are venues that require patrons to become members before they are eligible to use the premises. Many members' clubs often run at low overheads and with low profit margins, putting the revenue that they generate back into the club itself; as a consequence, drinks prices in some types of members' clubs may be lower than the standard 'high street' prices, although this is certainly not the case with exclusive and high-brow members' clubs. Members' club membership often involves at the very least a subscription fee, but as well as this, there may also be other 'rules' that members must fulfil, for example, some members' clubs are affiliated to a particular vocation, such as 'Servicemen's Clubs', which require members to be either serving or ex-members of the armed forces. Other clubs may also have strict codes of conduct, and breaching these may result in suspension or expulsion from the club. While all member's clubs were once 'exclusive', only allowing members (and sometimes their families/guests in), in an increasingly competitive business environment it is becoming ever more common for those who are not members to be able to visit and drink in at least some types of members' clubs. This in turn can dissuade existing members from renewing their membership, blurring the boundary between some members' clubs and bars/pubs.

Members' clubs offer the same types of entertainment as bars and pubs, but often on a larger scale, with function rooms that are specifically designed with entertainment in mind. A selection of the common types of members' clubs is featured in Table 4.2; please note that this list is by no means exhaustive.

Table 4.2. Members' clubs and their characteristics.

Type of members' club	Characteristics
Exclusive clubs	These are often considered high-end clubs, which are typically frequented by the very wealthy, and many of these are in decline, often due to their somber image, which lacks appeal among many younger people. With that stated, an ageing population in many Western societies may lead to this type of exclusive venue becoming more popular again in future
Occupational clubs	These clubs are frequented by members who are of a particular vocation, as highlighted in this chapter
Political clubs	These clubs typically require members to swear allegiance to a particular political party or a politically motivated organization. In northern England (once an industrial heartland of coal, steel and cotton), 'Working Men's Clubs' (WMC) were developed as a recreational space where co-workers could socialize outside of work. WMC traditionally had left-wing political sympathies, and strong affiliations with local trade unions
Smoking clubs	These are clubs where members go to smoke in an indoor environment. Due to the increasing spread of smoking bans, smoking clubs such as 'cigar clubs' are in terminal decline. In Germany, bars and pubs had the opportunity of continuing to allow smoking within their premises after their countries smoking ban took effect in 2008. Many bar and pub owners opted to do so, and had to become registered as smoking clubs, requiring patrons to complete a membership registration form upon entry
Sporting clubs	These are venues that have an affiliation to either a professional or amateur sporting team. The majority of members are themselves not athletes

NIGHTCLUBS

A nightclub is a venue (often referred to as a unit), which is a versatile space that can be themed with props and decor and utilized for a variety of purposes. The main function of a nightclub is the night-time entertainment on offer – typically music played by a DJ (see Fig. 4.5) often on themed 'club nights', as well as the sale of drinks (mainly alcoholic) and sometimes other refreshments. Visitors to a club typically pay a cover charge to enter, and once inside participate in recreational socialization activities, the predominant one being dancing, but attracting potential partners is also high on many people's agendas, and as such, nightclubs are perceived as being 'sexy' venues, which

Fig. 4.5. Clubbers dancing in front of a nightclub DJ.

is something that promoters often exploit, 'sex sells' is a very true adage. The core market for nightclubs is the 18–30-year olds, many of whom are unmarried, and are actively seeking partners.

Of course some clubs specialize in, and put on, particular nights aimed at specific market segments, for example, clubs that are also live music venues, which attract bands of a particular genre, may also operate 'club' nights that are targeted towards fans of the same music genre and not main stream 'pop'. Therefore, such clubs are mainly in competition with other clubs of a similar ilk, rather than 'mainstream' high street clubs. Growth in late-opening hybrid bars (particularly in the UK since the 2003 Licensing Act was implemented) means that many nightclubs are facing stiff competition from the bar and pub sector, which traditionally supplied them with customers after closing time, as opposed to competing with them.

The predominant types of nightclub are featured in Table 4.3.

Socio-economic Factor: Club Tourism

A growing trend from the 1990s onwards is the creation of club brands such as 'Cream' and 'Ministry of Sound', which began with humble origins as nights at venues based around niche offshoots of house and dance music (often associated with the much derided rave scene of the early 1990s). These have grown in popularity to such a point that club nights have become actual club venues, with additional venues opening, creating chains that have spread around the world, and a continual touring circuit of high-profile DJs including Carl Cox, Pete Tong, Paul Oakenfold and Sasha.

(Continued)

Socio-economic Factor: Continued.

These names attract dedicated clubbing enthusiasts who are willing to pay a premium price to participate in such an entertainment experience. In the Mediterranean, the Spanish island of Ibiza has specialized as a clubbing destination, with a high concentration of clubs in a geographically small area, mainly Ibiza Town and San Antoni, with clubs such as 'Café Del Mar', 'DC10', 'Manumission' and 'Pacha'. Synonymous with the club scene is hedonistic partying, which often involves alcohol and drugs, and which have been linked with music and youth culture since the 1950s, but the growth in drug use particularly is the cause for the concern when the knock-on effects often include increases in other crimes such as theft and violence. While the economic benefits of club tourism greatly help Ibiza, the downside of increased crime and antisocial behavior can dissuade other tourists from visiting the island, and bring local residents and authorities into conflict with clubbers and club owners, particularly when this involves creating and enforcing stricter laws and regulations upon them. Spanish tourism authorities are also keen to promote Ibiza as a more wholesome and family-orientated destination, aware that the island (which has several UN World Heritage Sites) cannot survive on club tourism alone. In the early 2000s, Ayia Napa a town on the Mediterranean island of Cyprus also became a popular clubbing destination; however, the speed by which this happened and the sharp increase in crime and the antisocial behaviour that followed caused the residents to protest to the authorities, who quickly clamped down, enforcing a range of rules including noise curfews and the eventual closure of some venues. This authoritarian stamp caused Ayia Napa to lose its popularity among many clubbers, and club tourism decreased as clubbers opted to go elsewhere including Malia on the Greek island of Crete and of course the ever-popular Ibiza.

Table 4.3. Nightclubs and their characteristics.

Type of nightclub	Characteristics
Gay club	A club targeted towards and frequented predominantly by homosexuals, with gay iconographic theming
Live music club	A club that features bands playing, as well as DJs within the same venue. Bands may play at any time during the night, but commonly play before the DJ takes over the entertainment
Mainstream club	This is the most common type of nightclub; it is a typical 'high street' city centre nightclub with a repertoire of largely chart music and well-known 'classics' for customers to enjoy
Niche club	A club that offers theming and music at niche markets, examples include: bondage and sadomasochism (S&M) clubs, line dancing clubs and clubs that specialize in a particular music genre

(Continued)

Table 4.3. Continued.

Type of nightclub	Characteristics
Strip club	An adult entertainment club that commonly offers (in addition to music) striptease, lap dancing and erotic stage shows
Supper club	A club that offers food and wine as a precursor to more laid-back late-night entertainment than other clubs, these are the only nightclubs where the target market are middle-aged and above
Superclub	This is a very large venue, often with many levels and numerous rooms that offer music played by a number of DJs. Many superclubs are high-profile venues with a worldwide reputation, and are wholly or partially owned by dance music producing record labels. Examples of superclubs include Godskitchen, Ministry of Sound, Ikon and Pacha
Ultralounge	This is a club that typically offers an ambient 'cool' and 'chilled out' environment with sumptuous comfortable furnishings including giant bean bags padded sofas and beds. Ultralounges often do not have dance floors
Warehouse and rave venues	Open and largely desolate venues, these are arguably the most 'underground' type of nightclub, which take a good deal of theming, decor and customers to give them the atmosphere and feel of a nightclub (see Fig. 4.6)

Nightclub promoters

In many towns and cities, there are several nightclubs, all of which are in competition with one another, and often in close proximity. Under such circumstances, effective nightclub promotion is a necessity in order to maximize patronage. A club promoter carries out this function, which is key to the marketing strategy of a nightclub, and one of the four Ps of the marketing mix. The relationship between clubs and promoters varies from club to club; it is very often the case that one is in a stronger position than the other, so can dictate terms. This can be influenced by a number of factors, but a strong and concurrent factor is that of competition. In an urban area where there are many clubs in close proximity, the competition is likely to be strong between them to attract customers, especially when the product

Fig. 4.6. Victoria Works, Leeds, UK, a warehouse venue, (a) by day, and (b) by night.

being offered is very often similar. In a scenario where a club is not reaching its potential in terms of footfall and bar revenue, a promoter is likely to be in a stronger position to be able to dictate financial terms with a club as to their involvement. A typical scenario is that the promoter keeps the entry revenue, and the club keeps the bar revenue, but there are also situations where a percentage of either may be shared with the other party. There is also the issue of entertainment within the club, and who will pay for that, the promoter or the club, this is typically down to the promoter, but there can be financial splits with the club also. This is a very simplified explanation, but at many clubs, it really is as straightforward as that. However, there is also a strong competition between rival promoters who are keen to expand their business, and where this happens, a club can be in a stronger position to dictate terms. All of these are examples of Michael Porter's Five Forces; the fifth 'force' (not yet mentioned) is the threat of other substitute products such as hybrid bars, late-opening bars or other night-time economy entertainment venues such as casinos, which is highlighted in Fig. 4.7.

The relaxation of both licensing and gambling laws means that competition for a share of the night-time economy is likely to continue to increase. The role of the promoter will become evermore crucial to the nightclub sub-sector; however, competition among promoters in cities with healthy night-time economies will also increase as more promoters compete with each other for seemingly lucrative nightclub contracts.

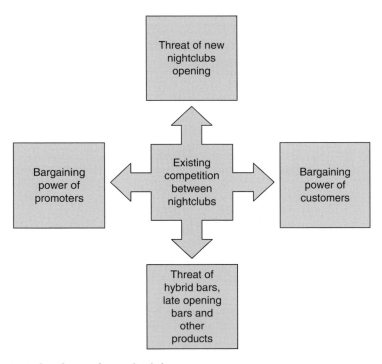

Fig. 4.7. Porter's five forces for nightclubs.

Social Factor: Student Cities

Students are a key target market for nightclub promoters for the following reasons: the majority of students are of the age of regular nightclub visitors; the majority of the students do not have the financial commitments of having families and owning homes; the majority of the students do not have to be at work or in class 5 days a week at 9 a.m., and so are inclined to 'stay out' later; and they can be used to capitalize upon unused capacity during 'the week' (Monday to Friday) when nightclubs are not normally operational or busy.

A student city is a city that has at least one large higher-education institution within its locality (usually a university) that has significantly large-enough student numbers to see the city's population 'swollen' by an influx of predominantly 18–21-year olds during term time. There are hundreds of student cities globally, including Boston, Dresden, Montreal, Nottingham and Oxford.

In the UK (and Canada), the academic year begins in September and ends in May or June with a long summer vacation period, although this is not necessarily the case in other countries, for example: the Australian and the New Zealand academic years run from January to December; the American academic year runs from August or September to August; and the German academic year runs from September to September. Academic years are generally divided into terms, semesters and/or trimesters; these are periods of study that are sandwiched between vacation periods. The busiest time for bars, pubs and nightclubs in any student city centre is the beginning of the academic year.

Figure 4.8 is indicative of the attendance at a nightclub during the UK academic year, an explanation now follows.

September – students move to the city; this is the time of the year when student finances are at their highest, predominantly due to 'student loans' being paid into student bank accounts and monies being taken to university 'from home'. Term begins with 'freshers' festivities, which traditionally involves 'partying' in bars, pubs and nightclubs. This is when nightclub promoters are competing most fiercely to get students 'on board' at their club nights. At this time of the year, promoters use a combination of both traditional and innovative methods to promote their nights, these include: posters; billboards; flyers; Web sites; Web 2.0 (particularly Facebook, Bebo and MySpace); giveaways including T-shirts, CDs, candies, glowsticks and drinks; eye-catching decorated vehicles such as monster trucks, smart cars and travelling billboards; and by paying big name acts or celebrities to appear at venues. This can often be a loss-leader as it is an investment for the longer term.

October – this is still an extremely busy month, although attendances at some venues dwindle, as students quickly establish a routine of which clubs provide the 'best' nights.

(Continued)

Social Factor: Continued.

'Promoter wars' may break out across cities as rivals go head-to-head in a bid to attract custom. Entry prices may be slashed as well as cheap drinks deals, and more celebrity appearances. This marks the beginning of the end of the loss-leading period, as those who cannot afford to compete, seek either diversification into niche markets (typically niche music markets) or accept lower attendances in the hope that they may pick up. Halloween at the end of the month is a very busy time in the student calendar and extremely busy in terms of themed fancy dress nights.

November – as this is mid-semester, assessment deadlines may begin, which results in more time being spent working on assignments, and less time on socializing. Student finances also begin to play a role in dictating how many nights per week they might 'go out'. Attendance figures begin to decline at most venues.

December – the run-up to Christmas is a difficult period for promoters, competition is fierce for the Christmas party-goers, and students typically begin their vacation shortly into December, often not returning until mid-January. Most students will go on at least one 'big' Christmas night out, but rapidly reducing finances, coupled with impending vacations and assessment deadlines (often in the week before vacation period) make this a difficult month, buoyed only slightly by the returning residents of the city who are students elsewhere and some students returning for New Year celebrations.

January – this is the quietest month during the academic year. Many students stay at home, and student finances are at their lowest point during the year, as student loans will for the majority have run-out, prior to their next payment in late January/early February. The period between January and May is also a time when students are looking for their next year's accommodation, which typically involves paying deposits, therefore impacting upon finance.

February – the second 'peak' of the year is when the second semester begins, and when students return to their universities. The second instalment of the student loan is paid into student accounts, and a second period of affluence and partying begins. February is very similar to September in terms of promoters going to great lengths to attract custom, and may also be a loss-leader for some. Valentines day on the 14th gives the opportunity for themed club nights and events. Previously underperforming club nights may be relaunched and rebranded in an attempt to attract custom.

March – mid-semester assessment deadlines make this a quieter month than February, with the peak in activity falling around St Patrick's Day on the 17th. In this month, many students concentrate on their work and competition between promoters is still very fierce, as the recognized and some newly perceived 'best' nights become the established venues for visitation.

April – this is a difficult month for nightclubs, as many students go home for the Easter vacation, which is typically 2- or 3-weeks long, although this may be offset by the residents of the city who are students elsewhere, returning. When students return, assessment deadlines are generally looming, impacting upon their free time to socialize. The third and final student loan instalment is usually paid towards the end of the month.

May – this is the formal assessment and exam period, many students begin to disappear for the summer, this is when the real 'slump' is felt as student cities depopulate. There are traditionally end of exam celebrations, but many students return home early to begin their summer vacations.

June – it is a quiet month for nightclubs and promoters, as many students spend this time at home.

July – student numbers (particularly those at levels two and three) rise in July as new accommodation contracts often begin, which results in an increase in nightclub visitation.

August – more students return to their new accommodation, although new first years (who are most likely to visit nightclubs) have not yet begun university, so their numbers will not be felt until term begins in September.

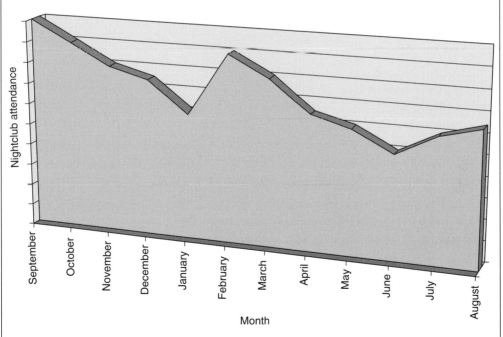

Fig. 4.8. Nightclub attendance during the academic year in a UK student city.

Case Study: Ministry of Sound (From Ministry of Sound, 2009)

The first Ministry of Sound (MoS) nightclub opened in South London in 1991 in a disused bus garage. Its entertainment offering was as an elite 'rave' venue specializing in various house music derivatives with DJs performing live mixes through a specialist sound system that appealed greatly to 'clubbing puritans'. MoS wanted to set themselves apart from other clubs, and did not want to attract those patrons who were into drinking and raucous partying; a trouble-free quality dance music experience was what MoS offered, and they did so by not selling alcohol, which meant that traditional licensing laws did not effect their operations, giving them the potential to open 24 h a day – which they often did. By not selling alcohol, MoS attracted a number of patrons who were heavily into the drug scene, which as mentioned previously in this chapter had become intrinsically linked with the club scene, particularly, LSD (acid), amphetamines (speed), and cocaine, all of which were easy to conceal and smuggle into the club. This caused concern for the local authorities.

Other venues began to open across the UK, Europe and North America that imitated the MoS model, although alcohol was sold in many of these. In order to be seen as the leading brand, MoS expanded and has opened licensed franchised venues globally up to this date, including venues in Australia, China, Egypt, India, Malaysia and the USA and owns other club music brands including Hedkandi, Euphoria and Hard2Beat. MoS have also diversified beyond clubbing venues into other areas that allow them to build their brand making it an even more recognizable one. MoS have diversified into the following areas:

- **Music festivals** – these are music festivals with MoS-themed tents and stages.
- **A record label** – this also has several sub-brands under the MoS umbrella, producing compilation mix albums as well as releasing CD singles.
- **Television** – MoSTV is a channel that can be accessed through the main MoS Web site and features various clubbing-related documentaries including: 'clubbers guides', festival diaries, features on DJs and music videos.
- **Radio** – MoS has had several digital and FM radio stations, but now solely use the Internet for transmission.
- **Clothing and accessories** – funky and stylish street and club wear that is popular among clubbers and young people is produced with the MoS logo, further strengthening the brand.
- **Electronic goods** – these include items that are popular with clubbers such as DAB radios and MP3 players.

This diverse range of products is already being imitated by rivals and gives an indication as to where superclub brands will go in the future. While the major global brands are particularly strong ones, there is still much room for competition and newcomers in this sector.

THE FUTURE

The immediate future for this entertainment industry sector is going to largely be dictated by factors in the external business environment that are out of the control of bar, pub and club managers. The global economic downturn combined with new laws that have banned or will ban smoking in these venues, and will regulate drinks promotions so as to discourage binge drinking will mean that more people will in future choose to frequent these venues either less, or not at all. The challenge for owners and managers will be to diversify the product that they are offering in order to attract potential new markets into their venues. The immediate future for selected parts of this diverse sector is highlighted in Fig. 4.9.

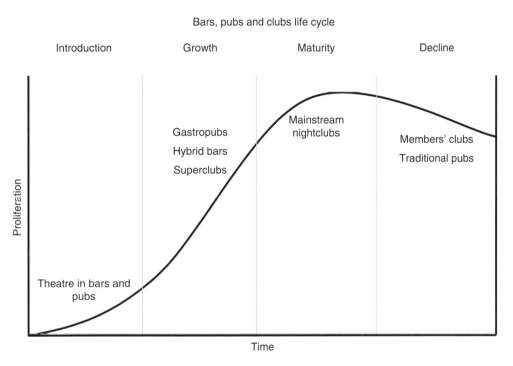

Fig. 4.9. Bars, pubs and clubs life cycle.

Introduction

Theatre in bars and pubs – as the process of feminization of bars and pubs continues, the range of live entertainment offered within them will continue, aspects of theatrical perform-ance will increase, particularly stand-up comedy, fringe theatre and readings/recitals.

Growth

Gastropubs – food sales have the potential to offer a much higher financial profit margin than drinks sales. Pubs that also offer food also have better daytime trade than those that do not, a combination of the above will see more pubs rebranding themselves as gastropubs, and offering an extensive range of snacks and meals, including 'novel' products such as tapas that can be enjoyed with a social drink, and traditional carveries with all-you-can-eat buffets.

Hybrid bars – more city centre bars will expand their entertainment offering to include DJs and dance floors, and open later into the night in order to keep their customers for longer, competing with mainstream nightclubs.

Superclubs – clubbing will become a more elitist pastime in future years; globally recognized superclub brands will continue to grow and diversify their product range into music, media, clothing and holidays, all built around an international network of key leading venues, and smaller satellite venues in towns and cities around the world. The ardent 'clubber' of the 2010s will be more club-brand loyal and music-genre loyal than in previous decades.

Maturity

Mainstream nightclubs – existing competition from hybrid bars and a saturation of venues in urban locations mean that growth in this sector has now slowed down. The opening of more hybrid bars, specialist clubs and superclub brands will mean that in future mainstream clubs will go into decline.

Decline

Members' clubs – overall, this sub-sector has been in decline for the past 2 decades, with numerous closures of venues such as occupational clubs and working men's clubs (WMCs). This trend is set to continue in the face of the smoking ban, and younger generations not being attracted to venues that they perceive to be either old-fashioned or outdated. The one saving grace which may slow the decline of some members' clubs is the global economic downturn, which may mean that some patrons choose these venues over more expensive bars and pubs.

Traditional pubs – again these are often not perceived as an 'attractive' option by younger customers who are more likely to want to frequent more trendy bars and pubs – particularly those with a good entertainment offering, according to the British Beer and Pub Association 36 pubs are closing per week in the UK (Hickman, 2008); this is highlighted in Fig. 4.10.

Fig. 4.10. A closed and boarded-up pub.

REFERENCES

Hickman, M. (2008) Pubs closing for business at a rate of 36 per week. *The Independent*, London. Available at: http://www.independent.co.uk/news/uk/home-news/pubs-closing-for-business-at-a-rate-of-36-per-week-922488.html

Ministry of Sound (2009) Welcome to Ministry of Sound. MoS, London. Available at: http://www.ministryofsound.com/

chapter 5

Cinema and Film

Rebekka Kill and Laura Taylor

The spectrum of organizations that are concerned with the production, distribution, and showing of big-screen movie entertainment.

Film was invented in the late 19th century, with the first theatre show for a paying audience screened by the Lumière Brothers in Paris in 1895. Early films only lasted a few minutes and were often shown at fairgrounds or in music halls. These fell into three basic categories: travel documentaries, comedies and news. By 1914, films became longer and storytelling became the dominant form. Films were now popular as they generated revenue, and movie theatres and large film studios began to appear in Europe, Russia, Scandinavia and the USA. The industry grew rapidly and production, distribution and exhibition networks grew, almost virally, across the world. The onset of the Second World War gave the US film industry the advantage, as Europe was under siege, and a talent drain proceeded across the Atlantic. Early films were described as 'silent' movies, as the technology to record and play back sound and film simultaneously was still very much in the early stages of invention up until the late 1920s (see Table 7.3 in Chapter 7, this volume). Sometimes the films would be accompanied by a live or separately recorded narrator, and often they would be accompanied by music, typically a pianist who would play mood music to accompany the storyline on screen (gentle high tones for romance, loud deep tones for suspense or danger, or fast piano playing when speed or action was being depicted on screen). Typically films would have 'inter-titles' which were black screens with white letters written on them which were designed to assist the audience's comprehension of the film by giving them an indication of what would follow in the next scene, audience participation was encouraged, and singing, clapping and cheering were the norm.

The next major phase in movie history was the glamour of sound, the widescreen format and Technicolor. America's Californian-based film industry was now riding high and so began the 'Golden Age of Hollywood', with *The Jazz Singer* in 1927. This film, starring Al Jolson, had two important success factors. First, it had a musical score, and second, lead actor Al Jolson's constant ad-libbing left the viewers feeling almost like they were eavesdropping on real conversations.

However, there was much criticism of many early talkies; to purist critics, the movie was a visual form, and often attempts to make these movies as a highbrow art form or 'illustrated radio' were often quite unsuccessful. During the 1930s, talkies really found their feet and especially popular were big-budget musicals that achieved real levels of sophistication through the work of people like Busby Berkley and Fred Astair. *King Kong* (1933), the story of a monster ape, directed by Merian C. Cooper and Ernest B. Shoedsack, proved to be a classic and demonstrated remarkable special effects for its era, and in 1937 Walt Disney released *Snow White and the Seven Dwarfs*, which was the world's first full-length animated feature film to be released (and would be followed by many others). This period is also described as the studio era; during this time, five major studios dominated Hollywood: Paramount; Metro-Goldwyn-Mayer (MGM); Warner Brothers; Radio Keith Orpheum (RKO); and Twentieth Century Fox, all of who owned studios where films were produced, as well as distribution companies, and large chains of movie theatres in major cities across the USA. These studios were huge, powerful and rich, and because of this they were able to mass-produce films, churning out around 50 movies per year per studio. Initially, many of the movies that were produced tended to be horror, westerns, melodrama, biopics and comedy.

The Second World War led to a lull in Hollywood production, but, by the late 1940s, going to the movies had become a core American leisure-time activity. However, the large producing houses, who owned their own movie theatre chains and dictated which movies would be shown where, were subjected to antitrust legislation by the US Government that led to them losing their movie theatres, ultimately benefiting audiences through greater choices being presented to them.

Movie going remained extremely popular throughout the 1950s and a number of technological advances helped it to compete against its new rival – television, particularly colour film and widescreen. The studios were extremely fortunate to have a wealth of writing, directing and acting talent at their disposal and the industry thrived. It was only in the 1960s that the major studio's dominance began to encounter problems, as audience profiles changed, and younger more educated patrons were seeking a higher-quality entertainment offering. Alfred Hitchcock provided a change in direction with complex psychological horrors and thrillers including *Psycho* (1960), and Ray Harryhausen's use of animation in the *Sinbad* and *Jason and the Argonauts* movies brought monsters to life like never before.

Towards the latter half of the 20th century, film makers who were independent of the studios, many of whom were educated in art and film theory (often in dedicated film schools), began to release movies for the artistic merit as well as for any financial gain. This led to a resurgence in critically acclaimed movies, many of which were criticized for bringing to the big-screen violent imagery and foul language – this only fuelled their popularity, notable titles include:

A Clockwork Orange (1971) directed by Stanley Kubrick, which featured numerous scenes of violence and a graphic rape and murder; *Straw Dogs* (1971) directed by Sam Peckinpah, which featured violence and a rape; and *Deliverance* (1972) directed by John Boorman, which featured violence and a graphic male rape scene. This was followed throughout the 1970s by numerous other movies that portrayed similar levels of violence and scenes of a sexual nature to take audiences on a complex emotional journey, and explore the dark side of cinema.

The late 1970s and beyond saw the use of complex special effects; George Lucas and Steven Spielberg being two names that became synonymous with the usage of computers, graphics, explosions, costumes, make-up and sound effects to give movies an even greater degree of realism. This translated so well on to the big screen that they saw numerous others trying to replicate their success.

From the mid-1980s onwards, such special effects were used to create a new genre of horror movies, which up to this point had been largely psychological in their ability to terrify. Special effects meant that movies were no longer only terrifying in their storylines, but were now capable of graphically depicting horrific torture and murder scenes, these included: *Friday the 13th* (1980), directed by Sean S. Cunningham; *A Nightmare on Elm Street* (1984), directed by Wes Craven; and *Child's Play* (1988), directed by Tom Holland; a new horror genre known as 'slasher movies' developed and remained popular to this day with the *Saw* franchise currently doing particularly well.

The 1990s saw gritty gangster movies reborn when *Reservoir Dogs* (1992), an independent movie directed by Quentin Tarantino, was released, which proved controversial for its violence and strong language. This propelled Tarantino on to the world stage, and several similar titles followed, most notably *Pulp Fiction* (1994). This decade also saw the rise of computer generated imagery (CGI) to replace traditionally hand-drawn cartoons. *Toy Story* (1995) became the first completely CGI movie to be released; since then numerous others have followed.

The turn of the millennium saw CGI and special effects create modern classics from notable works of fiction including: Peter Jackson's *Lord of the Rings* trilogy; the *Harry Potter* series; and the *Chronicles of Narnia*.

The North American industry dominates the market today, and there are several large studios that are seen as the 'giants' of the movie business: Metro-Goldwyn-Mayer, Viacom and Warner Brothers Entertainment all being prime examples of this. The studios take films through all the stages of production and distribution. Films are often made globally, and are financed by multinational companies, with thriving movie industries in China, India and Europe.

Bollywood films is the national cinema industry of India. Bollywood films can be defined as 'films [that] are produced in India, their language is Hindi (or Urdu) and they have a theatrical release across the usual distribution circuits of (north) India' (Dwyer, 2005, p. 1). The Indian movie industry is extremely productive; it is described as 'the biggest and fastest growing film industry in the world' (Parkinson, 1995, p. 226). A recent example of international collaboration between Bollywood and the British film industry is the multi-award-winning film *Slumdog Millionaire* (2008). This British movie was based on an Indian novel, set and filmed in India, and co-directed by the British director, Danny Boyle, with the Indian director, Loveleen

Tandan. In its first weekend, this (relatively low-budget) film broke box office records in three continents; however, box office revenue is only 'the tip of the iceberg' as a measure of the financial success of a movie. Merchandizing, product placement, technology and distribution rights are all economic factors in the film industry. It is also important to remember that economic achievement is not the only measure of success in the movie industry. There are thriving independent film companies worldwide that are not aiming for the big blockbuster, and they may make 'art' films or documentaries, and may have creative or political aims that are far more important than financial ones. Two good examples of successful independent filmmaking are: *Eraserhead* (1977) directed by David Lynch, shot over 5 years on a very low budget; and *Juno* (2007) directed by Jason Reitman, which went on to win an Oscar.

Producing movies is a financially risky business, and is never guaranteed to produce rewards, even for the large Hollywood studios. The main hurdles that impact the movie-making process are: completion of the film, performance at the box office, and finance, both in terms of making the film and making a profit. The four main processes within the Hollywood approach to movie making are sometimes called the movie-making value chain, featured in Fig. 5.1, and explained in more detail later.

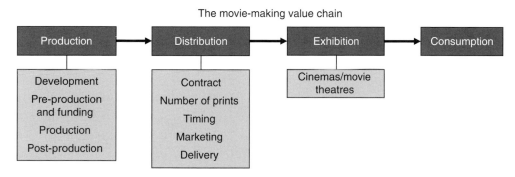

Fig. 5.1. The movie-making value chain.

PRODUCTION

Production is the actual making of the movie; this includes everything from the concept to the physical printing of the finished movie. It is a long and complex journey in which many different stakeholders are involved. The main crew members working on the movie such as the director of photography, sound recordist, production designer and editor are often referred to as Heads of Department (HoDs). They are in charge of their own specific area or department; the size of the department differs greatly depending on the size of the budget. The producer retains overall control on the movie throughout this phase. The director is there to ensure that the creative vision of the film is realized. They work intensely with the HoDs to ensure that they achieve this. The typical staffing structure for a movie is highlighted in Fig. 5.2.

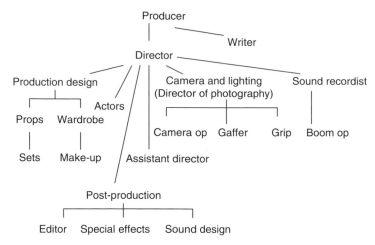

Fig. 5.2. Movie production management structure.

Development

The process starts with a concept or story, often presented in the form of a pitch. This is a short and snappy synopsis, or summary, of the idea, usually with an introduction to the main themes and description of the mood and genre of the film. It would be no longer than 3 min and is called 'the elevator pitch' because it has to be no longer than the time an elevator would take to get from the ground floor to the top of a large building, which is comparable to the maximum amount of time somebody would be given to catch a busy executive's attention. If the pitch is successful, then the writer may then be asked to produce a *treatment*, which is usually around 20 pages and develops the idea further; finally the full screenplay or script is developed.

Most professional writers have an agent who has working relationships with independent producers and producers within studios. Agents contact producers on behalf of the writers and it is then up to the individual producers to analyse a pitch, or script, and decide whether or not they want to take on the project. This is widely seen as the pivotal part of the process, a script that offers a great deal of potential may invoke a 'bidding war' at this early stage, as producers battle to secure the rights to purchase the script. Getting this right can be the difference between major gains or losses at the end of the value chain where risk is high, so only those scripts that show the greatest potential are successful. If the producer decides to go ahead with the project, they purchase the screenplay with what is known as an *option agreement*, which is the legally binding contract between the writer and the producer. The agent will typically charge a fee for their part in brokering the deal.

Funding and pre-production

A large amount of money is required to make the film; the producer starts the process by drawing up a budget and inviting a number of financiers to come on board and raise the full amount, and once this is raised the film can be made. If a studio is involved, then the funding is more straightforward as the studio would typically finance the whole process.

Pre-production is a busy phase, the producer needs to secure the cast, hire the crew, source locations and hire equipment – all of which takes time and money. The main members of the crew are hired and begin to start their work. Typically the production designer, production manager and location manager start working immediately. Design work begins on costumes, production design, storyboards and schedules for production, also known as the *shooting schedule*; the director starts to rehearse the cast; and crew and locations are finalized.

Production

During this stage each scene in the movie is filmed; this usually takes place in a studio or on location, or a mixture of both. By this point, the costumes have been made, sets constructed and production design completed. Shooting of the film usually goes on for a few months and this process is sometimes referred to as *principal photography*. It is potentially the most intense period of the chain and the crew will undoubtedly work for long hours. The set is often a highly charged place with many different crew members carrying out a number of different highly specialized tasks, all held together by the hierarchical system outlined in Fig. 5.2. The first assistant director is in charge of running the set and making sure that members of the crew understand what is happening at all times. Each day the *rushes* (the footage from the camera) are viewed by the producer, director and director of photography. This enables them to be flexible and evolve the project as they go along. It is important to have a clear chain of command at this stage so that problems are solved as quickly as possible. Once *principal photography* is complete, sets can be taken down, or *struck*, and work can begin on post-production. At this stage, many of the crew members who were present on the set will have reached the end of their involvement in the film and will no longer be required.

Post-production

Post-production is a costly business and can take many months to complete. It is during this process that the film is edited. The process starts with the director and editor working on editing the rushes together to create a rough version of the film known as a *rough cut*. This takes place in an edit suite on a computer-based program such as Avid or Final Cut Pro. At this stage, it is not unusual for the film to change significantly from the original script. Once the editing process begins it is about working with the rushes that have been filmed and making them work, rather than editing the film using the original script as a guide. Once the picture cut is finished or *locked off*, work on the sound can begin: music, sound effects and ambient sound are added. If the film includes special effects, then these are also added during post-production. Special effects and sound effects are used increasingly within movies especially as more complex technology evolves, and can have a huge impact on the look, style, time constraints and budget of a film. It is important to remember that the producer is still the principal overseer of the process at this point and may well step in to discuss changes, especially if he or she feels that there could be a financial impact on the film upon its release.

> ### Socio-economic and Technological Factor: the Democratization of Film-making
>
> In recent years, digital video technology has become affordable and accessible. The impact can be seen with relatively low-budget movies that have been created using camcorders. The example, the *Blair Witch Project* used hand-held cameras as a way of producing a film that seemed more 'real', so that the audiences believed that the central characters have made this film themselves, as opposed to the action being captured by a camera crew. Much more recently, due to the wide access to digital video technology, camcorders or even mobile phones, anyone can be a film maker. Web sites like YouTube are repositories for millions of these do-it-yourself (DIY) movies. The kinds of films available are sometimes highly personalized or amateurish, but increasingly high-quality short films, films for early career directors, and animations are viewed and distributed/downloaded by audiences across the world.

DISTRIBUTION

This is a multipart process that can vary from movie to movie; there are usually two types of distributors: major and independent. Major distributors include Paramount (Viacom), Buena Vista (The Walt Disney Company), Twentieth Century Fox (News Corporation) and Warner Bros. (Time Warner). These companies tend to produce, finance and distribute their own films, but they can sometimes distribute independent films, for example, *Star Wars: Episode One* was produced entirely by Lucasfilm but distributed by Twentieth Century Fox. It is not always clear who the majors and independents are, for example, The Walt Disney Company, one of the biggest distributors in the world, has an independent film subsidiary of their own, Miramax films. Most distributors will aim for a set number of movie releases per year.

Contract

Once a distributor is happy to take on a film, a distribution agreement is drawn up. The distributor must believe that the film will make a profit before he or she enters into this agreement; this is why it helps to invest in well-known cast and big directors as it is seen as less risky to employ crew and artists who have a proven track record and can bring crowds into the movie theatre. At this stage, it is not unusual for the distributor to have a hand in the re-editing of the movie in order to make the film more marketable.

Distributors are responsible for taking the film to the market place. In simple terms, the aim is to get the exhibitor to book the movie in return for the profit on ticket sales. Usually a blanket contract is set up between the distributor and an exhibitor so that it can then be applied to all films subsequently *leased* by the distributor. Sometimes though some of the terms, such as the percentage of the gross to be paid by the exhibitor, may be changed depending on the specific film, this is known as a *profit-sharing option*.

Number of prints

Prints of the film need to be made so that the films can be shown on projectors in theatres, the majority of which take the same kind of 35 mm print. There are a number of factors that enable the distributor to determine the number of prints to make, and these include: the price of the print itself (at least US$1000), the timing of the release (see section on 'Timing'), the budget of original film and also the type of film. The distributor starts by considering the number of theatres a movie can successfully open in. For example, in recent years, sequels such as *Spiderman 2* (2004) and *X2* (2003) have been seen as less risky releases as the originals were already hits. Characters, actors and storylines are already established and successful therefore making decisions like numbers of prints less of a gamble – although this is not always guaranteed. Geographical factors can also make a difference to the number of prints decided as films can often draw in different numbers from town to town, and there can be big differences from country to county.

Timing

In order to determine the best way of opening the film, the timing of the release needs to be agreed (the opening is the official debut of a movie). There are a number of elements to consider, and these include: other films being released at the same time, seasonal factors, cast popularity, promotion and 'buzz'. Even if the movie is backed by a major studio, has big stars and a great story and will probably do very well, it is still important to look at the best possible time for release in order to maximize profits. For example a feel-good Christmas story needs to be released at the right period (December) and has to have a reasonable amount of time for the lead up (for promotion). It would not make as much profit, nor make sense, to release it during the summer season. It is always very important for distributors to have a good idea of films that are ready to be released around the same time as their own and to look at the possible impact that this could have on their own movies opening.

Marketing

It is not just the print of the movie that the distributors obtain rights to. Most distributors also obtain the rights to distribute video home system (VHS), digital video disc (DVD), Blu-ray disc (BD), television, sound tracks, posters, games, toys and any other merchandize as well as the full range of movie advertising materials such as trailers and other film footage. Millions of dollars are spent on marketing during the run-up to the release of a film. It is the distributor's responsibility to make sure that this is done effectively. Traditionally, publicity starts at the theatre with the trailer and poster campaigns. At the same time, the cast and sometimes the director start to promote the film through magazine interviews and television appearances. This creates what is known as *buzz*, which gathers momentum and culminates in the opening or premier of the movie. The premier or the opening of the movie is at the height of the promotion and can be a very high-profile event involving the famous red carpet, parties and photo opportunities for the press. Famous stars are invited in a bid to create as much attention and frenzy as possible, sponsorship can also be factored in at this point. Merchandize is typically released as part of the end of the process, but this varies greatly depending on the type of product and success of the movie, and whether it is part of an already successful franchise. Festivals are also an excellent platform from which to promote a movie. *Pulp Fiction* was premiered at Cannes film festival where it won the Palme d'Or prize in 1994, creating a huge amount of buzz. The director Quentin Tarantino then travelled to other festivals and screenings to capitalize on the success of Cannes, so that by the time the film reached the masses it was already a huge hit. However, it is important to note that this process is rapidly changing; marketing for the movie *Cloverfield* (2008) took a very different path. The film was not officially named until very late in the day and until long after the trailer had premiered during which the only information provided was the release date of the film, along with a gripping selection of images. This caused a very modern buzz which led to a huge viral marketing campaign using Web site, Myspace profiles and other Internet-based mediums to promote the film, and was widely received as a very successful campaign (Thilk, 2008).

Delivery

The distributor is responsible for the delivery of the prints to the theatre in time for the opening night, as well as making sure that exhibitors show the film in the right theatre with the right technical specifications, including sound acoustics and visual qualities as previously agreed in the contract. This includes international shipping of all prints and all promotional materials including posters and merchandize, which would all be previously agreed and drawn up into the contract. At the end of this lease period, it is also the distributor's role to ensure that the prints are retrieved. It is not unusual for movies to have a second round of releases after the original primary release, so that the prints may be leased out again.

Movie theatres tend to use buyers to represent them when they are negotiating with the distributor. These buyers are usually full-time employees for big theatre chains and contractors for the smaller theatres. Negotiating the lease of a movie can be very complex and is often fraught with political issues. The theatre tends to make most of the money during the opening weekend and often subsequently loses once ticket sales have dropped off. During this subsequent phase, the movie theatre relies on the food and drink sales for their profit and this is the reason why eating and drinking is so expensive in movie theatres. At the end of the contract, if a movie is still running well, then the theatre can renegotiate to extend the lease agreement. This is called being *held over*.

EXHIBITION

Throughout movie history, the core movie medium has been 35 mm film, but in recent years an increasing number of movies have been made in digital format. This has a number of implications. There are significant differences in the distribution cost; 35 mm film is a very expensive medium costing in excess of US$1000 for each film reel. If a multiplex movie house has ten films showing, and a turnaround of 3 or 4 weeks, the cost can mount rapidly. Digital films can be encoded and delivered on a hard drive for a tiny fraction of the cost of 35 mm film, and are much more difficult to illegally copy. Piracy is estimated to cost the industry US$6 billion annually; digitized movies are encrypted in the studio and unlocked in the movie theatre minimizing the risk of theft. Movie theatres that are equipped with digital projection equipment can also project other material, meaning that their future may be much more varied than the showing of movies, including major televised events, computer gaming and conferencing. Various types of movie theatres are featured in Table 5.1.

Table 5.1. Movie theatres and their characteristics.

Type of movie theatre	Characteristics
Art House	These mainly screen independent/artistic films that appeal to a niche audience of viewers; see Fig. 5.3
Chain	Part of a larger chain of cinemas, these typically screen mainstream movies
Drive-in	Usually open air/outdoors, the cinematic experience is enjoyed from the comfort of audience member's own cars rather than from seats
IMAX	Movie theatres with very large screens, typically 22 m across and 16 m high; they usually show 'short' highly visual films, although some big screen movie titles do get adapted for the IMAX format, including *Batman: The Dark Knight* (2008).
Independent	These may screen both art house and mainstream content, but are solely owned and not part of a major chain
Megaplex	A complex of cinemas that has over 20 different screens, sometimes with as many as 50 different screens; megaplexes are usually part of a chain
Multiplex	A complex of cinemas that has up to 20 different screens; multiplexes are usually part of a chain; see Fig. 5.4
Planetarium	Cinemas with a dome-shaped roof that project films about astronomy from the ground into the concave side of the dome to an audience who sit beneath it and are looking upwards
Pornographic	These specialize in showing only movies with a highly sexual content

Fig. 5.3. The Hyde Park Picture House, an art house cinema.

Fig. 5.4. Vue Cinema at the 02 in London, a multiplex cinema.

CONSUMPTION

During the last decade or so, audience trends in movie theatres have changed significantly. Due to the affordability of high-quality equipment, many people prefer to watch films in the comfort of their own home; on DVD, television, pay-per-view cable or on the Internet. Research published by the Pew Centre for Social and Demographic Trends in 2006 shows a steady decline in movie going among American audiences between 1994 and 2006. However, movie watching is on the increase with more than 70% of people watching at least one movie per week (PEW Research Centre, 2006).

Case Study: Lucasfilm Ltd

American film maker George Lucas founded Lucasfilm in 1971. The company was set up in order to provide Lucas with the independence that he needed to create his own brand of films. Lucasfilm's first release was *THX1138,* but it was only after the success of *Star Wars* in 1977 that Lucas was really able to fulfil his dream of existing as a successful independent company. Today, Lucasfilm has grown into one of the most distinctly branded and successful film and entertainment companies in the world; there are now seven separate divisions within the company. These are highlighted in Table 5.2.

The Lucasfilm brand is responsible for a broad range of products and services, from movies and merchandise to multimedia entertainment and technical facilities and services. The most famous and long-standing products are undoubtedly the *Star Wars* (the third most successful film series of all time) and *Indiana Jones* merchandize including action figures, toys, clothes, mugs, computer games and DVDs. Lucasfilm has pioneered the use of cutting-edge technology in its movies; it has been increasingly responsible for services to external clients through use of technologies within their divisions. Industrial Light and Magic (ILM), Skywalker Sound and LucasArts have all contributed to films and multimedia platforms not produced or financed by themselves.

Case Study based upon Lucasfilm (2009).

Table 5.2. Significant events in the history of Lucasfilm.

Year	Event
1971	Lucasfilm Ltd was founded by George Lucas; it was responsible for the overall management including production and promotion
	THX 1138, the first film from Lucasfilm, was released
	Lucas Licensing was founded, responsible for licensing and merchandizing activities relating to Lucasfilm properties, e.g. *Star Wars* characters, as well as books and educational resources

(Continued)

Table 5.2. Continued.

Year	Event
1975	Industrial Light and Magic (ILM), a special effects facility, specializing in visual effects was founded Skywalker Sound, an audio post-production facility and producer of audio special effects, was founded
1977	*Star Wars* was released, winning six Academy Awards (Oscars): Best art direction/set decoration; best costume design; best film editing; best effects/visual effects; best music/original score; and best sound
1979	Lucas founded a graphics division that went on to specialize in computer animation
1980	*The Empire Strikes Back* was released and went on to win an Oscar for best sound, as well as a Special Achievement Award for visual effects
1981	George Lucas worked with Steven Spielberg to create *Raiders of the Lost Ark*, which won the following Oscars: best art direction; best film editing; best sound; best visual effects; and best sound effects
1982	LucasArts, a video and computer-based games development and publishing division, was founded
1983	*Return of the Jedi* was released and won an Academy Special Achievement Award for visual effects THX Ltd, a company that developed THX – a system that guarantees a specific standard of audio playback for movies, was founded
1984	*Indiana Jones and the Temple of Doom* was released and went on to receive an Oscar for best visual effects BallBlazer and Rescue on Fractalus became the first computer games to be released by Lucasfilm
1986	ILM created the first completely computer-generated character the 'stained glass man' in *Young Sherlock Holmes* Steve Jobs, co-founder of Apple Computers, bought Lucas's graphics division and rebranded it as Pixar Animation which went on to be bought by the Walt Disney Corporation
1989	*Indiana Jones and the Last Crusade* was released and won an Oscar for best sound effects editing LucasArts released a game based upon *Indiana Jones and the Last Crusade*
1997	Lucas Online was created, an online portal for entertainment, education, and e-commerce activities
1999	*Star Wars Episode I: The Phantom Menace*, the first of three prequels to the original *Star Wars* trilogy was released

(Continued)

Table 5.2. Continued.

Year	Event
2001	A 23-acre digital arts campus in San Francisco was started
2002	THX went independent
	Star Wars Episode II: Attack of the Clones won an Oscar
2003	Lucasfilm Animation was founded
2005	*Star Wars Episode III: Revenge of the Sith* the last of the *Star Wars* prequels was released
2008	*Indiana Jones and the Kingdom of the Crystal Skull* was released in partnership with Paramount
	Lucasfilm Animation released *Star Wars: The Clone Wars*

Environmental Factor: The Greening of the Film Industry

Since the late 1980s, the movie industry has become increasingly concerned with the environmental impact of film making. This focused on the impact that shooting movies on location might have on indigenous communities and local wildlife. More recently movie makers have begun to pay attention to recycling, green business practices and carbon footprints (Ingram, 2004).

The Environmental Media Association (EMA) was set up in 1989 (EMA, 2009), and this organization has become a progressively major Hollywood player. Its board has included major Hollywood stars like John Travolta and Jane Fonda. The EMA now runs numerous high-profile green schemes including awards acknowledging those organizations which have made significant improvements in their carbon footprint through attention to energy use, recycling and other 'green' initiatives. The EMA also encourages celebrity role models; for example, encouraging their celebrity supporters to drive hybrid-fuelled cars or carry canvas bags. Interestingly, EMA also offers advice on 'greening' plotlines in order to use the movies (and television) as a subtle public information vehicle. The EMA mainly focuses on the film industry in the USA; however, other countries are also building green initiatives, including the UK and Canada, under the banner of 'Green Screen'. Such environmental organizations also have support from respected industry figures, such as Anthony Minghella, writer, producer and Oscar-winning director of *The English Patient*, who spoke in support of the London Green Screen launch in 2008.

THE FUTURE

The movie industry will continue to evolve, and will be significantly impacted upon by the socio-technological advances and changes in how films are made and viewed by audiences. In the 21st century, audiences are increasingly choosing to watch movies on their portable media players, mobile telephones, computers and televisions that boast advanced home theatre systems. The movie industry, from producers to distributors, is taking this seriously. Audiences need to be tempted into the movie theatre and movie makers need to respond to changing audience needs in order to ascertain how to harness revenue in an increasingly convoluted technological environment; this is highlighted in Fig. 5.5.

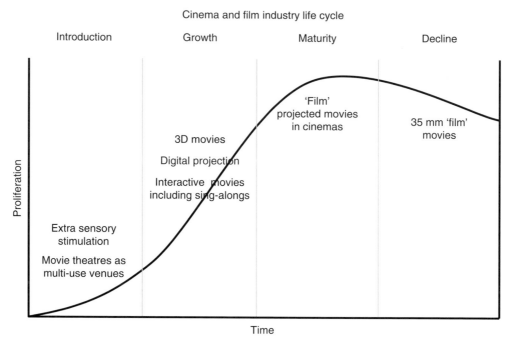

Fig. 5.5. Cinema and film industry life cycle.

Introduction

Extrasensory stimulation (ESS) – providing an all-around sensory experience, ESS will begin to appear in movie theatres in an attempt to provide a level of novelty that home viewing of films cannot replicate. ESS will include: vibrating seats; smells and odours; breezes; and fog and mist in cinemas, the London Eye 4D experience already offers this, and includes (amongst other things) wind and snow along with a 3D cinema experience.

Movie theatres as multi-use venues – the advancement of digital projection will allow an opportunity for movie theatres to become multi-use venues; it is likely that in future, televised events and big-screen computer gaming will also become common features of movie theatres.

Growth

3D movies – there have been various attempts at 3D film making since the 1950s. Early attempts were very blurry and hard to focus on, often causing headaches amongst audience members. Technology has now moved on considerably and good-quality 3D movies are being produced such as *My Bloody Valentine 3D* (2009), which is a horror film that uses 3D technology for the extra 'thrill' factor (Schiffman, 2008).

Digital projection – these will eventually become the norm in movie theatres providing a high-quality viewing experience. Digital projection may be prohibitively expensive for some independent movie theatres, who may continue to show 'old' 35 mm projected films as a novelty to film buffs. Some movie theatres will undoubtedly offer both formats.

Interactive movies including sing alongs – the release of *Mama Mia* (2008) proved to be a smash hit, as audiences interacted with the film and joined in by singing along with the songs. This created an entertainment experience on a scale that home viewing cannot easily replicate, and more releases of this type are likely.

Maturity

'Film' projection on to cinema screens – while this is still the most common method by which movies are screened, this is now old technology (see Fig. 5.6). Newly built movie theatres are likely to be 'digital', in order to be more 'future-proof' and eventually film-projected movies will go into a decline.

Decline

35 mm 'film' movies – the move to digitization is already seeing the 35 mm film going into a terminal decline as a production medium, as more titles are released electronically.

Fig. 5.6. Film reel projectors.

REFERENCES

Dwyer, R. (2005) *100 Bollywood Films: BFI Screen Guides*. BFI Publishing, London.

Environmental Media Association (2009) EMA. [Internet], Los Angeles, California. Available at: www.ema-online.org/

Ingram, D. (2004) *Green Screen: Environmentalism and Hollywood Cinema*. (Representing American Culture)

Lucasfilm (2009) Lucasfilm. [Internet], San Francisco, California. Available at: http://www.lucasfilm.com

The National Media Museum (2009) [Internet], Bradford, UK. Available at: www.nationalmediamuseum.org.uk

Parkinson, D. (1995) *History of Film*. Thames & Hudson, London.

PEW Research Centre (2006) A social trends report – Americans prefer going to the movies at home. [Internet]. Available at: www.pewsocialtrends.org/assets/pdf/Movies.pdf

Schiffman, B. (2008) Movie industry doubles down on 3-D. [Internet] Wired. Available at: www.wired.com/techbiz/media/news/2008/04/3d_movies

Thilk, C. (2008) Movie marketing madness: Cloverfield. [Internet]. Available at: http://www.moviemarketingmadness.com/blog/2008/01/17/movie-marketing-madness-cloverfield/

chapter 6

Broadcast Media

James Roberts

Entertainment that is produced for mass audiences and broadcast or transmitted from a distant source.

Broadcasting in a variety of forms has been at the centre of the entertainment industry for the last 50 years, and during that time it has grown and changed beyond all recognition. If we define broadcasting as a method of communication, which sends a single message simultaneously to multiple recipients, then its modern history in most countries typically begins with experiments in the radio medium. The early evolution of radio in a series of breakthroughs in wireless telegraphy throughout the late 19th and early 20th centuries by researchers like Tesla, Marconi, Popov and Baviera reveals the intimate and highly influential role of technology in the establishment of broadcasting as a medium. Hence the growth and commercialization of both television and radio could only proceed as technical developments were made in delivery platforms and reception equipments, as highlighted in Figs 6.1 and 6.2.

While the establishment of radio as a viable broadcast medium could perhaps be characterized as the result of scientific endeavour and enthusiasm rather than astute commercial acumen, its growth was certainly fuelled by commercial interests. Early stations in the USA were typically established by manufacturers and department stores to sell radio sets, and by media owners to sell their products, e.g. newspapers. This 'sponsorship' model was subsequently replaced by advertising from a wide range of sources as the main revenue for commercial stations.

The early history of radio also reveals a clear desire by governments to be intimately involved in operating and regulating the airwaves. Many early radio services were established by governments as part of a public service remit to serve the nation such as British Broadcasting Corporation (BBC) radio. Commercial stations were obliged to secure licences from early

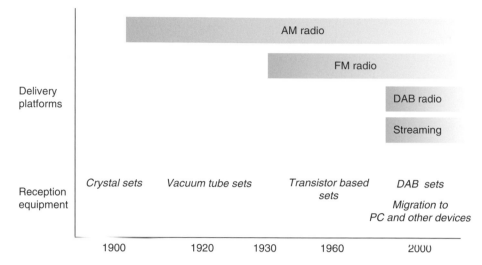

Fig. 6.1. Evolution of radio broadcasting systems and reception equipment.

government-appointed regulators such as the Federal Communications Commission (FCC) in the USA; a model that would soon be replicated in the television sector.

The early history of television was again driven as much by the ambitions and curiosity of scientists and engineers as by the men of commerce. Early experimental work was carried out by Rignoux and Fournier in Paris and Rosing and Zworykin in Russia during the early years of the 20th century. But if television is defined as the transmission of moving, monochromatic images, then it could be argued that John Logie Baird first achieved this privately in the UK on 2 October 1925.

Television broadcasts began in earnest towards the end of the 1920s, and Columbia Broadcasting System's (CBS) New York City station W2XAB began broadcasting its first regular 7 days a week television schedule on 21 July 1931, with a 60-line electromechanical system. The BBC began experimental broadcasts in 1932, and launched its own regular service in 1936.

While the diffusion of television technology among consumers was largely halted during the Second World War, the immediate post-war period was characterized by the rapid growth in consumer uptake of the technology. This was underpinned in Europe by the development of public service channels that were partly funded by public money such as the: BBC in the UK; Arbeitsgemeinschaft der öffentlich-rechtlichen Rundfunkanstalten der Bundesrepublik Deutschland (ARD) in Germany; and the Radio Audizioni Italiane, now known as Radiotelevisione Italiana (RAI) in Italy. Commercial channels that were funded by advertising also emerged including CBS in the USA; and Independent Television (ITV) in the UK. These were 'over the air' services, available to anyone with a television and an aerial (and in some cases payment of a licence fee, e.g. BBC, ARD and RAI).

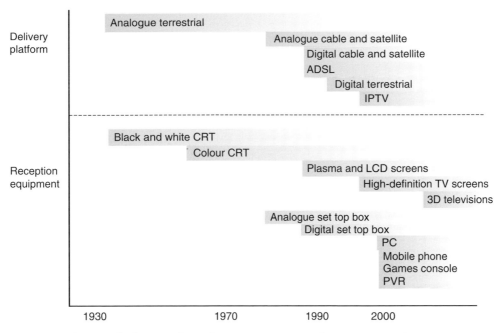

Fig. 6.2. Evolution of television broadcasting systems and reception equipment.

Up until the 1970s, television in most territories was dominated by a small number of broadcasters who controlled access to these over-the-air services. But then cable distribution in the USA moved from simply being a way of reaching homes that had difficulty in getting over-the-air broadcasts to a separate commercial operation with its own operators, channels and business model. It added a vital new source of revenue through subscriptions, whereby consumers paid a monthly fee to receive channels not available on the over-the-air services. These channels often aired premium content like sports and films unavailable on the terrestrial services.

Following this model, other 'pay-TV' services, which relied on subscription fees, were launched using new cable and satellite technology in the USA and Europe, examples being: Sky Television (now BskyB) in the UK; Canal+ in France; and Premiere in Germany. Such systems were initially based on analogue transmission technologies, and hence had limited bandwidth and programme offerings, though the 1990s saw the removal of many of these restrictions with the launch of digital services that were capable of carrying huge numbers of television and radio channels.

As broadcasting 'maturity' dawned in the West, television and radio were well established as the predominant forms of entertainment in many homes, often replacing the fire as the focal point of communal 'living rooms'.

As the first decade of this century ends, broadcasters may be seeing some worrying developments, as the mass audiences that broadcasting has traditionally commanded are increasingly fragmented over more platforms and time slots, changing the way in which we demand and consume radio and television. Equally, other recreation activities have emerged to challenge broadcasting's dominance of our leisure time. But in order to fully appreciate how companies are responding, it is necessary to establish some of the basic aspects of the broadcasting product, market and industry structure.

STRUCTURE OF THE BROADCASTING INDUSTRY

The broadcasting sector is typically divided up into five broad areas of activity, as described in Fig. 6.3 which provides some examples of companies undertaking each activity. Their principal activities are briefly described in Table 6.1.

PRODUCTS AND AUDIENCES

The broadcasting product has been examined from a number of different perspectives, each ascribing its different qualities and peculiarities. Common to many is a view that the broadcasting product is somewhat different to material products, specifically it is intangible and experiential (Holbrook *et al.*, 1990), and it contributes significantly to the creation and acceptance of cultural values, and how we perceive the world around us. The broadcast product is very varied and serves more than one market, as described in Fig. 6.4.

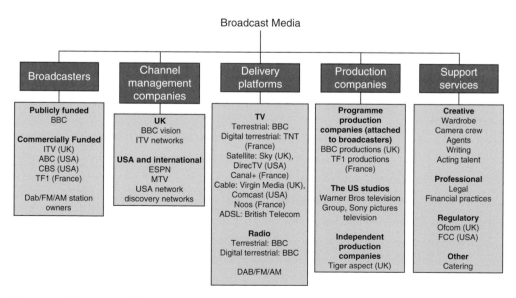

Fig. 6.3. Sub-sectors of the broadcasting industry with examples.

Table 6.1. Broadcast media sub-sectors and their characteristics.

Sub-sector	Characteristics
Broadcasters	Broadcasters typically acquire licences to broadcast services, create channels targeted at audiences and market them. They may or may not have internal production resources to make programmes themselves. Historically, they have also owned and operated delivery platforms such as over-the-air terrestrial television transmission systems, though increasingly third parties now run these
Channel management companies	Channel management companies aggregate their own and acquired programming to create channels. Some exist within the operations of broadcasters and delivery platforms and only work for those services. Others are independent such as Music Television (MTV), and Discovery Networks and work for a variety of different delivery platforms. Independent firms tend to focus on particular genres of programming including children's programming, music and non-fiction, unlike those aligned to broadcasters that tend to offer channels of mixed genres. The channel is then delivered as part of the broadcaster's core service, or licensed by an independent company to a delivery platform provider for a fee
	In the radio field, channel management companies typically own licences to broadcast in a particular area, or over a specific frequency. They typically acquire licences, programme the channel and secure funding from advertisers
	With the growth in the number of channels being offered, their positions have become more precarious as income available from advertising and subscriptions to pay for their operations has not grown as quickly. Many companies have developed channels in order to remain ahead of competitors. Hence, MTV has gone from one channel when it was first launched in the UK to nine today. Similarly Discovery has gone from being a single channel to offering seven channels in the UK. As the audiences for each new channel tend to be lower than that for the original channel, the fees received from platforms for each new channel have also declined. Hence, a number has come to rely on other revenue streams and activities like merchandizing or film and programme production
Delivery platforms	There are currently three major delivery platforms for television, these are: analogue and digital terrestrial; digital cable; and digital satellite. While some analogue broadcasting remains, most systems are planned to be converted entirely to digital in the next 5 years. Both cable and satellite delivery systems are now typically associated with pay-television operations, and hence

(*Continued*)

Table 6.1. Continued.

Sub-sector	Characteristics
	draw on subscription revenues as their primary source of revenue. Their key activities are to set up technical infrastructures including: laying cable; renting satellite transponders; setting up play out centres; aggregating channels; marketing the service to consumers; and managing customer service and billing
	Other platforms have been trialled, like programmes delivered via asymmetric digital subscriber link (ADSL), which utilizes digital telephone lines, but these are still relatively undeveloped compared to other platforms in the West. In some Asian countries (e.g. Korea), ADSL has become more rapidly established
	Radio can be carried on any of the above systems, but also broadcasted on its own dedicated AM, FM and digital audio broadcast (DAB) platforms
Production companies	Programme production organizations are sometimes part of broadcasters; Independent Television (ITV) productions mainly serves its parent organization, but they may also exist independently of broadcasters. Typically their role is to find and develop ideas that are subsequently made into programmes, usually with finance from broadcasters and channel management companies
	While for a long period production companies were reliant on production fees from broadcasters to fund their activities (and in return gave up all rights to subsequent exploitation of the programme), they are increasingly retaining the rights in their programmes and exploiting them in valuable secondary markets (see Endemol case study)
	Specialist production companies also exist in a variety of niches, to develop on-screen promotions and logos including Red Bee Media and Lambie-Nairn, and to work on developing new content for mobile and online services such as Digital Film
Service companies	The broadcasting industry regularly calls on the services of a range of support sectors. They extend from typical professional service firms like lawyers and accountants to much more creative services like advertising agencies, wardrobe provision, set construction, and of course the skills which support programme making more directly including camera and sound operators, editors, directors and actors
	While the large integrated broadcaster of 20 years ago typically maintained many of these functions in-house, a significant number have now been outsourced to independent companies. Hence, the broadcasting sector maintains a rich ecology of support firms which typically employ many more staff than are employed directly in broadcasting
	All of these groups are being affected by a variety of developments evident in the broadcasting industry, which will be covered further into this chapter

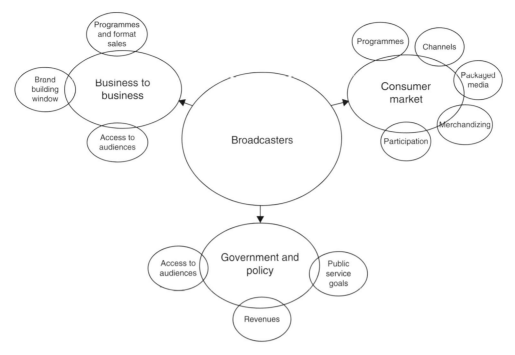

Fig. 6.4. Broadcast audiences and products.

CONSUMER MARKET

The consumer market can be broadly divided into two segments. The primary product market is made up of programmes and advertisements that are broadcast on television and radio channels to consumers. Such programmes may be one-offs, series or serials and in a wide variety of different genres including drama, news and comedy. The audiences' key benefits in watching or listening may vary and include: education, diversion, or a contribution to feeling part of a group or society. To less attentive audiences, broadcast media provides an audio and/or visual soundtrack for other activities.

The secondary product markets typically include packaged media, merchandise or online products that may enhance a viewing experience; deepen a consumer's relationship with a programme brand or carry it beyond the confines of a specific schedule, channel or the television set. Examples include: digital video discs (DVDs) (see Chapter 7, this volume); magazines and books (see Chapter 10, this volume); voting services and online information (see Chapter 8, this volume); and games. The success of such secondary products typically depends upon the success of the programme in its initial or subsequent transmission. The values of these secondary markets and the rights that underpin them have grown enormously in the last 20 years. Hence, they have become ever more important to those in the broadcast market, particularly with the threat of falling income streams from advertisers.

> ## Technological Factor: Do-It-Yourself Scheduling
>
> As technology has developed, devices have also emerged to allow the consumer greater control over their viewing and listening experience. Consumers can reschedule programmes to suit their individual circumstances, either through hardware devices like the set-top personal video recorder (PVR) as featured in Fig. 6.5 or software like the podcast or BBC's iPlayer which allows television programmes to be played back on PCs.
>
> One of the advantages that this technology offers to the consumer is that advertisements can be avoided, which is particularly popular on the American TiVo PVR service. This is not good news for advertisers who rely on broadcast services to reach audiences, or broadcasters who rely on income from advertisers to pay for their operations.

BUSINESS-TO-BUSINESS MARKETS

For commercial channels, whose main source of revenue is advertising, it could be argued that their primary customers are advertisers, and their primary product is the delivery of attractive

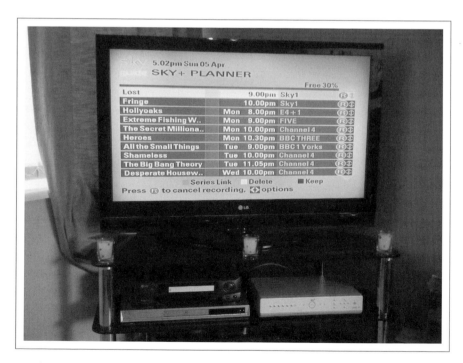

Fig. 6.5. Sky + PVR service allowing do-it-yourself scheduling on a 42" high-definition television.

audiences to those advertisers. Such audiences are sold in terms of their size and shape, which is their composition in terms of specific demographics including age, gender and social class, as well as how many times they are likely to be exposed to the advertisement.

What is being sold is the broadcasting service (channel or programme) as a 'brand-building window'. If a company wants to build demand for a new product, television and radio are a good place to rapidly reach a large number of appropriate potential customers, and raise awareness of the product. This extends to other types of product. Programmes and discrete pieces of content benefit from this brand-building window. As well as being an integral part of the channel offering, programmes benefit by being exposed to audiences. By building audience awareness and popularity, the value of a programme in secondary markets is significantly enhanced. A good example of this is the television and radio music channel, where promotional videos and music tracks not only create a broadcast product, but also create demand for the product in other markets, such as compact discs (CDs), downloads and concert tickets.

There is also a significant business-to-business market in the sale of programmes to channels by independent producers, and sale of channels to delivery platforms. Programmes can be sold in the form of ideas to be developed and produced (usually with the financial help of the broadcaster), and finished programmes, or formats which are remade in the context of foreign territories (see the Endemol case study). Channels, on the other hand, are typically paid a carriage fee per subscriber for their presence in the service of a delivery platform operator.

GOVERNMENT AND PUBLIC INSTITUTIONS

The broadcasting product offers the opportunity for governments and public institutions to benefit from their activities. This may at times have a negative association, with broadcasting as a vehicle for propaganda and state control of freedom of speech.

Broadcasting can equally offer governments and other public bodies a way of achieving more positive public goals like catering to the needs of minorities, and sustaining valuable cultural and linguistic differences such as: the Canadian Broadcasting Corporation's (CBC's) support of English–French bilingualism in Canada; and Sianel Pedwar Cymru (S4C) a Welsh equivalent of the English Channel 4 in the UK.

Governments may also benefit financially from broadcasting operations. Significant fees are often secured in exchange for broadcaster licences, directly through taxes on their profits and indirectly through the sale of the valuable national broadcasting spectrum.

Political and Legal Factors: Cultural Policy and Broadcast Media

Broadcast media is used as a cultural policy tool whereby governments can promote what they consider good or acceptable behaviour and values. Public information films were popular mediums by which to do this in the mid-20th century. In terms of legalities, sociocultural rules, values and norms are inscribed in censorship laws, and libel laws and advertising legislations exist which broadcasters must adhere to.

Cultural policy is also used for the purposes of citizenship and state promotion. It is arguable that the broadcasting of the last Olympics around the world was seen as an opportunity by the Chinese Government to promote the positive aspects of its rule, efficiency, effectiveness, tolerance and fairness. This in itself was controversial with accusations of pre-recorded and 'faked' firework displays being distributed to foreign broadcasters by Chinese state television, and a Chinese singer's voice being 'dubbed' over a more 'attractive' singer who allegedly mimed the words.

NEW CHALLENGES: DISTRIBUTION TO ATTENTION ECONOMY

Historically, broadcasters have been in a powerful position due to their dominance of access to distribution, the analogue broadcasting infrastructure and the limited competition it allowed. In an earlier broadcasting environment where three or four channels garnered the vast majority of viewing, choice was limited, both for programme makers (who had to go to a small number of broadcasters if they wanted their programmes to be distributed and seen) and audiences. Equally the advertiser had little choice but to advertise on these channels to reach mass audiences. But should a producer or advertiser be lucky enough to secure distribution, they had a good chance of reaching a large audience. This could be characterized as a distribution-based economy, where control of distribution (access to the airwaves) was the key strategic high ground.

However, we have seen significant changes in the broadcasting environment over the last 20 years including: the proliferation of television and radio services with more platforms and more channels on offer (particularly with the growth of digital pay-TV in the 1990s) and the proliferation of alternative ways to enjoy recreation time.

As a result, broadcast audiences have become spread across platforms, time slots, services and activities. With so many ways to consume audio-visual content, the attention of audiences is no longer fixed on a limited number of television channels; the traditional nuclear family gathered around a television for prime-time viewing is an increasingly rare sight. Just getting your programme distributed on a television channel, no longer guarantees viewers and attention. Power now resides not in distribution, but with those who can aggregate the attention of valuable consumers within, and across all of, these markets. These are as likely to be the brand owners of specific programmes, as they are the channels carrying them (see Endemol case study). Hence, we have moved from a distribution economy where securing distribution was difficult, but guaranteed large audiences and significant attention, to an attention economy where securing distribution is much easier, but does not guarantee any audience or attention at all. Ownership of the biggest brands does secure audiences and attention.

The challenge for broadcasters is to re-aggregate the large audiences that they have traditionally had for their channels by offering services on a variety of new platforms, and in developing new forms of content that are relevant to these new platforms. This is costly, and a particular challenge for public service broadcasters (PSB) whose 'universality' is often key to their public funding. The implications of the move from distribution to attention-based economies are huge and could affect a range of entertainment sectors. It has particularly relevance for the way supplier–buyer relationships are changing in broadcasting.

A phenomenon of the late 20th and early 21st centuries is the placement of large television screens in public locations, while these are mainly utilized for information provision, they are yet another medium by which broadcasters are attempting to reach members of the public, this is highlighted in Fig. 6.6.

Fig. 6.6. An audience sits beneath the 'big screen' in Millennium Square, Leeds, UK.

BUYER–SUPPLIER RELATIONSHIPS

Broadcasters who controlled access to airwaves and hence audiences have traditionally been dominant in their relationships with programme suppliers and enjoyed a powerful position in negotiations that often allowed them to secure secondary market rights in programmes beyond those needed for their core broadcasting service. This in turn left producers relatively impoverished and reliant on production fees from broadcasters to survive.

There are now more potential sources of distribution other than two or three major broadcasters. Producers are not limited to negotiating with a small number of outlets; however, the degree to which this has changed the balance of power in relationships should not be overstated. A small number of broadcasters still control access to the largest audiences.

However, added to the changes in terms of trade, investment from outside the broadcasting industry (often from investment banks and private equity companies) and an increased willingness to take on risk have led to a situation in which production companies increasingly retain and exploit rights. The value of those rights has increased significantly with the growth of secondary markets. Hence, a new competitive battleground in broadcasting is emerging over access to, and control of, rights, and also for access to staff to mange them.

Production companies have retained rights and recruited the talent to exploit them effectively, and have emerged as major organizations in the creation and management of brands. By controlling very strong brands that aggregate audience attention across platforms, they have secured dominant bargaining positions in relation to their broadcasting customers. A prime example of this is Endemol.

Case Study: Endemol

Endemol is an European production company that has moved beyond merely making programmes into being a major entertainment consultant and rights management company. Its growth is a case study in what producers can do to build strong production companies now and in the future.

Originally formed in 1994, through the merger of two major television producers in The Netherlands, the company rapidly expanded its geographic and product scope. Endemol now has operations in the USA, the UK, Italy, France, The Netherlands, Germany and Spain. In addition to producing programmes, Endemol now develops formats that are sold to other broadcasters and production companies. These are essentially an outline structure for a programme in terms of: core concept; suggestions for design of sets; elements of

(Continued)

Case Study: Continued.

the script; styles of production; and presentation. These are bought by broadcasters and made with local producers in each territory with advice from Endemol. The company is now responsible for some of the biggest formats in the world.

Over the last 5 years Endemol has (on average) created approximately 100 new formats each year. It now has a library of over 2200 non-scripted formats and more than 200 scripted titles (Endemol, 2008).

As well as creating show formats, Endemol is an expert in generating new revenue streams from programmes. In addition to being paid a production fee to make some programmes, Endemol generates revenues from: voting, online services, merchandizing and consultancy. While the majority of the company's total revenues come from production activities, the majority of its profits come from interactive and other services.

Endemol also took advantage of the interest that the financial markets showed in the broadcast media (particularly production) to secure funding, and has made a significant number of acquisitions to broaden its offering and skill base. In the UK alone, it has acquired a number of production companies including Brighter Pictures, Cheetah Television, Initial and Zeppotron. It has also acquired Digital Studios, an online and mobile content provider. Endemol has also set up a division (New State) to work with advertisers directly on programme and sponsorship ideas.

Endemol is a leading example of the future of independent production, a long way from the small underfunded broadcaster-reliant production company, typical of many firms in the industry 10 years ago. Endemol has established a range of businesses and services to match the evolving broadcast market for the next decade.

THE FUTURE

The next 10 years offer a number of significant challenges and opportunities to those in the broadcast media sector (see Fig. 6.7). For some commentators, broadcasting is already in terminal decline. But the sector is complex and diverse, and hence cannot be considered as a single entity as its major elements are at different stages in their life cycles, and hence, with different challenges to face; see Table 6.2.

Table 6.2. Key challenges to organizations in the broadcasting sector.

Broadcaster	Producers	Regulators
• Can we offer all things to all people – should we focus on specific day parts, genres or audiences – how might this affect our public service commitments?	• How do we need to change our products to adapt them to new platforms?	• How far should we protect public service broadcasting?
• Should we build internal production competencies or rely on independents?	• How do we secure preferential access to talent and rights?	• How do we regulate new types of content?
• How many services can we afford to have in-house?	• How do we access programme budgets from advertisers directly?	• How do we manage the increasing use of customer data by broadcasters?
• How can we best position ourselves to secure and exploit rights?	• Should our growth be organic or through merger/acquisition?	• How far do our remits extend into new platforms?
• How many and which platforms do we need to be on?	• Should we consider running day parts for broadcasters?	
• How can we maximize the value of our brand-building window?		
• Are our channel brands being eroded by PVRs?		

Introduction

Migration on to new platforms – for most in the broadcast industry, it is likely that at least some of their business will migrate on to new platforms, online, mobile, etc. and away from the traditional television or radio sets. This is at the very earliest stage of its evolution. This will require new skills, competences and significant funding to support the migration and capitalize on the opportunity. But as well as demanding new skills and talents, this does offer new opportunities for products and services. The effects of such changes will of course vary according to the type of organization, but all will be faced with some tough questions. Some of these are outlined below.

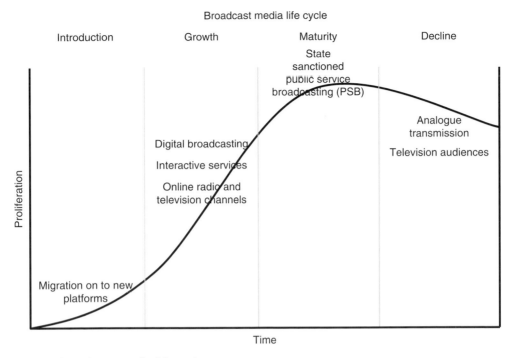

Fig. 6.7. Broadcast media life cycle.

Growth

Digital broadcasting – the most immediate challenge for broadcasters is the complete switch over to digital television from existing analogue systems. While this is far advanced in some territories, particularly in the realm of pay-TV, there remains a group of consumers who, even after 20 years of promotion by the pay-TV companies, stubbornly refuse to upgrade. They simply do not want 'enhanced TV' and certainly will not pay for it. The analogue service cannot be switched off (and the broadcasting spectrum sold) until virtually everyone has upgraded and purchased equipment capable of receiving digital transmissions. Questions remain: Should customers be forced to upgrade? Will governments step in and pay for consumers' new digital set-top boxes? What if customers have multiple televisions in their home and all of them need new digital 'set-top' boxes? This is potentially an expensive business for consumers, and could have ramifications for governments.

Interactive services – the combination of television and online platforms offers the potential for new interactive services from broadcasters. While in the past these have been largely unsuccessful from a commercial point of view (other than voting), they do offer the ability to enhance the viewers' relationship with the channel and programme through audience participation and on-demand services.

Online radio and television channels – Internet protocol television (IPTV) and radio will grow rapidly with the availability of broadband Internet and potential worldwide audiences.

Independently owned channels offering specialist content will grow particularly. The use of the Internet for broadcasting media will cause continued problems for policy makers, licence distributors and royalty collectors.

Maturity

State sanctioned public service broadcasting (PSB) – this has been a central part of the broadcasting environment in many countries for the last 50 years. But its future is in question. Many such services are funded by a combination of public and commercial money, and in some cases entirely from public funds. According to broadcasters, public funding has not kept pace with rising costs. As such, broadcasters must secure more funding from governments, take on more commercial activities or reduce their services. Many critics suggest that taking on more commercial activities would undermine the public service requirement for broadcasters to supply a diverse selection of high-quality programming.

At the same time, public service broadcasters are under pressure to maintain their 'available and applicable to all' remits, as the market and audience become more fragmented and diverse. At the very least, they are being forced to develop significant presence on new platforms like mobile and online, which is again squeezing already limited resources.

Decline

Analogue transmission – this will eventually be phased out altogether with the growth in digital and online technologies.

Television audiences – the ongoing erosion of television audiences has been evident for over a decade, as audiences move to new platforms and other forms of recreation. This may well continue; however, for the 'biggest' brand-building channels, this may be less of an issue in the short term. As it is more difficult to aggregate large audiences, those broadcasters that do (even if they are diminishing in relative size) remain important and valuable. Hence, even if a television channel can only deliver audiences of 5 million today, rather than 12 million for a similar programme 10 years ago, if this still represents the most efficient and effective way to deliver to the largest simultaneous audience, the value of its airtime will remain strong, and advertisers (and perhaps in the future even programme makers) will pay handsomely for access to these audiences to build their brands.

The broadcasting market has displayed constant change and evolution since its earliest days in the late 19th century. If history is anything to go by, the one thing we can be certain of is that new technologies will continue to change the face of broadcasting, offering new threats and opportunities, new ways to interact with the consumer audience and serve business-to-business markets and new products and services. While to some commentators, broadcasting may already appear to be in a state of terminal decline, perhaps it is merely on the brink of reinventing itself, as it has done many times before.

REFERENCES

Endemol (2008) Endemol UK. [Internet] London, Endemol. Available at: http://www.endemoluk. com/?q = taxonomy/term/1&tid = 1

Holbrook, M.B., O'Shaughnessy, J., and Bell, S. (1990) Actions and reactions in the consumption experience, the complementary roles of reasons and emotions in consumer behaviour. *Research in Consumer Behaviour*. 4, 131–163.

chapter 7

Audio-visual Media

Dr Stephen Henderson

Media formats that contain sound and/or images (still and/or moving) that require an electronic third-party device to be able to play/display their content.

In today's technologically advanced era, it is difficult to imagine that there was a time when the very idea of recorded entertainment would be unimaginable. Up to the end of the 19th century, performance art including live music and theatre was provided by travelling artists presenting a 'highbrow' product for the elite and wealthy classes. For those at the 'lower' end of the social spectrum, communal singing and storytelling would provide more accessible forms of entertainment. Storytellers and playwrights helped form early theatre but, until the 20th century, the concept of anything other than live entertainment would (to most people) have been too far-fetched to be imaginable.

There are seven recognized forms of mass media: these are print, audio recordings, cinema, radio, television, the Internet and, now, mobile telephones. This chapter will attempt to look at how those forms of mass media that are capable of storing and carrying audio and/or visuals in physical tangible formats were invented in the 19th century, developed and commercialized in the 20th century, before breaking free of their physical constraints and converging in the 21st century. It presents a timeline of where we were, where we are and where we may end up in term of audio-visual media, and relates directly to Chapters 3, 5, 6 and 8 of this book. Figure 7.1 denotes audio-visual media development throughout the 19th, 20th and 21st centuries.

VISUAL MEDIA

The manipulation of light and shadow to form shapes projected on to screens is where modern cinema and video products originated in the 17th century, while this was an enhancement

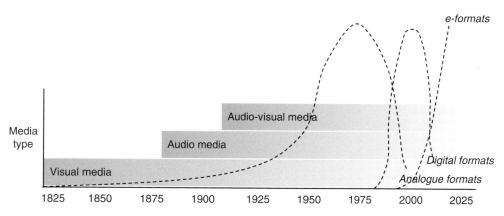

Fig. 7.1. Audio and visual media timeline.

or 'special effect' for live entertainment, it was not in itself a form of media, but a forerunner of this. The production of projection equipment designed specifically for this purpose followed including 'magic lanterns' which projected still images, and 'zoetropes' which gave the impression of movement through projecting numerous images in quick succession. The early 19th century saw physicists experimenting with light-sensitive chemicals to create shapes from shadows, a predecessor of the photograph (see Table 7.1).

Table 7.1. Visual media development, 1825–2010.

Year	Visual media development
1825	The first photograph was taken by French inventor Nicéphore Niépce
1837	Louis Daguerre invented the Daguerreotype, a type of photograph that used chemical exposure on a silver surface. This was followed by several similar forms of photography that used a 'hard' physical medium for their exposure
1839	The first photograph of a person was taken, a Parisian man having his shoes shined
1861	The first colour photograph was taken by Scottish physicist James Clerk Maxwell
1884	George Eastman developed flexible photographic film
1888	Louis Le Prince filmed moving images on a single lens camera, and patented a camera/projection system, George Eastman registered the trading name Kodak
1889	Kodak produced the first commercially available celluloid film
1895	The Lumière brothers held their first screening of projected motion pictures in Paris
1896	Louis Lumière and Victor Planchon developed photographic plate emulsion for use on celluloid roll film

(Continued)

Table 7.1. Continued.

Year	Visual media development
1897	Karl Ferdinand Braun invented the first cathode ray tube called the 'Braun Tube'; this was later developed for use in televisions
1907	The Lumière brothers' 'Autochrome' colour photography plate became commercially available, and dominated colour photography until the 1930s
1909	35 mm film became the standard size for the production of silent movies
1913	The 'Leica' camera that used 35 mm movie film for still photography was developed
1915	*The Birth of a Nation* a controversial film about racism in America was released at 190 min in two segments with an intermission in between each segment. It was considered the first blockbuster movie ever released and lead to a surge in the development of silent movies for the next decade
1927	Silent movies largely ceased production in the USA as new technology allowed audio to be added to the visual film
1934	135 film cartridges using 35 mm film were introduced by Kodak and became the most widely used still photography film cartridges right up to this present day
1935	Kodak invented Kodachrome colour film, which went on to be used in a number of formats including slides for photography, and various movie reel formats
1936	Agfa introduced Agfacolor-Neu transparency film
1947	Polaroid released the 'Land Camera'; the first commercially available instant camera, capable of taking self-developing photographs
1950s	The slide projector and Kodak 8 mm film projector grew in popularity as a home entertainment tool, family slide shows and home cinema became trendy among the middle classes and wealthy
1977	Polaroid invented 'Polavision' an 8 mm movie reel camera system that produced colour video film, which was encased in a protective cartridge
1986	Fujifilm developed and marketed the 'disposable camera'
1987	Compuserve developed the Graphics Interchange Format (GIF), an electronic compressed image file format, popular for use upon the World Wide Web (www)
1990	The first commercially available digital cameras appeared
1994	The Joint Photo Experts Group (JPEG or JPG) compressed image format was released as an alternative to the GIF format for photographs, JPG files also became popular for use upon the World Wide Web, as well as eventually becoming the standard format used by the majority of digital cameras

(Continued)

Table 7.1. Continued.

Year	Visual media development
1996	Kodak released the advanced photo system (APS) film cartridge under the brand name of 'Advantix'; this allowed users to take different formats of photograph including panoramic and high definition on the same film. The APS system was marketed as being simple for novices to use, and did achieve some success in the mid-1990s, but ended up losing out to digital photography
1998	Flat bed scanners became commercially available, allowing enthusiasts the opportunity to 'digitize' their photograph collections
1999	The first commercially available digital self-loading relay (SLR) cameras were released by Nikon and Minolta
2001	The first commercially available mobile phone with an integrated digital camera was released in Japan by J-Phone
2002	Compact digital cameras became widely commercially available; their popularity, megapixel photograph capability and affordability rose quickly throughout the decade to replace 35 mm as the most popular still photography format
2004	Kodak announced that they were going to cease marketing 'film' cameras; apart from disposable cameras, they also ceased production of slide projectors
2006	Minolta announced that it was to cease production of cameras; this is partly due to competition from the mobile phone market
2008	Polaroid ceased production of film cameras in favour of digital cameras. Nokia became the biggest-selling camera manufacturer in the world through their range of mobile phones with in-built cameras
2010	Mobile phones completely dominate the home photography market

The above table highlights the process of *creative-destruction*, which was highlighted over a century ago by philosopher Friedrich Nietzsche and applied to business and the economy by Joseph Schumpeter in the early 20th century, where he witnessed innovation and new product development by entrepreneurs being the force behind economic growth at the expense of previous developments. Creative-destruction is a never-ending process in competitive economic environments, and in the future is likely to see the decline of the present digital photography formats in favour of something 'even better'.

AUDIO MEDIA

The first 'proper' media formats that could play back sound which had been recorded on to them did not appear until 1877 when Thomas Edison recorded the words 'Mary had a little lamb', by attaching a needle to the diaphragm of his telephone and allowing the needle to prick holes in a tin-foil cylinder using a technology that he later commercialized as the phonograph (see Table 7.2).

Table 7.2. Audio media development, 1877–2010.

Year	Audio media development
1877	Thomas Edison invented the phonograph
1885	Alexander Graham Bell invented the graphophone
1887	Emile Berliner invented the gramophone using the flat disc
1898	Valdemar Poulsen patented the telegraphone, making the first magnetic recording using wire
1911	Thomas Edison moved from cylinder to disc – the forerunner of the vinyl record
1925	Round disc records adopted the standard speed of 78 revolutions per minute (RPM) with the introduction of the electrically powered synchronous turntable motor
1928	Joseph Begun created a magnetic tape using coated paper and, later, steel for a portable recorder
1934	Joseph Begun built the world's first tape recorder to be used for broadcasting
1945	The Radio Corporation of America (RCA) introduced the 7" 45 RPM single, which became a popular commercial format for the next 40 years
1948	The long playing (LP) 12" vinyl disc playing at 33 1/3 RPM was introduced. It dominated the 'album' format for 40 years
	Magnetic tape started to use a plastic backing and reel-to-reel tape recorders became the recorder of choice in the studio
1950s	Vinyl discs (records) continued to dominate the market, and stereo records became the norm for consumers
1958	RCA introduced an enclosed cartridge system for audio tapes known as a 'magazine cartridge'
1963	The Phillips company introduced the first 'compact cassette'
1965	The '8-track' cassette was developed by Learjet and branded as 'Stereo 8'; it later became popular for use in cars
1970s	The 12" single format was introduced for promotional purposes and disco DJs; it had wider grooves for better sound quality
	Battery and mains electrical-operated radio cassette recorders (also known as 'boom-boxes') were introduced, allowing listeners portability for their compact cassettes
1976	The 12" single format became commercially available for the general public playing at either 45 RPM or 33 1/3 RPM
1979	Sony made their 'Walkman' commercially available, allowing people to listen to their compact cassettes privately while on the move
1982	The compact disc (CD) was introduced to the market

(*Continued*)

Table 7.2. Continued.

Year	Audio media development
1980s	Compact audiocassette sales soared to rival vinyl records
	Sales of home high fidelity (hi-fi) units (also referred to as stereos) also soared; these units combine radio tuner, cassette player/recorder, and record player, and later include CD players and mini-disc player/recorders. Hi-fis were sold as 'midi-systems' that were combined units, or as 'separates' which meant that each component, record player (or deck); radio; cassette deck; CD player; mini-disc unit; and amplifier, were sold separately, and then wired together at the back using coaxial audio cables; typically this configuration would involve separate units being stacked upon each other with the record player at the top. Major brands for these units included: Pioneer, Toshiba, JVC, Sony, Phillips and Sanyo. Bang & Olufsen rose as a manufacturer of premium home stereo equipment for the 'high' end of the market
	Digital audio tapes (DAT) were released for the commercial market by Sony and offered a higher-capacity improved quality digital storage on a physically smaller media; they proved successful in professional circles; however, they did not achieve wide commercial success among the home-taping amateur market.
1990s	The CD dominated the market at the expense of vinyl records and the compact cassette tape
1991	The 'mini-disc' was launched as a smaller CD with similar capacity. The mini-disc challenged the compact cassette as offering a superior home-recording facility
1992	The waveform audio format (WAV) was created by Microsoft and IBM for use in personal computers (PCs) particularly for use in Windows 3.1
1996	Fraunhofer Institut established a patent for Moving Picture Experts Group-1 Audio Layer 3 (MP3) file format used to compress music files, reducing file size by around 90% from the earlier WAV format
1997	The compact disc rewritable (CDRW) became commercially available, as do single use 'CDRs'; their simplicity, affordability and ability to use them in both computers and audio equipment contributed to the mini-disc and compact cassette becoming obsolete
	SaeHan Information Systems developed their first digital audio player (DAP) called the 'MPMan'
1998	The MPMan became commercially available
	Diamond Multimedia developed and launched the 'Rio PMP300'
1999	DAPs became commercially known as MP3 players, although many play other formats including Windows media audio (WMA) and advanced audio coding (AAC) files
	Napster, the first of numerous free file-sharing programmes, was released, allowing users to easily share their MP3 collections (and other files) online

(Continued)

Table 7.2. Continued.

Year	Audio media development
2001	Apple launched the iPod, giving an elite stylish edge to MP3 players; the iPod quickly became the market leader in MP3 players. Apple released iTunes music management software for both the Apple Mac and Windows operating systems (Bosanquet and Gibbs, 2005)
	Sony Corporation and Ericsson combine to form the company Sony-Ericsson in order to make mobile phones with multimedia capabilities
2002	Bertelsmann (Bertelsmann Music Group (BMG), Arista and RCA) added digital rights management (DRM) to their audio CD titles in an attempt to prevent piracy; this rendered them unplayable in some older CD players. Other record labels later followed suit, although this proved unpopular and only lasted for 5 years
2003	MP3 players began to appear in mobile phones, the Sony Walkman brand was used on Sony-Ericsson phones that have MP3 playing capabilities
	Amplification systems were introduced for iPods which began to replace stereos and hi-fi units in the home
	iTunes music store opened allowing consumers to legally purchase music online in the AAC file format. Other rival online music stores quickly followed
2004	In December, legal MP3 downloads overtook CD sales in the UK for the first time
2005	Sony ceased production of DAT hardware
2007	EMI were the last major record label to announce that they were abandoning the use of digital rights management (DRM) on their titles
	The iPod touch was launched by Apple, and featured a touch screen for ease of use; this was followed by the iPhone which was virtually the same as the iPod Touch, but with communicative capabilities
2008	Thondheimsolistene a Norwegian orchestra released the first ever audio album on the Blu-ray format.
2009	Mobile phones completely dominated the MP3 player market
2010	E-audio formats comprehensively dominated the market, as all physical formats begin to go into terminal decline

From the early moments of recording, the search was on for the best materials to both hold the recording and play it back to the listener. Before Phillips introduced the audiocassette, magnetic tape became the tool for recording engineers who recognized its potential to record on different tapes and, later, splice them together in what is now known as the mixing process. In the 1960s, music fans marvelled at the fact that The Beatles recorded their classic *Sgt. Pepper's Lonely Hearts Club Band* on a 4-track recording equipment at a time when technology was developing to allow 24-track recording and a whole new range of possibilities for recording engineers. With this development, the music industry began to recognize the important role played by record producers, and artists such as The Beatles recognized that record producer George Martin was contributing as much to their music as their own composing skills were.

Case Study: the Rise and the Fall of the 8-track Tape

The possibility of recording multiple tracks on to one continuous tape sent both the professionals and the public into a spin during the 1960s. For professionals, the possibilities in recording studios were considerably increased, while the public gained by having a stereo recording looping four times across a tape in order to provide either an extended playing time or quadraphonic sound. Ironically developed by Bill Lear of Learjet fame, the 8-track player took off as in-car entertainment when he convinced Ford to add it as part of their dashboard equipment on some of their cars. The tapes, being bigger than the compact cassette, were described as cartridges and introduced yet another format for the public to consider. With disposable income increasing and cars being owned by more people, the 8-track cartridge became popular for car owners who wanted the finest of entertainment. Unfortunately, bulk worked against the format when compared to the compact cassette even though it arguably provided better quality. In addition to this, the 8-track developed a reputation as having problems when the tape switched across the four sections. Outside of the USA, the link to the car was much less obvious leading to patchy international adoption of the format. Despite the 8-track having its keen followers and record/tape clubs keeping the format alive via limited new releases, the 8-track was yet another defunct format by the early 1980s.

From the mid-1970s into the mid-1980s, the market for compact cassettes (audio tapes) grew at the expense of increased vinyl record sales; the advantage of having portable music for personal and in-car use was weighed against the problems generated by the mechanical aspect of tape. While consumers had got used to the idea of handling vinyl records with care at home, the outdoor use of tape within a machine could cause feed problems resulting in what was called 'wow' (slow changes in speed) or 'flutter' (fast changes in speed). Furthermore, tapes left lying about on a hot day (especially, in a car) could end being stretched rendering them useless due to the distortion of the music. Of course, much technical development went into developing materials that resisted these mechanical, heat-exaggerated problems. However, in the early 1980s, solid disc formats using digital technology began to appear, with compact discs (CDs) emerging as media that was not only stronger but also smaller, and able to carry more information than the earlier formats. Yet, they did not gain immediate acceptance with resistance coming from a market that was already in possession of earlier formats and players. Other, more traditionalist, views on the audio format suggested that the larger vinyl records were a better artefact to have due not only to their larger format making it easier for DJs to handle, but also because vinyl gave a 'warmer' sound due to the added detail allowed by the older analogue technology (Liversedge, 1995). The net results being that niche markets for vinyl products with the likes of DJs and hi-fi enthusiasts have developed despite the onslaught of further miniaturized products. For many years, as technology enabled media and players to develop faster and faster, the market for these products has regularly seen formats arrive and disappear in what are increasingly shorter life cycles. With all of these physical media formats, physical storage space can be an issue for those with large media collections, this is demonstrated in Fig. 7.2.

Audio media development has been driven by the consumer's passion for music. While the spoken word and storybooks make up a small proportion of the audio media content, the continual development of popular music genres throughout the 20th and into the 21st centuries has been the key driver in the audio media market. Quite simply people like music; it easily entertains and often is used as a source of inspiration through positive emotions and mental escapism experienced while listening to it. A musical background to our lives has almost become the norm, and with the development of portable audio player technologies, we can now listen to music at home, at work, while travelling and quite simply anywhere (see Fig. 7.3).

Fig. 7.2. Collecting music and video on media formats can present storage problems.

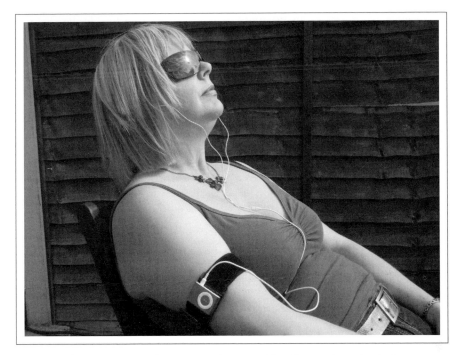

Fig. 7.3. An iPod can entertain almost anywhere, and hardly requires physical storage space.

While there is a continual demand for music, the same cannot be said for physical formats; as music collections grow, so does the need to create physical space to store them; so the advantage that electronic audio formats have in terms of space-saving is one of the key drivers, which will eventually see the almost complete loss of all physical audio media formats.

AUDIO-VISUAL MEDIA

It is logical that before an integrated audio-visual media format could be developed both separate audio and visual media technologies would first have to be created. In 1895, Thomas Edison developed the Kinetophone and 4 years later François Dussaud exhibited his Cinemacrophonograph in Paris both of which played images and sound to the viewer, but from separate sources. While still photography and audio without visuals have only ever grown in popularity, moving images without an audio soundtrack became unfashionable in the late 1920s after the introduction of 'talkies', but it was not until 1927 that audio-visual media really captured the imagination of mass audiences, as outlined in Table 7.3. Prior to this, movies were accompanied by a musical soundtrack, typically provided by a pianist, organist or orchestra (see Chapter 5, this volume).

In the mid-20th century, television engineers were starting to use videotape to record programmes for television broadcast. It was not long before bulky tapes found in recording studios were being reduced to a manageable size for the home. At this point of time, both audio and

Table 7.3. Audio-visual media development, 1907–2010.

Year	Audio-visual products
1907	Eugene Lauste patented sound-on-film
1919	Lee De Forest patented a version of sound-on-film for the commercial market
1923	The first commercial screenings of sound-on-film were made in New York
1926	*Don Juan,* the first feature-length film with a combined audio soundtrack (but no words), was released
1927	*The Jazz Singer,* starring Al Jolson, the first feature length movie with a combined audio soundtrack and spoken dialogue, was released
1951	Bing Crosby Enterprises demonstrated the world's first videotape recording
1956	Ampex developed their Quadruplex videotape machines which became the professional standard for the next 2 decades, but were prohibitively expensive for the amateur market 3M developed their first videotape
1957	3M offered the first commercial blank videotape for professional use
1965	The first 'colour' videotapes were produced
1971	The recently developed Dolby 'noise' reduction system was used on *A Clockwork Orange,* the first time it was used on a movie Sony introduced their U-matic videotape system for the commercial market
1975	Sony introduced 'Betamax' videotapes making home video viewing affordable and commercially available
1976	JVC and Panasonic developed video home system (VHS), which eventually won the 'home-video' war over Betamax
1978	The 'Laser Disc' was developed as an alternative to standard videotapes. However, its expense and lack of commercially available titles quickly lead to its demise as a commercial format
1982	JVC released the VHS-C format compact videotape for the commercial amateur and home camcorder market Sony introduced the Betacam system, which became a standard for the professional market
1983	Sony released the Betamovie BMC-100P a home camcorder that used Betamax videotapes
1984	Eastman Kodak released the Video8 8 mm videotape in a cassette format
1985	Sony released the Handycam for the commercial home-amateur market that used Video8 tapes

(Continued)

Table 7.3. Continued.

Year	Audio-visual products
	Hitachi and Panasonic released video cameras that recorded directly on to VHS videotapes, the advantage being that home users could watch recorded movies on their home video recorders. Unfortunately physical size and cost meant that these devices never achieved widespread commercial success among the home camcorder market, although they were used among the professional market
1986	Panasonic introduced the MII to rival Sony's Betacam for the professional market
1987	Super-VHS (S-VHS) is released as a superior alternative to VHS
1991	Apple released QuickTime software, which was capable of playing both video and audio files on Apple Mac computers and later PCs
	Microsoft released the Windows Media Player, which was capable of playing both video and audio files on PCs
1992	The first Moving Picture Experts Group (MPEG) file formats were patented for video compression, Microsoft released the Audio Video Interleave (AVI) file format
1995	A conglomerate of digital video camera manufacturers including Sony and Panasonic launched the digital videotape (DV) format, the first commercially available tape format that stored digital video signals
	Camcorders that recorded on to 30 min digital video discs (DVDs) were released, but proved prohibitively expensive to gain popularity among the home camcorder market
	DVDs as computer discs were launched
1996	DVD videos became commercially available
	Content scrambling system (CSS) was introduced for commercial DVD titles in an attempt to prevent illegal copying
1998	JVC launched their digital VHS camcorder, which allowed digital recordings to be stored upon VHS videotapes
1999	Apple released iMovie as a free programme within the Mac operating system; this allowed home users to create and edit movies using an Apple Mac. Subsequent versions including high-definition (HD) ones were later released
	Microsoft released the Windows Media Video (WMV) file format
	Surround sound was marketed to the commercial home-cinema market
	TiVo, a digital video recorder (DVR) was launched; this recorded television on to hard disc drive. DVRs later become known as personal video recorders (PVRs)
2000	Microsoft released Windows Movie Maker as a free accessory within the Windows operating system; this allowed home users to create and edit movies using a PC. Subsequent versions were later released

(Continued)

Table 7.3. Continued.

Year	Audio-visual products
2001	The increased penetration of broadband and fast Internet services globally meant that television programmes and movies were increasingly being illegally downloaded and shared online; this led to more file-sharing programmes becoming available, such as Kazaa, eMule, iMesh and Limewire
	Sky+, a PVR service is launched in the UK, which is a hard disc drive-based video recorder that allows users to pause, rewind and record live television
2003	Canon, JVC, Sharp and Sony formed the high-definition video (HDV) consortium developing technologies and products that allowed HDV to be recorded on MiniDV format videotapes
	Hitachi launched the first Blu-Ray camcorder
	Sony released the XDCAM, their first professional video camera that did not use videotapes, and recorded on to optical discs
	Toshiba and NEC launched high-definition DVD (HD-DVD)
2004	Mobile phones with in-built digital camcorder and video playback facilities became commercially available
	Digital photo frames became commercially available, these soon advanced to boast audio-visual capabilities, including playing MP3s along with photographs, and eventually video
2005	Advanced access content system (AACS) was released to protect HD-DVD and Blu-ray titles from illegal copying
	Apple released the fifth-generation iPod which featured video playback facilities, making movies on the move a reality in the pocket of consumers
	YouTube was established as a web site where users can upload their own videos and share them with the world; numerous similar others follow
2006	Advanced video codec high definition (AVCHD) was launched by Panasonic and Sony as their next tapeless high-definition recording format which would record on to DVDs, memory sticks and hard disc drives. The Sony Handycam HDR-UX1 was released the same year, which recorded on to DVD
	Toshiba released their first HD-DVD player along with numerous titles
	Sony, Panasonic and Samsung released Blu-ray players
	Sony and Acer released Blu-ray players for laptop computers
	Sony released the Playstation 3, the first games console that was also capable of playing Blu-ray discs
	The first commercial high-definition Blu-ray titles were released
2007	Canon released the HG10, a high-definition camcorder with an in-built 40 Gb hard drive for the home camcorder market
	Gnutella became the most used online file-sharing programme

(Continued)

Table 7.3. Continued.

Year	Audio-visual products
2008	Nokia became the biggest-selling video camera and portable media player manufacturer in the world through their range of mobile phones with in-built video cameras and media playing facilities (see Fig. 7.4)
	Warner Brothers announced that they were going to stop supporting HD-DVD in favour of the Blu-ray format; other major studios followed suit
	Toshiba ceased production of HD-DVD
2010	Mobile phones completely dominate the home video and portable media player markets

Fig. 7.4. Filming a video on a mobile phone.

visual media were relying on mechanical movement and brought along some of the associated problems mentioned earlier. All this changed when the use of digital formats was introduced and both audio and visual media were stored on CD and digital video disc (DVD). From then on, as new digital file formats developed, it became clear that technology convergence would allow both audio and visual media to be stored and played from the same players. The process of creative-destruction saw formats come and go throughout the 20th and into the 21st centuries, until we are now in a position where media itself has gone in favour of electronic files stored on the devices that play them back, instead of on playable media.

INDUSTRY ADAPTATION

The industry has separated into those who produce hardware (players) and those who provide the software (audio-visual media files) that are loaded on to the hardware. For example, those companies making MP3 players (hardware) are normally different to those producing music for downloads (software) to be played on these players. For the hardware producer, the industry is about a tangible product that needs to be manufactured in an efficient manner requiring knowledge of the most modern materials, that can provide safe storage for content.

Software manufacturers make copies of specific entertainment in standard intangible formats that later can be loaded on to the hardware. Though these formats change, software producers find themselves having to engage with the producers of entertainment and, hence, find their role is often more about managing human resources than physical resources. For example, Sony found that it had to learn lessons quickly when, in a shift from hardware to software, it decided to move into music production as well as music players. While technologists might argue for better funding of their developments, this was nothing compared to dealing with superstar musicians. Soon, it found its artists in revolt with George Michael accusing Sony of 'professional slavery' before becoming embroiled in a courtroom battle. Despite losing his case and returning to the Sony music label, this was a sign that working with talented artistic human resources needs very different skills to that of technological development (BBC, 2003).

The revolution in storage and miniaturization has been enabled by the change from analogue to digital data recording. The analogue format was traditionally produced by mechanical means such as the sound generated from the groves of a vinyl disc, whereas the digital format can be produced electronically. In sound wave terms, analogue data can be represented by a smooth wave where changes with time show no step change, whereas digital data approximate this smooth change to a series of discrete step changes. These step changes are small enough to look like a smooth wave though there is a slight loss of information, which was highlighted by the critics of the move from vinyl records to CD. To many consumers, this loss of quality is hardly noticeable, or in the case of younger listeners has never been experienced due to them having never heard analogue formats. People familiar with the physical products of the past such as vinyl records, DVDs and CDs can find the idea of downloading audio-visual media as strange due to it lacking in features such as artwork and information about who did what in the creation of the product. The great benefit offered from the portability and storage capabilities of digital file formats is their key strength which makes them popular among consumers.

For those seeking fame and fortune, it is now possible to create recordings on a computer while sitting in a bedroom rather than a large recording studio. All that is required is instruments that can be played and recorded (via microphone or direct to the personal computer (PC)) before manipulation using suitable software. Some record companies now find it more economical to offer their artists recording software, for example, Pro Tools (Digidesign, 2009), rather than expensive studio recording time. In addition to recording their own music, the musician might extract other pieces of music to be 'sampled' into the new material to provide a familiar sound to the potential listener.

In this way, new music has been developed as well as possibilities for other musicians to license the use of their popular material to others. This has numerous legal ramifications, particularly from the rise of hip hop music and its sub-genres which may include scratched samples, beats, voices and bass lines from other tracks. This emphasizes the rising importance of intellectual property in a digital world, and brings the discussion to one of the most controversial issues among recording artists (see Chapter 3, this volume).

Social, Technological and Economic Factor: the Rise of the Amateur

Home photography, film-making and music recordings have steadily grown in mainstream popularity since the mid-20th century. In days gone by, the technology to make any sort of recording was both scarce and expensive, but as rarity disappeared and equipment prices fell, the potential users of this new equipment grew. These users tend to fall into two categories, the amateur and the professional, with the former interested in amusing themselves, their family and friends (see Fig. 7.5), while the latter sees the recordings as having commercial value with its potential to sell to others.

Fig. 7.5. Amateur film-making on a high-definition digital camcorder.

(*Continued*)

> ### Social, Technological and Economic Factor: Continued.
>
> One of the main drivers of this has been the shift from analogue to digital media where storage and manipulation of the recordings have become much simpler. Though some areas of analogue recording, such as traditional film cameras, had been relatively simple to work, the switch to digital media not only made the latter easier still but also opened up opportunities such as having a portable recording studio. The days where touring artists needed large vehicles packed with equipment outside the venue are gone, as professional quality digital recordings can be made straight from the mixing desk in the venue itself. Even more dramatically, amateurs who wish to make their own recordings find this affordable and manageable whether for fun or with one eye on a future career.
>
> There are people ready for a revolution in recording that allows them to record in their own bedrooms and e-mail the results to their friends. The simple distribution of these recordings creates the possibility for direct sales to the consumer. Digital file formats require no packaging and all that is required is for the consumer to have some way to pay for the download of the music file. So, the record company, distributor and record shop can be cut out of the traditional supply chain by the new technologies leaving these businesses wondering about their future. In other words, a complete industry is facing restructuring due to the ease with which relative amateurs can enter the market (Byrne, 2007).

THE FUTURE

This chapter has presented a life cycle of audio-visual media, culminating with where we currently are, looking towards the immediate developmental future of audio-visual 'media' (or media-less as the case actually is); Fig. 7.6 highlights a number of trends.

Introduction

Online on-demand video downloads for mobile devices – the possibilities of downloading audio-visual media has been held back by both the storage demands of a larger file size compared to music and the need for broadband network speeds to further increase. However, as broadband network speeds improve and distribution via phone networks develops, it is possible to see that large files will download much more quickly. Furthermore, miniaturization continues to increase allowing the storage of enough files to make up a typical collection of audio-visual media. The commercial possibilities of this are already recognized in the sporting world where the top soccer leagues are already surrounded by speculators hoping to benefit from what gets termed a 'tri-cast'

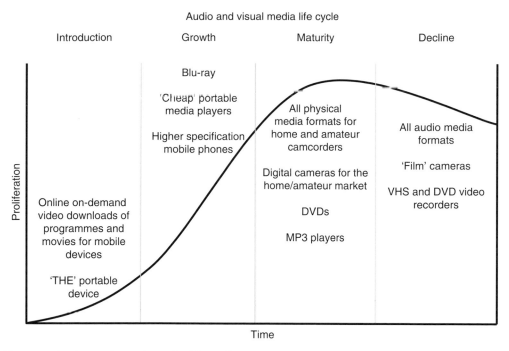

Fig. 7.6. Audio and visual media life cycle.

agreement for broadcasting to television channels, mobile phones and web site streaming (Henderson, 2010).

The portable device – The Apple iPhone is just the beginning, this refers to a device that incorporates all of the following (and more): mobile phone; video player; video editor; MP3 player; MP3 dictaphone; MP3 editor; streaming and digital television player/receiver; digital radio; camera; camcorder; organizer; diary; alarm clock; global positioning system (GPS) system incorporating Sat Nav; Internet browser; e-mail; e-book reader; game player; calculator; micro PC and applications; Bluetooth; Wi-Fi; huge memory; and wireless-syncing ability with computers and other media devices.

Growth

Blu-ray – the cost of Blu-ray players will continue to decrease as will the cost of discs until they are comparable to DVDs in price, and as this happens the DVD will go into decline.

'Cheap' portable media players – in an attempt to compete with improved mobile phone media capabilities, cheaper portable media players will become more common, although they will ultimately lose out to the mobile.

Higher specification mobile phones – mobile phones will continue to improve in specification.

Maturity

Physical media formats for camcorders – camcorders will go completely digital, recording on to hard drives only within the next 5 years.

Digital cameras for the home/amateur market – improved camera and storage capabilities of mobile phones will eventually lead to a decline in digital cameras for the home/amateur market, although demand will remain for professional standard devices.

DVDs – although these are currently the most popular physical audio-visual format, they will go into a decline as Blu-ray devices and players become more affordable.

MP3 players – improved MP3 playing and storage capabilities of mobile phones will lead to a decline in demand for MP3 players.

Decline

'Film' cameras – these will disappear altogether; disposable camera films will become a rarity as mobile phones become the norm for home photography; two 'film' cameras are featured in Fig. 7.7.

Fig. 7.7. Largely outdated and obsolete film cameras.

Fig. 7.8. Video home system (VHS) and audio cassettes, two defunct media formats.

All audio media formats – the continued rise of the MP3 will see all physical audio media formats eventually disappear.

Video home system (VHS) and DVD video recorders – the continued rise of personal video recorders (PVRs) will see video recorders that use physical formats (see Fig. 7.8) eventually disappear.

REFERENCES

British Broadcasting Corporation (BBC) (2003) George Michael goes back to Sony. [Internet] London, BBC. Available at: http://news.bbc.co.uk/1/hi/entertainment/3278909.stm

Bosanquet, N. and Gibbs, B. (2005) Class of 2005: The iPod generation. [Internet] London, Reform.co.uk. Available at: http://www.reform.co.uk/classof2005theipodgeneration_346.php

Byrne, D. (2007) David Byrne's survival strategies for emerging artists – and megastars. [Internet] New York, Wired. Available at: http://www.wired.com/entertainment/music/magazine/1601/ff_byrne?currentPage=all

Digidesign (2009) Digidesign. [Internet] Daly City, Avid Technology. Available at: http://www.digidesign.com/

Henderson, S. (2010) Football broadcasting – tipping point or bleeding edge? *Soccer and Society* 11(2) (Accepted for publication in March 2010).

Liversidge, A. (1995) Analog versus digital: Has vinyl been wrongly dethroned by the music industry? Omni. February 1995, 17(5), 28.

chapter 8

The Internet

Dr Erika Pearson

A technologically-supported social and information network that uses common protocols to link audiences with a wide array of content and each other in a global entertainment exchange.

The Internet has a relatively short but somewhat obscured history (Hafner and Lyon, 1998). Growing out of military-funded programmes to support widespread data transfer, the Internet is now used as a catch-all term to refer to online tools and exchanges such as e-mail, file transfer and the World Wide Web (WWW). For much of this nascent period, the Internet was tied to large corporations and institutions such as universities, and was very much a workplace tool (Kraut *et al.*, 1998) rather than a site for socialization or entertainment.

This began to shift as first personal computers and then the Internet began to migrate into the home (Kraut *et al.*, 1998). As the technology was domesticated, the Internet began to be adopted by users for non-commercial applications. Tools such as e-mail, bulletin boards (BBS), online forums and chat rooms began to attract the growing audiences that were now logging on. Even though, in this early period, the low bandwidth meant that it was mainly just text that was being transmitted, Internet users were beginning to experiment with the Internet as a site for entertainment.

The nature of the Internet, which supports many-to-many, one-to-many, and one-to-one communication, means that it is a tool and platform which can be adapted to suit numerous different types of entertainment, including text on web pages, multimedia, social networking and gaming. At the moment, many of these activities are undertaken from Internet-enabled personal computers, but there is a growing trend in portability, leading to many web pages and Web-based applications being accessed through portable personal devices (most commonly mobile phones), converging Internet-entertainment with other mass media, locations and activities; some examples can be found in Figs 8.1 and 8.2.

Fig. 8.1. Free public access to e-mail and the WWW, Newcastle, UK.

Fig. 8.2. Laptop computer connected to the Internet via free Wi-Fi access in a pub's beer garden.

Social Factor: Digital Nomads

Mobile Internet access is becoming increasingly commonplace. With growing Wi-Fi coverage, particularly in urban areas, and the decreasing cost of Internet-enabled portable devices such as mobile phones, laptop computers, netbooks and portable digital assistants (PDAs), an increasing number of users are accessing the Internet away from their desktop computers. As such, designers of web sites and online services need to become more conscious of designing interfaces and content delivery that can be accessed through these different portals.

Mobile Internet and computing (demonstrated in Fig. 8.3) has already begun to affect how people work, with some users choosing to eschew traditional offices in favour of working on the move, accessing information as well as telecommunications services through these online devices. But whether this will become a widespread trend in the long term, and what impact it will have on social behaviour, remains unclear.

Fig. 8.3. Accessing the Internet with a mobile phone.

WEB 2.0

The entertainment aspects of people's experience of the Internet leapt to the forefront with the rise of the so-called Web 2.0, which was originally a marketing term first used in 2004, and has been appropriated to be used more generally to refer to Internet tools, services and applications that revolve around interactivity, engagement, information and data exchange, socialization and user-generated content. These areas often overlap – for example, is social networking entertainment, socialization or part of a business strategy? It can be all three, and depends entirely on the surrounding context. As such, even though entertainment will be the primary focus of this chapter, it is difficult to completely divorce the Internet-as-entertainment from these other uses, as most online content and applications are intended to capture an audience, and invoke an emotional response among that audience.

In the current Web 2.0 environment, where the majority of users are still accessing online material via a desktop personal computer, there are some commonalities among the most successful online entertainment sites. Thanks in part to technological advances, there is a tendency towards multimedia experiences. This may include static images, video, animation, sound and (hyper)text working in combination to create the user experience. Secondly, and particularly in Web 2.0, this experience increasingly centres on user-generated content – content created, modified and consumed by the users of that site in a continuous self-renewing cycle that ensures novelty. Examples of this include YouTube, where users post their own short videos, or Second Life, where players create characters, environments, and engineer events and encounters. This exchange of creativity is fostered by a sense of sociability and of cross-user engagement. The most popular entertainment sites foster social experiences as part of, or alongside, the user-generated content. To continue these examples, YouTube users can comment on or post video replies to other videos, as well as subscribing to or becoming 'friends' with other users, and Second Life hinges on the interaction between users, mediated by their avatars.

This combination of user-generated content and sociability, which in the most successful sites explodes into a full-fledged sense of community, creates a sense of ownership of the site by the users themselves. This sense of ownership can be challenged when creators and hosts of such sites try to enforce policies in a top-down manner. A good example of this is the social networking site Facebook, which encourages users to develop their profiles and their social networks, as well as use and create small applications that run on the site. Facebook users subsequently developed a strong identification with the site, which was then challenged when Facebook altered the design of the site and introduced commercial material, selling user information to third parties, which in doing so revealed Facebook to be a personalized and intelligent global marketing machine.

Many recent entertainment web sites have begun to stress not only their accessibility and their user-generated content, but also the levels of user privacy and control. For example, Second Life allows users to own the intellectual property of the virtual items they create in-world. It may be valid to predict that future entertainment sites online will consider it necessary to enter into an equally creative relationship regarding the site and its contents.

Web sites are launched expecting to be the next *it* site for users looking for entertainment. The failure rate for such ventures (as with many other types of entertainment product) is high. Even if these sites engage users, allow content exchange, facilitate social interaction, guarantee privacy and security, and engage with their users on equal terms, most sites fail to thrive, and one of the main reasons for this is attention.

Though successful sites will always maintain a coterie of high-traffic users, such as *World of Warcraft*, which claims some users regularly play for 20 h per week (Hursthouse, 2005), most visitors to such sites fit their online activities around other time pressures, such as work and family commitments. For example, in 2007, the average time spent online by UK Internet users was 35 h per month (as of January 2007) (comScore, 2007). As such, users do not have a lot of time to spend trying out new sites, learning new interfaces or developing new content or social ties within new sites. Users tend to return to familiar sites, with their known interfaces and established social networks. Building a core group of users to drive content provision and foster social experiences is the key challenge for emerging online entertainment sites.

Keeping in mind the convergence nature of the Internet, it is possible to consider entertainment sites and portals online as belonging to one of six general categories. Though there is some overlap, these categories provide a useful starting point for considering the nature of online entertainment in a Web 2.0 environment, and are highlighted in Fig. 8.4.

A breakdown of each of these sub-sectors now follows.

THREE-DIMENSIONAL ENVIRONMENTS

Also referred to as virtual worlds, three-dimensional (3D) environments are graphical interfaces, which allow users to take on the aspect of an avatar (a virtual embodiment of self), to move through a representation of a 3D world. As computer processing power and broadband capacity increases, it can be expected that more and more information, play and social engagement online will take place in such constructed 3D environments (Table 8.1).

Table 8.1. Types of online 3D environment.

3D environment	Example site
MMORPG	*World of Warcraft*
	Everquest
Virtual Worlds	*Second Life*

Massively multiplayer online role-playing games (MMORPG)

MMORPG allow users to pit their skills against other users, or to team up with others online to complete challenges within the game environment. In many of the most popular MMORPG, such as *World of Warcraft*, this interactivity with other users is one of the major reasons for the continued engagement of the players (Griffiths *et al.*, 2003; Chen and Duh, 2007). The presence of other human players in the game increases the complexity of the play, provides a space for socialization, and helps users develop a sense of ownership and belonging which fosters their continued enjoyment of the game itself. Console-based games designers have taken note

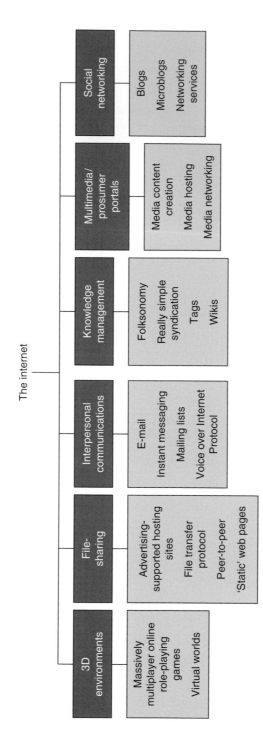

Fig. 8.4. Entertainment sub-sectors of the Internet.

of this, and networking is becoming an increasingly common feature across the games land-scape. As such, gaming is becoming a huge and growing entertainment industry sector (see Chapter 9, this volume).

Virtual worlds

Virtual worlds are constructed environments that people enter using mediated interfaces (such as 3D visual representations). Virtual worlds are platforms that may include a game-play element, or which may be more open-ended in their application. On these platforms, the user group can develop communal spaces, commercial environments or even spaces for training and education, political activity and protest, or fantasy constructs.

Economic and Legal Factor: the Value of Virtual Worlds

Massively multiplayer online games such as *World of Warcraft*, and virtual worlds such as *Second Life* have spawned their own in-world economies, based on their own currencies (such as the Linden Dollar, the currency of *Second Life*) that run parallel to the gameplay and are facilitated through online services such as eBay and PayPal. Even though the actual trade may revolve around a magic sword or a new set of virtual clothes for your *Second Life* avatar, these economies are at their core based on the familiar notions of scarcity and abundance. In-world economic activity, whether it be barter and trade or cash-based, revolves around the demand or desire players have for in-world artefacts, skills or abilities, and the resources the acquisition of these things requires. The major difference with in-world economies is that these resources are not tangible things (e.g. there is no wool in a virtual coat). However, the time and skill the creation of a 'wearable' virtual coat requires are valuable resources that can be traded, either for other in-game objects, in-game currency, or even currencies external to the game, such as the pound or the US dollar.

As such, many of the most popular games and virtual worlds now support thriving cottage industries of players who sell their time and skills in the online 3D environment as their job. This has led to a number of difficult and interesting questions at the intersection of the virtual and the real. For example, is this work, and the subsequent money earned, subject to taxation? If so, which set of tax laws has jurisdiction in a virtual world? Can virtual goods be stolen, and if so, how will thieves be prosecuted? As is often the case, the online experience has surged ahead of the law.

FILE-SHARING

File-sharing is a term that has received extensive media coverage in recent years in relation to the online exchange of copyright materials, but it can more accurately be thought of as the exchange of files between users, either directly, through hosting on a central server or

Table 8.2. Types of file-sharing.

File-sharing type	Example site
Advertising-supported hosting sites ('one-click' hosting)	Sendspace
	YouSendIt
	Megaupload
FTP	FileZilla
	SmartFTP
	In-browser FTP protocols
Peer-to-peer	The Pirate Bay
	Mininova
Web pages	Yahoo!pages

repository, or through a peer-to-peer network. When defined in this way, it can be seen that file-sharing is one of the central functions of the Internet (Table 8.2).

A Web 2.0-centric approach might consider file-sharing outside of the existing commercial entertainment models as a way for amateur creators of entertainment content to deliver their work to audiences. File-sharing in this sense is often closely interlinked with social networking sites, discussed below, to create communities of exchange in which these cultural artefacts circulate among a small but tightly linked community of interest and practice.

Advertising-supported hosting

Often referred to as 'one-click' hosting, this is an online service, which allows users to share large files with one or multiple selected users. Such sites often offer different levels of service depending on whether or not a membership fee is paid. Users who do not pay a fee have to navigate advertisements to transfer their files, whereas paid members are given a less cluttered interface and faster response times.

These sites provide an important service in the Web 2.0 environment. The dynamic nature of Web 2.0 content, plus the reliance on third-party sites such as social networking sites, combined with a growing volume of (often user-generated) multimedia content, means that users often need to exchange files that are either too large for e-mail services, or which have a large number of intended recipients. Prior to Web 2.0, such large-volume files would have been hosted on the users' own static HTML web page, but growing volumes of users and the declining cache and server space of free-hosting sites such as Yahoo!pages has meant that users needed alternate services to exchange these files. One-click hosting allows groups of users to circulate digital artefacts in a way that helps maintain social cohesion and information exchange, and gives users the opportunity to access files (such as video or audio) that then feed into other leisure habits.

File transfer protocol (FTP)

FTP is one of the older standard protocols for exchanging large files or volumes of data across a network. FTP refers more to a particular technological infrastructure, but FTP does require interaction between two or more end users (like a telephone – both a sender and receiver) to function. FTP creates a point-to-point relationship, where one end acts as the server, which delivers content to a client.

Peer-to-peer

Peer-to-peer is another method in which large files can be transferred around a network. Like FTP, peer-to-peer can function within a client–server relationship, but more frequently peer-to-peer (or P2P) is used to refer to distributed peer-to-peer networks. In distributed peer to peer, each member of the network (node) can act to both send and receive files simultaneously to multiple other points on the network. Distributed peer-to-peer networks are often ad hoc, with the network forming and dissolving based upon the demands made by the users on the network for the files it can access, as demonstrated in Fig. 8.5.

While peer-to-peer itself is not illegal, there is intense debate about the legality of activities on peer-to-peer networks. Peer-to-peer networks are often used to transfer copyrighted music and video files (as has been highlighted in previous chapters). Sites such as the Sweden-based Pirate Bay, which hosts the torrent files necessary to access such peer-to-peer networks, have come under strong legal pressures from groups such as the Recording Industry

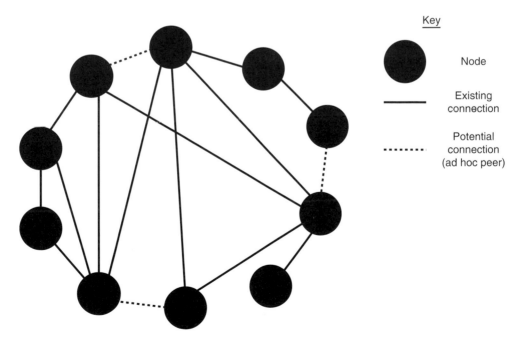

Fig. 8.5. Ad hoc peer to peer network.

Association of America and the Motion Picture Association of America, and as of August 2009 was blocked by the Swedish courts, however it has since re-emerged under a different guise, thus demonstrating the cat-and-mouse nature of enforcing copyright laws upon online file sharers. The global nature of peer-to-peer networks makes it difficult to apply a single national law or standard, and as yet the network users, copyright holders, Internet service providers and governments who are all stakeholders in this issue have been unable to reach a consensus.

'Static' web pages

Web pages are one of the most iconic features of the Internet landscape. Web pages are resources that can be accessed through a web browser. Web pages can be either *static*, where the web page is created and published online in a relatively fixed form, or *dynamic*, where the web page is coded so as to automatically update its own information and content by accessing other sites or services such as blogs or RSS feeds. Many other forms of Internet content and activity are often embedded in or accessed through a web page (sometimes referred to as a portal page) so as to be more easily located by intended users.

INTERPERSONAL COMMUNICATIONS

Interpersonal communications is one of the most enduring functions of the Internet. One-to-one or one-to-many communication that is not broadcast indiscriminately but rather targeted at specific users was one of the earliest services offered to users of the fledgling Internet (Table 8.3).

Table 8.3. Types of interpersonal communications.

Interpersonal communication type	Example site
E-mail	Hotmail
	Gmail
Mailing lists	Mailman
	Yahoo!Groups
Instant messaging (IM)	AIM
	Yahoo!Chat
	ICQ
Voice over Internet Protocol (VOIP)	GTalk
	Gizmo
	Skype

E-mail

For most users, interpersonal communication on the Internet means e-mail. E-mail is a communication form that is usually text-based, and involves messages being exchanged point-to-point between individual users using e-mail clients. A rudimentary form of e-mail predated the Internet, but in modern usage, e-mail retains this point-to-point nature, but can also refer to the act of e-mailing a mailing list or 'listservs' (automated mailing groups, usually centred on a specific interest or topic of discussion), which then resends the message to a larger audience.

Mailing lists

Mailing lists operate by enabling e-mail, which is normally a point-to-point communication method, to broadcast to a large subscribed audience. Mailing lists can be set up within an intranet by an IT administration, or by using free services such as Yahoo!Groups, to allow a group who share a common interest to share messages more easily than by doing a mass e-mail to each individual address.

Instant messaging (IM)

Instant Messaging is a form of real-time point-to-point communication. Most IM is text-based, such as the services offered by AOL IM (AIM), Yahoo!Chat, or ICQ ('I seek you'), and operates by allowing users to communicate via typed messages relayed through a desktop client. However, with increasing broadband capacity, IM has expanded to include audio transmissions, bringing IM together with simple voice-over-Internet services.

Voice over Internet protocol (VOIP)

VOIP, sometimes known as 'Internet telephony', uses the Internet instead of traditional telephone connections to exchange voice signals in real time. VOIP allows free or very cheap global voice connections, and as such competes with international calling rates offered for traditional international calls. It has only been recently that domestic broadband has developed in some areas to a sufficient quality to facilitate VOIP, but for many users VOIP is still too resource-intensive to deliver quality that is sufficient to make it the more desirable choice over traditional phone calls. However, as the resources and subsequent audio quality improve, VOIP may routinely replace telephony for some forms of contact. This is particularly relevant as services such as SNS expand people's social networks around the globe.

KNOWLEDGE MANAGEMENT

Knowledge management refers to activities online that help users navigate and search through the huge amounts of Web-based information. Knowledge management may not sound like

Social Factor: Instant Messaging and Teenagers

Instant messaging (IM) use among teenagers presents an interesting example of the ways in which interpersonal communication can be seen as entertainment. When the Internet is present in the home, IM provides teens with a way to supplement their social engagement, which is often limited by finances and mobility (Schiano *et al.,* 2002; Seepersad, 2004). Without a car, a private space to socialize, or extensive free time, IM provides teens with a way to maintain their social activity.

IM provides a number of useful benefits: it is low cost and low investment – teens can dip in and out of IM conversations, often around other online activities; it can be configured to communicate to a group or to a single individual; and screen names (the identifier of a user of an IM) can be discarded easily, and are therefore able to be exchanged with others with impunity. This helps to both maintain privacy as well as reflecting teens' shifting identities. The mediated nature of IMs make them sites of playful communication – for example, shy teens can practice flirting with their peers away from the pressures of face-to-face contact.

These factors all combine to create a space that teens can access to socialize, 'hang out', and maintain their social networks. The interactive, almost gossipy, nature of the messages, plus the fact that it is accessed through the same screen they use to do homework and other tasks, make it a popular alternative to other media available during a teen's leisure time.

a site for entertainment or leisure online, and it is certainly true that many of these tools have professional application, but it is a fact that many casual Internet surfers enjoy browsing through and even contributing to information portals such as Wikipedia. Delicious, a social bookmarking site, allows users to share brief information about web sites of interest, and many Delicious users contribute vast amounts of information to the service over extended periods of time. While a lot of this information is generated as part of professional practice, much of it is a product of users private online activity (Table 8.4).

Table 8.4. Types of online knowledge management tools.

Knowledge management	Example site
Tags	Embedded in SNS and portals such as Flickr
Folksonomy	Magnolia
	Delicious
Really Simple Syndication (RSS)	Atom
	RSS2
Wikis	Wikipedia

Tags

Tags are common keywords associated with particular pieces of information that are available online, such as blog posts, images or videos. Tags are assigned by the users themselves, and indexed so that a search for a particular tag brings up all uses of that tag. Tags are a form of metadata, or information about information, and as such only have meaning in relation to the information system in which they operate. Because tags are assigned by users, different tags might be used for the same piece of information, making tags highly subjective and contextual.

Folksonomy

Folksonomy describes the communal act of assigning tags within a system. Folksonomy is supported by tagging social sites such as Delicious, which track sites assigned tags by users and collate clouds or aggregates of information about sites and information that shares a communally assigned tag.

Really simple syndication (RSS)

RSS is used to distribute information, including metadata, about sites that update frequently, such as blogs. RSS, sometimes referred to more generically as a Web feed, can be received by individuals using RSS Readers, which collate and present information culled from multiple feeds, or by dynamic web sites which use the information to update their own content.

Wikis

Wikis are perhaps the most well known of the Web 2.0 knowledge management services, with Wikipedia being the eponymous example. Wikis use simple update interfaces to allow users (either members of a specific group, such as a business or social group) or the general public (such as with Wikipedia) to create, update and edit information on a topic. Wikis rely on the concept of crowdsourcing for their information, where it is assumed that the aggregate knowledge and judgement of a group will find the best or most accurate result.

Multimedia/prosumer portals

Along with SNS, multimedia portals such as YouTube are among the most recognizable sites on the Web 2.0 Internet. They are also the sites that are most explicitly linked with entertainment. Multimedia portals are a key element of the prosumer (producer–consumer) revolution, with audiences of content becoming producers of content in turn, as they come up with their own media content or react to content posted by other users (Table 8.5). These sites also allow users to repost content to external locations: for example YouTube videos can easily be embedded in Blogger and Facebook pages.

Table 8.5. Types of multimedia/prosumer portal.

Multimedia/prosumer portal	Example site
Media content creation	Indaba Music
	Minimum Noise
Media hosting	YouTube
	Vimeo
	Hulu
	Flickr
	Deviart
Media networking	Last.fm
	Pandora

Media content creation

The rise of desktop media content creation and online distribution, combined with the increasing popularity of online social networking, has led to sites being developed that allow content creators to network with other creators to develop collaborative works. Sites such as Indaba Music and Minimum Noise invite members to post works-in-progress and invite other creators to contribute to those works. As the tools and channels for multimedia content creation continue to improve, demand for such creator-specific social sites will continue to grow.

Media hosting

Media hosting is one of the more rapidly growing sub-sectors of Web 2.0, as users are able and interested in sharing media content. Sites such as YouTube and Flickr offer intuitive and easy-to-use channels to reach large online audiences without requiring the technical sophistication necessary to stream multimedia online. However, media hosting services are facing difficult questions regarding copyright and control of the files that they host.

Media networking

Media networking is another emerging area of Web 2.0 content service. Media networking revolves around users connecting and sharing with others based upon content tastes and preferences. last.fm, perhaps the most popular of the media networks currently operating, allows users to develop playlists, offers new music suggestions and facilitates connections with other last.fm users based upon stated music tastes and preferences. In the future, media networking may converge with hosting and even creation services to create one-stop portals for new media prosumers.

SOCIAL NETWORKING SITES (SNS)

Social networking sites including Facebook, MySpace and Bebo have become a key part of the core experience of the Web 2.0 Internet. Internet users have been using the technology to interact in virtual social environments for much of the history of the Internet, the Whole Earth 'Lectronic Link (WELL) established in 1985 being a famous example of early online social networking communities (Rheingold, 1993), but new platforms and services have seen an explosion in social networking online (see Table 8.6).

Table 8.6. Types of social networking sites.

Social networking site	Example site
Blogs	Blogger
	Livejournal
Microblogs	Twitter
	Dodgeball
Networking services	LinkedIn
	Facebook
	MySpace
	Yammer

Case Study: Hulu

Though many users create their own material to post on hosting sites such as YouTube, the site was also used extensively to post clips taken from commercial media in violation of copyright. Copyright holders could demand the take-down of material in violation, but these clips were often simply reposted by other users. In response to this, and the growing threat online multimedia posed to traditional broadcast media, two commercial content providers, NBC Universal and News Corp, combined to form Hulu (Hulu, nd), a YouTube-like multimedia portal for commercial content providers to post content for Web audiences. At the moment, much of the content on Hulu is, for copyright reasons, limited to users logging in from US Internet addresses, a fact which has generated a lot of bad press for Hulu among international users.

Despite this, Hulu has become an important portal for users seeking multimedia entertainment online. Even though desktop multimedia production technology has improved dramatically over the last decade, home-made videos for the most part cannot compete with the slick professionalism of the media output of the studio system. The high quality of the media on Hulu has made it a strong competitor to the do-it-yourself (DIY) ethos of sites like YouTube as to the consumption choices made by online viewers in their limited leisure time.

Blogs

An abbreviation of the portmanteau 'Web Logs', blogs are sites that allow users to publish content. Typically this is text, but now also includes multimedia content, which is frequently hosted by a third party, such as a one-click hosting site, which is then broadcast over the Web to an online audience. This audience then often has the opportunity to respond on the blog to the contents, creating the situation for dialogue and social interaction. With the increasing volumes of DIY multimedia content, the types of blogs have expanded to include video blogs, photo blogs and music blogs. As their names suggest, these blogs prioritize forms of communication other than text, and are made possible through the convergence of desktop production technologies, increased broadband speeds, and new channels for uploading and sharing such content.

Microblogs

Some of these sites require significant investments of time and effort. Others, like the newly emerging microblogging sites, demand only passing attention as the user moves through other tasks. Microblogs function by giving bloggers only a limited space in which to communicate to others. As such, microblogs encourage off-the-cuff remarks or observances, rather than a more thoughtful or formalized extensive blog post. The spontaneous nature of microblogging also fosters a sense of immediacy among participants.

Case Study: Twitter

Twitter is currently the most used microblogging service. Its users respond in 140 characters or less with their answer to the question 'What are you doing right now?' Users post their answer to this question, and can read in a list known as a 'tweetstream' the responses of other users they have chosen to follow. Twitter is instantly searchable, and can be accessible through a number of portals include a web site interface, third-party clients or mobile phones.

Development and Current Operations

Started in March of 2006, Twitter's user-base grew rapidly, causing early difficulties with service reliability. Such service outages threatened the viability of the service, but Twitter overcame many of these problems with a structural overhaul, which created a much more stable platform. It is unclear now exactly how many people use Twitter, with figures varying from millions to tens of millions of users.

During its early expansion phase, the Twitter user group featured a large cohort of early-adopters and technology enthusiasts. However, as Twitter was more frequently referenced in the media (both newspapers and broadcast media, and social media such as blogs), its use became more widespread, with users spanning the globe, including many in Asian countries, most notably Japan.

(Continued)

Case Study: Continued.

Twitter's strongest points are its immediacy and the low entry point. It is also free to use, though accessing Twitter through a mobile device may incur usage costs from the telecommunications service provider. Because Twitter posts are so short they encourage spontaneity, rather than more carefully crafted and longer blog entries. Twitter feeds are constantly updated in real time as new posts are made. Twitter users have also developed their own lexicon, with the @name and the #hash tag protocols allowing users to hold conversations or follow popular topics on the site as a whole.

In keeping with the themes of convergence that are common across Web 2.0, Twitter also supports an application programming interface (API) that allows other developers to create applications that feed into Twitter. These includes tools to allow users to scan across Twitter for common news items, or Twittervision (http://twittervision.com), which combines the geolocation data on Twitter posts (known as tweets) with Google Maps data to create a real-time map of tweets as they are posted.

Twitter and the Future

Is Twitter a passing fad, or will it endure? Unlike other Web 2.0 tools that went before, Twitter strongly fosters immediate and casual interactions. In many ways, Twitter and other microblogging sites act as an electronic 'water cooler', a place for quick and casual interaction that has a trickle-down effect in terms of socialization and interaction. This cumulative effect is arguably Twitter's greatest strength.

Though there is always a sense of a transitory nature to any Web 2.0 platform (Friendster went to MySpace went to Facebook and now Twitter), Twitter's ability to be integrated into other platforms, technologies and tools suggests that, in some form or other, the microblogging style fostered by Twitter will endure into the future. The biggest threat to Twitter and similar services is its economic viability. Currently, despite its popularity, Twitter has no functioning business model. For long-term sustainability, a workable business model that maintains the user features of the site will need to be developed.

Networking services

These have become much more mainstream with the development of commercial Web 2.0 sites and their associated applications. The sophistication of SNS platforms means that users do not require high levels of technological skill to manipulate the site, but can instead point and click to create a slick online presentation of themselves. As such, the barriers to entry are much lower. This, combined with extensive mainstream media coverage of these sites, has brought SNS usage out from being a 'geek hobby' to being an essential part of everyday life for much of the wired world.

Case Study: Facebook

In 2009, Facebook was the most used SNS globally. It was originally designed to facilitate networking among students at US universities, but expanded beyond the campus to include users from all walks of life. With its point-and-click interface; support for text and images; and the ability to facilitate chat, e-mail and interactive programs known as 'apps', Facebook is a popular destination for many Web users. Though there is increasing interest in Facebook as a tool for commerce, for most users, it is part of their leisure time (sometimes in work time, which has in itself proved controversial).

Despite early concerns that Facebook usage was detracting from other activities (the so-called Facebook addiction), there is a growing consensus that, for most users, Facebook provides a platform which helps facilitate existing or offline activities. For example, users organize parties, announce events and even facilitate political activism through the site. Instead of making a face-to-face visit or a phone call, friends stay in touch through the chat, e-mail or apps operating on the site. The development of a Facebook interface for mobile phones and portable devices can only accelerate this trend. As such, the use of Facebook may soon exemplify the convergence of the Internet more generally into everyday life.

THE FUTURE

Once tools intended for work and productivity, computers and the Internet now support a wide variety of entertainment, which blurs with other uses like professional development, productivity, communication, and information exchange, in ways that make it difficult to distinguish between leisure and non-leisure time. The immediate future for the Internet as a facilitator of entertainment is highlighted in Fig. 8.6.

Introduction

Microblogging – with its reduced demands on time and low barriers to entry, microblogging is attracting users who were not engaged in more intensive social networking activity.

Mobile Internet nomadism – the introduction of cheap, light-weight laptops, PDA/phone hybrids such as the iPhone, and more extensive Wi-Fi coverage has seen a dramatic increase in interest in Internet use away from the desktop environment.

Growth

Networked media editing – as more users experiment and become comfortable with becoming media producers, demand for services that allow them to network and share their creations will increase.

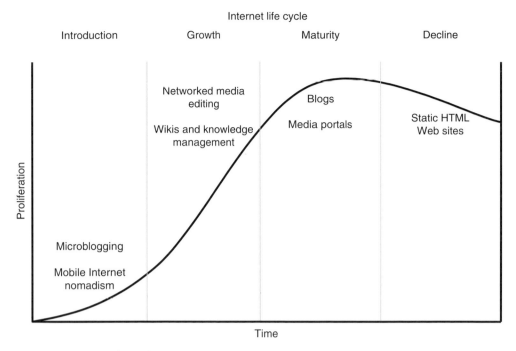

Fig. 8.6. Internet life cycle.

Wikis and knowledge management – overcoming initial concerns about reliability and accuracy, wikis and knowledge management systems are now becoming part of general research activity and large-group information coordination.

Maturity

Blogs – from their initial boom, blogs have now settled down, with clear striation between the so-called A-, B- and C-list blogs. A-list blogs such as The Huffington Post have developed a large following and now command similar respect and privilege from its newsprint rivals.

Media portals – despite the prevalence of low-quality limited-interest footage, YouTube has become a landmark site on the Internet, and the proliferation of competitor sites reveal continued interest in such portals. The development of professional media equivalents such as Hulu contributes to the authority and maturity of portal sites.

Decline

Static HTML web sites – with dynamism and novelty being watchwords of Web 2.0, the static web site is now in decline, replaced by more dynamic web sites that use media portals, RSS feeds, tags and other metadata to create portals that give site users constantly updated and renewed streams of information and entertainment.

REFERENCES

Chen V.H.-H. and Duh H.B.-L. (2007) Understanding social interaction in World of Warcraft. In Bernhaupt, R. and Tscheligi, M. (eds) *Proceedings of the International Conference on Advances in Computer Entertainment Technology*. ACE, New York, pp. 21–24.

ComScore (2007) Worldwide internet audience has grown 10 percent in last year. [Internet] Reston, Virginia, ComScore. URL available from: <http://www.comscore.com/press/release.asp?press = 1242>.

Griffiths, M.D., Davies, M.N.O. and Chappell, D. (2003) Breaking the stereotype: the case of online gaming. *Cyber Psychology and Behavior* 6, 81–91.

Hafner, K. and Lyon, M. (1998) *Where Wizards Stay Up Late: The Origins of the Internet*. Simon & Schuster, New York.

Hulu. About Hulu. [Internet] Los Angeles, Hulu. URL available from: <http://www.hulu.com/about>.

Hursthouse, J. (2005) MMOG Demographics: Perspectives from Industry Insiders. IGDA, New Jersey. [Internet] URL available from: <http://www.igda.org/online/quarterly/1_2/mmogdemographics.php>.

Kraut, R., Mukhopadhyay, T., Szczypula, J., Kiesler, S. and Scherlis, W. (1998) Communication and information: alternative uses of the internet in households. In: Karat, C.M., Lund, A., Coutaz, J. and Karat, J. (eds) *Conference on Human Factors in Computing Systems: Proceedings of the SIGCHI Conference on Human Factors in Computing Systems*. ACM Press, Los Angeles, California, pp. 368–375.

Rheingold, H. (1993) *The Virtual Community: Homesteading on the Electronic Frontier*. Addison-Wesley, New York.

Schiano, D., Chen, C.P., Ginsberg, J., Gretarsdottir, U., Huddleston, M. and Issacs, E. (2002). Teen use of messaging media. In Terveen, L. (ed.) *Proceedings of CHI2002*. ACM Press, New York, pp. 594–595.

Seepersad, S. (2004) Coping with loneliness: adolescent online and offline behavior. *CyberPsychology and Behavior* 7(1), 35–39.

chapter 9

Gaming

Stuart Moss

Entertainment that involves participation in a structured activity, usually undertaken for purposes of enjoyment, where a challenge or challenges are presented to participants, who must follow rules in order to achieve particular goals, and where outcomes are uncertain.

People have played games for thousands of years, typically (but not always) as a recreational pursuit, participated in for personal satisfaction or gain (skills, education and financial), to pass the time, or as a social activity. The depth and power of human imagination has led to thousands, if not millions, of games being created across all societies throughout history. In the gaming sector, both the entertainment industry and the leisure industry meet head-on, as gaming requires an audience, and games (like leisure activities) require participants. The characteristics of gaming are such that it can be considered as both a form of active entertainment, and a form of passive leisure. Not all categories of games are included in the gaming sub-sector of the entertainment industry, for example children's games such as 'hide and seek', 'tig' and other similar forms of play are largely free to participate in, and therefore are characteristically not a part of the more commercial entertainment industry. These types of games often rely on made up or improvised rules, and are largely reliant on the imaginations of the participants, as opposed to purchased gaming equipment.

The debate as to how exactly gaming fits within the entertainment industry is slightly more complex, for example a person playing a game of *Solitaire* with a deck of cards is engaging in a recreational activity, which can involve emotional involvement, ranging from the euphoria felt from a win to the disappointment of a loss. Although this emotional outcome can be the same as with other forms of entertainment, the question needs to be asked, is this genuinely an entertainment experience, or another 'form' of recreation? A game of *Solitaire* with a deck of cards passes the time, so it is a pastime, it involves participation so it is also leisure, if it is participated in regularly it may also be a hobby, but whether it can also be considered entertainment hinges on the philosophical debate as to whether the player who is generating the activity can also be the audience to it. In other words, is it possible to be both the entertainer and the audience at the same time? There will undoubtedly be various viewpoints on this, some who will believe that it is, as well as those who do not. In the same manner, it could be asked do persons singing entertain themselves? And does a person sculpting entertain themselves? They are all likely to be occupied and involved in what they are doing, they may be doing what they are doing as part of a recreational pursuit, their activities may also be amusing, enjoyable and satisfying, but is this really entertaining to them while they are doing it? An activity that is occupying or enjoyable is not necessarily entertainment, the ability of the human brain to be capable of both concentrating on an activity it is controlling, and be captivated by the outcome of that same activity simultaneously must be considered.

As mentioned in Chapter 1, there is no globally accepted definition as to what exactly constitutes entertainment, leisure and recreation. Until a globally accepted definition of 'all of the above' can be given, this debate will remain a largely philosophical one, and sectors such as gaming will always struggle in terms of identity as to whether they belong wholly, partially or not at all within the entertainment industry. Figure 9.1 denotes the sub-sectors that make up the gaming sector.

COMPUTER GAMES

Computer games generally involve the use of any electronically operated system whereby challenges are presented, and an input device is used to manipulate images (and usually sounds) produced by a computer or microprocessor on some kind of display. As well as providing audio and visual entertainment, some of the most modern systems also provide touch stimulation through vibrating handsets, or gaming chairs, all of which can lead to a range of emotive responses from the player (gamer) including: elation at a win, anger from making a mistake, disappointment at losing and fear from something unexpected happening.

In the 1970s, the first electronic large arcade video games began to appear; in the 1980s home game consoles were developed which meant that these games could be played in the home; from then on, technological advancements and the rise of home personal computers (PCs), the Internet, mobile phones, and hand-held gaming devices have revolutionized this highly competitive and growing sub-sector. As with most things technological, physical size and the actual cost of gaming devices has decreased, while computer processing power has increased, meaning that games are becoming increasingly life-like in the graphics that they display, and complex in their soundtracks, formats and features.

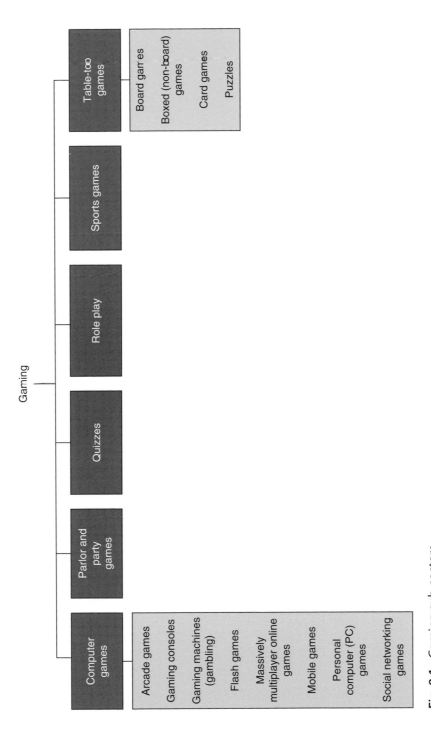

Fig. 9.1. Gaming sub-sectors.

Popular computer games genres based upon game themes and player interaction are:

- card games – simply playing card games, where the cards are usually controlled via the mouse, e.g. *Solitaire*;
- fighting games – the player controls a character who usually fights an opponent stood opposite them, fights are often unbalanced through characters having special powers, e.g. *X-Men vs. Street Fighter*;
- platform games – the player controls a character who has to move around the screen (often from left to right) and manoeuvre around obstacles, sometimes collecting objects along the way, e.g. *Sonic Adventure*;
- simulation games – the use of strategy, knowledge and skill to take the player through a simulation of a real scenario, e.g. *Microsoft Flight Simulator X*;
- shoot 'em ups – the use of a gun or other weapon to protect the player as they move around a hostile environment, e.g. *Halo 3*; and
- sports games – competitive games that simulate real sports, e.g. *Wii Sports*.

Table 9.1 gives information about the most popular forms of computer games and gaming devices.

Table 9.1. Forms of computer games and gaming devices, and their characteristics.

Forms of computer game and gaming devices	Characteristics
Arcade games	Arcade games are coin-operated, and are usually found in either arcades themselves, or places where it is likely that those interested in them (predominantly young males) will congregate (shopping malls, swimming baths, bars, tourist destinations and leisure centres). There are three predominant types of arcade games, which are amusements with prizes (AWPs), video arcade games (VAGs) and quiz machines
	AWPs are the exception to the computer game rule, in that they do not usually have any kind of video output, as the game involves physical movement of pieces within the game, usually through an input device. Modern AWPs are considered computer games, as at least part of the game is controlled by a microprocessor, even if it is only a minor game element such as a score board or musical sound effects. Common examples of AWPs are pinball machines, 'claw grabber' machines, coin-push machines and shooting galleries. The ancestors of today's AWPs pre-date video-based arcade games by over 40 years (see also Chapter 11, this volume)

(Continued)

Table 9.1. Continued.

Forms of computer game and gaming devices	Characteristics
	Video arcade games (VAGs) are computer games that are built into large cases whereby the user stands or sits at the machine (see Fig. 9.2), and uses in-built input devices such as joysticks or guns to manipulate graphics on the screen. The first popular VAG was *Pong* in 1972, although this was the third coin-operated VAG released after *The Galaxy Game* and *Computer Space*. *Pong* was based on table tennis; it was a black-and-white game that involved the player 'bouncing' a moving 'ball' across the screen where it was deflected by either a computer-controlled opponent or a second player. Every successful player deflection of the ball accrued a score, and it was the competitiveness of this game that made it so popular
	Since *Pong*, numerous classic VAG titles have been released including *Space Invaders*, *Asteroids*, *Pac-Man* and *Frogger*, all of which have since been developed into console games as well as other forms of computer games. Many current VAGs are based upon console games such as *Grand Theft Auto* and *Tomb Raider*. In the early days, Atari Inc led the market with VAG development, although today, there are numerous competitors
	Quiz machines are aimed at the adult market, and as a consequence are often found in bars. One machine can commonly offer a number of game formats, including quizzes based on TV programmes such as *Who Wants to Be a Millionaire*; board games such as 'Monopoly'; and music quiz machines. In quiz machines cash prizes can be payable to those who gain high scores by answering questions correctly
	In recent years there has been a slow down in arcade game usage, most likely due to the availability of console and online alternatives
Gaming consoles	These play commercially available computer games that are viewed through a television. They are therefore aimed at the 'home' market. The first games console was the 'Magnavox Odyssey' in 1971. Games for this console came on circuit boards that were plugged into a slot on the console. In the years following this, Atari Inc developed several game consoles,

(*Continued*)

Table 9.1. Continued.

Forms of computer game and gaming devices	Characteristics
	where the games were contained on cartridges and pushed into a slot in the machine. Magnavox released several other consoles and titles including one which played a *Pong*-type game
	Several other manufacturers released unsuccessful consoles, then in 1977 Atari released its 2600 console. However, it wasn't until 1980 after Atari released *Space Invaders* that the success of this console skyrocketed. Atari went on to turn many of their VAG titles into console games (and vice versa). Activision also began developing games that could be played on the 2600 (after a lawsuit with Atari), Activision's range of titles helped to cement the 2600s popularity. Following the 2600 Atari release, and the 5200 in 1982, which never fared as well commercially, especially with competition from 'Intellivision' (which had the first computer keyboard) and the *Coleco Vision* (both of these were cartridge game systems
	Competition from games aimed at home computer users caused game consoles to lose popularity until 1985 when Nintendo released the Nintendo Entertainment System (NES), and then the Super Nintendo Entertainment System (SNES). The NES proved immediately popular due to the *Super Mario Bros.* game. Mario immediately became a gaming icon, which then main competitors 'Sega' and their 'Mega Drive' could not compete with, until *Sonic the Hedgehog* was developed in 1991, putting Sega ahead as market leader, who followed the Mega Drive with the 'Master System' and the 'Saturn' consoles. Sega consoles differed from the competition in that its games were on a compact disc (CD)
	In the early 1990s, competition arose again from Atari; however, their 'Jaguar' system failed in the face of market dominance from Nintendo and Sega, almost causing Atari to go out of business.
	In the mid-1990s, the Sony Playstation was launched to mass acclaim. It quickly became the most popular gaming console, and Nintendo responded with the *N64* and Sega with the Dreamcast, but neither of these outlived the Playstation's

(Continued)

Table 9.1. Continued.

Forms of computer game and gaming devices	Characteristics
	popularity, due to a wide number of quickly released hugely popular games such as *Tekken*, *Rayman* and *Streetfighter*. As market leaders, Sony released the 'Playstation 2' or 'PS2' in 2000, which was marketed as a games console that could also play DVDs. DVD players were still expensive at this time, so the PS2 was potentially a money saver for those who wanted up-to-date games and movies
	Nintendo responded with their 'Game Cube' in 2001, which was popular among fans of previous Nintendo consoles and games, but was never as popular as the PS2. The serious competition for the PS2 didn't come until 2002 when Microsoft released the 'Xbox', which boasted a DVD player; its own hard disc drive; various media facilities (including the ability to 'rip' audio from CDs); and the capability of going online to 'Xbox Live', a subscription-based gaming service where players could compete globally. The game *Halo* was also released for the Xbox which immediately made the console a hit. An upgraded version of the Xbox was released in 2005, with the 'Xbox 360' which was high definition (HD), had a larger hard drive, and increased media capabilities, including the ability to play some software video formats
	Microsoft remained market leaders for a year until the near simultaneous release of the 'Playstation 3' and the Nintendo 'Wii'. The Playstation 3 was released with HD capability, as well as Bluetooth capability and a Blu-ray disc player. Nintendo's Wii was heralded as being ground-breaking for the innovative and 'energetic' manner by which its game controllers are used. The Wii has the 'Wii Fit' which is a balance board that allows players to exercise while they play games. Although the Wii is heavily publicized for its 'active' form of gaming, it was not the first console to offer this; 'dance mats' were used by other consoles before the Wii Fit was released, and as far back as the late 1970s 'pistol' hand sets were available for shooting gallery games

(Continued)

Table 9.1. Continued.

Forms of computer game and gaming devices	Characteristics
	At present, the console market is dominated by Sony, Microsoft and Nintendo, and history has demonstrated that innovative features and popular games have been two ingredients for success with games consoles. The future will bring greater gaming 'power', increased capacities, more multimedia capabilities and greatly increased integration with the Internet, particularly through social gaming networks, where friends and players can compete at a distance
Gaming machines (gambling)	Similar to arcade games, gambling machines present players with challenges, where money can be won. Popular gaming machines are 'poker' machines (based upon the card game), as well as 'fruit' machines that feature supposedly random configurations of characters on a reel, and prizes are awarded for similar characters landing next to each other. This format is based upon old mechanical 'one-armed bandits' that had been in existence since the turn of the century. Modern fruit machines are so-called because most of the characters on their wheels are based upon fruits. Modern fruit machines also feature skill tests beyond the reels including 'higher or lower' card games, and speed tests. The availability of gaming machines is dependent on gambling laws; relaxation of gambling laws in a number of countries has recently led to a greater proliferation of high-payout gaming machines (see also Chapter 11, this volume)
Flash games	Flash is a Web-based programming language, which is one of a family of languages known as 'Dynamic HTML'. Flash games are reasonably quick to load and are usually quite simple in their formats. They are accessed and played on Internet-connected computers through Web browsers such as 'Internet Explorer' or 'Firefox'. There are currently thousands of flash games available online, and more of greater complexity are constantly being developed. 'Miniclip' is a subscription-based provider of Web Flash games, which is popular among children and teenagers
Massively multiplayer online games (MMOGs)	These are games which can be played online simultaneously by thousands of people at once. MMOGs are played through both personal computers (PCs) and games consoles

(Continued)

Table 9.1. Continued.

Forms of computer game and gaming devices	Characteristics
Mobile games	Hand-held electronic games that used bulbs and light-emitting diodes (LEDs) in displays, and took large batteries as well as smaller liquid crystal display (LCD) games have been around since the 1970s. In the 1980s and 1990s, Nintendo dominated the hand-held gaming market with the 'Gameboy' and its successors. Today, the hand-held gaming market is dominated by Sony with their 'Playstation Portable' and Nintendo with their 'DS' (see Fig. 9.3). There is some stagnation in the hand-held gaming market, with developers wary that the new generation of mobile telephones are more than capable of playing good-quality games. Nokia led this development in 2003 with the 'N-Gage' mobile phone/hand-held gaming device. Numerous other manufacturers have now challenged, particularly with the onset of 'tilt and swivel', whereby the physical movement of the phone can be used to control game play
Personal computer (PC) games	These are games that are purchased as software and installed on to the hard disc drive of personal computers. These are increasingly being used online as part of MMOGs. Prior to the commercial availability of PCs in the late 1980s, home computers (HCs) such as those made by 'Commodore', and the 'ZX Spectrum' series were used by gamers to load games on to – often very slowly from audio cassette tape, where games were held in memory until the computer was reset or turned off. Crashes were common and eventually HCs lost out to the PC and console markets
Social networking games	These are generally simple games that are embedded within online social network environments such as 'Facebook', 'Bebo' and 'MSN'. Social networking games allow groups of 'friends' to play each other while being geographically dispersed. They are particularly popular among teenagers

PARLOR AND PARTY GAMES

Parlour and party games became popular in the 19th century, particularly among wealthy 'socialites' that would host and visit dinner parties on a regular basis. Parlour games such as 'Charades', 'Consequences', 'Eye Spy' and 'Twenty Questions' were traditionally played as entertainment after dinner.

Fig. 9.2. Motorbike-style video arcade game.

Fig. 9.3. Mobile gaming on a Nintendo DS.

Fig. 9.4. A giant Jenga set which is a popular party game.

All of the above-mentioned games are still played today, and at some point have been turned into commercial gaming products, either as board games, boxed (non-board) games, electronic games, computer games or a combination of the above. 'Pictionary', 'Articulate' and 'Jenga' (see Fig. 9.4) are examples of parlour and party games that have been turned into boxed (non-board) games. A more contemporary example of a boxed party game is 'Twister', which was developed in the 1960s and was originally considered a risqué 'adult' game due to the use of people as playing pieces, where contorted bodies would come into close proximity during game play.

QUIZZES

Quizzes are a popular social gaming activity that allow participants to compete singularly or in teams against other participants, where mental challenges are presented (often questions), and where the highest score usually wins a prize. The entertainer that hosts a quiz is known as the 'quizmaster', and it is the quizmaster's responsibility to either ask or distribute the questions or other challenges, and ensure that participants enter into the quiz fairly. Quizzes have been popularized through television game shows, examples include *Who Wants to Be a Millionaire*, *Wheel of Fortune* and *The Weakest Link*, which have subsequently become popular in table-top and computer game formats.

Quizzes are commonly offered as a form of entertainment in pubs; the 'pub quiz' is usually held on traditionally quiet evenings in order to boost attendance and drinks sales, as such, the pub quiz is also a form of sellertainment.

ROLE PLAY

Heavily reliant on participant imagination, role playing involves the use of acting and make-believe to create stories and scenarios. Structured role play involving storylines and rules has evolved as spin-offs from books, television programmes and movies, particularly in the science fiction and fantasy genres, with *Dungeons and Dragons*, *World of Warcraft* and *Warhammer* being popular role-playing games. Ardent role players go to the extremes of dressing in costume, and playing their games in settings such as woodland or disused buildings.

Online role-playing has become extremely popular through the use of social role-playing environments such as *Second Life* and fantasy games such as *World of Warhammer*.

Case Study: *Warhammer*

Warhammer was first published in 1983 by 'Games Workshop' as a table-top fantasy game, and it came boxed with fantasy books and pieces. It is set within a world inhabited by fantasy figures such as elves, dwarfs and wizards, and where conflict and gothic humour are everyday realities of life. From 1986 onwards, incarnations of the game included role-playing variants, where the game would be controlled by a 'games master' who would dictate a story and rules to players, that were required to approach problems presented to them with novel reasoning, and often the shake of multi-faced dice. Over the years there have been numerous spin-offs from *Warhammer*, including six further additions, and other materials such as books, models and character kits based around the *Warhammer universe* (WU).

From the late 1990s onwards, computer games set in the WU were released for both the PC and the Playstation. These achieved success as 'shoot-em-up' and 'strategy' titles, and kept the now 'cult' *Warhammer* brand alive for new generations of dedicated gamers. In 2008, *Warhammer* went back to its role-playing routes with the 'Mythic Entertainment' release of *Warhammer Online: Age of Reckoning*, which is a MMOG that allows people from around the world to interact and role-play in the WU. The game has proved extremely popular and a number of sequels and spin-offs are currently under development. Over the past 2 decades, *Warhammer* has made the transition from a niche product aimed specifically at fantasy enthusiasts, to a mainstream audience. This may have been helped with blockbuster fantasy film releases such as the *Lord of the Rings* trilogy, as well as the popularity of rival role playing MMOG *World of Warcraft*, but ultimately the WU's success has been down to its ability to transcend both media formats and game types. Commercial exploitation of the *Warhammer* brand will result in an expanded portfolio of *Warhammer* entertainment, including quite possibly movies, DVDs and books.

SPORTS GAMES

Participation in sporting activities is a sport and leisure activity that does not constitute being entertainment for the participant. However, the spectating of sports games, matches and tournaments by an audience is entertainment for that audience (see Chapter 12).

TABLE-TOP GAMES

These are so-called because they are played by one or more individuals while sitting at a table; some of the most popular types of table-top games are identified in Table 9.2.

Table 9.2. Forms of table-top games, and their characteristics.

Types of table-top games	Characteristics
Board games	Modern board games traditionally consist of a patterned board that presents players with challenges as they move pieces along a route on the board. They are typically aimed at the family market and participated in by more than one player at a time; board games are designed to offer a fun social experience. The earliest known board game dates back to ancient Egypt over 5500 years ago. Today there are thousands of types of board games, some of which have historic origins, an example being chess, which has been played globally for around 1500 years. Numerous contemporary games have been mass-produced commercially over the past century. Many of these comparatively 'modern' games have carried a theme; some popular examples include 'Monopoly' (making money); 'Clue' and 'Cluedo' (crime detection); and 'The Game of Life' (life, education and vocation)
	The dominant players in the board games sub-sector as well as boxed party games are Hasbro (which owns the MB Games and Parker Brothers brands) and Mattel. While Mattel is the larger of the two companies, the majority of its revenue is generated by toys such as Barbie, rather than games. Toys are used for non-structured play at the imagination of the user (typically children) and are a leisure–pastime rather than an entertainment product. Both Hasbro and Mattel have diversified their range, to offer products in the computer gaming sub-sector
	New variants of old titles are constantly produced in order for them to remain up-to-date and 'attractive' to young players, such as Monopoly, which is now available in editions based around popular television programmes such as *The Simpsons* and *Family Guy*, as well as hundreds of 'local' editions around the world based upon countries, institutions, and

(*Continued*)

Table 9.2. Continued.

Types of table-top games	Characteristics
	major urban centres (see Fig. 9.5). Monopoly, and its variants, is the biggest-selling board game of all time (Armstrong, 2008). Another example of a 'classic' board game that has been reproduced in more modern editions (although to a lesser extent than Monopoly) is Scrabble, which was first trademarked in 1948 (History, 2008), and has since been reproduced in numerous international versions to accommodate non-English alphabets, as well as other versions with unique novelties, including Scrabble Deluxe (rotating three-dimensional (3D) board with raised surface to avoid tiles moving); Travel Scrabble (small-scale board with raised surface and tiles); Kids Scrabble (with graphic clues); Party Scrabble (with a countdown timer that relates to variable scoring); and the latest Diamond Anniversary Edition Scrabble (with a folding storage case that opens to become the board). The addition of novelties to existing game formats is one method by which board game manufacturers have been able to boost sales when they begin to go into decline; another way by which this has been done is the exploitation of new formats
	Board game manufacturers have been keen to exploit electronic media in order to remain at the forefront of competition and to tap into new markets. It is now possible to purchase official software for games such as Monopoly, Trivial Pursuits, Sorry!, and Scrabble to be played on a PC, although the trend now among games manufacturers, is to shift electronic content online, which helps to control distribution, and to combat piracy. Pirating a board game, and all of its pieces, is a complex large-scale operation; however, copying a CD or DVD is very straightforward, and such unauthorized copying can be damaging on sales (as mentioned in Chapter 7, this volume). Subscription-based online content can overcome the problem of piracy, but what it cannot prevent is imitators stealing patented and registered game formats, and then producing their own unofficial versions without the permission of the original game owners
Boxed (non-board) games	Similar to board games, these are table-top games that are commercially available and come supplied in boxes, but have more elaborate playing areas than board games. Numerous boxed (non-board) games have been developed for the commercial family market, and titles that have proved popular globally include *Connect 4*, *Yahtzee* and *Jenga*
Card games	Traditional card games are based upon a standard 'Western' playing card deck, which has four suits of 13 numbered cards, plus two 'jokers'

(Continued)

Table 9.2. Continued.

Types of table-top games	Characteristics
	Most games are based around the following themes: number sequences (e.g. Gin); similarities of cards (e.g. snap); and numerical value (e.g. Poker). Most playing card games are also widely available as computer games
	Top Trumps are themed playing cards based upon specific genres, such as *Aircraft*, *Hannah Montanna*, *Dr. Who* and *Dinosaurs*. Each card in a pack of trumps contains numerical data, that is used to try and *Trump* (beat) your opponent by being the highest value (categories are chosen randomly)
	There are also trading (or collecting) card games, where players either purchase unseen packs of cards, or search for free cards that are packaged in other products (in England, themed cards used to be given in packets of English tea). The object of the game is to make a full set. Examples of trading card sets are *Pokémon*, *Star Wars* and *Basketball* cards, and these are particularly popular among children who often swap their doubles with friends for cards that they want, hence the 'trading' name. While reading and looking through sets of cards may be entertaining to collectors, this is also a hobby for many people. A variant of trading card games are trading stickers which are typically available for a limited period, and are placed in an album, completed sticker albums, as well as completed sets of cards can become valuable over time to collectors
Puzzles	Puzzles are typically undertaken by one player at a time. They offer players a specific problem that challenges the player's initiative and resourcefulness. Popular types of puzzles include jigsaws; crosswords, word searches and Sudoku. Most puzzle formats have grown beyond their traditional physical boundaries, are now available as both electronic and computer games

Case Study: Battleship

Battleship was invented at the turn of the 20th century, as a strategy game that was played on paper between two players. In 1943, it was patented by Milton Bradley Company (now MB Games), where it was produced commercially under a number of guises (sometimes *Battleships*) before becoming a popular boxed game with plastic three-dimensional playing kit in the 1970s. Since the 1980s, it has been available as a computer game on various consoles, and hand-held gaming devices, and has also been replicated many times online as a Flash game. Battleship is an example of an old party game that has a simple format, which has not dated, and its reproduction using new media to attract new markets has been part of the reason for its continued success throughout the 20th and into the 21st century.

Fig. 9.5. The Leeds edition of the Monopoly board. (Image courtesy of Stuart Rhodes.)

Legal Factor: Hasbro and Mattel Versus RJ Software and *Scrabulous*

Scrabulous was an online game created in 2005 in India by brothers Rajat and Jayant Agarwalla (RJ Software), based upon the board game Scrabble. *Scrabulous* featured a near identical board design, letter tiles and rules to Scrabble, the rights of which are owned by Hasbro in North America and Mattel in most of the rest of the world. *Scrabulous* was originally launched as a game on a stand-alone web site, but due to a lack of exposure and publicity only had a limited user base of around 20,000. The game was then developed for use as an application on social networking site Facebook, where a combination of the viral nature by which Facebook adds applications, and the popularity of the original Scrabble board game among Facebook users, led to the *Scrabulous* user base increasing by over 4000% to 840,000 Facebook users globally (Stone, 2007), leading to *Scrabulous* becoming the most used game on Facebook, attracting over five million hits daily (Madhavan, 2007). As the user base for *Scrabulous* increased, so did publicity surrounding it, with the media dubbing *Scrabulous* a 'Facebook phenomenon'. This of course did not go unnoticed by both Hasbro and Mattel, who then began legal proceedings to have the *Scrabulous* game removed from both Facebook, and the rest of the Web due to infringement of trademarks and copyright.

In August 2008, Facebook banned the *Scrabulous* application in all countries apart from India, where the high court ruled that the concept to the game of Scrabble could not be copyrighted, but that the similarities between *Scrabulous* and Scrabble were too great, particularly the names. In September 2008, the stand-alone non-Facebook *Scrabulous* web

(Continued)

Legal Factor: Continued.

site was also taken down by its server providers. In response to all of this, RJ Software made a number of changes, wherein they agreed to change the name of *Scrabulous* to *Lexulous*, the layout of the board, the value assigned to certain letters, and some tile values. In this period of 'down time' a great many Facebook users removed the *Scrabulous* application believing it to be gone permanently. In December 2008, the *Lexulous* application was launched on Facebook, and all previous *Scrabulous* users who had not removed the Scrabulous application were automatically granted access to the new *Lexulous* application. However, by January 2009, the Facebook user base for *Lexulous* had been drastically reduced to 33,000 active users from the peak days of *Scrabulous* usage. By 2009, there were also two official Facebook Scrabble applications, one for use in North America, and one for use in the rest of the world.

The lesson learned from this case, is that there is potentially a large demand on social networking web sites such as Facebook for traditional board games. After all the concept of playing a game socially with friends is just the same online as it is offline. Well-known 'classic' games such as Scrabble, where the format and rules are already known, stand a good advantage over lesser-known online multiplayer games on social networking web sites. There is some anecdotal evidence to suggest that sales of the board game Scrabble actually increased at the height of *Scrabulous'* popularity, although this was never confirmed by Hasbro or Mattel, but this kind of online exposure is potentially cost-effective advertising for board games, as well as being a potential revenue generator, through charging other companies for adverts to be placed on their web pages. *Scrabulous* was reported to be earning its creators US$25,000 per month from advertising revenue alone (Bowser, 2008).

THE FUTURE

Overall the future for the gaming sector is a healthy one. The integration of computer games and the Internet will help gaming remain a growth sector, although the influence of the Internet and free games will impact upon the sector as a whole causing game manufacturers to rethink how their revenue is generated. In future, subscription-based online games that are wholly or partially subsidized by advertising revenues will become the norm, as free games that are offered online will continue to grow in complexity and quality. Gaming will become integrated more into our everyday lives, and be something that is participated increasingly outside of traditional recreation time. This is highlighted in Fig. 9.6.

Introduction

Cell phone gaming devices including mobile MMOG – the cell or mobile phone will rise greatly in significance to gaming companies, 'tilt and swivel' technologies have already reinvented these as gaming devices, and titles will become available specifically for phones.

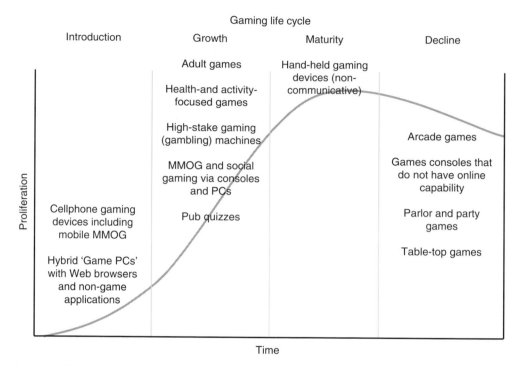

Fig. 9.6. The gaming life cycle.

An increased rate of mobile Internet access combined with social networking sites developing applications specifically for mobiles will lead to a great increase in social gaming. MMOG will also take advantage of the rising mobile Internet market.

Hybrid 'Game PCs' with Web browsers and non-game applications – the games console and the PC will grow closer in format, and the hybrid gaming PC will be developed from a gaming console that offers non-gaming applications, such as word processors, media players and Web browsers, as well as the ability to install third party software on them, and use non-gaming input devices and peripherals that are compatible with PCs.

Growth

Adult games – while families and teenagers will remain the main markets for games designers, a generation of middle-aged gamers who grew up in the 1980s with games consoles will lead the demand for more games geared towards the adult market, and this trend is set to continue. There will be demand for more games with adult themes including sex, violence and strong language.

Health-and activity-focused games – the recognition of the Wii format (see Fig. 9.7) has set the tone for future games console design. The negative publicity that gaming has received, especially with regards to inactive youth and childhood obesity, will lead to more games being

(a)  (b)

Fig. 9.7. Physical movement using the Wii Fit.

developed that require physical movement from players. The success of the Wii Fit will not have gone unnoticed by console manufacturers, who will be keen to emulate this with similar fitness boards of their own.

High-stake gaming (gambling) machines – the relaxation of gambling laws, and a worldwide growth in casinos will lead to increased demand for high-stake gaming machines.

MMOG and social gaming via consoles and PCs – the demand for competitive game play among friends that are geographically dispersed will continue to increase, and this will include MMOG.

Pub quizzes – smoking bans and a trend to 'feminize' pubs and bars as more general entertainment venues will lead to more demand for live gaming entertainment such as pub quizzes, which are likely to become more elaborate, so as to attract wider audiences.

Maturity

Hand-held gaming devices (non-communicative) – the future focus for hand-held and portable devices will be communicative. It is likely that successors of previous formats will be communicative and integrated into cell (mobile) phones and/or made wi-fi compatible.

Decline

Arcade games – the demand for arcade games will decrease in the face of 'free' competition from consoles, the Internet, PCs and mobile devices. New arcade game production will centre on major titles only.

Games consoles that do not have online capability – games consoles that do not have an online capability will no longer be produced for the mass market, and the ability to play online via consoles will become the expected norm.

Parlour and party games – these are now rarely played in the face of other forms of in-home entertainment. Sociable computer games such as the Playstation's *Singstar*, team-quiz games and Wii Fit games will continue to dominate the party games market.

Table-top games – these will continue to decline (almost terminally) in the face of competition from various computer games formats. Board game manufacturers will shift the focus of their output into computer games.

REFERENCES

Armstrong, R. (2008) Board games – the best selling games of all time. [Internet] EzineArticles.com. URL available at: <http://ezinearticles.com/?Board-Games—The-Best-Selling-Board-Games-Of-All-Time&id=33554>.

Bowser, J. (2008) Facebook army mobilises to save Scrabulous. [Internet] London, Brand Republic. URL available at: <http://www.brandrepublic.com/News/777806/Facebook-army-mobilises-save-Scrabulous/>.

History (2008) Toys and games – Scrabble. [Internet] Manhattan, A and E Television Networks. URL available from: <http://www.history.com/minisite.do?content_type=Minisite_Generic&content_type_id=57162&display_order=4&sub_display_order=4&mini_id=57124>.

Madhavan, N. (2007) Kolkata brothers 'scrabble' Facebook's hottest game. [Internet] New Delhi, *Hindustan Times*. URL available from: <http://www.hindustantimes.com/StoryPage/StoryPage.aspx?id=195219c6-5a29-4672-aacb-b5383c39648e&&Headline=Kolkata+boys+build+hottest+online+game>.

Stone, B. (2007) In Facebook, investing in a theory. [Internet] New York, *New York Times*. URL available from: <http://www.nytimes.com/2007/10/04/technology/04facebook.html?_r=2&pagewanted=2&ref=business>.

chapter 10

Printed Media

Dr Alexandra J. Kenyon

Entertainment that is typically paper-based, involving the use of printed text and graphics.

The body of all written work is referred to as 'literature'. The Samarians of Mesopotamia began structured 'writing' on clay tablets between 3300 and 3200 BC by listing the names of people and also food and drink items. However, Egyptian hieroglyphics are considered to be the earliest form of symbolic writing (Fischer, 2004). For several thousands of years their pictures and symbols were used to make records of important events and stories. Stories included battles, general news, religious teachings and ghost stories for children. The stories were also sung, acted out in plays or recited by travelling storytellers for the entertainment of the masses. As most people could not read and understand symbolic writing, they enjoyed the travelling entertainers. As time passed, the Greeks (900–800 BC) invented the alphabet of 24 letters, similar to the alphabet we use today. Having a structured alphabet enabled scholars and storytellers the opportunity to write down their teachings, yarns or fairy tales. Still only scholars, those taking religious orders and the very rich used the new alphabet as a formal education system did not exist. The most famous early Greek writings came from Homer who wrote two epic poems known as the Iliad and the Odyssey, which people still read for pleasure.

Reading is a cognitive process, wherein we read strings of words and our minds process these mentally, converting them into images and thoughts, invoking a wide range of emotional responses. Printed media is potentially a very powerful form of entertainment; at one end of the 'spectrum' it can generate extreme emotional responses such as delight, resulting in laughter, and at the opposite end it can invoke extreme sadness resulting in tears – all from words on pages. Ask yourself 'What is my favourite book?' then ask yourself 'why is that my favourite book?' Considering *how* that book made you feel emotionally may help you to appreciate this point.

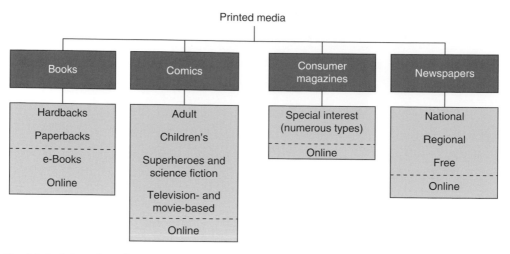

Fig. 10.1. Printed media sub-sectors.

For hundreds of years, stories, poems and general news were handwritten on large manuscripts. However, in 1447, the first printing press was invented and soon afterwards mass production of books, newspapers and later magazines occurred. Mass production brought down the prices to an affordable level for the middle classes. In time, particularly during the Victorian period (1837–1901), more people became educated and literate. The opportunity to read stories and fairy tales in a *printed format* is now being challenged, as the Internet has revolutionized this once wholly paper-based sector. The printed media sector of the entertainment industry comprises of books, magazines and newspapers, as highlighted in Fig. 10.1, and remains a very popular source of entertainment.

BOOKS

Generally divided into fiction ('made-up' stories or fantasies that are untrue) and non-fiction (factual), books are a collection of written sheets (leafs) that are bound and published. Most published books have an International Standard Book Number (ISBN) which is a 9- or 13-digit numeric code that is unique to each publication allowing them to be identified by stockists and retailers. Books tend to have either 'hard' covers and backs, typically thick inflexible cardboard, known as 'hardbacks', or thinner flexible cardboard covers and backs known as 'paperbacks'.

Hardbacks

These were originally produced to protect the contents of books from the rigours of everyday wear and tear. Today they are produced for new titles, and retail at premium price as a luxury item, as featured in Fig. 10.2.

Fig. 10.2. A book can entertain during a long car journey.

Paperbacks

A printing phenomenon of the 20th century meant paperback books became (and still are) affordable to the masses, and made owning a private book collection or library within the reach of everybody and not just the wealthy. One of the earliest, prolific publishers of paperback books was the Tauchnitz Edition series in Leipzig, Germany, which published series of British and American authors with over 5000 titles (Strout, 1956). Penguin paperback books, launched in 1935, revolutionized printed media in the UK and America (Briggs, 1974). At the time, private vehicle ownership was rare, so the majority of people travelled by train, tram and bus.

Penguin's pocket-sized (181 × 111 mm) novels were ideal for travellers and commuters to be entertained while on their journeys. Allen Lane launched the Penguin series with ten books, and calculated that he needed to print 20,000 copies and sell 7000 immediately. In the first few weeks Lane did not sell his books, so he sought out a new distribution channel – Woolworths (general retail stores). A new book-reading public was born and within 2 years the ten Penguin book titles grew to 200. Most books are eventually printed in paperback format, and as the print and production costs are low, paperback books can be sold between a third and half the price of a hardcover book, making them more accessible to the public.

e-Books

These are not printed media, however e-books (and online books, discussed below) have been included to give an indication as to the strategic direction that the traditional printed book publishing industry is going. e-Books are contained on digital media and are usually displayed upon, and read from computers, or on e-book readers, which are portable electronic devices that are of a similar size to a paperback book. Other portable devices such as mobile telephones are increasingly being fitted with software capable of displaying e-book electronic files.

Online books

These are books that are displayed online and viewed through Web browsers, often in Portable Document Format (PDF). Google have championed this book format with their 'Google Books' service – http://books.google.com, which was launched in 2004 as a digitized book service, where pages from thousands of texts (including magazines) are available online and searchable via a Web browser. Some texts are displayed in full, while others are displayed only in part.

Techno-legal Factor: Copyright Challenges in a Digital Age

Each and every sentence written, photograph taken, cartoon drawn for a comic, and all other intellectual property is owned by the creator and subject to copyright. The creators can choose whether to share their work with others, or keep it for themselves. If they wish to share what they have created so that it can be appreciated by the general public, the owners have the option of publishing their own work (typically via the Internet), or assigning their exclusive rights to a publisher to publish their creation; the publisher then becomes the new owner of the work. The exchanging of ownership has worked reasonably well and fairly for many years. However, as has been mentioned in several previous chapters, peer-to-peer file sharing over the Internet has challenged the fair exchange of ownership. For example, a person can pay for an e-book and download it on to their hard drive. If the same person makes their downloaded e-book available through a peer-to-peer file-sharing network, many people can access it at no cost, which means the publisher and the author do not receive the payments to which they are entitled.

It should be noted that any written, photographic, dramatic play or musical work that is not assigned to publishers, performers or broadcasters remains in the hands of the author or creator during their lifetime and for a further 70 years after their death, after which it 'goes out of copyright'. Since 2006, Google Book Search has scanned thousands of 'out of copyright books' as well as thousands of other 'in-copyright' books online. This caused the Author's Guild, the Association of American Publishers and several other publishers and authors to file a lawsuit against Google, claiming that Google were infringing copyright laws. After 3 years of discussions the agreement reached is that Google Book Search consumers can download the 'out of copyright books' free of charge on to their hard drive, to read on-screen or to print as they see fit. 'In-copyright and in-print books' that are available in shops or online bookstores such as Amazon can be previewed or

(Continued)

Techno-legal Factor: Continued.

purchased through Google Book Search; and books which are 'in-copyright but currently out-of-print' can also be previewed or purchased. This agreement gives the general public the opportunity to view, download or purchase over seven million books through Google Book Search.

There are other copyright laws that can infringe the rights of the creators and publishers. Amazon was reported in the *Wall Street Journal* (10 February 2009) to be infringing audio copyright laws. Amazon have recently launched Kindle 2, which is an e-book that is capable of 'reading aloud' the downloaded e-book. Stories include Stephen King's 2009 release – *Ur*, which was published exclusively for the Kindle 2. However, it is reported that Amazon do not have audio rights for Kindle 2 and the Authors Guild claim that authors are not being awarded audio-licensing fees to which they are entitled (Fowler and Trachtenberg, 2009). Once again, it can be seen that technological advances are challenging established rules and laws.

COMICS

Typically comics are soft-back 'magazine'-style publications, and come in a variety of guises with thousands of different titles. Comics are highly graphic in nature, and tell stories in picture form, with an accompanying narrative, as well as characters' spoken words and thoughts written in 'bubbles'. Due to their relative ease to read, and the assistance of images to tell a story, comics are popular among children, where titles such as *Thomas the Tank Engine* and *Beano* attract loyal followings (Mintel, 2008a). Some comics develop a 'cult' status, as readers get older but still loyally read them. Many titles are collected and accrue a value far in excess of their original cost (sometimes thousands of dollars). This is often the case with 'superhero' comics, particularly special editions; issues where a famous character first appears; issues where a famous character dies; 'round number' issues, e.g. 100th, 500th or 1000th; and 'first' issues such as Action Comics No.1, which featured the first appearance of *Superman*; it originally sold for US$0.10 in 1938, but at a 2009 auction an original sold for US$317,200. This demonstrates how comic books have become valuable and collectible like antiques and fine art. There was a 'boom' in comics from the mid-1980s until the early 1990s, when media attention of their value to collectors caused publishers to increase the number of collectible editions, by printing comics with shiny or holographic covers, or including 'limited edition' features such as trading cards and other free gifts.

Similar to comics are 'annuals', which are usually hardback compendiums of a comic taken over a yearly period, and graphic novels, books that consist entirely of comic-style cartoons; the most renowned of these is *Watchmen*, which began as a comic series, before being adapted into an annual, and later adapted for the 'big screen' in 2009. Some of the most common comic formats are listed below.

Adult comics

These are comics that contain strong adult themes that graphically depict stories involving violence, death, rape and sex. They are particularly popular in Japan where the 'Manga' format tells stories aimed at all ages, but many aimed specifically at adults. 'Hentai' is another Japanese genre of adult comics, which typically tell sexually explicit stories.

Children's comics

Titles such as the *Beano* and *Thomas the Tank Engine* have been popular for decades, and parents who read the comic as children often purchase it for their own children. Children's comics typically contain stories with a moral ending, as well as cheeky stories to help recruit new readers.

Superheroes and science fiction comics

By far the most successful comic genres has been those that depict superhero and science fiction characters. Leaders in this field are Marvel Comics and DC Comics, which between them have spawned characters including *Batman, Blade, Catwoman, Captain America, Flash Gordon, Iron Man, Spiderman, Superman, Teenage Mutant Ninja Turtles, The Incredible Hulk, The Fantastic Four, Wonder Woman,* and *The X-Men.* Marvel Comics is now a part of Marvel Entertainment, (now a part of The Walt Disney Company) and DC Comics is now wholly owned by Warner Brothers Entertainment, which has assisted in adapting comic book superheroes for movies and television series, as well as books and a wide range of merchandise.

Television and movie comics

These are comics based on popular television series and movies that often have a 'cult' following of fans. Titles include *Futurama, Indiana Jones, Star Wars,* and *The Simpsons.* Comic stories often retell episodes that have already been broadcast or screened, as well as 'side stories' involving characters from the programmes or movies in stories that are not screened, but may be linked in some way to the overall 'screened' storyline, for example *Star Wars* comics often told stories about 'what happened' in between the main movies, as well as giving 'background' stories about *Star Wars* characters.

Online comics

These are not printed media, but serve as both an extension of, and a marketing tool for, the printed version of the comic. The online format allows for a multimedia element that is unavailable in the paper version of the comic. *Peppa Pig* and *Jim, Jam & Sunny* are two titles to the children's comic market that have supporting web sites so that the children can feel part of a community and watch videos of characters found in the comic. This makes the entertainment value for children a dual experience. First they can take the comic with them to school, in the car or on vacation, and read stories, colour pictures and follow the daily lives of different characters and then visit the web site to take part in interactive elements including games.

CONSUMER MAGAZINES

Consumer magazines have been in existence for almost 300 years, with the first magazine published in the UK in 1731 called *The Gentleman's Magazine*, which delighted wealthy gentlemen with articles regarding current affairs, social opinion, science and poetry. The first fashion magazine for women entitled *The Lady's Magazine* was published in 1790. It contained drawings of fashionable dresses and commentary of the dresses worn by princesses at court. Later editions included embroidery patterns. Over 200 years later, women's magazines still contain pictures and opinions of fashion and handicraft suggestions. Magazines (and indeed comics) each have an International Standard Serial Number (ISSN), which serves the same purpose as what an ISBN does for books. Today there are thousands of different titles managed under 23 distinct subcategories.

Table 10.1 demonstrates the diverse subcategories of the *special interest* consumer magazines of which there are thousands of different titles. The number is approximate because new titles join the market regularly and existing titles disappear through lack of readers, and lack of finance or takeovers. This is known as *magazine churn*. Each subcategory has numerous magazine titles vying for readers who wish to be gain knowledge, relax, be amused or just be inspired. Many new titles are released in the New Year as weekly publications that come with a free collectable item, such as a figurine or a DVD. Deagostini and Eaglemoss are two publishers that specialize in this area with titles such as 'The Dog Collection' each issue of which comes with a free toy dog, and 'The Combat Tank Collection' each issue of which comes with a 1:72-scale model of a tank. This type of publication is aimed at collectors, with the 'free gift' an incentive to purchase the magazine, as well as to commit to buying it in order to complete the collection. Many magazines are aimed at people of a certain age or targeted specifically at men or women (see Fig. 10.3, below).

Monthly lifestyle or fashion magazines such as *Cosmopolitan* and *Hello!* are strong brands that are growing; however, there are numerous other similar titles including *Grazia*, *Glamour* and *Bella*. Churn will take place due to the high number of similar magazines in competition. Magazines that do not change, do not include excellent supplements and have poor quality stories will lose popularity and close. Women share magazines more than children, who prize their comics and claim immediate ownership. Therefore, publishers find success in circulation figures and also readership figures. It is predicted that the women's magazine sector will grow further (Mintel, 2008b).

Table 10.1. Subcategories of consumer magazines.

Buying and selling – general, cars, houses at home and abroad	**General interest** – almanacs, humour, lonely hearts, retirement	**Motoring** – general, buying & selling, classics, driving, 4 × 4, kit car
Computing – hardware, Internet, Nintendo, PC games, Saga & Sony	**Health & Fitness** – general, disabled, fitness	**Music** – general, blues, brass bands, classical, country, jazz and so on
Country, town and local interest – city and country guide magazines	**Home entertainment & electronic equipment** – audio, mobile phones, TV equipment	**News & cvurrent affairs** – General, court & society, environment & conservation, religion
Education and careers – alumni, college and university, education, jobs and careers	**Home interests** – general, DIY, gardening, home movers	**Outdoor pursuits** – bicycles & cycling, boating & sailing, country pursuits & field sports, guns & shooting and so on
Entertainment & leisure guides – film reviews, hotels & clubs, restaurants, TV & radio listings, national and regional	**Leisure interests** – antiques, history, nature & wildlife, painting, pets, photography, science fiction & paranormal trains, wood working	**Personal finance** – credit cards & bank accounts, investments & savings
Ethnic & expatriates – general, Africa, Americas, Asia and so on	**Men's magazines** – gay lifestyle, general lifestyle, top shelf (over 18 years of age)	**Sport** – general, american football, angling, athletics, badminton, basketball & netball, bodybuilding, bowls & bowling, boxing, cricket, croquet, cycling, darts and so on
Food and drink – general, slimming, vegetarian	**Motorcycling** – general, biker, buying and selling, classics	**Travel & tourism** – camping & caravanning, in-flight, on-board, tourism UK, travel overseas
Women's magazines – business women, hair, lesbian lifestyle, parenthood, weddings & brides fashion, women's weeklies/monthlies, women's associations	**Youth** – boys magazines, comics, girls magazines, pre-school, primary, style & fashion, teenage & pop	

Fig. 10.3. A selection of women's magazines on a store shelf.

Case Study: *Hello!* Magazine

Hello! was established in 1998, by Eduardo Sánchez Junco, a Spanish publisher, who also produce *¡Hola!*, which is the magazine that *Hello!* originates from. *Hello!* is a highly respected magazine for its photojournalism of aristocrats and A-list celebrities. The magazine is published in the UK, but sold in a number of countries including Canada, Greece, Mexico, Turkey, Russia and the United Arab Emirates. For every *Hello!* magazine sold 4.55 people read it, and this encourages organizations to buy advertising space in it.

News coverage of events relating to the British royal family often boosts sales, examples being the wedding of Princess Anne's son Peter Philips to Autumn Kelly in May 2008 (Mintel, 2008b); and the breakup of Prince Harry and Chelsey Davey. Alongside such articles is A-list celebrity news, examples being pictures of Hollywood stars such as Angelina Jolie, details of Geri Halliwell's (Ginger Spice) wedding and Sir Paul McCartney's love life.

Hello! has a fixed formula, so their readers can become familiar with the format and enjoy the continuity. Each issue has 'Diary of the Week' – photographic coverage of high society and celebrity events such as royal news; 'Panorama' – a review of current world events with many stunning photographic images; 'Cookery and Travel'; and 'Fashion and Lifestyle' (*Hello!*, 2009). The target market is women aged over 25 in the higher social classes A, B and C1 (BRAD, 2009).

Men's magazines (particularly in the general lifestyle category) have grown exponentially in the last 10 years (Mintel, 2006). This has coincided with the changes in men's behaviour and consequently their desire for fashion and grooming advice. However, many men have never bought lifestyle magazines, as they do not see any relevance in the articles that are contained within. Additionally, younger men, teenagers and those in their early twenties are turning to the Internet for advice, knowledge of fashion and news of the latest cars or sports. Therefore, while the men's consumer market is much larger than it has ever been, it may decline if younger men do not feel that reading magazines should become part of their leisure time activities in the same way that women do. While the market in terms of magazine sales has seen recent steady growth, it may reach saturation in terms of the number of titles offering the same diet of stories and features, and it is likely that the number of magazines in each category will reduce

---

Case Study: *Viz*

Viz is a comic–magazine hybrid, aimed at an adult male readership. It is a highly fun, 'tongue-in-cheek' publication with a great deal of 'toilet humour'. It was launched in Britian in 1979, but is popular in countries around the world with a monthly circulation of 88,000 copies that are read by 396,000 people – approximately 4.49 readers per *Viz* bought. The magazine contains 'adult' humour in the form of cartoons and comic strips; parodies of the news; spoof adverts for fake products that make a mockery of real adverts and products; claim to lame (lame claims of encounters with 'celebrities' by readers); features; letters pages; Profanisaurus (dictionary of swear words and rude terms); and Top-Tips where readers send in comedic tips, an example being 'Geography teachers. Attach pitta bread to the elbows of your tweed jacket for a tasty alternative to leather patches' (*Viz*, 2009, p. 10: Top Tips). The Letter Bocks pages also comment on current affairs in a humourous way, for example 'In 2001 Dennis Tito paid $20 million for seven days in space. Yet next October, some worms from the University of Nottingham will enjoy a fortnight's holiday on the International Space Station completely free. It hardly seems fair' (*Viz*, 2009, p. 10: Letter Bocks). Regular characters that have appeared in *Viz* include *Buster Gonad; The Fat Slags; Finbarr Saunders and his Double Entendres; The Modern Parents; Roger Mellie, the man on the Telly; Johnny Fartpants and Sid the Sexist*. As the names of the characters suggest they are extremely crude in nature, but ultimately very fun.

Online magazines

See online books.

NEWSPAPERS

Newspapers are important guides for the general public, as they provide knowledge of cultural events, politics and current affairs both locally and internationally. They also provide practical information such as television listings, sports results, share prices, weather forecasts, gardening tips, and financial advice; interest stories, such as celebrity gossip; comic strips; and games including crosswords and Sudoku. Newspapers are used to educate, sell, and provide fun. Newspapers were historically concerned only with current affairs, and read only by the wealthy and educated; however, today they are read by the masses.

Newspapers are divided along two lines: *periodicity* – when newspapers are available typically daily, weekly, monthly, bimonthly or quarterly. Additionally, the time of day is a further sub-category of periodicity such as morning, afternoon or evening news; and *type* – tabloid and broadsheet. Tabloid newspapers are usually sized around 380 × 300 mm, and broadsheets are usually around 600 × 380 mm.

National newspapers

These are most commonly daily publications, and come in both tabloid and broadsheet format. Tabloid newspapers specialize in 'fast food' news, short disaster stories, an abundance of photographs, celebrity scandals and sports results. They are often referred to as 'the gutter press', as journalists often report salacious news such as pictures of drunken celebrities having fights. Tabloid journalists and editors of newspapers tend to work with the 'paparazzi', who are photographers that typically: set up camp outside the homes of celebrities, sit outside night-clubs and bars frequented by celebrities and attend 'red carpet' events. Tabloids often contain 'cross heads', which are titles above paragraphs within articles that are indicative of the following content. Tabloid newspapers are highly popular and easy to read, and they are particularly attractive to audiences in the 'lower' socio-economic groups C2, D, E. The most popular national daily tabloid newspaper in the UK is *The Sun* with over three million copies sold daily (Keynote, 2008). In the USA, the most popular tabloids are *The New York Post*, *Philadelphia Daily News* and the *Chicago Sun-Times*.

Broadsheets are known as the 'quality press' because they report on current affairs, politics, the economy, international affairs of state, the arts and theatre. The news stories are longer, and provide more detail in an objective, pragmatic manner. Broadsheet journalists also provide cutting-edge reports on world issues that educate readers on events and cultures, hitherto unavailable to the reader. Some journalists risk their lives by venturing into danger zones or living with unique tribes of people to provide thought provoking reports. Newspapers such as these attract audiences from the 'upper' socio-economic groups A, B and C1. The most popular national daily broadsheet newspaper in the UK is the *Daily Telegraph* with over 900,000 copies sold each day (Keynote, 2008). Other renowned broadsheets worldwide include *Die Ziet* – Germany; *The New York Times* – USA; *Corriere Della Sera* – Italy; *Philippine Daily Inquirer* – Philippines; *Khaleej Times* – United Arab Emirates; and *L'Osservatore Romano* – Vatican City.

In the UK, the reason for the larger size of broadsheets is economics. Two hundred years ago, newspapers were taxed by government based upon the number of pages contained within the newspaper. To save money, newspaper bosses decided to print larger sheets meaning fewer pages. *The Independent* recently took a bold step and launched a compact edition and downsized their newspaper. There has been a 'social divide' between tabloid and broadsheet newspapers, i.e. tabloids for the working classes and broadsheets for the middle and upper classes, so moving a national, quality daily broadsheet newspaper to a compact size could potentially have alienated readers who 'feared' they would be 'seen' as reading 'gutter press' because of the size of the newspaper they were reading. However, *Independent* readers soon downsized to the 'easier to handle' newspaper, and now most broadsheet newspapers offer a downsized newspaper in addition to one their usual size.

Early newspapers were revolutionary in nature, but bland in comparison with the highly visual media we see on newspaper stands today. Photographs have been in newspapers for over 100 years, but historically few newspaper publishers could afford to include them. Modern newspapers are abundant with photographs because printing techniques are much less expensive, and consumers now expect to be stimulated by written text *and* creative images. Indeed front-page photographs on newspapers are used to motivate consumers into purchasing them.

The World Press Photo Contest has acknowledged the outstanding contributions that photojournalists make to the success and sales of newspapers. The organization began in 1955 and has been awarding outstanding photography ever since. There are many awards for current affairs, nature and sporting events. Figure 10.4 was taken by Ivaylo Velev, from Bulgaria at FREERIDE QUEST, Flaine, France, at Skiing and Snowboarding event in March 2008. Skier Phil Meier was skiing off-piste during his freeride (unlike the carefully managed slopes, off-piste skiing is unpredictable and avalanches can occur). This photograph encapsulates a dramatic avalanche and the skill of Phil Meier who had to ski ahead of the avalanche at breakneck speed. Phil Meier finished his freeride safely. Ivaylo Velev won the First Prize in Sports Action – Singles category at World Press Photo 2008 contest due to his skill in beautifully capturing a scene filled with danger (World Press Photo, 2009).

Fig. 10.4. ©Award-winning press photograph by Ivaylo Velev.

Political, Legal and Ethical Factor: Freedom of the Press

'Freedom of the Press' means that journalists provide news and current affairs honestly, truthfully, without bias – AND on any news story they wish. Notable news and current affairs stories include reports on the tsunami in Indonesia on 26th December 2004; Tibetans demonstrating during the Olympic Games in China 2008; and Madonna and Guy Ritchie's divorce. Generally, it is important for journalists to advise the public on all current affairs, however, many countries do not allow journalists freedom to report on topics that may affect national security. Other non-democratic countries 'own' the newspapers and use them for propaganda; therefore, journalists have very little freedom to report the truth. According to the Worldwide Press Freedom Index: Iceland, Luxemburg, Norway, Estonia, Finland and Ireland offer their journalists the greatest freedom to report on current affairs, and Vietnam, Cuba, Burma, Turkmenistan, North Korea and Eritrea restrict their journalists. Governments also ban journalists from viewing events for political reasons. For example, the Israeli government banned all journalists from Gaza during the 2008 period of conflict.

A recent BBC World Service survey asked newspaper readers if they thought a *free press* is important; 56% stated that to keep a free society it is important that journalists have the opportunity and freedom to report on current affairs. However, 40% of consumers worldwide stated that it is beneficial to keep peace and social harmony and if this means limiting what journalists report – so be it.

Source: Douglas (2007); Freedom House (2009); and Reporters without Borders (2008).

Regional newspapers

It is common for people not to live or work in the same, city and town and in some cases the country in which they were born. This means that people may not have a strong affinity with their locality, which in turn means they are less interested in regional news. Additionally, young people often move away from home to go to university; these people have traditionally been the new customers for regional newspapers. These cultural changes, therefore, are having a detrimental effect on the sales of all regional, daily newspapers.

Weekly regional newspapers have a special niche in the marketplace. Their news stories are at a local level such as school entertainment events, local sports results and community news such as recycling opportunities. Regional weekly newspapers are renowned also for classified advertisement sections containing details of local job vacancies, property for sales and other items 'for sale'.

Free newspapers

Free newspapers consist almost entirely of paid-for advertisements, and have been delivered to the homes of consumers for many years. There is now a growing trend for 'city'-based free newspapers such as *Metro London*, which was launched in the UK in 1999. This newspaper has

Fig. 10.5. *The Metro,* a free newspaper.

now expanded into many other UK cities including Manchester, Liverpool, Bath, Leeds and Edinburgh. *The Metro* has international and national news, but also regional music concerts and local cinema listings. Like tabloid newspapers the articles are compact and consist mainly of current news, celebrity gossip and popular culture. *The Metro* is distributed through public transport networks (see Fig. 10.5), advertisements facilitate the printing and circulation costs of free newspapers.

Online newspapers

Although these are not printed media, the inclusion of online newspapers is to give an indication as to the direction that this traditionally print-based industry is going. The majority of newspapers offer online additions to complement their printed newspapers, but these do take audiences away from buying printed versions. News stories online are often shorter than what they are in printed media.

THE FUTURE

Printed media is going through a transitionary period, with many once popular printed formats now facing decline, and increased competition contributing towards 'churn' of titles. Printed media will stay in circulation, the experience of relaxing with a magazine on a bus, or curling up in bed with a good book has its special place in our lives that online viewing will not easily replace, at least in the short term. With that said, the penetration of online and e-formats will impact upon this traditionally paper-based sector, although to what extent remains unknown. The experience of the music and movie sectors has been that e-formats have replaced physical media all too easily; the printed media sector cannot be wholly immune to this. The immediate future for the printed media sector is highlighted in Fig. 10.6.

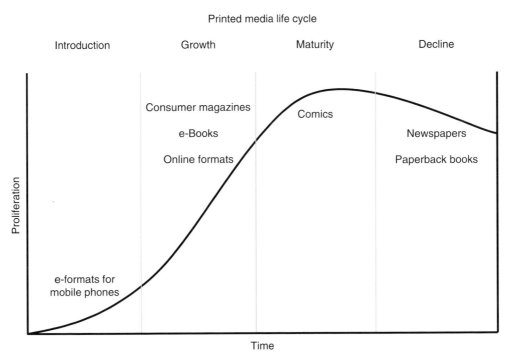

Fig. 10.6. Printed media life cycle.

Introduction

e-formats for mobile phones – the most used cameras and MP3 players are contained in mobile phones, will these devices also become the next 'challenges' for the printed media sector? One might expect competition for less graphic formats such as paperback books will more easily come from mobile e-formats than with highly visual items such as consumer magazines. The disadvantage that mobile devices currently have for displaying some forms of printed media is the physical size of screens being too small – although with advances in screen technology and electronic paper this may change. As more titles become offered in this format their purchase or subscription and take-up will most likely increase. The equivalent to an 'iTunes' solely for e-formats of printed media is not far away.

Growth

Consumer magazines – these are in the late stages of growth and nearing maturity, which is being exacerbated by a flood of 'similar' titles and magazine churn. New innovations such as 'hand-bag'-sized editions may help to prolong the life of some titles, but overall competition from other portable entertainment, and electronic formats may bring consumer magazines into maturity from growth, sooner rather than later.

e-Books – although still not accepted among the masses, these will steadily grow in popularity as more titles become available, and gadgets such as mobile phones become increasingly capable of displaying them.

Online formats – online formats of all printed media will continue to increase in popularity. With the advantages that they offer, there will be disadvantages. These include slow download times during peak periods; restricted availability, i.e. less chance to read online while waiting at the train station or travelling on the bus; and reading online strains the eyes, however, all that may change as technology improves (Rosen, 2009).

Maturity

Comics – the readers of comics (typically young males) are generally within the same demographic as those who are embracing the Internet. As more children grow up in an 'online' world, it will be much easier to convert them wholly to online formats that offer greater multimedia capabilities than what paper does. Subscription-based games web sites that are aimed at children (such as Miniclip) already exist – could comics follow a similar path? Online subscription-based comic formats could prove to be a testing ground for other formats, leaving fewer physically printed titles, but making those that are printed highly valued and sought after items, in essence this could spark a fresh period of growth.

Decline

Newspapers – alternative news sources offered via radio, television and the Internet, combined with some social issues highlighted earlier in the chapter, as well as technological ones such as the availability of alternative forms of entertainment that are just as portable as newspapers have all contributed to the decline in newspaper readership. Migration on to online platforms may eventually lead to a new period of growth in terms of readership, although as to whether this is in paper or electronic format remains to be seen.

Paperback books – increased competition from portable entertainment formats (including e-books) delivered via mobile devices is contributing to the decline in paperback book sales, this is expected to be a continued and growing trend, causing publishers to shift the way by which they do business away from print. Books are likely to be seen as a luxury item in future as more titles are produced in electronic format in order to appeal to the 'online' generations. The questions remain – is this the thin end of the wedge, and will all other printed formats follow suit.

REFERENCES

Brad Insight (2009) British rate and data. [Internet] London, Brad Insight. URL available at: <http://www.brad.co.uk>.

Briggs, A. (ed.) (1974) *Essays in the History of Publishing*. Longman Group Limited, London and Colchester, UK.

Douglas, T. (2007) World 'divided' on press freedom. [Internet] London, BBC. URL available at: <http://news.bbc.co.uk/1/hi/in_depth/7134918.stm>.

Fischer, S.R. (2004) *A History of Reading*. Reaktion Books, Chicago, Illinois.

Fowler, G. and Trachtenberg, J. (2009) New Kindle audio feature causes a stir. [Internet] New York, *The Wall Street Journal*. URL available at: <http://online.wsj.com/article/SB123419309890963869.html>.

Freedom House (2009) Freedom of the Press. [Internet] Washington, DC, Freedom House. URL available at: <http://www.freedomhouse.org/template.cfm?page=16>.

Gentleman's Magazine *The Gentleman's Magazine in the Age of Samuel Johnson, 1731–1745*. Introduced by Thomas Keymer, 16 Vols. Indexed. Pickering & Chatto, London.

Hello! (2009) Hellomagazine.com. [Internet] London, Hellomagazine.com, URL available at: <http://www.hellomagazine.com>.

Mintel (2006) *Men's Magazines: UK – April 2006*. Mintel International Group, London.

Mintel (2008a) *Children's Comics and Magazines: UK – October 2008*. Mintel International Group, London.

Mintel (2008b) *Women's Magazines: UK – October 2008*. Mintel International Group, London.

Reporters Without Borders (2008) Only peace protects freedoms in post-9/11 world. [Internet] Paris, Reporters Without Borders. URL available at: <http://www.rsf.org/article.php3?id_article=29031>.

Rosen, J. (2009) Jayrosen_nyu. [Internet] New York, Twitter. URL available at: <http://twitter.com/jayrosen_nyu>

Strout, D.E. (1956) *Paperback Books – Boon or Bane? The Nature and Development of the Library Collection*. Allerton Park Institute No. 3. University of Illinois Library School, Champaign, Illinois.

Viz (2009) ISSN 9 770952 796146 83, p.10.

World Press Photo (2009) World press photo. [Internet] Amsterdam, WPP. URL available at: <http://www.worldpressphoto.org>.

chapter 11

Commercial Gambling

Marc W. Etches

Entertainment that involves risking the loss of money over a possible financial gain.

Gambling is a form of entertainment that engenders for the vast majority of people a sense of fun, excitement and exhilaration without causing any harm. However, there is a small minority that may gamble excessively beyond their personal financial means causing harm to themselves and their dependents (Wardle *et al.*, 2007). Concerns about 'problem gambling' allied to different religious and secular moral perspectives mean that gambling generally, and commercial gambling specifically, is a controversial sector of the entertainment industry.

A mistake that is often made by those that seek to advance arguments either for or against the legalization and regulation of commercial gambling is to treat gambling as if it is a homogeneous activity. This is not the case; people participate in a variety of different gambling activities in diverse circumstances for a range of reasons, sometimes with quite varied economic and social outcomes. There is not the space within this text to examine in depth the complexities of what is, for some at least, a fascinating aspect of human behaviour; the intention is simply to introduce the reader to a range of activities that, in contemporary Western societies, have collectively been 'reclassified as part of the entertainment business and integrated into mainstream economic development' (McMillen, 1996a, p. 11).

Commercial gambling is essentially concerned with participation in various kinds of games where money may be won, and is primarily engaged in for fun or pleasure (Collins, 2003). There are three components, all of which must exist if an activity is to constitute gambling: Something has to be staked, or put at risk; there has to be the prospect of winning something; and there has to be uncertainty about the outcome as to whether one will win or lose. Gambling does not necessarily depend on chance, but there does have to be uncertainty about the outcome.

Commercial gambling providers charge for supplying a gambling service, most commonly by imposing odds and other conditions that ensure 'the house' (which is the commercial enterprise operating the gambling activity) will always win over the long term. Gambling requires the consumer to accept that the 'house' has a statistical advantage that ensures it wins a proportion of the money staked. Participation in commercial gambling, for most people, will not result in generating a profit for the gambler. In the long term 'gambling retains the distinguishing feature that, over time, for gamblers as a group, their gambling will inevitably cost them money – it is more like consumption than investment' (Productivity Commission, 1999, p. 6).

Gambling providers are able to calculate the ratio of 'wins' in their favour over the long term for gambling on mechanical devices such as a roulette wheel, slot machine, playing 'blackjack' or throwing dice. Some gambling activities such as sports betting more generally involve making better judgements about probabilities, and may involve pitting the wits and knowledge of players against the 'house', 'bookmaker' or some other party or device (Collins, 2003). There is universal confusion between the amount of money wagered, sometimes called the 'handle', and the amount of money actually spent by the gambler, which sometimes accounts for the widely varying estimates of the size of the legalized gambling industry. Gross gambling revenue or yield (GGR or GGY) is the total amount of money wagered minus the winnings returned to players, a true measure of the economic value of gambling. GGR or GGY is the figure used to determine what gambling businesses earn before paying out salaries, supplies and taxes – the equivalent of sales revenue but not company profits.

Although the 'price' of gambling may be not always obvious to the consumer, the consumption of leisure time that gambling involves might be considered directly analogous to watching a movie or some sporting event.

A BRIEF HISTORY OF COMMERCIAL GAMBLING

Ashton (1898), France (1902) and Steinmetz (1870) offer many references for gambling among a variety of cultures ancient and otherwise, including Egyptians, Chinese, Persians, Indians, Japanese, Greeks and Romans. The origin of modern commercial gambling is recognizable in the early manipulation of cards and dice, which were in turn derived from the ancient casting of lots. Playing cards, like dice, originated within the context of magical–religious ritual and early forms were used to predict future events or outcomes, as well as to provide amusement (Reith, 2002). Backgammon, or at least a race game similar to backgammon known as tables, quickly became popular after its introduction into Britain in the 11th century, probably from the Middle East, where it still remains popular. In Europe, by the 12th century, there were ten different dice games recorded including hazard, a game with two dice that was to become the most popular dice game in gaming houses in the 18th and 19th centuries (Munting, 1996). Other popular dice games in medieval taverns included queek and chequers. The earliest card games were simple, required little if any skill and substituted for dice games such as 'basset' and 'faro', which was a betting game that relied on the value of the next card turned over from the pack, and became one of the most popular games in the 19th century both in Britain and in the USA.

The earliest recorded lottery in Europe was on 24 February 1446 in Bruges, and the first in Britain was in 1569 (Ashton, 1898). The progressive development of public lotteries in European cities and emerging nation-states during the 16th and 17th centuries belied an 'uneasy symbiotic relation to the development of a capitalist system of production' (Reith, 2002, p. 55). They were revenue-raising for public projects without the need for politically sensitive taxation, in tension with religious and secular concerns about undermining Divine authority and the virtues of work. Lotteries played an early and important role in America's development. The Virginia Company of London successfully petitioned for the right to operate lotteries for the purposes of raising funds to support its Jamestown settlement. The first draw was conducted in London in 1612 (Ashton, 1898); however, by the early 1700s the level of dishonesty and corruption in the American colonies provoked the instigation of government regulation starting in Massachusetts in 1719 (Pierce and Miller, 2004), and by 1776 only Maryland and North Carolina did not require state lotteries to be subjected to legislative authorization (Abt, 1996).

The subsequent success of state lotteries in early America is illustrated by the fact that by 1832 eight eastern state lotteries were raising US$66 million per year, equivalent to four times the entire federal government budget (Blakey, 1979 in Pierce and Miller, 2004). However, the era of Jacksonianism social reform ensured that by 1860 twenty-one of the twenty-four states to allow lotteries had banned them; Delaware, Missouri and Kentucky were the exceptions (Pierce and Miller, 2004). In Britain, lotteries were banned between 1699 and 1710 but subsequently thrived before social concerns caused their prohibition again in 1823 until the emergence of the National Lottery in 1994.

The period of the Industrial Revolution in the 19th century shaped the contemporary commercialization of gambling. As Reith (2002, p. 74) puts it, 'as the calculation of odds became more fully understood, the nature of games played changed so that they became more amenable to commercial organisation, more homogeneous and, ultimately, more sellable'. This is the era that gave rise to mass market gambling via casinos, racetracks, betting offices, mechanized slot-machines, bingo and pools.

Increased secularization and religious tolerance combined with the growing economic and political power of the so-called middle class in most Western countries has significantly reduced, although not removed, societal anxiety about gambling (McMillen, 1996b). New political and economic challenges in the last four decades have enabled the re-emergence of state lotteries globally and the widespread development of casinos, particularly in North America (Pierce and Miller, 2004). New technologies are driving the development of remote gambling via the Internet, television and mobile devices, particularly in relation to poker and sports betting. In the 21st century, gambling is indisputably an integral component of contemporary popular culture (McMillen, 2003).

COMMERCIAL GAMBLING SUB-SECTORS

A convenient taxonomical approach might be to categorize different gambling activities by venue such as 'casino' or 'betting parlour'; however the categorization of commercial gambling is not so straightforward. Increasingly the distinctions between what may be referred to as traditional gambling venues are blurred, not least due to technological changes in the past decade, indeed most forms of gambling can now be participated in remotely.

Commercial gambling may be regarded as consisting in four possible types of gambling activity, outlined in Fig. 11.1.

BETTING

Profit gained in 'making a book' is dependent on offering odds that imply that the outcome is more likely than it really is; the art of bookmaking lies in the ability of the betting business to make better judgements about likely event outcomes, and to do so more often, than the betting public.

Betting exchange – a form of betting that allows gamblers to bet online at odds set by, and requested of, other gamblers, rather than with a professional bookmaker. Bettors can place bets to 'back' a selection to win, and 'lay' bets against a selection to win, paying a commission to the commercial enterprise providing the Web-based platform.

Fixed-odds – involves the payout being agreed at the time the bet is sold on the basis of the prevailing odds. In relation to horse racing and greyhound racing, the odds available in the on-course betting market at the precise starting time of the relevant race are referred to as

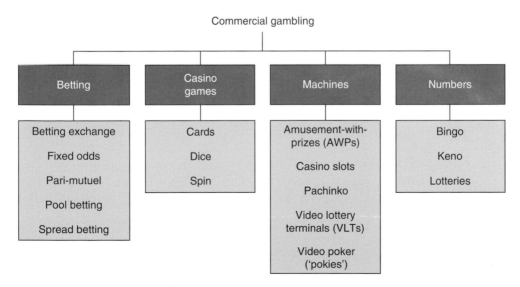

Fig. 11.1. Commercial gambling sub-sectors.

the starting price (SP). Fixed-odds betting are also available on a wide range of other events including elections, television competitions and the weather.

Pari-mutuel – a betting system in which all bets of a particular type are placed together in a pool, taxes and a house percentage are removed and pay-off odds are calculated by sharing the pool among all winning bets. This system is used in many jurisdictions on gambling on horse racing, harness racing, greyhound racing, and other sporting events in which participants finish in a ranked order.

Pool betting – a variant of pari-mutuel betting where gamblers pay a fixed price into a 'pool', and make a selection on the outcome of an event or a number of events. There are no odds involved and the payout is determined on the basis of the total 'pool', less taxes and house percentage, divided by the number of winners.

Spread betting – betting on the outcome of an event, where the payout is based on the accuracy of the wager, rather than a simple win or lose outcome. For example, in relation to a cricket match between England and Australia, a spread-betting business may set a 'spread' of between 220 and 240 runs to be scored by England in its first innings. The bettor specifies the unit stake, for example UK£5 per run, and chooses to either 'buy' or 'sell' against the offered 'spread'. That is, the bettor either 'buys' because he thinks England will score more than 240 runs, or 'sells' because he thinks they will score fewer than 220 runs. In the scenario in which England scores 280, the 'buyer' wins UK£200 (280 – 240 × UK£5), and the 'seller' loses UK£300 (280 – 220 × UK£5). However, if England only scores 200 runs, the 'buyer' loses UK£200 (240 – 200 × UK£5), and the 'seller' wins UK£100 (220–200 × UK£5) (based on Miers, 2004, p. 356).

CASINO GAMES

In US casinos, gambling machines (slots) offer the most popular form of gambling (56% of people surveyed), followed by blackjack (24%), poker (8%), craps (6%) and roulette (4%) (AGA, 2008). The most popular casino game in the UK is American roulette, which accounts for 51% of the total national casino 'drop' (money exchanged for playing chips), followed by blackjack (18%), electronic roulette (16%; see Fig. 11.2), punto banco or baccarat (8%) and three-card poker (5%) (Gambling Commission, 2008).

Cards – poker is one of very few gambling games where the balance between skill and chance can permit some to earn a living. Blackjack or '21' is also a game that blends chance with skill to the extent that a skilful player is able to reduce the casino advantage to anywhere between 0.0% and 1.0% depending on the number of decks and the exact rules of the game. However, for the average player, the 'house advantage' is about 2% (Hannum and Cabot, 2001).

Dice – craps is played by betting on the outcome of a roll of a pair of dice. There are 36 possible combinations with seven being the most likely to be thrown, with a probability of 6 in 36, or 16.67%. The myriad of possible wagers makes this a complex game with the 'house advantage' ranging from 0.12 to 16.67% (Hannum and Cabot, 2001).

Fig. 11.2. Roulette terminals video linked to the roulette table in a casino.

Spin – American roulette offers various bets on the numbers 1 to 36 plus '0' and '00'. The house advantage or 'edge' (the percentage of money that is wagered that the casino can expect to retain in the long run) for American roulette is 5.26%, or US$0.053 for every US$1 bet. In traditional European roulette, the lack of a '00' reduces the 'house advantage' to 2.7% (Hannum and Cabot, 2001).

MACHINES

The popular and commercial interest in mechanization that emerged in the 19th century in Europe and in North America gave rise to coin-in-the-slot machines dispensing such items as chewing gum and cigars (Schwartz, 2007). The first gaming machine (or 'slot machine') is reputed to have been built in 1895 by Charles Fey in the USA as an offshoot to the increasing sophistication and competition of the automatic weighing and vending machine industry (Miers, 2004). Fey's simple spinning three-reel design continues to form the basis of contemporary machine design, and many of the early symbols that were used including bells (representing the 'Liberty' bell) and fruit (flavours of chewing gum) remain popular (Schwartz, 2007).

Amusement with prizes (AWPs) – these are predominantly British gaming machines offering a range of stakes and prizes located in many different venues including seaside amusement arcades (see Fig. 11.3), adult gaming centres, betting offices, clubs and licensed public houses (pubs) which remain the most popular venue, accounting for 64% of all gambling machine play (Gambling Commission, 2008).

Fig. 11.3. 'Coin push' AWP game in an amusement arcade.

Casino 'slots' – in most international jurisdictions, these are dependent on Random Number Generators (RNG) controlled by microchip technology. Random does not mean totally unpredictable, only in the short term, and typically casino 'slots' offer players between 90% and 95% payback – proportion of money wagered returned. In most casinos around the globe, slots dominate the gaming floor with hundreds if not thousands on offer, many of them offering unlimited stakes and prizes; see Fig. 11.4.

Pachinko – a pinball-like slot machine game available in privately run pachinko parlours throughout Japan. It attracts 20 million regular players. Although not officially considered as gambling by the Japanese government, the machines payout in the form of additional balls that players exchange for prizes, which are in turn 'sold' for cash (Schwartz, 2007).

Video lottery terminals (VLTs) – introduced by lottery companies to enhance revenues, New Brunswick was the first Canadian province to utilize them in 1990, and by 2004 there were 39,000 VLTs in age-restricted venues in eight provinces. Although Ontario and British Columbia have no VLTs, they do share 60% of the country's 48,000 casino 'slots'. Nearly 10,000 casino 'slots' are located in racing centres in Alberta and Ontario (Azmier, 2005).

Video poker – particularly popular in Australia where there are more than 180,000 gaming machines, the majority of which are video poker machines or 'pokies'. Only 6% of all machines are located in casinos, 61% in clubs and 33% in hotels (Productivity Commission, 1999).

Fig. 11.4. Casino slots.

NUMBERS

Lotteries and bingo have been characterized as 'soft' forms of gambling (Miers, 2004), but illegal betting on numbers has a long and colourful history. Challenged by the need to 'draw' random numbers in a manner that was transparent, illegal numbers operators in the USA in the middle of the 20th century developed innovative solutions, including relying on numbers published by legitimate business institutions, such as stock exchanges, sports attendances, the US Treasury, and pari-mutuel pools (Schwartz, 2007).

Bingo – also known as 'housie' in Australia and New Zealand, bingo operates on the basis that players mark off or cover numbers on purchased playing cards that correspond to numbers that are randomly drawn. The winner is the first to declare a specified 'pattern' (typically a straight line of marked-off numbers) or a 'full house' (all numbers being marked-off) is achieved. Revenues are derived from participation fees, which players pay per game. In Britain, bingo continues to be the only gambling activity which men are less likely to play than women.

Keno – a lottery-type game with a touch of bingo that is generally played 'live' via screens in casinos, bars and convenience stores. The game requires players to select one or more numbers between 1 and 80, who hope to match them with 20 numbered balls drawn at regular intervals during the day.

Lotteries – a form of gambling that involves the drawing of 'lots' for prizes. In Britain, 70% of adults gamble on the National Lottery, spending around UK£2.5 billion annually (NLC,

2008), and in the USA nearly half of all adults participate in a lottery (AGA, 2008) accounting for 27% of total gross gambling revenue. Although lotteries will often offer life-changing prizes, the odds against winning are generally extremely high.

INTERNATIONAL CASINO DEVELOPMENT

The first recorded European casino was Il Ridotto ('the retreat'), authorized and taxed by the Republic of Venice between 1638 and 1744 (Barnhart, 1997). The later success of casinos such as those at Baden-Baden in Germany and at Monte Carlo encouraged other European nation-states to consider legalizing casinos to increase government revenues from gambling tourists. In 1907, casinos were legalized in France and were purposefully located in several resort areas including Deauville, Cannes and Biarritz. With an emphasis on elegance, dignity and refinement, casinos were subsequently developed in Italy, Belgium, Spain and Portugal (McMillen, 1996c).

Britain did not legalize commercial casinos until 1960 and is distinct from most nation-states in that casino legalization and regulation has not to date been undertaken on the basis of promoting tourism. In the USA, casino gambling was prohibited everywhere except in Nevada from 1931 to 1978, and was then authorized only in Nevada and New Jersey between 1978 and 1989. Variations of commercial casino settings have developed in the USA, including casinos on riverboats, at racetracks, in historic mining towns, in urban and suburban locations, and on Indian lands. By 2008, the number of US states offering casino gambling had expanded to 37. It is estimated that more than 25% of adults visit a casino and the combination of commercial casinos and those owned by Native American Indian tribes account for 56% of total annual gross gambling revenues (Christiansen Capital Advisors LLC, 2006).

As in the USA, the legalization and consequent spread of casinos in Canada, Australia and New Zealand began in the early 1990s following the successful introduction of state and national lotteries. Canadian casinos generally replicate the urban-centred, regional monopoly model used in Australia, although they are government-owned, rather than being owned by the private sector. In New Zealand, the 1990 Casino Control Act provided a framework for casino development as a means to stimulate economic and regional development.

Social Factor: Cost Benefit of Casinos

The polarized debate around casinos tends to overstate both the positive and negative impacts (Reith, 2006); an enduring issue in impact assessment is establishing that gambling is the definitive cause of social change (May-Chahal et al., 2007). It has been suggested that gambling research may be divided on the basis of academic discipline (economics and psychology), as well as on ideology; one is either for or against gambling (McGowan, 1997). There is criticism that some academics and researchers are guilty of focusing only

(Continued)

Social Factor: Continued.

upon that which best fits their research interests (Shaffer, 1997), while there are also claims that the casino industry lobby is so powerful that unbiased information is 'drowned out' by industry-sponsored studies (Goodman, 1995).

In particular, disagreement continues about the methodology in the cost–benefit analysis of casinos (Walker, 2007), including:

1. what may or may not count as a 'social' cost (external) versus a cost borne entirely by the 'individual or household' (internal);
2. what counts as a 'transfer' and what counts as 'displacement';
3. accounting for 'consumer surplus', that is consumer well-being;
4. the calculation of crime rates;
5. defining so-called 'problem gambling' and its comorbidity with other problematic behaviour;
6. multi-causality of negative and positive economic and social outcomes of casino development; and
7. the opportunity costs of legalization or expansion of gambling.

There are legitimate concerns regarding the relative benefits and costs of permitted casino-style gambling. Consumer well-being (consumer surplus) is not usually given much priority in the legalization and regulation of casino gambling, and so the typical policy trade-off is between economic benefits and social costs, where the economic benefits are mostly attributable to tourism. The liberalization of commercial gambling markets inevitably leads to more competition, which in turn enhances customer choice and generally drives down the price of participation. However, the consequence of this with regard to casino development is that 'economic rents' – the surplus profits that can be directed to projects in the public interest – will be lost if the supply is not sufficiently constrained (Eadington, 2002).

Case Study: Development of Las Vegas

Las Vegas, in the Mojave Desert in the south-western USA, is synonymous with gambling and entertainment, and with more than 39 million annual visits in 2007 is one of the world's most successful visitor destinations (NCoT, 2008).

Following the arrival of the railroad and the subsequent auction of land in 1905, Las Vegas was established. It was not until the 1930s that this isolated, dusty desert town began its meteoric rise to becoming the world's favourite playground. Two events were crucial. First, the building of the Boulder (renamed 'Hoover') Dam between 1931 and 1935 just 30 miles south created thousands of jobs, attracted thousands of tourists and provided an unprecedented economic stimulus to Las Vegas, which marketed itself as 'The Gateway to Boulder Dam'. Second, on 19th March 1931 the Nevada state legislature legalized 'wide-open' gambling.

(Continued)

Case Study: Continued.

By the 1940s, the central business district of Las Vegas, centred on Freemont Street, was dominated by casinos and neon signs, and the city's tourist base continued to broaden as a result of the rapid population growth of Los Angeles and the wider catchments of southern California. The opening of the El Rancho Vegas on 3rd April 1941 a few miles south of the Las Vegas city limits on Highway 91 marked the beginnings of the Las Vegas Strip (Schwartz, 2003). This casino development by Thomas Hull, a motel operator from California, was significant in terms of both its location and structure. Two miles south of Freemont Street, the location of a casino business on the direct car route between Los Angeles and Las Vegas is likely to have provided Hull with an advantage over his downtown competitors in terms of prominence at the very least. The location permitted Hull the freedom to create a new, expansive casino concept without the strictures of a crowded urban landscape, and with the financial benefit of lower land and tax costs (Chung, 2007). El Rancho Vegas was conceived as an integrated resort including 65 'cottages' with porches and private lawns, paved and lighted streets providing car access, restaurants, shops, nightclub-style entertainment and other recreation facilities, offering its guests an 'escape from the rigors of suburban life by relaxing in a facsimile of it' (Schwartz, 2003, p. 35).

This operational model became the blueprint for other casino resort development on Highway 91 that quickly followed including: Hotel Last Frontier (1942), Flamingo (1947), The Thunderbird (1948), Desert Inn (1950), Sahara (1952) and Sands (1952). The nine-storey Riviera opened in 1955 as the first high-rise casino property on the Strip. Liberace was paid US$50,000 a week as the casino's headline entertainer, however within 3 months the owners were bankrupt. Other properties opening in the same year suffered similar financial difficulties including Royal Nevada and Dunes (Chung, 2007).

The early development of Las Vegas casinos required both operational knowledge and access to sufficient capital funds. The fact that casino gambling was prohibited in the USA outside of Nevada until 1976 meant that home-grown operational experience could initially only be gained illegally. In these circumstances, mainstream financial institutions and businesses were disinclined to invest in a nascent and volatile industry, especially if it involved backing people who by definition were 'criminals'.

The development of the Bank of Las Vegas headed by E. Parry Thomas, a Utah Mormon, in the late 1950s, and the arrival of Howard Hughes at the Desert Inn in November 1966 and his subsequent acquisition four of Strip properties – Desert Inn, Sands, Frontier and Landmark – are important events that contributed to the gradual process 'where the traditional syndicates of "boss gamblers" with underworld financing gave way or evolved into publicly traded corporations that were more palatable to mainstream investors' (Schwartz, 2003, pp. 147–148).

The opening of the US$25 million Caesars Palace on 5 August 1966 marked 'a new era in the creation of lavish casinos' (Schwartz, 2003, p. 133). With 680 rooms in a 14-storey

(Continued)

Case Study: Continued.

hotel tower and a 980-seat theatre, Caesars Palace was significantly bigger than the Riviera but what made this new venture stand out was the extensive and detailed Greco-Roman theming, including US$150,000 worth of imported Italian marble statuary (Chung, 2007). In addition, there was 25,000 ft² (1 foot = 30.48 cm) of meeting and exhibition space ensuring that Caesars Palace could operate as a convention hotel as well as a holiday resort.

The decade that followed the opening of Caesars Palace saw the introduction of the first 'mega-resorts'. Kirk Kerkorian's International and the original MGM Grand were both designed by the architect Michael Stern Junior, who utilized a Y-shaped 'triform' hotel tower to meet the requirement for 1000 hotel rooms each offering a pleasant view. This construction form allied to a spacious 'porte cochere'; attached multilevel parking; expansive casino, entertainment and shopping spaces on the ground floor and set the modern industry standard not only on the Strip, but throughout the USA and in many other international jurisdictions.

In November 1989, Steve Wynn opened The Mirage with a dramatic volcano to entertain and entice potential customers outside on the Strip, a dolphin exhibit, and what became the world famous and long-running Siegfried and Roy illusionist act with disappearing tigers and elephants. The Mirage heralded a new period of massive growth throughout the 1990s, indulging entrepreneurial enthusiasm for heavily themed resorts and expensive production shows, to emerge into the 2000s as the undisputed convention and entertainment 'capital of the world'.

On the Las Vegas 'Strip', in 2008, there were 23 casinos with annual gross gaming revenues exceeding US$72 million. Key statistics for these top venues include: non-gaming revenue – 61% of total revenue; music and entertainment – 3.2% of gross gaming revenue; employees – 99,080; room nights – 24.2 million; physical occupancy – 95.1%; total assets US$44.8 billion; and average return on invested capital – 7.4% (NGCB, 2008).

In 2008, there were 170,000 slot machines distributed across 260 'non-restricted' casinos generating at least US$1 million of annual gaming revenue throughout Nevada. Employing more than 200,000 people, the Nevadan casino industry generated US$12 billion of gross gaming revenues, representing 48% of total revenues. More than 80% of total gross gaming revenue is produced by 78 casinos that are owned by 21 publicly traded companies (NGCB, 2008).

Enlightened commercial self-interest

Because commercial gambling makes many people uneasy, public opinion demands that gambling opportunities be less than what a free market would normally make available, and that the conduct of gambling businesses be subject to abnormally strict regulation. This means that profits depend crucially on what governments allow; forbid; and require gambling businesses to do, including paying taxes. It also means abnormal (monopoly or oligopoly) profits can be made by charging more for playing time – worse odds and/or higher minimum bets – than would be possible in a fully free market (Collins, 2003).

Pleasing government and being thought well of by the public are therefore essential to profitability, and ensuring this, is consequently a key skill for managers in the industry, and a major priority, which should influence all aspects of operations.

Ethical Factor: Responsible Gambling

In contemporary Westernized democratic societies, where religion no longer dominates cultural norms as it may have once done, the principal issue around which opponents to gambling legalization or liberalization coalesce is 'problem gambling'. The term itself is problematic, and despite the uncertainty as to the precise nature and consequences of problem gambling (LaPlante *et al.*, 2008), this is the issue that dominates any political debate about gambling generally. The general sense of unease about there being too much gambling – a proliferation of gambling generally and gambling machines specifically – and the particular focus on 'problem gambling' puts pressure on commercial gambling providers to act responsibly, and vitally that they should be thought well of by the public and policy makers alike. Problem gambling results, in part, from erroneous perceptions about the probability of winning. From a public health perspective, the gambling industry, in collaboration with governments and community leaders, can assist individuals by providing access to accurate information and advice about making responsible gambling choices (Blaszczynski *et al.*, 2008). For those individuals that gamble excessively beyond their financial capacity, the industry may implement 'self-exclusion' policies and assist in the funding of appropriate treatment services.

Eadington (2002) warns that if the negative consequences of gambling liberalization, particularly in relation to 'problem gambling', really are as substantial as gambling opponents suggest, then the current course of expansion will lead to future prohibitions. However, if any impacts of 'problem gambling' can be sufficiently mitigated, or are considered to be outweighed by benefits to society as a whole, the development of commercial gambling will continue unabated.

THE FUTURE

Rose (2003, p. 114) warns that 'gambling spreads in a haphazard manner, with long-term recurring patterns played out against a background of local politics and unpredictable technology'. Gambling has twice before in American history enjoyed popular and legal sanction, only to be prohibited in response to political scandal and moral concern. Rose characterizes the current proliferation of gambling in the USA as a 'third wave' born out of the Great Depression of the 1930s; a 'wave' that he suggests may be destined to come crashing down in a repeat of past prohibitions. On the other hand, Sauer (2001) observes that a reversal of the current trend of gambling liberalization would require a significant fiscal strengthening of governments via increased efficiency in alternative taxation instruments and reductions in government spending before the current wave of gambling expansion recedes. In light of the global financial crisis emerging in 2008, Sauer's perspective will be tested. The immediate future for the commercial gambling sector is highlighted in Fig. 11.5.

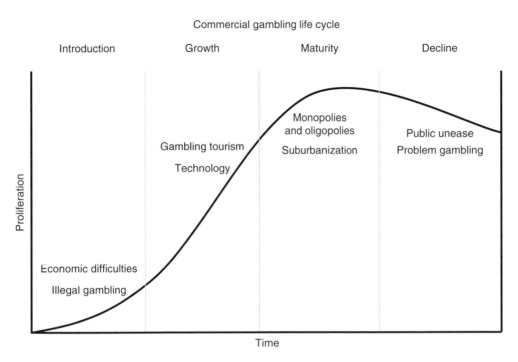

Fig. 11.5. Commercial gambling life cycle.

Introduction

Economic difficulties – legalizing commercial gambling is typically associated with economic development and state budgetary politics (Pierce and Miller, 2004). In the USA, in response to the fiscal challenges of the 1970s, many states introduced lotteries; and in the early 1990s economic recession sparked widespread development of casinos, and a proliferation of slots at racetracks.

Illegal gambling – when gambling is prohibited, just as with the prohibition of alcohol consumption, there are political pressures to legalize it in some form at least. This is largely because popular activities will always find an outlet whether legal or not, and in the case of gambling criminal prosecution of what may be thought of as a victim-less crime is unpopular, particularly if it diverts public resources away from what may be considered more serious criminal behaviour.

Growth

Gambling tourism – the success of places such as Monte Carlo, Las Vegas, Atlantic City and Biloxi continues to inspire many other locations around the globe to utilize resort-style casino development to act as a catalyst to sustainable economic growth by attracting and facilitating national and international leisure and business tourism.

Technology – the development of the Internet and chip-based technologies are driving the explosive growth in commercial gambling; every form of gambling can now be engaged in at any time, in any place via mobile phones, personal computers and other hand-held devices.

Maturity

Monopolies and oligopolies – the nature of commercial gambling causes it to be regulated in ways that typically gives rise to just a few licensed operators who are naturally highly motivated to maintain their competitive advantage; for example, in Britain four companies operate 82% of the national casino estate, and three companies own 68% of a total of 9000 betting shops.

Suburbanization – urban casinos and the increased availability of other gambling products on the 'door step' tend to draw a high proportion of their custom from local areas, rather than exporting tourism, and is generally regarded as a legitimate constituent of the wider entertainment industry.

Decline

Public unease – the politics of gambling may be characterized as 'morality politics', which readily engages widespread public debate on the basis of core values, moral principles and religion (Pierce and Miller, 2004). The prevailing sense, a democratic consensus if you will, is typically that there should not be too much gambling too easily available (Collins, 2003).

Problem gambling – the principle issue around which opponents to gambling legalization or liberalization coalesce is 'problem gambling'; its political potency lies in its capability to erode the libertarian argument that individuals ought to be free to do that which they choose for themselves including making 'bad' choices so long as no harm is caused to others.

REFERENCES

Abt, V. (1996) The role of the state in the expansion and growth of commercial gambling in the USA. In: McMillen, J. (ed.) *Gambling Cultures: Studies in History and Interpretation*. Routledge, London and New York.

American Gaming Association (2008) State of states: the AGA survey of casino entertainment. [Internet] Washington, DC, AGA. URL available at: <http://www.americangaming.org>.

Ashton, J. (1898) *A History of Gambling in England*. Duckworth, London.

Azmier, J. (2005) Gambling in Canada 2005: statistics and context. [Internet] Calgary, Canada West Foundation. URL available at: <http://www/cwf.ca>.

Barnhart, R.T. (1997) Gambling with Giancomo Casanova and Lorenzo Da Ponte in eighteenth century Venice – the Ridotto: 1638–1774. In: Eadington, W.R. and Cornelius, J.A. (eds) *Gambling: Public Policies and the Social Sciences*. Institute for the Study of Gambling and Commercial Gaming, University of Reno, Reno, Nevada, 451–479.

Blakey, R.G. (1979) State conducted lotteries: history, problems, and promises. *Journal of Social Issues* 35, 62–85.

Blaszczynski, A., Ladouceur, R., Nower, L., and Shaffer, H. (2008) Informed choice and gambling: principles for consumer protection. *The Journal of Gambling Business and Economics* 2(1), 103–118.

Christiansen Capital Advisors LLC (2006) In American Gaming Association Factsheet. [Internet] Washington, DC, AGA. URL available at: <http://www.americangaming.org>.

Chung, S.K. (2007) *Las Vegas: Then and Now*. Salamander Books, San Diego, California.

Collins, P. (2003) *Gambling and the Public Interest*. Praeger, London.

Eadington, W.R. (2002) The spread of casinos and their role in tourism development. In: Pearce, D.G. and Butler, R.W. (eds) *Contemporary Issues in Tourism Development*. Routledge, London and New York.

France, C.J. (1902) The gambling impulse. *The American Journal of Psychology* 13(3), 364–407.

Gambling Commission (2008) Gambling industry statistics, 2007/08. [Internet] Birmingham, Gambling Commission. URL available at: <http://www.gamblingcommission.gov.uk>.

Goodman, R. (1995) *The Luck Business: The Devastating Consequences and Broken Promises of America's Gambling Explosion*. Free Press, New York.

Hannum, R.C. and Cabot, A.N. (2001) *Practical Casino Math*. UNLV, Institute for the Study of Gambling & Commercial Gaming, Las Vegas, Nevada.

LaPlante, D.A., Nelson, S.E., LaBrie, R.A. and Shaffer, H.J. (2008) Stability and progression of disordered gambling: lessons from longitudinal studies. *The Canadian Journal of Psychiatry* 53(1), 52–60.

May-Chahal, C., Volberg, R., Forrest, D. *et al.* (2008) Scoping study for a UK Gambling Act, 2005 impact assessment framework. The casino scoping study (ITT 636) for the Department of Culture, Media and Sport, June 2007.

McGowan, R. (1997) The ethics of gambling research: an agenda for mature analysis. *Journal of Gambling Studies* 13(4), 279–289.

McMillen, J. (1996a) The globalization of gambling: implications for Australia. *The National Association for Gambling Studies Journal* 8(1), 9–19.

McMillen, J. (1996b) Introduction. In: McMillen, J. (ed.) *Gambling Cultures: Studies in History and Interpretation*. Routledge, London and New York.

McMillen, J. (1996c) From glamour to grind: the globalization of casinos. In: McMillen, J. (ed.) *Gambling Cultures: Studies in History and Interpretation*. Routledge, London and New York.

McMillen, J. (2003) From local to global gambling cultures. In: Reith, G. (ed.) *Gambling: Who Wins? Who Loses?* Prometheus Books, New York.

Miers, D. (2004) *Regulating Commercial Gambling: Past, Present and Future*. OUP, Oxford.

Munting, R. (1996) An *Economic and Social History of Gambling in Britain and the USA*. Manchester University Press, Manchester and New York.

National Lottery Commission (2008) National Lottery Commission. [Internet] London, NLC. URL available at: <http://www.natlotcomm.gov.uk>.

Nevada Gaming Control Board (2008) Nevada Gaming Abstract, 2008. [Internet] Carson City, NGCB. URL available at <http://www.gaming.nv.gov>.

Nevada Commission on Tourism (2008) Discover the facts: a digest of statistical information on the Nevada tourism industry. Qtrs.1–4, XV. [Internet] Nevada, NcoT. URL available at: <http://www.travelnevada.biz>.

Pierce, P.A. and Miller, D.E. (2004) *Gambling Politics: State Government and the Business of Betting*. Rienner, London.

Productivity Commission (1999) Australia's Gambling Industries, Report No. 10. Canberra, AusInfo.

Reith, G. (2002) *The Age of Chance: Gambling in Western Culture*. Routledge, London.

Reith, G. (2006) with the Scottish Centre for Social Research (ScotCen). Research on the social impacts of gambling: Final report. The Scottish Executive, Edinburgh, Scotland.

Rose, I.N. (2003) Gambling and the law: the new millennium. In: Reith, G. (ed.) *Gambling: Who Wins? Who Loses?* Prometheus Books, New York.

Sauer, R.D. (2001) The political economy of gambling regulation/management and information issues for industries with externalities: the case of casino gambling. *Managerial and Decision Economics* 22(1/3), 5–15.

Shaffer, H. (1997) Gambling research and science: toward a mature relationship. *Journal of Gambling Studies* 13(4), 275–278.

Schwartz, D.G. (2003) *Suburban Xanadu: The Casino Resort on the Las Vegas Strip and Beyond*. Routledge, New York and London.

Schwartz, D.G. (2007) *Roll the Bones: The History of Gambling*. Gotham Books, New York.

Steinmetz, A. (1870) *The Gaming Table Its Votaries and Victims in All Times and Countries Especially in England and in France*. Tinsley Brothers, London.

Walker, D.M. (2007) *The Economics of Casino Gambling*. Springer, New York.

Wardle, H., Sproston, K., Orford, J., Erens, B., Griffiths, M., Constantine, R. and Pigott, S. (2007) *British Gambling Prevalence Survey Prepared for the Gambling Commission*. National Centre for Social Research, London.

chapter 12

Spectator Sports

Stuart Moss, Phil Clements and Nicola Mccullough

Entertainment that involves the spectating of sporting activities that incorporate both physical exertion and fair competition.

The competitive nature of humankind has led to the participation in challenging physical activities for thousands of years. The origins of the Olympic Games are estimated to go back around 2,800 years to ancient Greece, where the games were held as part of ritualistic celebrations in honour of Greek gods and legends. Games would fuse competitions such as running races (see Fig. 12.1) and 'throwing' events with worship to the ancient Greek gods, and ceremonies that included animal sacrifices. Throughout the centuries, sporting activities developed, and many of these activities were often combative, which was a reflection of the world's volatile political history. Training for combat meant that men particularly were taught to throw stones and spears, as well as fire arrows, wrestle and fight with swords, clubs and knives. Practising these combative arts involved competition, which would draw spectators. Outside of any military realm, sporting competitions were confined to days of celebrations and 'feasts', although many sporting activities such as archery, horsemanship and hunting were practised by the ruling and upper 'classes' as part of their educational development and in their own leisure time.

In mediaeval Europe, the lower classes would participate in 'rough and tumble' tournaments that lacked rules, often between adjoining villages. This typically consisted of 'teams' from each community competing against one another to get an object placed at a neutral distance between the villages and back to one of the villages – by any means necessary. The object in question could be any of the following: a scarf; a log; a rock; a purposely made effigy or statue; a crude ball made from animal hide stuffed with fur, leaves or feathers; an animal carcass; a pig's bladder; or even according to some tales a human head. The winning village would be the first one to get the object in

Fig. 12.1. A running race viewed by spectators, these have ancient origins.

question back into the centre of their village, where the object would be displayed and the village would celebrate the win over their local rivals. Such sporting rituals developed over hundreds of years into playing for a cup (the object was revered like a cup by the winning village); the phenomenon and passion of 'derby' games; and actual sports such as soccer and rugby (which has since been exported from England to North America and developed into American Football). Sport was often used as a means to excuse violence between communities; as such, tournaments would often descend into anarchy resulting in mass brawls venting pent-up frustrations and aggression caused by a variety of political, social, economic and religious factors. In England, King Edward II banned football in the 14th century as he believed the resulting disorder could lead to wider civil unrest (Ingle and Hodgkinson, 2001); from an audience perspective, this association of sports and violence was to re-materialize briefly in the 1880s and then from the mid-20th century onwards as crowd violence at soccer matches (and sometimes other sports fixtures).

Only boys and men participated in the early sports mentioned above, and the audience watching and cheering would typically be the women of the villages as well as those too old or young to participate. Over the centuries, significant developments were made in creating sports that today are world recognizable and played/spectated by millions of people globally. There has been significant development in the last 200 years with regard to formalizing rules around sports; creating leagues of competing teams; and forming governing bodies to ensure that teams adhered to rules. Such governing bodies include: Fédération Internationale de Football Association (FIFA) formed in 1930; the International Cricket Council (ICC) formed in 1909; the International

Olympic Committee (IOC) formed in 1894; the National Football League (NFL) formed in 1920; and the National Hockey League (NHL) formed in 1917. Most of these organizations (and the plethora of other organizations for other sports) have their own local and national governing bodies and leagues, in which games are played by various sporting teams. Many of these teams attract thousands of spectators who spend money not only on game tickets, but on food, car parking and merchandise. This potentially makes them big business, although it must be stressed that in many sports a minority of teams tends to control the majority of the wealth, as is the case in Scotland, where the 'big two' soccer teams (Glasgow Celtic and Glasgow Rangers) hold more wealth between them than the majority of other Scottish soccer teams combined.

The marketability and fan base of many teams have outgrown the ability of stadiums to hold fans, and, as such, global audiences are now possible due to broadcast media and the Internet. The growth and diversity of media outlets and this increased accessibility have also led to an unparalleled growth in sports sponsorship and a radical shift in the professionalism of sports in terms of business management. The level of interest in sports has made players, teams, leagues and stadiums (among other things) the target of sponsors, who wish their brand/product/logo to be seen by as many people as possible.

A simplified example of how this may work in practice is as follows: a soccer team may have their shirt sponsored by a particular company on the front, and sometimes a different one on the back, with both sponsors getting a prominent logo display on the shirt, the higher the profile of the team, the more lucrative the sponsorship deal. Soccer kits are manufactured by a clothing company whose logo will also be displayed on the shirt and shorts (and sometimes socks); clothing manufacturers are also in high competition to supply the higher-profile teams with kits. Each individual player may also have their own individual sponsorship deal to wear a particular brand of boots – again the bigger the name of the player, the more lucrative the deal. Sports stadiums are decorated with both static and animated billboards (particularly at pitch side), so that during a game the logo that they display is extremely prominent and very visible, sports stadiums are also often named after sponsors, e.g. 'The Emirates Stadium', which is the home of Arsenal FC.

A sporting game or tournament attracting a global audience of millions is one scenario whereby sponsors are prepared to pay a premium price for such a high level of exposure. As media audiences increase, so will the level of sports sponsorship so that multiple sponsors are highly visible and become a part of the 'uniform' as is currently the case with Formula One motor car racing.

There are literally hundreds of recognized sports in the world today; some attract minimal audiences, while others attract millions. Some sports are well established and will seemingly always be popular among audiences (soccer, golf, tennis, rugby, hockey, handball, football, basketball, baseball, athletics and cricket), while other sports which were once popular, now seem less so among audiences, crown green bowing being a particular example of a game that has been in steady decline for several decades. The most popular sports are those which have global appeal; soccer is by far the most popular sport in the world, with other sports having less of a global and more of a regional appeal, and the soccer world cup is the only global sporting mega

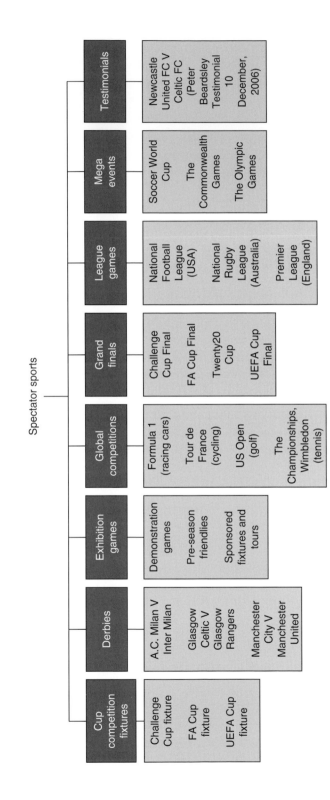

Fig. 12.2. Typology of spectator sports events.

event that features only one sport. Other mega events in sports include the Olympic Games and the Commonwealth Games, both of which feature multiple sports.

So-called extreme sports involving fast-paced action have been growing in popularity since the 1980s, when the Bicycle Moto-Cross (BMX) bike became popularized in movies such as *BMX Bandits* and *ET*, and James Bond got in on the action with a snowboarding scene in *A View to a Kill*. In the 1990s, the movie *Point Break* reintroduced surfing culture, and since then numerous movies have featured an element of extreme sports, including several bond films, the *xXx* series and numerous martial arts releases. Artistic and daredevil sports have developed to the point where they now have their own annual international championships (the X-Games and the Winter X-Games), which are becoming ever more popular (and mainstream) each year. It is worthy of note that at the 2008 Beijing Olympics, BMX racing was featured for the first time in an Olympic Games.

The myriad of the different types of sports that exist is too numerous to mention in this chapter alone, but key types of sporting events and fixtures that can have varying levels of attendance based upon fan motivation to attend are featured along with some examples in Fig. 12.2 and Table 12.1.

Table 12.1. Spectator sports events and their characteristics.

Type of spectator sports events	Characteristics
Cup competition/ fixture	This is a fixture that takes place outside of a standard league fixture, where a team or athlete may have chance to compete against a team or athlete which they may not normally play in their standard league. Many cup competitions have a knockout format, whereby the winning team or athlete progresses to the next round of fixtures, to be randomly drawn against another winning team or athlete, and the losing teams or athletes are out of the competition. The surprise element of the draw itself is what makes cup competition fixtures so novel; in team sports particularly, fan attendance at a particular fixture is often down to whom the draw is against, and a novel draw against a team or athlete from a different league often draws greater audiences
Derby	This occurs when a team plays another team from a geographically close location, giving the element of local 'bragging rights' to the winners. These are often passionate fixtures drawing large numbers of fans who are keen not to see their team lose against their local rivals
Exhibition game or match	This is a game where the outcome of the fixture has a lesser significance than most other types of fixtures. Exhibition games

(Continued)

Table 12.1. Continued.

Type of spectator sports events	Characteristics
	may be demonstration games, whereby a particular sport is being demonstrated to an audience who may not have seen it before, making it a novelty, or it could be for financial reasons such as English Premier League football teams being invited to play a one-off game in the Middle East. Exhibition games are also used by managers to 'try out' teams and formations against other teams as preparation for the beginning of a league, and these fixtures are often referred to as 'friendlies' as the final result is of most significance to the fans (see Fig. 12.3)
Global competition	This is a fixture in a competition that attracts teams and athletes from around the world. Many of these competitions are very high profile, and in terms of audience size come a close second to mega events
Grand final	This is the culmination of a cup competition whereby the two teams or athletes to reach this position have beaten all competition up to this point and the winner will be *the* champion. Grand finals often attract tens of thousands of fans to the fixture (see Fig. 12.4), and many more as television audiences. They are often criticized for their 'corporate' nature allowing corporate sponsors and associated others to take up seats in limited-capacity venues, thereby depriving 'real' fans of attending in person
League game	Most sports are organized into leagues (or divisions); a league is a collection of teams or athletes of a similar ability or financial standing which compete against all other teams or athletes in the league accruing points along the way, depending on whether the game was won, lost or drawn (tied). At the end of a season, a particular team or athlete with the most points will finish at the top of the league becoming champions. This often comes with financial rewards from league sponsors, as well as promotion to a higher league or invitation to other competitions. Teams or athletes who finish at the bottom of their respective league may be relegated to the league beneath
Mega event	These are the biggest and most viewed sporting events in the world, and involve numerous fixtures in a competition format played out over several weeks. Mega sporting events are few and far between (a 4-year cycle is common) due to the level of preparation and organization involved, and the financial cost of staging such events

(*Continued*)

Table 12.1. Continued.

Type of spectator sports events	Characteristics
Testimonial	This is a fixture that is designed to 'thank' a player for his or her long years of loyalty or service to a particular sporting team. They are very much games for the fans who also want to show their appreciation by turning up. Testimonials are often against teams that a particular team would rarely play against, giving them a 'novel' element; profits from the gates receipts or a percentage of them often go to the player whose testimonial it is, as well as to a charity or charities of the player's choice

Fig. 12.3. Small crowds at a small-scale 'friendly' soccer fixture.

AUDIENCE MOTIVATION

Bill Shankly (1913–1981), one of Britain's most successful football managers, once stated: 'Some people think football is a matter of life and death. I don't like that attitude. I can assure them it is much more serious than that'. This quote is hardly a recommendation for sports being an entertainment, but for millions of live event attendees and those who view sports

Fig. 12.4. Huge crowds at a grand final.

through the media, it is just that. For passionate sports fans (fan is short for fanatic), spectating sporting fixtures can invoke the full spectrum of emotions from the joy and delight of seeing the team/player that he or she is a fan of win to the anger and disgust of seeing the team/player that he or she is a fan of lose. Followers of soccer in Italy, Indian cricket fans, and the rugby union fans of New Zealand could be described as so dedicated that they are fanatical in their support.

Economic Factor: the Value of Fans

Carey and Lynn (1999) noted that in the USA, around 50% of the population consider themselves to be a sports fan and 22% are self-described fanatical fans spending millions of dollars on sporting events, sports-related paraphernalia and sports apparel. Good regular attendance at sporting fixtures is key to the marketers of sports and sports-related products in that they depend on a core base of fans to buy tickets (including season tickets), souvenirs and clothing (often replica kit). Competitive and financial pressures from not only other sports but other forms of entertainment in general have resulted in programmes where fan retention as well as the attraction of new fans is vital to maintain financial viability of many professional sporting organizations.

(Continued)

Economic Factor: Continued.

Fan attendance is deemed as vital to an organization's business survival. As the size of venues expand, competition for leisure time and a share of available monies increases, with those monies often being spent on entertainment that is perceived to be of greatest perceived value. Sweeney and Soutar (2001) see perceived value under four dimensions: emotional value – the affective state the game generates; social value – the degree to which a product enhances self-concept; functional value – price/value for money based on the reduction of short- and long-term costs; and functional value – performance as derived from the perceived quality and performance of the product. Plans for stadiums in excess of 200,000 are becoming more common, e.g. Penn State University in the USA. This reinforces the need for a greater understanding of the factors that influence attendance. It is not just the gate or ticket revenue from regular attendees that sporting organizations rely upon, but the revenue streams from food and drink, and team-related merchandise and the power of positive word-of-mouth publicity that fans engender.

Smith and Stewart (1999) created a typology for Australian Rules Football supporters: aficionado – the fan who seeks quality performance, game-loyal but not team-loyal; theatre goer – seeks entertainment and wants a close contest; passionate partisan – wants his/her team to win and identifies with team successes and losses; champ follower – brand switcher based on winning; and reclusive partisan – fan identifies strongly with a team, but does not often attend.

Although this acknowledges segmentation based on psychographic criteria, it should be noted that there is a definite emphasis on attendees who have a strong affiliation to the sport and even a specific team. What about attendees who do not have this affiliation? What or how can non-attendees be attracted to attend an event where they do not have such affinity and what factors might they consider when deciding on whether or not to attend? In other words, loyalty to a team or specific sport is not an issue. So is it about a perception that the event will offer something more, such as entertainment?

For those who are less passionate about sports but still watch it anyway, emotions experienced may not be as strong, but can also be wide-ranging. Sporting fixtures are often 'enhanced' by turning the fixture into a longer event with other forms of entertainment featured on the 'bill' (see Figs 12.5, 12.6 and 12.7). This can be pre-, mid- or post-fixture entertainment, including singers, cheerleaders, fireworks, dancers and mini sports tournaments. The American Superbowl grand final is a particularly good example of this, with previous half-time entertainment featuring some of the biggest names in music, including Aerosmith (2001), U2 (2002), Paul McCartney (2005), The Rolling Stones (2006), Prince (2007), and Bruce Springsteen (2009) who played for 30 min each when the game itself consists only of 60 min play; as well as this, there is a pre-game build-up and post-game celebrations. The Superbowl event is the most viewed US television broadcast each year.

Fig. 12.5. Entertainment and sports: pre-match festivities.

Fig. 12.6. Entertainment and sports: celebrations after a cup final.

Fig. 12.7. A sound and lighting mixing desk that is used for entertainment and to create 'an atmosphere' before, during and after an ice hockey fixture.

Many sports events organizers and businesses are driven by the competitive need to understand what their audiences are looking for; i.e. what motivates people to attend and watch sports events. As business success depends on the provision of products and services to meet these needs, it has become more apparent from academic and industry research that there are many and varied motivations to attend, of which 'entertainment' is often cited. The difficulty is what constitutes 'entertainment' from a sport event attendee's point of view, and how high it is valued when choosing to attend a sporting fixture (or even between competing fixtures).

Wann (1995) developed the 'Sport Fan Motivation Scale' (SFMS), where eight factors were identified: eustress, self-esteem, escape from everyday life, entertainment, economic factors, aesthetics, group affiliation and family needs. These motivating factors were related to gender, age and education, and later studies showed significant gender differences with males having higher levels of eustress, self-esteem, escape, entertainment and aesthetic motivations than females. Gender differences in the behaviour of sports fans found that females see themselves as fans for mainly social reasons and attend matches with friends and family (Dietz-Uhler *et al.*, 2000).

Mehus (2005) compared attendance motivation between soccer and ski-jumping competitions, claiming that both fall under the term 'entertainment sport' where there is an emotional link between athletes and spectators and that satisfaction is gained from 'social contacts' and 'arousal'.

While gender differences were relatively insignificant, education and age showed that the higher the age and education of a spectator, the lower the motivational ranking of 'entertainment' factors.

There are many factors which can impact upon the number of people who attend sporting fixtures, and a significant one is the amount of game coverage given through the media – in particular television, and increasingly the Internet.

Economic and Technological Factor: Media Audiences

The majority of high-profile sporting leagues, tournaments and teams have exclusive and often lucrative media deals, giving their fans live access to games through a particular medium. These typically include radio, television and Internet deals often with one service provider per country of distribution. It is common for sporting leagues to sign blanket deals with particular providers, which all teams within that league are then covered by, with each team receiving an equal share of revenue from the deal. Prior to the 1980s, live media coverage for the majority of games would be via local radio stations only; however, the onset of pay-TV services and the proliferation of specialist sports channels through cable and satellite meant that there was growing demand for live audiences at locations geographically distant from the stadium itself, and often on foreign shores. In 1994, Manchester United Football Club was reported to be the highest-grossing sellers of merchandise of any sports team in the world, and their success on the field (they won at least one trophy per season between 1989 and 1994) was broadcast around the world, giving them fanatical long-distance support on every continent, and particularly in Asia. Media coverage of the team's success was directly responsible for their brand getting world exposure, and thus growing a global fan base.

While media deals can provide leagues and clubs with an income stream, they can also have an adverse effect upon attendances at games. For example a televised Monday night football game is much less likely to draw as large an audience as a game that is not televised. In order to minimize such negative impacts, various rules are put in place including staggered start times (so that broadcast games are not actually live, but run slightly late), and games at particular times not being allowed to be screened, for example, in England it is illegal to screen a Saturday afternoon football match with a kick-off time of 3 p.m. (apart from cup finals) – although this rule does not apply to such a game being screened in another country. Audiences do manage to circumvent such rules. In the 1990s, it was not uncommon to find equipment that was capable of viewing satellite broadcasts that were intended for another country, although in this advanced era of Web technology, the most common way nowadays in which audiences illegally watch live sports games is through the Internet. One such Web-based program that allows this is *Sopcast*, which uses peer-to-peer technology to allow viewers to 'share' television programmes that they are watching with other users globally. So a live Saturday 3 p.m. Premier League game that

(Continued)

Economic and Technological Factor: Continued.

is legitimately screened in China can be found and viewed using *Sopcast* anywhere else in the world. The implications of this for broadcasters are that television audiences are likely to reduce in future, meaning that advertising revenues may reduce. Web technology will continue to improve as audiences watching games freely but illegally continue to grow, and the full ramifications of this for sports teams are yet to be seen.

Case Study: the Olympic Games

'The Games have always brought people together in peace to respect universal moral principles' (IOC, 2009).

The Olympic Games (the Summer Games) is the largest mega sports event in the world. What is now known as the 'modern' Olympics began in 1896 in Athens, Greece, as homage to the ancient Olympics practised in Olympia, Greece, 2700 years before. While the modern Olympic Games began as one competition, there are now four different competitions, and these are as follows: the Summer Olympic Games – this is staged every four years and features numerous sports including team 'pitch' games, gymnastics, track and field, equestrian, golf and tennis and this is the most high-profile of all of the Olympic Games; the Paralympic Games – this follows the Summer Olympic Games and features only athletes with disabilities, and while its popularity is increasing, it is less high-profile than the main Summer Games; the Winter Olympic Games – this is based around winter sports such as skiing, ice-skating and curling, and while it is not as popular as the Summer Games among audiences, it is growing rapidly with much emphasis on the 'extreme' element of some of the featured sports; the Youth Olympic Games – this will be a shorter tournament for the 14–18-year olds only to compete in, and there will be both a Summer and a Winter version, with the Summer version beginning in 2010. In effect, this means that there will be both a Summer and a Winter Olympic tournament somewhere in the world every 2 years.

The Summer and Winter Olympics have been held in various locations globally, and these are highlighted in Table 12.2.

Table 12.2 demonstrates a trend for each game to surpass the previous one in terms of size and scale with an increasing number of nations, athletes and events becoming the accepted norm for future games. Larger-scale games mean more lavish settings, bigger stadiums, and more spectacular opening and closing ceremonies. The Olympic Games draw a global audience through the given media exposure. According to sports programming experts, the Olympic Games in Beijing were followed by a record 4.7 billion television viewers across the world. This is aside from 'live' attendees, and any other media such as the Internet. The games always begin with an elaborate opening ceremony, featuring speeches, parades of athletes, theatre, live music, cultural displays, fireworks and of course the lighting of the Olympic flame.

(Continued)

Case Study: Continued.

Prior to an Olympics taking place, a 'Cultural Olympiad' occurs; this is a celebration of the art and culture in the country that is hosting the following Olympics. The Cultural Olympiad often includes displays of art work, festivals, ceremonies and events, each of which attracts audiences of varying sizes, and is recognized as the beginning of the official build-up to the actual games.

Each Olympic Games has its hub in an Olympic stadium; however, the events themselves are often staged at various locations around the host country. This often requires stadium and infrastructure development costing billions of dollars. For a country to be awarded the Olympics, they must satisfy the IOC that they have the resources to make them capable of undertaking this phenomenal commitment. Such developments are a necessity as the Olympics attract visiting audiences in the hundreds of thousands. The economic benefits of staging the games are (allegedly) increased tourism and associated expenditure either through visitors to the games or through exposure given to a country through staging the games attracting foreign investment. However, history has demonstrated that this is not always the case: the 1976 Montreal games are still being paid for over 3 decades later with an Olympic 'Cigarette Tax'; and the 2004 Athens Olympics were estimated to cost US$1.3 billion, but, this cost rose to US$14 billion – enough to increase Greece's budget deficit (Evans, 2005). The 1984 Los Angeles Games did, however, make a profit, credited to the massive media interest and large sums paid by television networks and sponsors, and the fact that little infrastructure development was needed in what was already a very modern city (Evans, 2005).

Being such a high-profile event also unfortunately makes the games a target for terrorism by those who wish their 'cause' to be given global exposure: in 1972, at the Munich Games, 11 Israeli athletes and coaches as well as a German police officer were murdered by the terrorist group 'Black September'; at the 1996 Atlanta Games, a pipe-bomb killed one woman and injured further a 111 people; and in July 2005, the day after the announcement that London had been chosen as the location for the 2012 Olympics, four suicide bombers killed themselves and a further 52 people and injured another 700 on London's public transport system – something which will play a vital role in moving the hundreds of thousands of visitors who are expected to visit the city during the 2012 games. The security bill alone for the staging of the 2012 London Olympics will cost US$840 million (BBC, 2009), with specialist army units, police officers, security stewards, various volunteers, medics and firefighters being mobilized.

The Olympic Games will continue to grow, attracting additional athletes from more countries, developing an even larger global audience. In future, media revenues and sponsorship will play a more central business function to the Olympic Games, in the face of increased costs associated with their planning and implementation. As games grow in size, the spread of where events take place will increase, until Olympic Games shared between more than one hosting nation becomes the norm.

Table 12.2. Summer and Winter Olympic statistics 1896–2012. (From IOC, 2009.)

Year	Summer Olympics	Number of nations involved	Number of athletes	Number of events	Winter Olympics	Number of nations involved	Number of athletes	Number of events
1896	Athens	14	241	43				
1900	Paris	24	997	95				
1904	St Louis	Unknown	651	91				
1908	London	22	2,008	110				
1912	Stockholm	28	2,407	102				
1920	Antwerp	29	2,626	154				
1924	Paris	44	3,089	126	Chamonix	16	258	16
1928	Amsterdam	46	2,883	109	St Moritz	25	464	14
1932	Los Angeles	37	1,332	117	Lake Placid	17	252	14
1936	Berlin	49	3,963	129	Garmisch-Partenkirchen	28	646	17
1948	London	59	4,104	136	St Moritz	28	669	22
1952	Helsinki	69	4,955	149	Oslo	30	694	22
1956	Melbourne/ Stockholm	72	3,314	145	Cortina d'Ampezzo	32	821	24
1960	Rome	83	5,338	150	Squaw Valley	30	665	27
1964	Tokyo	93	5,151	163	Innsbruck	36	1,091	34

(Continued)

Table 12.2. Continued.

Year	Summer Olympics	Number of nations involved	Number of athletes	Number of events	Winter Olympics	Number of nations involved	Number of athletes	Number of events
1968	Mexico	112	5,516	172	Grenoble	37	1,158	35
1972	Munich	121	7,134	195	Sapporo	35	1,006	35
1976	Montreal	92	6,084	198	Innsbruck	37	1,123	37
1980	Moscow	80	5,179	203	Lake Placid	37	1,072	38
1984	Los Angeles	140	6,829	221	Sarajevo	49	1,272	39
1988	Seoul	159	8,391	237	Calgary	57	1,423	46
1992	Barcelona	169	9,356	257	Albertville	64	1,801	57
1994					Lillehammer	67	1,737	61
1996	Atlanta	197	10,318	271				
1998					Nagano	72	2,176	68
2000	Sydney	199	10,651	300				
2002					Salt Lake City	77	2,399	78
2004	Athens	201	10,625	301				
2006					Turin	80	2,508	84
2008	Beijing	204	10,500	302				
2010		Unknown	Unknown	Unknown	Vancouver	Unknown	Unknown	Unknown
2012	London	Unknown	Unknown	Unknown				

THE FUTURE

The future for spectator sports will largely be effected by two factors: technology; and the actual entertainment offering. Throughout the 20th and into the 21st centuries, we have seen sports audiences develop in locations away from the action itself as various media channels have given sporting events global audiences. This will continue further through the Internet. Spectator sports today are competing with many other forms of entertainment; in order to remain ahead of the competition, they need to be seen as offering a value-for-money experience, irrespective of the outcome of the fixture. While the sporting performance itself is paramount, the emphasis on the whole event being more entertainment-focused will rise in significance. The immediate future for the spectator sports sector is highlighted in Fig. 12.8.

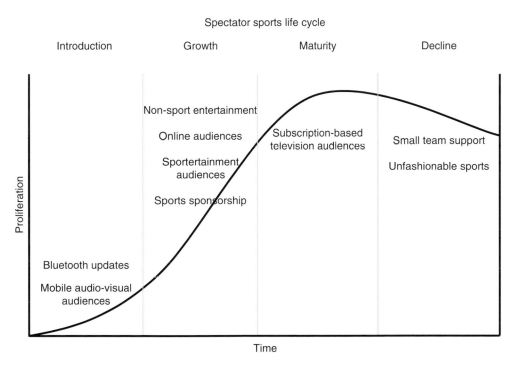

Fig. 12.8. Spectator sports life cycle.

Introduction

Bluetooth updates – this will be used as an alternative way to reach fans within sports stadiums who have Bluetooth-enabled devices, particularly mobile phones. Bluetooth will be used to send a combination of publicity and game information direct to customers. This could include: pre-match news; squad line-ups; the details of officials and sponsors; kick-off times; special offers; details of future ticket sales; player profiles; team ring tones; goal replays; half-time analysis; and post-match reviews.

Fig. 12.9. A crowd of spectators who would be easy to reach via Bluetooth.

Mobile audio-visual audiences – as technology advances, games will eventually be streamed live to mobile phones via the Internet. This will mean that mobile audiences, who have thus far only been allowed to listen to games while on the move, will also be allowed to watch games on their mobiles while out and about.

Growth

Non-sports entertainment – the whole sport-viewing experience will become more of a varied entertainment spectacle. Pre-match, half-time and post-match entertainment will become of more central importance to the match-day experience, with audiences staying for longer overall. While there are additional costs with this, the financial benefit will be in a higher volume of match-day sales, particularly clothing and other team-related merchandize.

Online audiences – these will continue to grow, although the legitimacy of which web sites that broadcast live sports fixtures get the most viewers remains to be seen. As existing broadcast media providers continue to develop online content, including live content (see Chapter 6, this volume), more illegitimate web sites such as *Sopcast* will appear, often with origins in countries that inhibit them from being subject to the rule of law.

Sportertainment audiences – the blending of legitimate sports with theatre (sportertainment) is mentioned in Chapter 2 (this volume). These types of sports are growing rapidly in popularity and will continue to do so, and their displays will continue to attract growing audiences as young people in particular are keen to watch them. The X-Games and Winter X-Games (the Olympics and Winter Olympics of sportertainment and extreme sports) will become accepted as more mainstream sports events with even larger international audiences and greater media prominence. It is also likely that sports with a theatrical element will feature more prominently in more mainstream competitions such as the Olympics.

Sports sponsorship – this will continue to increase as sports gain larger global audiences, giving wider global exposure.

Maturity

Subscription-based television audiences – in the face of less expensive and more interactive online technologies, the current model of subscription-based sports channels through cable and satellite television has now peaked, and the challenge for broadcasters is to adapt to new online business models and methods of distribution.

Decline

Small team support – unfortunately the money in sports all too often is with the largest teams which attract the largest audiences. The incredibly strong brands that the large teams have means that their fan base continues to grow, while smaller 'grass roots' teams are losing out as local younger supporters choose higher profile and more glamorous teams to support.

Unfashionable sports – a lack of interest among young people and an evermore adventurous ageing population will lead to some particularly gentile sports becoming less popular as audiences dwindle in favour of more vibrant and fast-paced competition. Sports considered 'at-risk' include: crown green bowling (not ten-pin), snooker, darts and table tennis.

REFERENCES

British Broadcasting Corporation (BBC) (2009) Peers urge EU role in 2012 plans. [Internet] London, BBC. Available at: http://news.bbc.co.uk/1/hi/uk_politics/7936121.stm

Carey, A.R. and Lynn, G. (1999) USA snapshots. *USA Today* 4 January, C1.

Dietz-Uhler, B., Harrick, E., End, C. and Jacquemontte, L. (2000) Sex differences in sport fan behaviour and reasons for being a sport fan. *Journal of Sport Behaviour* 23, 219–231.

Evans, S. (2005) The Olympics and the need to make money. [Internet] London, BBC. Available at: http://news.bbc.co.uk/1/hi/business/4653491.stm

Ingle, S. and Hodgkinson, M. (2001) When did football hooliganism start? [Internet] London, Guardian News and Media Limited. Available at: http://www.guardian.co.uk/football/2001/dec/13/theknowledge.sport

International Olympic Committee (IOC) (2009) The Olympic Games. [Internet] Laussane, IOC. Available at: http://www.olympic.org/uk/games/index_uk.asp

Mehus, I. (2005) Sociability and excitement motives of spectators attending entertainment sport events: spectators and ski-jumping. *Journal of Sport Behaviour* 28(4), 333–352.

Smith, A. and Stewart, R. (1999) *Sports Management: A Guide for Professional Practice*. Allen & Unwin, Crows Nest, NSW, Australia.

Sweeney, J.C. and Soutar, G.N. (2001) Consumer perceived value: the development of a multiple item scale. *Journal of Retailing* 77(2), Summer, 203–220.

Wann, D.L. (1995) Preliminary validation of the sport fan motivation scale. *Journal of Sport and Social Issues* 19, 377–396.

chapter 13

Thrillertainment

Stuart Moss

Entertainment that is intended to thrill, excite, and sometimes cause fright.

The world in which we live was once filled with great danger for humans, going out to find food or water carried inherent dangers as humans were not always at the top of the food chain and were actively hunted by predatory carnivorous mammals, reptiles and even birds. Even those animals that did not want to eat us may have taken exception to our very presence and chased after us. A knock, stamp, gorge or bite from the likes of a woolly rhinoceros could quite easily have proved to be fatal to a human. Yet our world had to be shared, and our basic survival instincts helped humans to endure, as did our body's natural defence systems, including *adrenalin*, which is a hormone and a neurotransmitter within the body that stimulates our senses, increases our heart rate and blood flow, sending oxygen and glucose to the muscles and brain. Adrenalin production occurs within the body's adrenal gland, which goes into overdrive when we sense danger or stress, thus preparing us for 'fight or flight'. If you have ever been chased by somebody or something, and you were afraid of the consequence of being caught, your body's production of adrenalin will have helped you to run faster than what you might normally have been capable of.

Adrenalin saved lives in a world filled with danger; today, many of us are fortunate enough to live in 'developed' nations which have secure housing and a system of law enforcement and health care in place that is designed to protect us and preserve life. While it must be acknowledged that there are still many parts of the world where this is not the case, our lives are not filled with the same levels of danger that our ancestors' lives may have been. A person on a trip to buy food from the grocery store no longer runs the risk of being eaten alive, and provided they take note of man-made dangers such as road vehicles and loose paving slabs on footpaths, such a trip should not be a dangerous one.

Particular feelings and emotions are causes of adrenalin production, and the entertainment industry invokes these same feelings and emotions through sensory stimulation. Some products within the entertainment industry are specifically designed to increase adrenalin production among audiences who actively seek out experiences that are harmless, but can leave them feeling fearful and stressed. People in such audiences are referred to as 'thrill-seekers'. These people enjoy the seemingly near-to-dangerous experiences which thrill-ertainment can give them. The experience of being thrilled causes sudden and intense emotions including excitement and fright, which can cause adrenalin to flow, and leave audiences in a variety of bodily states including: being in a heightened state of alert; 'weak at the knees'; and having 'butterflies in their tummies'. These are all experiences that many (but not all) people enjoy. Thrillertainment appeals mostly to younger people, particularly those in their mid- to late-teens and early 20s. This younger segment of the market is actively seeking out experiences that are new and exciting as a part of their growing and learning process. Thrillertainment is provided in both 'media' and 'live' forms, and these are outlined in Fig. 13.1.

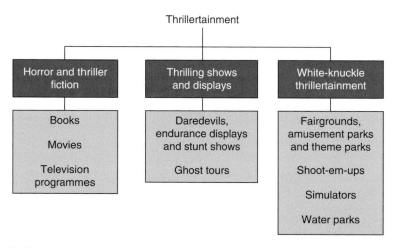

Fig. 13.1. Thrillertainment sub-sectors.

HORROR AND THRILLER FICTION

The imagination of creative writers has been thrilling and terrifying audiences for centuries; monsters such as 'the Minotaur', 'Medusa' and 'Cyclops' appeared in ancient Greek mythology, and since then stories involving ghosts, goblins, werewolves and witches have terrified audiences. Horror and thriller fiction is designed to take the audience out of the reality of their lives and immerse them in a story, which is both unsettling and frightening, where the empathy of the audience towards characters in such stories is pivotal in the audience feeling the true thrilling effects (emotions) of the fiction.

Books

While horror and thriller writing has taken place for many centuries, the commercial boom in such fiction did not take place until the 20th century. Prior to this, horror stories were based mainly upon classic tales and folklore. In the 18th century, Donatien Alphonse François de Sade – known as Marquis de Sade – wrote a series of novels that featured murder, rape, torture and necrophilia, most of which were written while de Sade was being held within mental health institutions; the word 'sadism' was a direct reference to his written genre, and is today used to describe acts of brutality and torture. Nineteenth-century literary horror classics including *Dracula* by Bram Stoker and *Frankenstein* by Mary Shelley went on to inspire many more writers with similar tales. In the 20th century, the emergence of authors such as Thomas Harris, James Herbert, Howard Phillips Lovecraft, Stephen King (see Fig. 13.2), Dean Koontz, Richard Laymon and Anne Rice led the way in providing hundreds of works of horror and thriller fiction. Many of these stories provided tense storylines with uncertain but potentially terrifying outcomes, such as: *Misery* by Stephen King (which is a dark psychological horror); and *Dragon Tears* by Dean Koontz (which is a horror story based upon the paranormal), while others graphically described scenes of death, rape, torture and gore including: *American Psycho* by Brett Easton Ellis (which graphically describes all of the above); and *The Rats* by James Herbert (which included graphic descriptions of death and human mutilation). It is worthy of note that both of the latter titles received widespread criticism and derision in the media at their time of publication due to their graphic content.

Fig. 13.2. Some novels written by Stephen King, one of the 20th and 21st centuries most celebrated writers of horror and thriller fiction.

Movies

The first horror movie lasted approximately 2 min, and featured devilish characters and witches concocting a potion to create demons. Today, this sounds more like a children's Halloween story rather than something that was meant to terrify. Many horror movies are based upon existing works of fiction, these include: classic fairytales such as *Little Red Riding Hood*, which was the inspiration for the movie *Freeway* (1996) where the 'big bad wolf' was represented as a serial killer, and 'Red Riding Hood' as an abused girl; classic horrors such as *Dracula*, which has been adapted into dozens of 'vampire' movies; and more contemporary works of fiction, that are simply transformed into movie format, this applies to a number of works by Stephen King, including, *Carrie, Misery, It* and *The Shining*.

Horror and thriller movies for the most part contain at least one human death, and more often than not, numerous deaths. The death of a fellow human is something that (thankfully) the majority of us rarely experience in our own real lives (particularly murders), and it is an extremely difficult and unpleasant time for many when somebody whom they know dies. With that stated, it seems incredulous that in the movies it is an accepted, standard fare to kill people (characters) in the name of entertainment, horror movies particularly thrive upon this, allowing the audience to 'witness' something that the vast majority of them will (hopefully) never witness in real life.

Social and Legal Factor: Movie Certification and Changing Attitudes

Horror and thriller movies have developed from being not only tense and psychological to graphic and brutal, largely due to the developments in special effects (this is discussed more in Chapter 5, this volume). This has led to them being awarded 'age ratings' or certification based upon their content, and suitability to be viewed by minors. Typical ratings include U, PG, 12A, 12, 15 and 18. U- and PG-certificated movies may be viewed by anybody of any age, those for 12, 15 and 18 may only be viewed by people of those ages and older, a 12A may be viewed by anybody aged 12 or older, and people younger than 12 may view a 12A if they are accompanied by an adult. In the UK, cinemas also used to have an additional X certificate for movies that featured 'extreme' sex or violence. When *Dracula* starring Christopher Lee was released as a movie in 1958, it was awarded the X certificate by the UK movie censors. Changing times, attitudes and an increase in graphic horror movies, including 'slasher' movies, led to the same *Dracula* movie being awarded a 12A certificate when it was re-released in time for Halloween 2007.

Television programmes

Thrillers particularly have become popular as a genre of television programmes, notable titles from the 20th and 21st centuries include: *Tales of the Unexpected*; *Lost* and *Prison Break*. Thrillers are becoming increasingly fast-paced, action-packed and often promote a lead character as the 'hero'. Some popular thrillers also transcend genres into science fiction, and notable titles include: *Dr Who;*

The X-Files and *Torchwood*. Horror television series are less common than thrillers, and this may be due to stricter rules governing what is and what is not acceptable to broadcast, particularly at 'prime time' and before the 'watershed' (usually 9 p.m.), after which more graphic content (including expensive special effects) may be screened, but when viewing figures are likely to be reduced.

THRILLING SHOWS AND DISPLAYS

These take thrillertainment from a media-based environment into live theatre, involving real people who are involved in predetermined routines that carry either a real or a perceived element of danger, or the fear of the unknown.

Daredevils, endurance displays and stunt shows

These involve specially trained performers undertaking tasks, or carrying out feats that carry a real element of danger about them. To the majority of audiences, the thrills associated with watching such acts come from the stress of willing the performer to succeed and hoping that nothing will go wrong. Performers in these shows may be undertaking a range of activities, and these include: tightrope walking; fire-walking; sword swallowing; escapology; stunt flying/driving; high diving; dangerous animal handling; and acts of physical endurance. Examples of performers who have become famous or gained notoriety for participating in such acts include: Bubba Blackwell, David Blaine, Derren Brown, Jonathan Goodwin, Harry Houdini, Evel Knievel and Jim Rose (along with his Circus Sideshow of performers).

Inevitably things do go wrong, and performers do get injured, and sometimes killed. Evel Knievel was a motorbike stuntman who performed 'death-defying' jumps upon his motorbike over all manner of objects including: cars, buses, lions, sharks in tanks, fountains and boxes of rattlesnakes. Knievel did not succeed in all his jumps, and became as famous for his crashes as he did for his successes. During his career Kneivel had numerous accidents while attempting jumps which left him with many broken bones, as well as time spent in a coma. British escapologist Jonathan Goodwin had to be cut free from a hangman's noose after failing to escape from it during 'cheating the gallows' – one of his televised stunts, and this led to complaints from viewers and the television regulator (BBC, 2006).

Ghost tours

These involve the audience becoming a live part of the show itself, and may take place around city streets, such as York or Edinburgh in the UK, or around more eerie locations such as parks and gardens at night. Ghost tours are generally led by a tour guide, who will tell stories along the way, and some tours feature performers playing ghosts and ghouls throughout the tour, which are designed to create an atmosphere and instil a sense of fright among participants. This may involve costumed performers making a sudden appearance or noise causing the audience to jump, which is usually followed by hysterical laughter.

Beyond traditional ghost tours are the more contemporary visitor attractions that feature elements of ghostly or gruesome storytelling, accompanied by costumed performers and gruesome props such as cadavers, and fake blood daubed on walls. One such example of this type of attraction is the 'Dungeons' owned by Merlin Entertainment. The London Dungeon features sets that are designed to replicate: the Great Plague; the Great Fire of London; Sweeney Todd; and Jack the Ripper. Other similar attractions are located elsewhere in the UK, as well as Germany, Holland and Italy. This type of attraction may also feature human performers who suddenly appear and cause fright to audiences sometimes even giving a chase to them.

WHITE-KNUCKLE THRILLERTAINMENT

The term 'white-knuckle ride' was originally used to describe the whiteness of the knuckles when grip bars were being held tightly on a thrilling ride. The development of modern gaming consoles also means that 'white-knuckle' can apply to games that can thrill or frighten the player; hence, game controllers are gripped tightly, giving a white-knuckle effect. White-knuckle thrillertainment (WKT) is often fast-paced and involves active and live participation of the audience in the entertainment experience. The thrill of WKT is down to the perceived 'dangerous' position that the audience (or their persona) is seemingly put in, be that strapped into a ride seat (see Fig. 13.3) or being sat in front of a screen.

Fig. 13.3. A white-knuckle ride that spins riders in circles and turns them upside down.

Fairgrounds, amusement parks and theme parks

These are collections of rides of varying sizes and scales that are designed to thrill riders and spectators alike, usually supported by side stalls that sell food and drinks, and at larger attractions there may also be stages where shows are held, as well as animals in 'zoo'-style environments. The difference between fairgrounds, amusement parks and theme parks is largely in their size, although theme parks often (but not always) carry additional theming.

Fairgrounds (fairs) originated centuries ago as communal celebrations of a number of things, including: important figures, religious deities, national days and successful harvests. Fairs would bring gatherings of people together who would celebrate, with food, dance and song. While the majority of early fairs were temporary, permanent fairs began to appear in Europe as locations to relax and for amusement as early as 1583 (see Table 13.1); many were formed in coastal locations where early tourists would visit to bathe in sea water.

Table 13.1. The ten oldest amusement parks in the world that are still in operation. (From NAPHA, 2009.)

Year founded	Name of the park and location
1583	Bakken, Klampenborg, Denmark
1766	The Prater, Vienna, Austria
1838	Widam Park, Budapest, Hungary
1842	Blackgang Chine Cliff Top Theme Park, Isle of Wight, UK
1843	Tivoli, Copenhagen, Denmark
1846	Lake Compounce Amusement Park, Bristol, Connecticut, USA
1853	Hanayashiki, Tokyo, Japan
1865	Grand Pier, Teignmouth, UK
1868	Blackpool Central Pier, Blackpool, UK
1870	Cedar Point, Sandusky, Ohio, USA

Entrepreneurs realized that gatherings of pleasure-seeking folk could bring financial gain, and so fairs were often targeted by them with stalls selling goods and wares, which often included foods and ales. Some fairs became known as feasts (a name which still persists in parts of the UK), due to the emphasis placed upon food and drink at them. Traders became more elaborate, and visiting shows (including 'freak shows') and circus-style acts with clowns and animals would often provide entertainment for audiences at fairs; such shows were transient and would move across country from one location to another. P.T. Barnum was an entrepreneur who had numerous shows that travelled around the world in the 19th century, and is considered the world's first entertainment millionaire.

Early 19th-century rides included roundabouts that featured wooden horses for the riders to sit upon, which were turned by either man or animal (NFA, 2007). Other rides included slides, swings and roundabouts, not dissimilar to what might be found on a children's playground today. These were still new innovations, and while tame by today's standards, rides like 'gondola swings' where the riders would make the swing go higher by pulling ropes were certainly considered to be the great thrill rides of the day. The invention of steam-powered technology for railways led to the development of steam-driven merry-go-round in the UK in 1861 (NFA, 2007); the novelty of such a machine proved to be a great draw to the visiting public, and the popularity of the ride saw it featured at numerous fairs. Entrepreneurs realized that having a large significant ride as the centrepiece to a fairground would draw in fee-paying crowds. Companies began to create such rides for fairgrounds as demand soared, with new innovations such as 'galloping' horses that would move up and down powered by pneumatics and roundabouts that had 'ups and downs' to give additional thrills to riders.

Other powered rides would soon follow including powered swings and big wheels. Fairground ride development throughout a great deal of the 20th century followed several common design features: rides that travelled in a circular motion (roundabout-style); rides that relied on gravity to bring riders down to earth (safely); rides that spun around; and rides that went up, before coming back down again. Many rides incorporated several of these features setting new benchmarks for would-be thrill-seekers. Notable rides based upon the concept of the roundabout include: the waltzer – where riders sit in cars that also spin around; gallopers – where riders sit on horses that move gently up and down as the roundabout turns (see Fig. 13.4); the octopus – where riders

Fig. 13.4. A 'gallopers' carousel ride.

sit in cars that are on arms which go up and down as the ride spins; chairoplanes – where riders sit in swing seats and are spun so that centrifugal forces cause chairs to spread outwards and in doing so tilting riders towards earth; and the caterpillar – where riders sit in a car that not only goes on a track which goes up and down, but also partway through the ride the cars are plunged into darkness through a mechanized cover. Other notable rides found at fairgrounds included big wheels, dodgems and mini train-rides – the precursor to the roller coaster.

Technological developments meant that larger and more spectacular rides were being developed; many were elaborate, achieving seemingly death-defying feats for those brave enough to ride them. Large-scale rides did not only provide thrills for riders, but the sight of them has proven to be an entertaining spectacle for fascinated and thrilled audiences of onlookers. The traditional roundabout-style design of rides, while still popular, has been eclipsed by large-scale tracked rides that are not only expensive for fairground owners to buy, but also more difficult to transport from one location to another. This has contributed to the formation of permanent fairgrounds, in locations that would guarantee large numbers of visitors, giving birth to the modern-day amusement park.

Amusement parks were developed predominantly in urban and coastal locations that would guarantee a high number of visitors. Notable parks developed throughout the 20th century include: Blackpool Pleasure Beach, UK (1896); Luna Park, Coney Island, USA (1903–1944); Great Yarmouth Pleasure Beach, UK (1909); Luna Park, Melbourne, Australia (1912); and Astroland, Coney Island, USA (1962). The success of early amusement parks, in a market with few competitors did not go unnoticed. In the UK, several parks opened in coastal locations with the name 'Pleasure Beach' and globally 'Luna Parks' appeared that tried to emulate the success of the Coney Island original. What the majority of Luna Park owners did not realize is that 'Luna' was the name of the sister of the original Luna Park founder.

Legal Factor: Image Rights Usage and Intellectual Property Theft at Fairgrounds and Amusement Parks

It is common practice for fairground and amusement park rides to be given a theme, so as to make them more appealing to potential customers. Traditionally themes may have been related to a particular genre of movie such as a space/science fiction or Western theme. In more recent times, rides have been themed based upon products that are popular with the target audience of riders, e.g. 'The Pepsi Max' roller coaster at Blackpool Pleasure Beach. Theming a ride involves painting and decorating it with particular images, and providing music and sound effects, all of which should be reminiscent of the theme that they are portraying. Providing that the artwork used to theme the rides is original there should not be a problem, but when rides are decorated with images or photographs of celebrities, and copyrighted images without permission of the celebrities or owners of the images, laws may have been broken.

(Continued)

Legal Factor: Continued.

With regards to the images of celebrities, 'consumers and businesses identify with celebrities and are often influenced into purchasing products which claim a connection with the individual marketing the product' (Lawdit, 2005). Therefore, to use an image of a celebrity on a ride could suggest that the celebrity had endorsed that ride. Some rides are decorated with the images of numerous celebrities; Fig. 13.5 contains the images of (among others) 'Usher' and Carl Cox, and if they have not given permission for their images to be used on this ride, the ride owners could potentially be liable.

Some rides are decorated with images that are easily recognizable such as cartoon characters and movie logos (see Fig. 13.6), all of which are owned by either somebody or a major corporation. This is particularly an issue in the UK where traditionally fairgrounds and amusement parks have been family-run, with rides swapped, hired and borrowed from other fairgrounds or parks. Tracing ownership of a particular ride can prove to be a hindrance in enforcing intellectual property laws. In the face of rising intellectual property theft from 'across the board', major corporations are likely in future to put more effort into following ownership 'paper-trails' and enforcing such laws upon fairgrounds and amusement parks. This could mean for such ride owners compliance, fines or closure.

Fig. 13.5. Celebrity images painted on a UK fairground ride.

Fig. 13.6. Bart Simpson's image on a simulator ride.

Amusement parks opened with increasingly large 'signature' rides, for which they would become well known, and these rides were designed to thrill. Roller coasters led the way as being the centrepiece and core attraction of amusement parks, and a list of the most common types of roller coaster is featured in Table 13.2. Roller coasters were traditionally constructed from wood, although today steel has taken over as the primary construction medium. The majority of roller coasters rely on gravity to release riders in cars along tracks; wooden roller coasters tend to feature a series of tight turns, dips, rises, slopes, curves and inclines. Comparatively modern steel roller coasters additionally feature even greater thrilling features including corkscrews, spirals, loop-the-loops, and near vertical drops. Roller coasters are a multimillion dollar investment for a park, and their development has seen them become progressively longer, taller and faster.

Table 13.2. Roller coasters and their characteristics.

Type of roller coaster	Characteristics
4th-dimension coaster	A coaster where riders are placed on either side of the track rather than above or below it and where seats spin on a horizontal axis
Bobsled coaster	A coaster that does not run on a rail track but has wheeled cars that roll within a U-shaped chute

(Continued)

Table 13.2. Continued.

Type of roller coaster	Characteristics
Dark coaster	A coaster that is indoors and runs in darkness, so that dips, twists and turns are not seen in advance, usually with some special-effect lighting including strobes and lasers
Diving coaster	A coaster that has wide rather than long cars, and features a 'vertical' drop as the main feature of the ride (see Fig. 13.7)
Floorless coaster	A coaster where riders sit in cars with their feet suspended, giving an additional sense of danger
Kiddies coaster	A small-scale and usually portable coaster that has minimal height restrictions and only mild dips and twists
Jet coaster	A coaster that has an immediate high-speed powered launch, often through the use of hydraulic or pneumatic power, giving the car a high momentum making it capable of tackling steep climbs quickly at the beginning of the ride
Spinning coaster	A coaster where the cars do not only run down a track, but also spin on a vertical axis
Standing coaster	A coaster where riders stand rather than sit in the cars
Steel coaster	Any type of roller coaster that is built with a steel frame
Suspension coaster	A coaster where the cars are suspended below the track rather than above it (see Fig. 13.8)
Wet coaster	Part of the track of this roller coaster is either immersed in water or passes by shooting water so that riders are at a risk of getting wet
Wooden coaster	Any type of roller coaster that is built with a wooden frame

New 'ground-breaking' roller coasters open every year in theme parks around the world. A theme park is generally a more large-scale amusement park that includes the additional element of theming for the whole park. Due to the extensive costs and spatial requirements of roller coasters, theme parks – which tend to be the largest of man-made purpose-built visitor attractions, often with financial backing from multinational corporations – tend to be the predominant buyers of new roller coasters, although large-scale amusement parks also periodically add new roller coaster rides. Theme parks tend to have the advantage of being built in areas that provide large open spaces, so that new development is less of a problem than it can be with some of the comparatively smaller amusement parks.

The importance of theming rides so as to entice potential customers has already been mentioned; theme parks tend to be themed around one subject that is then localized for individual rides and attractions. Subjects that parks are themed around tend to be fun and attractive to the core target market of such attractions which mainly comprises: young families; teenagers;

Fig. 13.7. A diving coaster, Alton Towers, UK.

Fig. 13.8. A suspension coaster, Blackpool Pleasure Beach, UK.

and those in their early 20s. Some theme parks make very little attempt at overall theming on a particular subject outside of the general theme of being 'fun' or having 'big scary rides'; some parks are divided into zones where sub-themes may be apparent, for example, Drayton Manor Theme Park in the UK has no overall park theme, but does have five zones within the park, each of which carry a theme: aerial, nautical, pirates, action and a children's themed area.

Table 13.3 features the worlds most visited theme parks in 2007; it is interesting to note that six of these are themed around movies and movie characters; six of these are owned by The Walt Disney Company; the top eight all have a Disney connection; and five of these parks are in the USA.

Table 13.3. The ten most visited theme parks in the world in 2007, based upon TEA/ERA (2008).

Name of park	Number of visitors	Country	Owner	Theming
Magic Kingdom (see Fig. 13.9)	17,060,000	USA	The Walt Disney Company	Disney characters and movies
Disneyland	14,870,000	USA	The Walt Disney Company	Disney characters and movies
Tokyo Disneyland	13,906,000	Japan	The Oriental Land Company	Disney characters and movies
Tokyo Disneysea	12,413,000	Japan	The Oriental Land Company	Nautical exploration
Disneyland Paris	12,000,000	France	The Walt Disney Company	Disney characters and movies
EPCOT	10,930,000	USA	The Walt Disney Company	International culture and technological innovation
Disney's Hollywood Studios	9,510,000	USA	The Walt Disney Company	Hollywood movies, music and television
Disney's Animal Kingdom	9,490,000	USA	The Walt Disney Company	Animal conservation
Universal Studios Japan	8,713,000	Japan	NBC Universal	Universal movies and characters
Everland	7,200,000	South Korea	Samsung	Various

Some large-scale amusement parks label themselves (or are labelled as being) as theme parks, due to the methods by which visitors pay to use the park. At fairgrounds it is common practice to pay per ride; at amusement parks it is common practice to buy tokens which are used

Fig. 13.9. The iconic Cinderella Castle – the centrepiece of Disney's Magic Kingdom theme park.

as currency to pay for rides, or to buy wristbands which entitle the wearer unlimited access to specified rides. At theme parks, it is common practice to pay to enter the park, then once inside be granted unlimited access to the rides within. Some large-scale amusement parks have begun to charge an entry fee in the same way that theme parks do, e.g. Blackpool Pleasure Beach introduced an entry charge of £5 in 2008, unless a wristband allowing access to all rides was purchased. At the Disney theme parks in Florida, a system of fingerprinting is in operation (see Fig. 13.10), so that each individual's entry ticket is matched to only one person, and in this way a park user cannot 'sell-on' their tickets to somebody else after they leave the park.

Case Study: Disney's Hollywood Studios

Opening in 1989 as Disney-MGM Studios, Disney's Hollywood Studios (DHS) is one of the four major theme parks within Disneyworld, Florida. DHS is themed upon a celebration of Hollywood's creative output, including movies, music and television programmes. In 2007, DHS was the seventh most-visited park in the world with 9.51 million visitors (TEA/ERA, 2008). Within the park there are six distinctly themed areas: Animation Courtyard; Echo Lake; Hollywood Boulevard; Pixar Place; Streets of America; and Sunset Boulevard. The centrepiece of the park is Mickey Mouse's hat from *Fantasia* (see Fig. 13.11).

The park has attractions to suit all age groups, and thrillertainment-specific attractions are listed below.

(Continued)

Fig. 13.10. Fingerprint scanner at Disney's Hollywood Studios.

Case Study: Continued.

The Indiana Jones Show – this is a live re-enactment of a number of iconic scenes from the movie *Raiders Of The Lost Ark* including a sword fight in an Egyptian Bazaar and a fight between Jones and a German soldier by an aeroplane; the show includes perfectly timed and well-rehearsed stunts, as well as blank firing machine guns and pyrotechnic explosions that are guaranteed to thrill audiences. The show is also annotated with technical explanations given by experts.

Lights! Motors! Action! Extreme Stunt Show – this is a stunt show that involves cars and motorbikes being driven into near-collisions and over ramps.

Rock 'n' Roller Coaster – this is a jet-powered dark coaster themed upon a limousine ride being taken with the band 'Aerosmith'.

Star Tours – this is a simulator ride, where riders are seated in a spaceship that 'flies' around the *Star Wars* universe.

The Twilight Zone Tower of Terror – the first part of this ride is a 'hotel', where costumed cast members invite riders to watch a suspense building video, and then the riders are taken into the 'guts' of the building – the basement, before being shepherded into a lift, which rises up the tower. The ride includes video footage and voices from the *Twilight Zone*, riders sit in cars that are transported along rails, the real thrill comes when the car is pulled downwards at a speed

(Continued)

Case Study: Continued.

faster than gravity alone, before coming to a stop and then shooting back up into the air, and this is followed by a series of drops and lifts. During this time riders see the briefest glimpse of daylight through an open window in the ride (which from the outside looks like a hotel, as highlighted in Fig. 13.12), which gives the crowds below a snapshot of them, but more importantly – the crowds below hear the riders scream, thus building further suspense and anticipation.

Case study based upon Disney (2009) and Moss (2007)

Fig. 13.11. Mickey Mouse's *Fantasia* hat.

While Disneyworld is currently the world's largest theme park area, plans are afoot to eclipse this in Dubai with Dubailand, which will be twice the size of Disneyworld and comprise of $107\,\text{mi}^2$ ($1\,\text{mi} = 1.609\,\text{km}$) of theme parks that will be built upon what is currently desert. Dubailand will feature 26 theme parks built at an estimated cost of US$60 billion; these parks will be in seven different 'zones' with each park having a specific theme, and confirmed parks so far include: Marvel Super Heroes, Universal Studios, Dreamworks, Thomas the Tank Engine, Legoland and Bob the Builder. This project will involve a theme park opening every 6 months from December 2010, and is expected to be completed by 2018 (Keenan, 2008).

The popularity of theme parks globally means that they will enjoy a bigger and brighter future, although this may be at the expense of smaller more regional fairgrounds and amusement parks, that simply cannot afford to compete with the glitz and glamour associated with major theme parks.

Fig. 13.12. The Twilight Zone Tower of Terror at Disney's Hollywood Studios.

Shoot-em-ups

These are violent computer games that can also be frightening to play due to the fast-paced action within them. Shoot-em-ups tend to involve the player moving through an environment that is filled with danger, in which the player's character is at risk of being killed throughout the game. In order to survive, enemies must be killed, and this is often graphically depicted. This has led to a system of age ratings being put in place to prevent overly violent games falling into the hands of children which are currently: 3 – contains content suitable for all ages; 7 – contains some content which may be frightening for very young children; 12 – contains realistic violence towards fantasy characters; 15 – contains some realistic violence and sexual swear words; 16 – contains realistic and sustained violence; and 18 – contains extreme violence, sex scenes and the liberal use of sexual swear words (ELSPA, 2009). As gamers grow older, the number of violent shoot-em-ups will undoubtedly increase as demand for such games grows.

Simulators

These are a type of 'white-knuckle' ride that can be found in numerous locations outside of the traditional amusement park sphere including: museums, shopping malls, and video games arcades. Simulators involve the riders sitting within a 'pod' or 'capsule' and watching a video or computer graphics simulation on screen. The images viewed on screen depict forward movement, and as the images move the simulator physically moves around, giving riders the feeling of motion, a ride that begins gently soon becomes quite violent as the action on screen quickens, as do the movements of the simulator. In terms of white-knuckle rides, these are reasonably technologically advanced, but quite small and certainly tame when compared to roller coasters. Simulators are particularly popular with children and young teenagers.

Waterparks

Generally located in warm climates such as the southern US states and the Mediterranean, waterparks feature pools and lagoons that have slides of varying magnitudes going into them. The slides at waterparks provide the thrills, and are often given names that conjure up danger, such as 'Kamikaze' and 'Death-Drop'. Waterpark slides can be extremely steep, and riders can achieve very fast speeds as they enter the water. Some slides are elaborately shaped and use inflatables for riders to ride upon giving additional novelty value.

THE FUTURE

The demand for thrills will not go away, and overall the thrillertainment sector is one to experience growth. Technological advances mean that future thrills will be even more death-defying as thrill-seekers urge to get as close as they can to danger without actually being hurt themselves. The predicted future for some thrillertainment sectors is featured in Fig. 13.13.

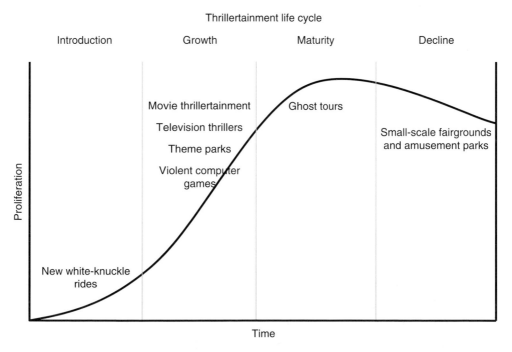

Fig. 13.13. Thrillertainment life cycle.

Introduction

New white-knuckle rides – in order to remain a step ahead of the competition new white-knuckle rides will continue to be developed that are either of a greater magnitude than existing rides; or find new ways to thrill riders.

Growth

Movie thrillertainment – graphic and realistic special effects will lead to more movie violence and gore as boundaries are pushed to terrify audiences.

Television thrillers – the popularity of this genre means that it is a safe investment for studios and television companies alike, and there will be a continuation of new (particularly American) series being released that are designed to thrill audiences.

Theme parks – these will not only grow in size and scale, but they will grow in number; more countries will open glamorous large-scale theme parks in an attempt to boost tourist revenues.

Violent computer games – as existing gamers get older, the demand for adult-orientated games will also increase, and this will include violent and realistic shoot-em-ups.

Maturity

Ghost tours – while they do carry thrills, younger audiences are aware that these are simulated theatre rather than real danger. Thrill-seekers will in future look for something that is more terrifying.

Decline

Small-scale fairgrounds and amusement parks – the tired image and unfashionability of many of these will cause many to close, as customers are tempted by more big-named parks in glamorous settings.

REFERENCES

British Broadcasting Corporation (BBC) (2006) TV hanging show sparks complaints. [Internet] London, BBC. Available at: http://news.bbc.co.uk/1/hi/entertainment/4667224.stm

Entertainment and Leisure Software Publishers Association (2009) How age ratings are applied to games. [Internet] London, ELSPA. Available at: http://www.elspa.com/docs/aag_leaflet_artwork.pdf

Keenan, S. (2008) World's biggest theme park rises in Dubai. [Internet] London, *The Times*. Available at: http://www.timesonline.co.uk/tol/travel/news/article3886979.ece

Lawdit Solicitors (2005) Image rights: the UK view. [Internet] Southampton, Lawdit Solicitors. Available at: http://www.lawdit.co.uk/reading_room/room/view_article.asp?name=../articles/Image%20 Rights.htm

Moss, S. (2007) The Disney experience part 2: Disney MGM Studios. [Internet] Leeds, Entertainment Planet. Available at: http://entplanet.blogspot.com/search?q=MGM

National Amusement Park Historical Association (2009) Worlds oldest operating amusement parks. [Internet] Lombard, Illinois, NAPHA. Available at: http://www.napha.org/nnn/Default. aspx?tabid=70

National Fairground Archive (2007) Fairground rides – a chronological devlopment. [Internet] Sheffield, The University of Sheffield. Available at: http://www.nfa.dept.shef.ac.uk/history/rides/ history.html

Themed Entertainment Association/Economics Research Associates (2008) Attraction attendance 2007. [Internet] Burbank, TEA. Available at: http://www.connectingindustry.com/downloads/ pwteaerasupp.pdf

The Walt Disney Company (2009) Disney's Hollywood Studios. [Internet] Burbank, TWDC. Available at: http://www.disneyworld.disney.go.com/parks/hollywood-studios/

chapter 14

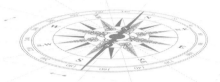

Edutainment

Stuart Moss

Entertainment that is designed to promote knowledge and learning.

Once upon a time education was accessible only to the elite or those who could afford it. This is still the case today in some parts of the world, where the functions necessary for survival (providing food, water, shelter and security) dominate daily life and take precedence over other activities. In contrast to this, in the majority of the industrialized societies, some form of school education system usually exists for children, and often for adults via further and higher education (colleges and universities). Education is often considered as being a means to an end, for example, passing school qualifications may allow entry into college, passing college qualifications may allow access into university, and gaining a degree may be a requirement for an individual to get a particular job, which will allow that person to begin their chosen career along a path of their choice. In that sense, each educational 'milepost' becomes a stepping stone along the path of life, where participating in education has been a necessity to move from one stone to the next. This is a traditional view of education, but what about participating in educational experiences for recreation, rather than as a means to an end? Edutainment promotes recreational learning and knowledge transfer in non-traditional informal settings, including: the home, museums, information centres and observation platforms. Edutainment also promotes 'lifelong learning', which revolves around the concept that learning should not be limited by targeting it solely towards those of school age.

Edutainment typically involves an entertaining method of educational delivery in that it can hold the attention of an audience, very often with an emotional response among audience members, and can potentially draw in people who may have otherwise been 'turned-off' by the notion of participating in education as a recreational activity. The concept of combining recreation and education is not a new one. In ancient Greece, 'mouseion' existed as collections of artistic and cultural artefacts where scholars could visit and study (Findlen, 1989), and the Greeks were well known for worshipping a number of gods, and among these were the 'Muses' who were goddesses that inspired art and creativity; from the words mouseion and muse, we now have 'museums' which are a major edutainment sub-sector. The sub-sectors within the edutainment sector are highlighted in Fig. 14.2.

Social Factor: Edutainment Needs To Be VARK

There have been numerous studies about the way people take in information and learn from it. One such study is VARK, which stands for visual, aural, read/write and kinaesthetic. Each of these categories depicts how information may be presented to promote learning. According to Fleming (2008b), visual means information that is presented in graphical form including diagrams, graphs and charts; aural is the spoken word, and can include listening to information from a person or in a pre-recorded format; read/write is the use of written words to convey information; and kinaesthetic is the use of examples such as demonstrations, videos and actual practice. Most people either have a preference for the way by which they take in information and learn from it; some people will have a specific

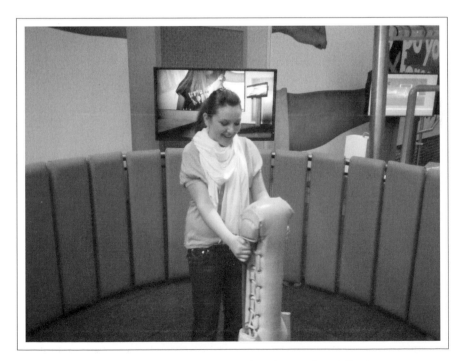

Fig. 14.1. A ride at the Science Museum, London, kinaesthetically demonstrates centrifugal and gravitational forces.

(Continued)

Social Factor: Continued.

VARK category, while others are known as 'multimodal' which means that they may share preferences from two or more categories.

In order to appeal to all members of their audiences, edutainment venues need to provide information in all VARK formats. Otherwise the messages that the venues are trying to convey may be lost on certain members of their audience. Museums have a stereotypical image among some people as being 'stuffy' and 'boring' due to the perceptions (possibly from childhood) that all they contain are exhibits in glass cases. This may still be the case with some museums, but many modern museums now go much further than this to convey their messages to members of their audience in a number of different formats. Figure 14.1 demonstrates kinaesthetic learning in practice in a museum.

BUILT ENVIRONMENT EDUCATIONAL FACILITIES

The built environment consists of man-made constructions that have been created to facilitate society and human existence. In any urban area, the built environment including houses, office blocks, roads, railway lines, factories, bridges and churches surrounds us. The majority of the local built environment is unremarkable to those who live within it, but occasionally something within the built environment is created, which is unique, becomes a spectacle, and as a consequence an attraction. When this happens it is largely due to the novelty of what has been created. Built environment attractions can be novel due to their uniqueness, architecture, history, notoriety, usage, size or any combination of these factors. When something has been created within the built environment that becomes an attraction, this is often capitalized upon with the introduction of educational facilities so that visitors to the attraction can learn more about it. The creation of visitor centres and associated facilities such as car parks also help to manage visitor numbers and flow. The majority of built environment attractions were not originally created as attractions; however, in some cases their importance as attractions has become central to their existence. An example of this could be the ruins of the Colosseum in Rome, Italy, that once formed an important functioning building, but today has no function other than to draw in visitors. Table 14.1 contains some typical examples of built environment attractions, along with actual examples of edutainment venues.

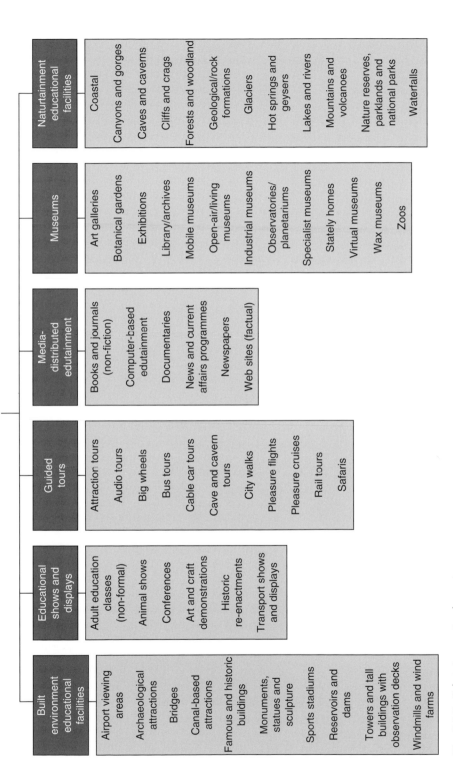

Fig. 14.2. Edutainment sub-sectors.

Table 14.1. Built environment attraction types by category.

Built environment attraction	Example edutainment facilities
Airport viewing areas	• Aviation Viewing Park, Manchester Airport, England (see Fig. 14.3, below) • Dusseldorf Airport Viewing Deck, Dusseldorf, Germany • Panorama Terrace, Schipol Airport, The Netherlands
Archaeological attractions	• An Creagán Visitor Centre, Omagh, Northern Ireland • Bath's Big Dig Visitor Centre, Bath, England • Kingsland Archaeological Center, Texas, USA
Bridges	• Golden Gate Bridge Gift Center, San Francisco, USA • Millau Viaduct Visitor Centre, Millau, France • Sydney Harbor Bridge South East Pylon, Sydney, Australia
Canal-based attractions	• Falkirk Wheel, Tamfourhill, Scotland • Ohio and Erie Canal Visitor Center, Cuyahoga National Park, USA • Standedge Tunnel Visitor Centre, Huddersfield, England
Famous and historic buildings	• Alcatraz Jail, San Francisco Bay, USA • The Colosseum, Rome, Italy • Fountains Abbey, Ripon, England
Monuments statues and sculptures	• The Angel of the North, Gateshead, England (see Fig. 14.4) • The Sphinx, Giza, Egypt • The Statue of Liberty, New York, USA
Reservoirs and dams	• Hoover Dam Visitor Center, Colorado, USA • Thames Barrier Visitor Centre, London, England • Upper Derwent Visitor Centre, Derbyshire, England
Sports stadiums	• Ajax Stadium, Amsterdam, The Netherlands • Old Trafford, Manchester, England • Santiago Bernabeu Stadium, Madrid, Spain
Towers and tall buildings with observation decks	• Blackpool Tower, Blackpool, England • Eurotower, Rotterdam, The Netherlands • Main Tower, Frankfurt, Germany
Windmills and wind farms	• De Valk Windmill, Leiden, The Netherlands • Denver Windmill, Norfolk, England • Scroby Sands Wind Farm Visitor Centre, Great Yarmouth, England

Fig. 14.3. Interpretive spectator facilities at Manchester Airport Aviation Viewing Park, UK.

Fig. 14.4. 'The Angel of the North' and interpretive information board, Gateshead, UK.

Technological and Political Factor: High-rise Edutainment

Generally located in large urban areas, observation decks and towers allow visitors a unique opportunity to view vast expanses of land from a height. Many observation decks are built on top of, or within, tall buildings that have primarily been built as office blocks or for commercial/residential usage. In contrast to this, observation towers have been built with the sole purpose of providing a unique high-rise tourist attraction. In Frankfurt, Germany, the Main Tower has a roof-based observation deck, but the majority of the building is used for offices, whereas the Sydney Tower, in Australia, was built with the primary purpose of being an observation tower (and communications/broadcast media transmitter).

Most observation decks and towers provide educational resources about their creation and history, as well as audio and visual information about the areas that can be seen from the tower, and typically there are also guides on hand to answer questions that visitors may have. As additional features some towers also provide hospitality in the form of bars and restaurants (sometimes revolving), as well as novelty areas such as glass-floored 'walks of faith', adding a little thrillertainment into the mix.

From the perspective of governments, having the world's tallest building or tower is a unique status symbol that demonstrates superior technological capability. As a consequence of this, the world's top ten tallest buildings and towers change frequently, see Fig. 14.5.

EDUCATIONAL SHOWS AND DISPLAYS

GUIDED TOURS

Guided tours involve an audience of people being taken around a specific location by a tour guide who imparts his/her knowledge about that location. Typically this will include facts about any one or more of the following aspects of that location: history, geography, culture, religion, society, arts, architecture, business, politics, environment, science and nature. The duty of a tour guide is to aid visitors with interpreting the area that they are being guided around, and consequently a tour guide needs to be expertly knowledgeable, able to control an audience and be a clear, confident public speaker – as such, they are storytellers and entertainers in their own right.

From a tourism context, guided tours can be traced back to the mid-17th century and the days of 'the grand tour' when young male European socialites were taken across Europe by a guide to 'finish off' their education and immerse them in languages, culture, politics and art that were largely 'alien' to the area from which they were from. Participants in the grand tour would take educational instruction from their tour guide. The grand tour was especially popular among young British noblemen who would travel on horseback across Europe on a journey that could take several years.

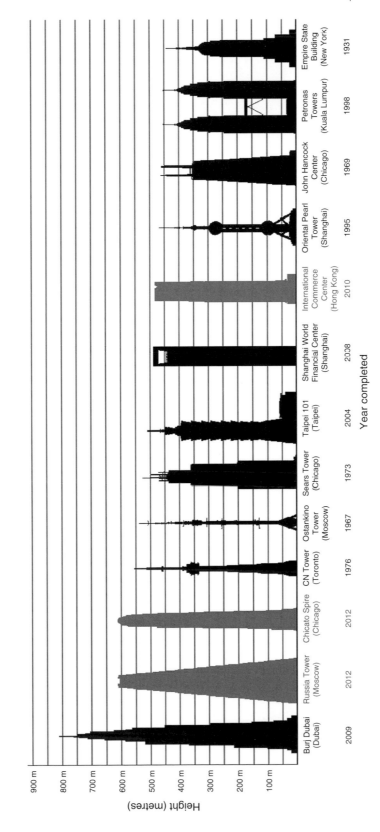

Fig. 14.5. The tallest buildings and towers in the world with public viewing facilities. (Image courtesy of Declan Warda.)

Fig. 14.6. A falconry display, Costa Del Sol, Spain.

Table 14.2. Educational shows and displays by category.

Type of show/display	Characteristics
Adult education class (non-formal)	This is something outside of the formal education system, where adults attend classes (recreationally and for socialization) that are designed to impart upon them new skills. The tutor is the entertainer and leads the group in a way which is intended to be perceived as being enjoyable, satisfying or rewarding by participants
Animal shows	Often found within zoos, aquariums and theme parks, animal shows involve novel routines being performed by trained animals, while the host or facilitator provides explanative commentary about the animals (see Fig. 14.6)
Conference	This involves a number of presenters leading discussion and debate on a particular theme or topic, and really is on the periphery of entertainment due to the fact that most attendees or delegates are present for the purposes of work, business or education. There are, however, a minority of attendees or delegates at many conferences who attend recreationally to be entertained by those who are speaking at the conference

(Continued)

Table 14.2. Continued.

Type of show/display	Characteristics
Art and craft demonstrations	This involves an individual with a particular creative skill, practically demonstrating his or her skill to an audience, who are often then encouraged to purchase these 'hand-crafts' (also sellertainment)
Historic re-enactment	This involves a group of people performing a routine that depicts a particular event from history while a commentator gives explanative commentary to the audience. Historic re-enactments usually take place outside, sometimes in very large open areas due to the size and scale of the number of participants involved
Transport show	This is a large-scale, and often, open-air display that involves a particular kind of transport being displayed statically or driven/flown/manoeuvred around a particular location while explanative commentary is broadcast to the audience

Fig. 14.7. An open-top bus tour around Belfast, Northern Ireland.

Fig. 14.8. An official tour guide explains local plant and wildlife to an audience in a forest in The Gambia.

The concept of guiding an audience for pleasure or recreation around a specific area or location goes even further back than this; in ancient Greek, Roman and Chinese societies, selected and well-connected fee-paying audiences could be guided around sites of political or religious significance.

Today tour guiding can be found in a variety of guises and in a plethora of locations. Some of the more common locations are: urban areas, where groups of people may be guided around a town or city; historical edutainment attractions, where a tour guide may act as a storyteller or heritage interpreter; rural areas, where a guide may provide information relating to the bio-diversity, land formations and highlight the natural phenomena. Table 14.3 highlights some of the more common forms of guided tour that take place today.

Table 14.3. Guided tours by category.

Type of guided tour	Characteristics
Attraction tours	While the word 'attraction' is slightly ambiguous, this type of guided tour refers specifically to an audience being taken around an attraction's premises, such as a building and/or its grounds, rather than a wider area such as a city. Attraction tours commonly take place in heritage

(Continued)

Table 14.3. Continued.

Type of guided tour	Characteristics
	attractions such as stately homes and castles. In North America, tour guides of heritage attractions are often referred to as docents (a term rarely used elsewhere). Attraction tours may also take place in sports stadiums where there could be a need to regulate visitor movements, as well as industrial and scientific attractions that may require interpretation to aid the audience's understanding
Audio tour	A relatively modern innovation, the audio tour often involves an audience of one listening to information and following instruction from a hand-held electronic audio device. While listening, an individual is guided towards specific locations within an attraction's premises, such as a building and/or its grounds. Audio tours commonly take place in heritage attractions such as stately homes and castles. Audio tours may also take place in industrial and scientific attractions that may require interpretation to aid the audience's understanding
Big wheel	This involves an audience of people being taken for a ride on board a large big wheel ride that offers unique views over a particular location. Big wheels are usually guided by a running audio commentary, but sometimes a tour guide is present dependent on the size of the passenger capsules
Bus tour	This involves an audience of people being driven around a specific area such as the streets of a town or city, or on a longer distance cross-country journey while a tour guide addresses the audience via a public address system about location-specific information (see Fig. 14.7). Longer tours usually involve 'stop-offs' at points of interest, and can sometimes form the basis of a holiday when accommodation is included. Buses can be anything ranging in size from a 'mini-bus' to a 'double-decker' bus, and are sometimes novelty vehicles such as ex-military amphibious 'ducks' or converted yellow school buses
Cable car tour	This involves an audience of people being taken on a cable car ride that offers views over a particular location. Cable car tours are guided by either a tour guide or a running audio commentary. This is usually determined by the size of the cable car/gondola
Cave and cavern tour	As the name suggests, Cave and cavern tours take place underground, usually in large caves or caverns that can accommodate an audience of several people or more. An audience on one of these tours is guided by an expert guide who can speak extensively about the geology, history and any wildlife associated with the cave(s) or cavern(s) they are in

(Continued)

Table 14.3. Continued.

Type of guided tour	Characteristics
City walk	This involves an audience of people being taken on foot around the streets of a town or city, while a tour guide addresses the audience about aspects of that location. Some city walks have specific themes such as architectural walks, historic walks and ghost walks
Pleasure flight	This involves an audience of people being taken on a journey in some form of aircraft, usually an aeroplane, helicopter or hot air balloon. The audience is accompanied by an expert guide (who may also be the pilot) who usually gives information about the aircraft, and the area over which the aircraft is travelling
Pleasure cruise	This involves an audience of people being taken on some form of boat along or across a body of water, while either a prerecorded tape or a tour guide addresses the audience about location-specific information via a public address system. Pleasure cruises are common in cities that have major rivers running through them, as well as coastal locations that are popular with tourists. There are specific types of pleasure cruise such as 'whale-watching' tours, 'crocodile cruises', and tours in glass-bottomed boats where the audience are in attendance to witness the spectacle of 'naturtainment'
Rail tour	Rail tours (sometimes referred to as scenic railways) involve the transportation of audiences in rail-based mass transport systems, namely trams, steam locomotives, loco-hauled trains and mono-rails. Rail tours are slightly unique for two reasons: first, the motivation to participate in them is often down to the experience of travelling on a particular type of train, and typical examples of this are a preserved steam locomotive being run on a cross-country journey or a tram ride around a major city; and second, rail tours do not always include a 'guide' as such or any form of running audio commentary. Instead rail tours are often staffed by costumed 'cast members' to help make the experience of the journey more authentic, these people can often be called up for questions about the train or journey. Long rail tours on trains may include accommodation which can form the basis of a holiday for participants
Safari	This is a land-based guided tour which is most common in large eco-sensitive areas that are largely unspoiled by man, and where natural flora and fauna flourish. Consequently safaris usually take place in less-developed countries (particularly African countries). Safaris often involve an audience of people travelling in vehicle(s) (although walking safaris

(Continued)

Table 14.3. Continued.

Type of guided tour	Characteristics
	are also commonplace; see Fig. 14.8) along with experienced guide(s) who are there to share their knowledge of the local environment, particularly its plants and animals. The major attraction of safaris is the ability to witness animals in their own natural environment, which is another example of 'naturtainment'. Some safaris form the basis of holidays, and can last a number of days

MEDIA-DISTRIBUTED EDUTAINMENT

Media-distributed edutainment is distributed or broadcast using an electronic or paper-based format. As media-distributed edutainment is media-reliant, it transcends several sectors of the entertainment industry (broadcast media, printed media and the Internet). The main forms of media-distributed edutainment are detailed in Table 14.4.

Table 14.4. Media-distributed edutainment by category.

Type of media-distributed edutainment	Characteristics
Books and journals (non-fiction)	Written paper-based printed media publication that includes informative books and periodical magazines/journals that focus upon a particular non-fictitious subject
Computer-based edutainment	Advances in computing technology have led to the development of programmes that are designed to educate those who interact with them. This may be direct knowledge development programmes such as training software for a specific function, e.g. first aid or languages, or this could be game-based software such as flight simulators
Documentaries	Programmes broadcast most commonly by television, but also radio, which focus on a particular non-fictitious subject
News and current affairs programmes	Programmes broadcast by television and radio that focus on current and topical happenings
Newspaper	Written paper-based printed media publication that contains news, information and often advertising. Newspapers are typically printed daily or weekly
Web sites (factual)	Internet sites on the World Wide Web (WWW) that contain non-fictitious factual information, often on a particular subject

MUSEUMS

A museum is an institution that is dedicated to the collection, care, study and display of items that are typically historical, scientific, natural, cultural or artistic in nature. Museum exhibits are displayed along with explanative and interpretive information for visitors to learn from. There are a variety of different types of museum; Table 14.5 gives their characteristics and provides examples.

Table 14.5. Museums by category.

Type of museum	Characteristics
Art gallery	This is typically a building that is used for the display and appreciation of predominantly visual artistic exhibits. This can include both traditional and contemporary (modern) art such as paintings, collages, sculptures, statues and moving images, as well as sounds. Art galleries are sometimes referred to as art museums
Botanical garden	This is an institution that typically holds large collections of plants. Botanic gardens are primarily scientific institutions that are concerned with plant research and conservation. Plants are displayed alongside information boards to be viewed by the visiting public
Exhibition	This is a temporary display often based around a specific theme. Exhibitions are often displayed in existing museums or buildings that can offer large versatile spaces. Large-scale exhibitions of this nature are now relatively rare, unless they are related to commercial purposes such as trade shows (this is also sellertainment)
Library[a]/archive	This is typically a building that contains collections of information. This is commonly in the form of printed media (usually books), as well as audio/visual materials, and archived information stored in other formats such as micro-fiche or CD-ROM
Mobile museum	This is typically a collection that is housed and displayed in a type of vehicle or trailer/container/coach that can be transported from one location to another. The contents of a mobile museum may be borrowed from a fixed collection or collections that are permanently mobile in order to maximize their exposure to new audiences
Open-air museum	This is typically a collection that is not housed in a building but instead outside in a specified area. This may be due to the size of the exhibits being too large to enclose (a good example of this being preserved railways), the necessity of enclosing exhibits being unnecessary or for artistic or realistic appreciation. Some open-air museums are recreations of times gone by where communities

(Continued)

Table 14.5. Continued.

Type of museum	Characteristics
	have been reconstructed to demonstrate how life was in a particular era, often with the use of actual people in period costume who act as 'cast members'. Others may be preservations of an actual area or site so that future generations can see how people lived – or died
Industrial museum	This is a museum based in an existing and fully operational industrial facility, where visitors get to see 'behind the scenes' with regards to manufacturing and operational processes
Observatory/ planetarium	These are themed science museums that are concerned with astronomy and the study of the universe. They often contain interactive exhibits aimed at children. The unique feature of planetariums is a concave circular ceiling-based cinema screen that is projected on to from a central floor-level camera, which vertically projects a full circular cinematic image on the ceiling above. The audience sit beneath this, looking upwards and listening to explanative commentary. Many planetarium buildings have a distinct domed roof due to the cinema inside
Stately homes	Typically buildings that have a historic significance, as being the ex- or current home of a person or family of some nobility or wealth, in which a collection of art and/or artefacts is displayed for the appreciation of visitors. The uniqueness about these types of museums is their rich history which makes the buildings attractions in their own right, especially preserved or restored structures and estates/gardens
Specialist museums	Typically a collection of a specific type that is housed within a building or other venue for the appreciation of visitors. These collections can be extremely varied in nature, but often have either a historical, artistic or cultural theme
Virtual museums	An archive or collection of audio/visual resources that has been stored on the World Wide Web for the appreciation of visitors to the virtual museum web site. These are sometimes online representations of actual museum collections, as well as archives of materials that are no longer on public display
Wax museum	This is a museum which features exhibits that are effigies of celebrities and other famous people that have been created and sculpted using wax

(Continued)

Table 14.5. Continued.

Type of museum	Characteristics
Zoo	This is a museum that features living animal exhibits in a 'mock-up' of their natural living environment. Zoo is an abbreviation of the term 'zoological garden'. The first zoos were private collections owned by wealthy collectors, and can be dated as far back as ancient China and Egypt over a thousand years BC. Many zoos today have a conservation remit to help endangered species, as well as carrying out research and providing education. There are several specialist types of zoos that concentrate on particular animal groups. Some of the more common ones are: • Aquarium – specializing in the display of aquatic animals and plants (see Fig. 14.9). • Aviary – specializing in the display of birds. • Safari park – an open area of parkland in which animals can roam almost freely and which visitors can usually drive through. These often feature African and Asian mammals.

[a] It is worthy of note that libraries are not always considered to be museums, particularly in the UK.

Fig. 14.9. An audience stand mesmerized at an aquarium.

Ethical Factor: Dark Tourism

Dark tourism is a term used to describe the visitation of sites that were once associated with death, suffering or disaster. Creating edutainment facilities at these sites is something that does not sit comfortably with many people and raises the ethical and moral question as to whether it is 'right' to do so. Auschwitz-Birkenau Concentration Camp in Poland is one of the sites of the world's single largest atrocity in history, the genocide of Jews by Nazi Germany in the Second World War. The 'final solution' at Auschwitz led to over a million people – mostly Jews, but also prisoners of war, political objectors, homosexuals and gypsies (among others) – from all over Europe being gassed, worked, starved and tortured to death. In 1947, a museum was built at Auschwitz to commemorate those who had died and educate visitors as to the true atrocities that occurred there. In 1979, Auschwitz was made a world heritage site by the United Nations Educational, Scientific and Cultural Organization (UNESCO), in recognition of the unique role that it played in history, and to promote peace among future generations through education of past atrocities. To date 25 million people have visited the museum (Auschwitz-Birkenau State Museum, 2008), with this number set to rise even further with the increase in the number of budget airlines that are flying to nearby Krakow from other European destinations. The very notion that such a setting could be considered an entertainment venue is a very uncomfortable one for many. But this is considering the word entertainment as something 'light' or 'happy' which is an outdated use of the word. Auschwitz exhibits are designed to educate visitors, and in doing so often cause an emotional response among those who feel an empathetic connection with what they are seeing, hearing and reading about. This is edutainment at its most raw controversial edge, but it is undeniably edutainment, which is both captivating and educational, and participated in by (mostly) tourists as part of their recreation.

Case Study: the National Media Museum, Bradford, UK

Britain's National Media Museum (NMM) opened in June 1983 as the National Museum of Photography, Film and Television (NMPFT). It is a subsidiary of the London-based National Museum of Science and Industry (NMSI), which is the overseeing government body for several of Britain's National Museums, and apart from the NMM, these include: The Science Museum (London), The National Railway Museum (York) and The Locomotion Museum (County Durham).

The 1970s and 1980s witnessed many towns and cities in Northern England experiencing economic downturns, in the face of local primary industries (coal, steel and textiles) being downsized or closed altogether in the face of cheaper foreign imports. This led to high unemployment, and in many areas unused, decaying and often polluted 'brown-belt' (former industrial) land, which contributed to much of northern England gaining a

(Continued)

Case Study: Continued.

negative image in comparison to the more affluent south, often referred to as 'the north–south divide'. Bradford is a city with an industrial past centred on the wool industry, which by the mid-20th century had almost disappeared, leaving the city in financial decline. The city of Bradford was targeted by the government for a number of social improvement schemes including the location of the then NMPFT which, as a national collection, was hoped to help bolster tourism in Bradford City Centre. Many areas around Bradford already had relatively high levels of tourism (Howarth with its preserved railway, cobbled streets and Bronte sisters connection, and Saltaire as a UNESCO world heritage site), and the hope was that the NMPFT could tap into this visitor market – even helping to make Bradford the base for holidays as well as day visits, with the ultimate aim of the city undergoing a modern urban renaissance.

The National Media Museum name change occurred in December 2006 with a good deal of publicity. The rationale for the name change being as follows:

- Advances in computing technology, gaming and particularly the Internet were having a profound impact upon the ways by which media such as television, radio and photographs were being created, stored, distributed and accessed. The museum's collections needed to become increasingly technological in order to keep up with this. This has included public Internet facilities and other interactive computer terminals, as well as new areas dedicated to gaming technology which are outside the parameters of 'photography, film and television'.
- Although the museum has attracted 12 million visitors since it opened in 1983, it had seen a steady decline in visitor numbers since 2001; in 2003, it received 750,000 visitors, and in 2006, this had further fallen to 652,400. It was believed that a new stronger brand identity that better reflected the museum's more technological content might help boost museum admissions. After the name change in 2007, the museum had 715,800 visits (up 9% on the previous year). It could be argued that rebranding has contributed to increased visitor numbers, although The Association of Leisure Visitor Attractions (ALVA) reported similar increases in admissions for a number of Britain's museums over the same period (ALVA, 2008).
- The old 'National Museum of Photography, Film and Television' name was cumbersome, and often erroneously referred to in local media and newspapers, as well as being incorrectly named by people in the locality as a variety of names including: 'The Film Museum'; 'The Film, TV and Photo Museum'; 'The Bradford Museum; and 'The IMAX'.

As technology advances and 'media' breaks new boundaries, the museum will begin to cover more areas, the most recent of which is gaming, where new interactive displays and consoles have become available for visitors to use. It is likely that the proliferation

(Continued)

Case Study: Continued.

and integration of the Internet into our everyday lives will lead to new areas for the museum to showcase – including audio exhibits – particularly radio, as well as greater integration of National Media Museum exhibits with other areas from within the National Museum for Science and Industry. Future exhibitions may also celebrate lasting media influences from the 20th century, including television, film, news/journalism and popular music. At present, the museum does not have exhibitions dedicated to the printed media, and this could also be a future growth area. It is likely that with a growing number of exhibits and collections that there will be a future need for the museum to expand further or create a second site.

Case study based upon NMM (2008a,b) and Moss (2006).

Table 14.6. History of the National Media Museum.

Year	Feature
1983	The museum opened on 16 June as the National Museum of Photography, Film and Television with a remit to cover the art and science involved in these mediums. It was built with Europe's first IMAX cinema
1985	The Bradford Fellowship was launched, allowing local artists to develop and exhibit their work at the museum
1986	Two television galleries were developed to mark the 50th anniversary of the first public television broadcasts
1989	The Kodak photography gallery and a live television broadcast studio were opened at the museum
1992	The Pictureville Cinema was opened, where movies in a variety of formats could be screened
1993	A three-projector cinerama system was installed in the Pictureville Cinema complete with a panelled curving screen. The TV Heaven facility was also opened, whereby visitors could watch old archives of television programmes
1994	The Bradford Animation Festival was launched in June
1995	The Bradford Film Festival was launched
1997	The museum closed its doors in August for a 19-month period of refurbishment and extension
1999	The museum was reopened on 16 June by the then James Bond actor Pierce Brosnan. The Cubby Broccoli Cinema was also opened, and the IMAX cinema was also upgraded so that it could show 3D films. A new television studio as well as a cafe and a shop also opened

(Continued)

Table 14.6. Continued.

Year	Feature
2000	The museum had 1 million visitors boosted by the 'Art of Star Wars' exhibition, which had attracted over 30,000 extra visitors to the museum by December (Bradford Telegraph and Argus, 2000)
2001	Visitor numbers rose further when the British government made all National Museums and Collections free to enter. This in itself caused the museum problems with congestion (consequently a lack of seating between galleries was identified); additional wear and tear on facilities; and extra frontline staff being required. There was expansion of the retail, catering, pay-in attractions (such as the simulator) and conferencing facilities to help finance this
2002	The hugely successful James Bond exhibition visited the museum in time for the 20th Bond film *Die Another Day* which was also released later that year
2003	The Royal Photographic Society Collection was acquired by the museum with the aid of a National Lottery grant. BBC Bradford Studios opened within the museum allowing for live broadcasts by BBC Radio Leeds, BBC Asian Network and BBC Local News to be seen by museum visitors
2006	The Experience TV gallery opened, and in December the museum was renamed the National Media Museum
2008	Twenty-fifth anniversary celebrations were held at the museum, including a new exhibit charting the museum's history

NATURTAINMENT EDUCATIONAL FACILITIES

Naturtainment is a term for spectacles and phenomena that occur in the natural world, which can engage or captivate an audience. There is often a high degree of novelty in naturtainment, in the sense that what the audience experience is something that they rarely get to witness. Examples of naturtainment include: large dramatic waterfalls, an erupting volcano, flocks of migrating birds, geysers, tidal bores and unusual rock formations. Naturtainment is not controlled or managed by man, but naturtainment spectacles and phenomena are controlled entirely by events in the natural world, and consequently naturtainment is *not* a part of the entertainment industry.

Many naturtainment sites are recognized as being visitor attractions, and subsequently have had educational facilities built, such as visitor centres or observation platforms. The intention of these is usually to help audiences interpret and understand the naturtainment that they are witnessing, and, as such, these facilities are edutainment venues. Table 14.7 contains some typical examples of naturtainment sites, along with actual examples of accompanying edutainment venues.

Table 14.7. Naturtainment attraction types by category.

Naturtainment attraction	Example edutainment facility
Coastal	• Gulf Coast Visitor Center, Florida, USA • The Isle of Wight Coastal Visitors Centre, Isle of Wight, Great Britain • Scottish Seabird Centre, North Berwick, Scotland
Canyons and gorges	• Cheddar Gorge Visitor Centre, Somerset, England • Grand Canyon Visitor Center, Arizona, USA • Red Rock Canyon Visitor Center, Nevada, USA
Caves and caverns	• Mammoth Cave Visitor Center, Kentucky, USA • Waitomo i-SITE Visitor Centre, Waitomo, New Zealand • White Scar Cave Visitor Centre, Ingleborough, England
Cliffs and crags	• Creswell Crags Visitor Centre, Derbyshire, England • Knockan Crag Visitor Centre, Ullapool, Scotland • The White Cliffs of Dover Gateway Visitor Centre, Kent, England
Forests and woodland	• Afan Forest Park Visitor Centre, Neath, Wales • Sherwood Forest Visitor Centre, Nottinghamshire, England • Tilamook Forest Center, Oregon, USA
Geological/rock formations	• Giant's Causeway Visitor Centre, Bushmills, Northern Ireland • Uluru-Kata Tjuta Cultural Centre, Northern Territory, Australia • Blue Mountains Visitor Information Centre, Katoomba, Australia
Glaciers	• Begich Boggs Glacier Visitor Center, Alaska, USA • Fox Glacier Visitor Centre, Westland National Park, New Zealand • Mendenhall Glacier Visitor Center, Alaska, USA
Geothermal	• Calpine Geothermal Visitor Center, California, USA • Gjáin Visitor Centre, Gjáin, Iceland • Old Faithful Visitor Center, Wyoming, USA
Lakes and rivers	• Kabetogama Lake Visitor Center, Minnesota, USA • Loch Ness Visitor Centre, Loch Ness, Scotland • The River Thames Visitor Centre, Surrey, England
Mountains and volcanoes	• Mount Snowdon Visitor Centre, Snowdonia, Wales • Mount St Helens Visitor Center, Washington, USA • Mount Fuji Visitor Centre, Yamanshi, Japan

(Continued)

Table 14.7. Continued.

Naturtainment attraction	Example edutainment facility
Nature reserves, parklands and national parks	• Brecon Beacons National Park Visitor Centre, Brecon, Wales, UK • Salim Ali Visitor Centre, Keoladeo, India • Sweetwaters Game Reserve Visitor Information Centre, Kenya
Waterfalls	• Great Falls Visitor Information Center, Montana, USA • Linville Falls Visitor Center, North Carolina, USA • Niagara Falls Visitor Center, Niagara Falls, USA

THE FUTURE

The future for the majority of the edutainment sector is bright, with forecasted increases in tourism globally and the recognition that attractions are the key drivers in most tourism systems (Swarbrooke, 2001). Edutainment attractions will get bigger, larger museums will house ever-growing diverse collections, and vaster more spectacular creations in the built environment will lead to growth in the number of built environment edutainment attractions. Novelty, status and prestige will become the 'selling points' for edutainment (see Fig. 14.10).

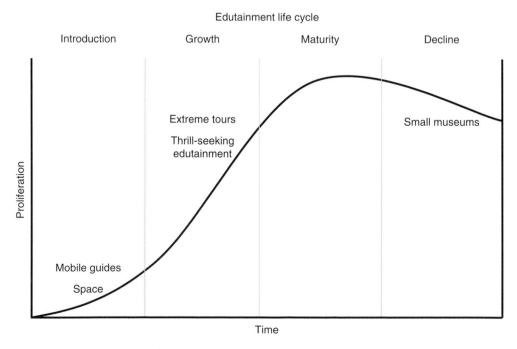

Fig. 14.10. Edutainment life cycle.

Introduction

Mobile guides – there will be a proliferation of services offered at edutainment attractions (venues, and larger areas such as cities) to people with their own mobile devices. Official podcasts and guides will be available to download from attraction web sites, as well as there being Bluetooth on-demand services at the sites themselves, e.g. 'press this button if you would like a podcast guide transmitting to your mobile device'.

Space – commercial pleasure flights in space are no longer the dreams of science fiction writers. In July 2008, Virgin Galactic showcased an aircraft that will be used to take tourists into space. As of July 2008, more than 250 people have already paid US$200,000 per head to be among the first to make this journey (BBC, 2008).

Growth

Extreme tours – in the natural environment, growth edutainment areas will include guided walks and tours through unchartered and hostile wilderness areas, which are increasingly being brought to our attention through television programmes such as *Bear Grylls* (*Born Survivor/ Man Vs Wild/Ultimate Survival*), *Ice Road Truckers*, *Survivorman*, *Deadliest Catch*, and *Ax Men* (to name but a few documentary series). This will be further fuelled by big screen movie adaptions of these titles, such as Twentieth Century Fox's purchase of the movie rights for *Ice Road Truckers* (Fleming, 2008a).

Thrill-seeking edutainment – growth in thrill-seeking recreational pursuits continues, a current example of this is at Sydney Harbour Bridge, which has had its own museum and visitor centre for a number of years; however, since 1998 visitors can now go a step further and go on a guided walk on the bridge structure – at a premium price of around US$180–280 per head, and this has proven to be a success with over 2 million people climbing in the first 10 years of operation (BridgeClimb, 2008). In 2007, a glass-floored horseshoe shaped 'skywalk' was unveiled at the Grand Canyon, Arizona. This allows visitors to walk on a see-through floor at a height of 1200 m above the canyon floor. To access this, visitors must pay almost US$60 per head for both passage to the attraction site, and then access to physically walk upon the sky walk. This will not have gone unnoticed among managers of other large and spectacular attractions (particularly in the built environment), and others will very possibly imitate this with outside sky walks becoming features of tall buildings and towers (such as Sydney Tower Skywalk), or at a very extreme level, we may even see the first bungee jumps or 'swings of faith' appearing hundreds of metres above our city streets.

Decline

Small museums – small independent museums that appeal to niche markets and operate on a limited budget that cannot afford to update their facilities as regularly as large heavily funded and sponsored collections will face closure. This has already happened in the UK with the Cumberland Toy and Model Museum closing in 2005 due to increasing costs and reduced visitor numbers (Moore, 2005).

REFERENCES

Association of Leading Visitor Attractions (2008) Visits made in 2007 to visitor attractions in membership with ALVA. [Internet] London, ALVA. Available at: http://www.alva.org.uk/visitor_statistics/

Auschwitz-Birkenau State Museum (2008) Auschwitz-Birkenau Memorial and Museum. [Internet] ABSM, Poland. Available at: http://www.auschwitz.org.pl/new/index.php?language=EN&tryb=start&id=675&menu=g

Bradford Telegraph and Argus (2000) Star Wars show out of this world. [Internet] Bradford, Newsquest Media Group. Available at: http://archive.thetelegraphandargus.co.uk/2000/12/7/146392.html.

BridgeClimb. (2008) About us. [Internet] Sydney, Otto Holdings. Available at: http://www.bridgeclimb.com/aboutUs/default.htm

British Broadcasting Corporation (2008) Branson unveils space tourism jet. [Internet] BBC, London. Available at: http://news.bbc.co.uk/1/hi/sci/tech/7529978.stm

Findlen, P. (1989) The museum: its classical etymology and renaissance genealogy. *Journal of the History of Collections* (1), 59–78.

Fleming, M. (2008a) Fox drivers 'truckers' to big screen. [Internet] Los Angeles, Variety. Available at: http://www.variety.com/article/VR1117980821.html?categoryid=13&cs=1&nid=2565

Fleming, N. (2008b) The VARK categories. [Internet] Lincoln, New Zealand, Neil Fleming. Available at: http://www.vark-learn.com/english/page.asp?p=categories

Moore, R. (2005) Cumberland toy and model museum. [Internet] Cockermouth, Rod Moore MBE. Available at: http://www.toymuseum.co.uk/

Moss, S. (2006) Visit: The National Museum of Photography, Film and Television. [Internet] Leeds, Entertainment Planet. Available at: http://entplanet.blogspot.com/2006/11/visit-national-museum-of-photography.html

National Media Museum (2008a) Celebrate our 25th anniversary. [Exhibition] Bradford, National Media Museum. Viewed 30 July 2008.

National Media Museum (2008b) Museum's future and history. [Internet] Bradford, NMM. Available at: http://www.nationalmediamuseum.org.uk/General/MuseumFutureHistory.asp

Swarbrooke, J. (2001) *The Development and Management of Visitor Attractions*. Butterworth-Heinemann, Oxford.

chapter 15

Sellertainment

Stuart Moss

Entertainment that is designed to increase uptake among the audience of a product, belief or ideal.

Advertising has been around for many thousands of years; archaeologists have found the remnants of written advertisements in ancient Egyptian, Roman and Greek ruins. A formally recognized advertising industry did not appear until the 17th century, when improvements in technology led to printing presses being developed, and improvements in education meant that a more literate population could actually read advertisements that were printed as posters or leaflets. It would be another 200 years before newspaper space would be sold to advertisers in order to help subsidize printing costs. Radio advertising first appeared in the 1920s, and was followed by television advertising in the 1950s. Advertising slogans and storylines began to appear in cohesive promotional campaigns utilizing a number of promotional mediums in the 1960s. In the 1980s, shopping channels and channels dedicated to specific products began to appear in the USA on cable television, and in the 1990s, the launch of the commercial Internet heralded a brand new media by which to convey advertising messages. Nobody really knows exactly how many advertising messages we are exposed to each day. An interrogation of several respected business journals, asking this very question for US citizens, revealed a number of studies that gave answers ranging from 247 to 3000 – whatever the answer actually is, there are *lots*. In an increasingly competitive business environment, promotion through advertising has taken on many forms in order to remain ahead of the competition. Many sellers and advertisers are now using entertainment in order to capture the attention of an audience and get their message across – this is sellertainment.

In order to have an impact upon those exposed to sellertainment, it needs to be attention-grabbing, sensory-stimulating (typically visually, audibly or both), and engaging. Sellertainment that is effective follows the principle of AIDA, it grabs the audience's attention – by being noticeable and captivating; interest – telling a story that provokes an emotion; desire – the emotional impact leaves the audience wanting; and action – the audience buy into what the sellertainment is promoting. In order for sellertainment to effectively achieve this, it is usually professionally designed and managed, and, as such, is a creative art form; the advertising industry is classified as being within the creative industries (DCMS, 2008). Donaton (2005) notes that the advertising and entertainment industries are intrinsically linked, and predicts an ever-strengthening unity between these formerly distinct areas, with an increasing uptake of promotional creative entertainment to sell products.

The sellertainment triangle is a variant on the 'sales funnel'; it is intended to demonstrate the stages that are traversed in the relationship between a successful sellertainment tool and its audience, as featured in Fig. 15.1.

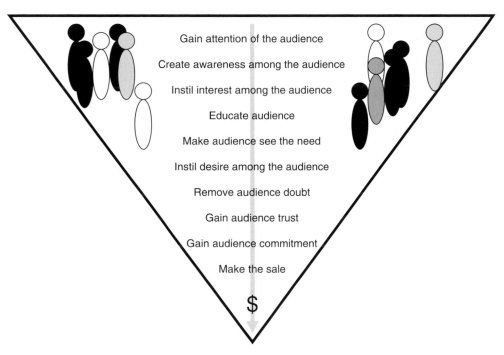

Fig. 15.1. The sellertainment triangle.

It is clear from the Figure 15.1 that a sellertainment tool must convince its audience that what it is promoting is right for them, and it must also instil trust and belief in the seller's integrity.

Sellertainment is promotion, but not all forms of promotion are sellertainment. Promotion is 'the publicizing of a product, organization, or venture so as to increase sales or public awareness. Also: a publicity campaign; the activity of organizing publicity campaigns' (OED, 2008). It is one of the four Ps of Kotler's marketing mix (price, product, place and promotion) (Kotler *et al.*, 2008), and is typically demonstrated through advertising, branding and publicity (public relations) activity. Within the service sector, where products being offered to markets are variable and not always obligatory, promotion is necessary, so that potential customers can be kept informed about what is available for acquisition.

A theatre is an example of a venue that offers a variety of products, the predominant one being staged performances, but typically also catering facilities, bars, cloakrooms and education space. Staged performances tend to play for a set period of time, some may last one night only, while others may last for several weeks. In order for potential customers to be kept informed of when performances are taking place, as well as information about performance contents, times and the prices, it is necessary to promote this information. The methods by which theatres undertake promotion can vary significantly depending on a number of factors including the suitability of promotional mediums, cost and who the target audiences are for the product(s) being promoted.

Typical examples of the ways by which theatres promote their products include the following:

- brochures that contain information about performances over a specific time period (often monthly, bimonthly and seasonal);
- mail shots to existing customers who have disclosed their contact details and agreed to be put on a mailing list;
- posters including those placed outside and within theatres, as well upon billboards next to roads, and in areas with a high volume of passers-by such as transport interchanges;
- leaflets and flyers for specific performances or detailing special offers and loyalty or membership schemes;
- newspaper and magazine advertisements, particularly those with a high regional or local distribution;
- banner advertisements placed upon buses for specific performances;
- advertisements placed upon local commercial radio stations, usually to promote specific performances;
- advertisements placed upon local commercial television stations, usually to promote specific performances;
- web sites (both official web sites and a social network web presence) that should contain detailed information about the theatre, performances, facilities (typically disabled, parking, catering) and sometimes 'other information' including history, job vacancies, loyalty or membership schemes, location information and contact details;
- e-mail information bulletins, bulletins to those who have subscribed to e-mail lists; and
- text message information bulletins to those who have elected to give their mobile phone numbers.

It is typical to use a variety of the above methods when undertaking an advertising campaign (sometimes referred to as a marketing campaign or a promotional campaign); there are advantages and disadvantages to all of them, as well as variable costs, which make some forms of promotion more appealing than others to advertisers. Sellertainment sub-sectors are identified in Fig. 15.2, overleaf.

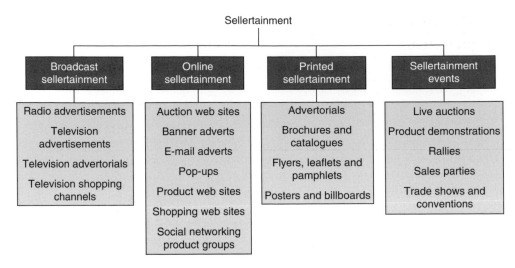

Fig. 15.2. Sellertainment sub-sectors.

The above sellertainment sub-sectors include both 'push' and 'pull' promotional techniques. Push promotion sends out a blanket message to an audience, and it is typically high in volume and visible. The disadvantage of push promotion is that those who are exposed to it may not be interested in it, and therefore costs can be incurred that are 'wasted', and it is also difficult to track at the point of promotion *who* exactly was interested in the promotion. Pull promotions are not specifically audience-targeted or distributed, but are accessed by those who are seeking information, therefore they 'pull' in an audience, and in theory can be more cost-effective than push promotions. Some forms of sellertainment demonstrate characteristics of both push and pull promotions. Table 15.1 demonstrates which sellertainment methods are push and pull promotions.

Table 15.1. Push and pull promotional sellertainment.

Push promotion	Pull promotion
Advertorials	Auctions
Banner advertisements	Auction web sites
Brochures and catalogues	Banner advertisements
Commercial radio advertisements	Brochures and catalogues
Commercial television advertisements	Flyers, leaflets and pamphlets
E-mail advertisements	Product demonstrations
Flyers	Product web sites

(Continued)

Table 15.1. Continued.

Push promotion	Pull promotion
Leaflets	Rallies
Newspaper and magazine advertisements	Sales parties
Pop-ups	Shopping web sites
Posters	Social networking product groups
Television advertorials	Television shopping channels
Television shopping channels	Tradeshows and conventions

BROADCAST SELLERTAINMENT

Possibly the most visible form of sellertainment, it is that which is broadcast through the media – particularly television. Broadcast sellertainment is typically professionally made by production companies and film makers, who seek to produce a high-impact promotional product that is only seen and/or heard for a short period of time. Broadcast sellertainment types are outlined in Table 15.2, below.

Table 15.2. Types of broadcast sellertainment and their characteristics.

Type of broadcast sellertainment	Characteristics
Radio advertisements	Scripted radio advertisements have been in existence since the 1920s, and they tend to feature a combination of the spoken word and/or music often combined with sound effects. Some radio advertisements take a storyboard format, so that the listener can visualize and imagine what is taking place, which can be potentially powerful. The main disadvantage of radio advertising is the fact that listeners can easily be distracted from it, and so its potential to captivate an audience is lessened. Some radio advertisements take the form of programme sponsorship announcements prior to, and after, programmes have been broadcast, as well as at the beginning and end of commercial breaks
Television advertisements	Television advertisements or commercials have been in existence since 1941, when the first television advertisement was aired in the USA upon channels owned by retailers (see Chapter 6, this volume). Drama programmes were named 'soap

(Continued)

Table 15.2. Continued.

Type of broadcast sellertainment	Characteristics
	operas' (abbreviated to soaps) due to advertisements by soap manufacturers being featured within them. This highlights the importance of advertisements being targeted towards the right audiences; a major audience during the 1960s and 1970s for drama programmes was women, who would often be home during the day while their husbands were working. Advertising that would be appealing to woman (cleaning, sanitary and pharmaceutical products) was therefore broadcast. Contemporary society is now very different, and soap operas are viewed by a much wider audience, and as such, they feature a much wider array of advertisements. Television advertisements are mostly under a minute in length, and involve a storyline that is typically portrayed through the use of any of the following: actors, graphics, special effects, words displayed on the screen; artistic cinematography and music. Television advertisements have been used for a wide variety of reasons including: product sales, political broadcasts, highlighting global issues, and public information films. Television advertising has proved to be a good source of revenue generation for channel operators, but not always popular with viewers who may not like interruptions throughout the programmes that they are watching. In the USA and Australia, television advertisements are particularly regular, an example being up to five commercial breaks being incorporated into an episode of *The Simpsons* making a 23 min programme last well over 30 min in some cases. This gives a fragmented viewing experience. Personal Video Recorders (PVRs) such as TiVo are now available and can record programmes without commercial breaks, which is of course a concern to many broadcaster stakeholders who do not want to see advertising revenue cut because of this. Some television advertisements take the form of short programme sponsorship advertisements prior to, and after, programmes have been broadcast, as well as at the beginning and end of commercial breaks, and some advertisements are actually broadcast on-screen during programmes, although this is predominantly in North America

(Continued)

Table 15.2. Continued.

Type of broadcast sellertainment	Characteristics
Television advertorials	Generally longer than television advertisements (and also much more rare), television advertorials tend to be broadcast on cable or satellite channels where the 'air time' is cheaper. Television advertorials are often used in the same way as television advertisements, but tend to feature longer storylines so that the viewer is more likely to be captivated by it
Television shopping channels	The availability of cable/satellite and digital television has led to the segmentation of channels with many solely providing specialist content – this includes 'shopping' channels that are entirely made up of advertising content such as QVC and Bid TV. These channels allow viewers to buy products as they are being advertised in a seemingly live environment by chatty hosts who often 'play act' or demonstrate these products to the viewing public. Some shopping channels 'share' their frequency with other channels that may only broadcast at certain times of day, allowing shopping channels to take up unused broadcasting capacity

ONLINE SELLERTAINMENT

The Internet is host to many forms of advertising; it offers a predominantly visual experience, although audio promotion via the Internet is also feasible. Internet promotion is typically via the World Wide Web (web) and often involves the creation of online content that is hosted on a web server. There are costs involved in this; web design is something that may be practised in-house or a paid-for service from a design agency. The cost of hosting content on a web server is another expense that web sites require, as is the registration and 'rent' of a domain name (.com/.org/.co.uk, etc.). The cumulative cost of producing and publishing a web site is usually less than placing advertisements on radio or television, and is very often less than producing large-scale paper-based promotional media. There are no distribution costs with web-based promotion, which can also attract a potentially global audience. 'It is becoming increasingly important for venues to have an online presence; e-mail listings and reminders can be sent to regulars detailing up-and-coming events' (Mintel, 2007). The various types of online sellertainment can be found in Table 15.3, overleaf.

Table 15.3. Types of online sellertainment and their characteristics.

Type of online sellertainment	Characteristics
Auction web sites	The excitement of bidding for, and winning, an item at auction has easily transferred from the physical to an online environment. The Internet has transformed auctions into a 21st-century phenomenon. Online auctions involve sellers advertising a product through written descriptions and photographs on to an auction web site. In order to do this, membership and a payment is usually required on behalf of the seller. Buyers browse auctions and enter an amount that they are willing to pay for a product before committing to bid. Most auctions last for a set period of time (an hour, a day, a week, a month) at the end of which the person who has bid the most wins, and is required to pay the seller either directly, or through a third-party web site (such as PayPal) for the item. There is also usually a shipping fee added to the final purchase price. Online auction site 'eBay' has proved incredibly popular since the late 1990s onwards, seeing off a number of competitors including 'Yahoo! Auctions' which ceased trading in the USA and Canada in 2007, and in most of the rest of the world during 2008
E-mail advertisements	E-mail and text promotions are controlled via Internet applications, and are considerably less expensive than many other forms of push promotion. However, in many countries they are governed by privacy legislation that limits their usage so as to avoid exposure to unwanted text messages and 'spam' e-mail. Those who are interested in receiving such promotions can 'opt-in' which makes those being targeted more likely to have an interest in the promotion. Due to misuse of e-mail by spammers, and criminals spreading viruses, or 'phishing' for user details, e-mails are often blocked by service providers, and their interactive content is often not displayed by e-mail programmes such as Microsoft Outlook. Consequently e-mail promotion is no longer perceived to be a good thing by many marketers, although if the problem of e-mail misuse can be completely overcome, e-mail promotion may rise again
Banner advertisements	These are advertisements placed upon web sites that are usually graphical in nature with some wording along them. The use of Flash and dynamic HTML often allows advertisements to run at video quality with the addition of sound and without taking too long to load. Banner advertisements are 'click-through' advertisements, which rely upon users clicking upon them if they are interested in

(Continued)

Table 15.3. Continued.

Type of online sellertainment	Characteristics
	going further into what they are promoting. Users that click upon them are typically taken to a different web page via their browser. Banner advertisements are both push promotion in the sense that they are placed upon web sites for all to see, but pull promotion in the sense that interested users must click upon them to find out further information. Banner advertisements are sometimes blocked so that their content cannot be seen by the security settings in web browsers
Pop-ups	An annoyance to many users, pop-ups are web pages that open in new windows, and they are genuinely 'triggered' to open when an area of the screen is clicked upon, or after a certain period of time upon a particular web page. Pop-ups can easily be blocked via pop-up blockers that are installed in most modern web browsers, as well as antivirus and security software. Variants of pop-ups are pop-unders which appear beneath web pages, and dynamic HTML overlays, which a user may have to view to see other content. Dynamic HTML overlays are particularly favoured by commercial broadcasters, with online television programme content, where the broadcaster requires the viewer to watch an advertisement before proceeding to see the content that they actually wanted to see
Product web sites	Web sites that are designed to sell a product or service are now commonplace, and typically contain information, photographs, contact details and the facility to place orders, or request further information
Shopping web sites	The online equivalent of brochures and catalogues, shopping web sites are designed to tempt interested users into making a purchase, either via a credit or debit card, or through a third-party web site such as PayPal. Shopping web sites are rapidly replacing printed brochures and catalogues due to their cost-effectiveness
Social networking product groups	These are often set up by those who wish to share information about a product/service/belief/cause with others. Social networking groups allow social networking users to join them and become a part of a community of practice, where discussion can take place and information be shared among group members. Facebook groups are a typical example of the kind of facility used for social networking product groups

Case Study: eBay Inc.

eBay Inc. is an online provider of retail, commerce and communication products. The company is most noted for its founding and ownership of eBay.com (the world's largest online auction site); however, in recent years, the company has expanded its business portfolio, particularly in the face of a challenging financial climate, which has impacted upon online retailers as it has in other areas. In the first trading quarter of 2007, eBay.com's sales had risen by just 1%, which is lower than in previous years (Friedlos, 2007), and consequently eBay Inc. has expanded to source alternative revenue streams. In the third-quarter of 2008, eBay Inc. stated a revenue of US$2.12 billion, up US$228 million from the same period last year (eBay Inc., 2008), its expanded portfolio of acquisitions was largely credited for this. Information about the eBay portfolio of companies is listed below.

eBay.com: The world's largest online auction web site began in the USA in 1995 under the name AuctionWeb. In 1998, it was floated on the US stock exchange. As of 2006, eBay had a web presence in 33 countries, with 193 million registered users globally that traded US$1600 worth of goods per second. At any given time, there are almost 90 million items listed for sale globally, with 6 million new items added on a daily basis, in over 50,000 categories of item type. There are almost three-quarters of a million professional eBay sellers in the USA who use eBay for their primary source of income (eBay, 2006). eBay.com remains the core revenue generator for eBay Inc. and at the heart of its business activities. In addition to being the world's largest auction site, the ability to 'Buy it Now' for a fixed price and the eBay shops make eBay.com one of the largest shopping web sites in the world, and certainly very recognizable as a global brand.

Gumtree.com: Particularly popular in the UK, where it claims to be the number one classified advertisements web site, Gumtree is a web site that is dedicated to classified advertisements, particularly for property sales and rentals. Other popular advertisements placed upon Gumtree are for jobs, dating, miscellaneous items for sale and services to business. Gumtree has localized web sites in 30 countries including Australia, Ireland, New Zealand, Singapore, China, Poland, the USA and South Africa.

Kijiji.com: Similar in what it offers to Gumtree.com, Kijiji is a more localized classified advertisements web site that places advertisements within 'city' directories, and encourages users to shop locally using it. Kijiji has an international presence and its growth has been aided by eBay Inc. purchasing similar international web sites and in most cases rebranding many (but not all) of them under the name of Kijiji. Spain's Loquo.com is a similar type

Fig. 15.3. eBay Inc. companies.

(Continued)

Case Study: Continued.

of site to Kijiji which is now under the ownership of eBay Inc., but has been left under its original name. eBay Inc. has rebranded its Indian Kijiji operations as Quikr.com.

PayPal.com: A provider of e-commerce services, PayPal was purchased by eBay Inc. in 2002 to support the organization's main business – eBay.com. At the time of purchase, over 50% of eBay users were paying for their goods via PayPal, and charging users a percentage for each transaction, and so it was a logical step for eBay Inc. to make this acquisition and further integrate PayPal into their ebay.com web site. The use of PayPal is now being wholly encouraged by eBay. com, to the point that certain countries and certain sellers now have to offer PayPal as a payment medium to users. PayPal is also extensively used outside of eBay.com, and is a reasonably simple way for persons to transfer funds online, from one location to another (particularly internationally) without going through formal banking channels, but with a percentage of fee involved in the amount being transferred. Unfortunately this has made PayPal attractive to fraudsters, who are in a continual cat-and-mouse battle with PayPal security systems. PayPal currently has 164 million account holders, spread across 190 countries globally.

Skype.com: Acquired by eBay Inc. in 2005 with 65% of shares being sold to 'Silver Lake' in September 2009, eBay Inc. still retains a minor shareholding in this company. Skype specializes in communications, with telephone services, instant messaging, video conferencing and file transfer all being elements of the Skype package. Skype users can communicate with each other globally at no cost, and charges are made for communications from Skype to non-Skype telephone lines. Skype is particularly useful for those in areas without a telephone infrastructure, or for those who are continually on the move, and want to be accessible wherever they go (that has an Internet connection).

eBay Inc. has demonstrated the necessity for online retailers to integrate with a range of online services in order to support their revenue streams, and where possible to integrate them into their core business activities. By purchasing businesses in growth areas such as e-commerce and communications, potential stagnation in eBay.com's core revenue streams has easily been offset, and considering the current global financial crisis, these have been wise investments for eBay Inc.

PRINTED SELLERTAINMENT

Typically paper- or cardboard-based, printed sellertainment involves the mass production of a variety of printed formats. Although it is commonplace, printed sellertainment is on the decline, predominantly due to its associated costs, which typically include: design, printing, courier and distribution. The major costs incurred with paper-based promotional media are those related to distribution, as few clients requesting printed sellertainment have the infrastructure to also broadcast and display it. It is typical to employ the services of a distribution agent, who can physically take paper-based media to specific locations, and then display them in the correct manner. Printed sellertainment types are outlined in Table 15.4, overleaf.

Table 15.4. Types of printed sellertainment and their characteristics.

Type of printed sellertainment	Characteristics
Advertorials	Typically found in newspapers and magazines, advertorials are advertisements that are disguised as interest stories to get readers interested in the product, belief or ideal being sold. In most countries, there is a legal obligation for advertorials to be labelled as being advertisements, although to some readers, this may not always be obvious
Brochures and catalogues	These demonstrate both push and pull promotional characteristics, in the sense that they may be distributed to an audience en masse (push), but may only be viewed by those who are interested in their contents (pull). In the case of product retailers, brochures and catalogues are often produced by those who generally do not have large 'shop' capacity, and instead may have small front of house reception areas backed up by large storage facilities, or those who do not have any shop frontage at all and only storage/distribution facilities. Brochures are commonly used within the travel industry to showcase holiday destinations and products (see Fig. 15.4), and, as such, they are often highly visual, featuring professional, attractive photography, as well as written information. There are typically high distribution costs associated with brochures, although some are collected from retailers' premises
Flyers, leaflets and pamphlets	Similar to brochures and catalogues these demonstrate characteristics of both push and pull promotion. The main difference between each of these is size. A flyer consists of a sheet of printed paper or card that can be printed on both sides. A leaflet is 2–4 pages, and a pamphlet is 5–48 pages long (UNESCO guidelines), beyond 48 pages it is considered a book, which some brochures and catalogues are. The content of flyers, leaflets and pamphlets is necessarily abbreviated to fit into the limited available space, but typically incorporates eye-catching graphics as well as written information including 'punchy' slogans, and contact information to find further details. Flyers, leaflets and pamphlets can be found in many places, often pushed through letter boxes as 'junk mail' or distributed by hand to passers-by; in 'student cities' these are particularly used to advertise club nights
Newspaper and magazine advertisements	Advertisements placed in magazines and newspapers contribute heavily towards their production costs, they are typically highly visual with the use of eye-catching graphics and written content. Perfume and eau de toilet advertisements often contain 'rub and

(Continued)

Table 15.4. Continued.

Type of printed sellertainment	Characteristics
	sniff' areas, making them particularly sensory-stimulating. In some cases, advertisements can completely pay for the production and distribution of newspapers – this has become a trend in the UK with *The Metro* available nationally via the public transport network, and many major cities having free newspapers. Many magazines are often 'loaded' (and heavily subsidized) with numerous full-page and smaller advertisements that are targeted towards their readership, for example fashion and lifestyle magazines that are aimed at woman, typically carry advertisements relating to items such as perfume, jewellery, cosmetics, clothing and accessories
Posters and billboards	These typically consist of highly visual display art that can be found in numerous locations; large billboards are often displayed by road sides so as to attract the attention of the occupants of passing vehicles. They generally contain a limited message, but are used to create brand awareness, as well as awareness of current or forthcoming special offers that may be available for a limited period of time (see Fig. 15.5)

Fig. 15.4. Brochures displayed by a travel agent.

Fig. 15.5. A poster display advertising theatrical performances.

Socio-technological and Environmental Factor: Responsible Sellertainment

Much printed sellertainment is wasted as it is never used or seen, or invariably becomes out of date. In this age of environmental concern and carbon emissions, producing large print runs of advertising materials is not perceived to be particularly 'green' or eco-friendly. Companies are now charged for the waste that they incur, including a raft of environmental taxes and charges that are being introduced by governments to encourage recycling. In recent years, there has been a trend to decrease the quantity of their paper-based printed output in the face of this, combined with a socio-technological shift to 'browse' online for products, rather than through brochures. The growth of online shopping has now caused a number of traditional users of printed promotional media to shift their operations online, which includes: travel agents who now produce fewer brochures; catalogue shopping where customers are being encouraged to shop and manage their accounts online; and universities who now produce fewer prospectuses with a concentration on online alternatives. There are obvious advantages in using online sellertainment mediums, including: the ability to easily make changes and rectify any mistakes, no print costs, no distribution costs and the fact that online facilities are more easily searchable by users. The printed sellertainment sub-sector faces some challenging times ahead.

SELLERTAINMENT EVENTS

In order to showcase some products to great effect, sellertainment events are often held that allow potential buyers to interact with: products; sellers; interested stakeholders (such as finance and insurance organizations); and each other. The predominant types of sellertainment events are featured in the Table 15.5.

Table 15.5. Types of sellertainment events and their characteristics.

Type of sellertainment event	Characteristics
Live auctions	Haggling or bargaining for goods at markets has gone on for thousands of years; auctions are more formal events that involve audiences haggling competitively for goods that are displayed as being for sale. For centuries live auctions have attracted not only interested buyers, but also audiences of spectators that are fascinated by the spectacle of the auction process. The origins of auctions are agricultural, but today all of items are put up for auction, with property, vehicles, businesses, antiques and art all being popular items to send to auction. Premises where auctions take place are often referred to as 'auction houses'. The world's oldest auction house that still functions today is 'Stockholms Auktionsverk' in Sweden. Possibly the most famous auction house in the world is 'Sothebys', which has offices in both London and New York and holds the world record for the most expensive piece of contemporary art ever sold, which was Mark Rothko's 1950 *White Center* (Yellow, Pink and Lavender on Rose), which sold for US$72.8 million in May 2007. At a live auction, items are typically paraded in front of an audience, who are then invited to make bids to purchase them by the auctioneer. Bids are competitive and usually increase by a certain amount, which is dependent on the perceived value of the item; at some auctions, bids can be made by telephone. Once bids are no longer forthcoming, the auctioneer counts down before striking a hammer or similar device to mark an end to the auction. Some auctions are timed, and the highest bid by the end of the allocated time period is the winning one
Product demonstrations	These take place in a live environment and may be both theatrical and artistic in nature. A product showcase involves the exhibition or demonstration of an actual product to a potential audience. This could be as simple as a market vendor demonstrating a cleaning product on a carpet, or a more elaborate technological demonstration involving specially

(Continued)

Table 15.5. Continued.

Type of sellertainment event	Characteristics
	designed mobile 'sets' (see Fig. 15.6). Static product demonstrations can be found in highly artistic window displays (which are not strictly speaking 'events') that are enticed to capture the attention of passers-by
Rallies	These are large organized events, which typically involve a speaker, or speakers appearing before a massed audience. Rallies are very often political in nature, and sometimes involve an element of protest or demonstration. The development of numerous communicative mediums has led to a decline in the number of rallies that take place; they were once a major attraction that brought in large audiences. The first ever rail excursion was organized in 1841 by Thomas Cook, and it took passengers from Leicester to Loughborough in England to a temperance rally to listen to speakers talk about the wrongs of alcohol consumption. In the recent US elections, the political campaigning cost both parties over US$1 billion, much of which was spent on large-scale rallies where both Republican and Democrat parties attempted to 'sell' themselves to the US electorate; both candidates and their vice presidents spoke to thousands of people, and in doing so became entertainers to their audiences
Sales parties	Tupperware, Pampered Chef, Virgin Vie and Ann Summers parties (which all have the broadest appeal to women) are held in a person's home. With the use of a kit/starter pack or instructions, the 'host' typically has to prepare by buying food and drinks for their invited guests. When the party is held, an organizational representative arrives to demonstrate products, as well as organizing tasks and games. The idea of the party is that the audience will be tempted to commit themselves to buying a product or products there and then. The host, for their involvement, gets a small percentage of the sales revenue – often in the form of 'points', which is typically traded for products from the promoting company. Sales parties are viral, and part of their intention is to stimulate an audience member into volunteering to host their own party at a later date
Trade shows and conventions	From the fashion shows of Milan, Paris and London, to the British International Motor Show, trade shows and conventions are commonplace. They typically involve a large number of sellers

(Continued)

Table 15.5. Continued.

Type of sellertainment event	Characteristics
	converging at a specific large-scale venue, where thousands of visitors flock to see demonstrations of what is being sold, in the hope that some of those visitors will themselves make purchases either then, or at some point in the future. As well as products being displayed, there are typically other forms of entertainment being offered, including guest speakers, live music and screened films and documentaries. At the 'World Travel Market' (which is held annually at ExCel in London), countries from around the world showcase themselves to potential buyers, including tour operators, students and trade body representatives. In order to have appeal to passing potential customers, stands are visually eye-catching, and often use entertaining promotional methods such as: cultural crafts and artworks (see Fig. 15.7); musical performances; traditional costumes; gastronomic delights (see Fig. 15.8); dance displays; and many different types of 'giveaways'

Fig. 15.6. A mobile product demonstration unit, set up on a pedestrianized street.

Fig. 15.7. Traditional crafts being used to 'sell' South Africa at the World Travel Market, London.

Fig. 15.8. Culinary crafts being used to 'sell' catering school at an educational fair in Dresden, Germany.

THE FUTURE

Sellertainment's future is going to be most significantly effected by technology; the Internet will absorb most of the printed sellertainment sub-sector, and the increase in global television channels and methods by which to circumvent advertisements will impact upon the methods used by advertisers to promote their products. This is further demonstrated in Fig. 15.9.

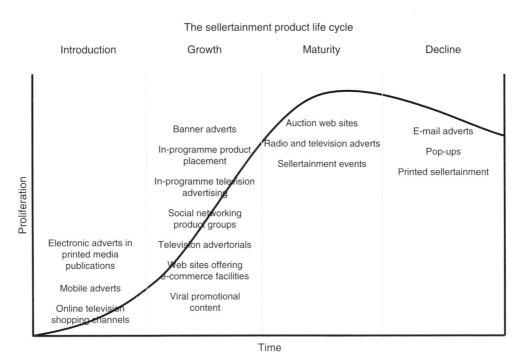

Fig. 15.9. Sellertainment life cycle.

Introduction

Electronic adverts in printed media publications – these will feature audio (at first) and then eventually small screens with moving images, that are activated by the press of a button or by motion and powered by tiny batteries (similar to the ones in audio greeting cards). In the early days these will be of such novelty value that they will become collectable (particularly to fans of what is being advertised), however in later years as technology advances and prices fall they will become the norm for some of the glossier and more luxury titles, particularly fashion magazines.

Mobile advertisements – advances in mobile technology will lead to video-quality advertisements being created specifically for mobile telephones, which can be forwarded virally or via Bluetooth to other users. Advertisements are likely to be of high impact, possibly humorous in nature and will have to be viewed or downloaded in order to view or download other online content.

Online television shopping channels – the relative expense of broadcast media compared to online media and the increases in Internet bandwidth and speed will lead to a complete shift for some shopping channels to an online environment.

Growth

Banner advertisements – these are likely to continue to grow in usage as more providers offer online content, and banner advertisements that have high-quality video content will become the norm.

In-programme product placement – as television advertising revenues decline, especially as the use of personal video recorder (PVR) technology advances, more thought will need to go into how products are promoted, and one way will be to incorporate named products into television programmes, either through placement or in storylines.

In-programme television advertising – it is an alternative to commercial breaks that may also get around PVR technologies and are advertisements streamed along screens during programmes. Although unpopular, they may soon be seen outside of North America.

Social networking product groups – it is a very cost-effective medium by which to communicate product information to those who are interested in particular products, usage will increase, particularly among product manufacturers, thereby reducing marketing budgets.

Television advertorials – these are scheduled advertisements disguised as actual television programmes, with real storylines and episodes that will grow in number, in order to try and get audiences 'hooked'.

Web sites offering e-commerce facilities – why pay other parties to promote and sell products when you can do-it-yourself? It will become standard practice for most product manufacturers to develop their own e-commerce facilities.

Viral promotional content – often funny, or risqué, possibly including content that would not be allowed on television, viral advertisements (e-mail, social networking web sites, and eventually mobile advertisements) will significantly increase in number, whereby the distribution costs are picked up by the audience.

Maturity

Auction web sites – these experienced a boom in the mid-1990s, and today there is only ebay.com left of any global significance. The few smaller rivals will not experience significant growth, and eBay Inc. will dedicate more of its business away from online auctions to other online revenue streams.

Radio and television advertisements – advertising as we know will go through a period of stagnation as more people view online content, and circumvent advertisements using PVR systems. This will lead to new methods of advertising, as highlighted above.

Sellertainment events – growth in sellertainment events is expected to stagnate, as communicative technologies now mean that there is less need for people to travel to trade shows and conventions. Product information and launches can largely be found online, and only the very committed will continue to visit these events. Some consolidation between previously rival events is likely.

Decline

E-mail advertisements – no longer seen as being politically correct, and too often abused by criminals, e-mail advertisements will continue to decline.

Pop-ups – technology to circumvent these will lead to their cost-effectiveness being questioned and a reduction in usage.

Printed sellertainment – concerns over costs and the environment, coupled with the increased use of electronic alternatives, will put this sub-sector in terminal decline, and it will be reserved for 'luxury' items only.

REFERENCES

Department for Culture, Media and Sport (2008) Creative industries. [Internet] London, DCMS. Available at: http://www.culture.gov.uk/what_we_do/creative_industries/default.aspx

Donaton, S. (2005) *Madison and Vine: Why the Entertainment and Advertising Industries Must Converge to Survive*. McGraw-Hill, New York.

eBay (2006) eBay fact sheet. [Internet] Sydney, eBay.com.au. Available at: http://pics.ebaystatic.com/aw/pics/au/new/eBayFactSheetApr06.pdf

eBay Inc. (2008) eBay Inc. reports third-quarter 2008 results. [Internet] San Jose, eBay Inc. Available at: http://files.shareholder.com/downloads/ebay/61908212x2078731x241175/694bc74d-6b11–434c-85c6-fe1c8ec37748/eBay_FINALQ32008EarningsRelease.pdf

Friedlos, D. (2007) Online retailers must keep evolving. [Internet] London, Incisive Media Ltd. Available at: http://www.computing.co.uk/computing/analysis/2192971/online-retailers-keep-evolving

Kotler, P., Armstrong, G., Wong, V. and Saunders, J. (2008) *Principles of Marketing*, 5th edn. Prentice-Hall, Harlow, UK.

Mintel (2007) *Live Entertainment*. Mintel International Group, London.

Oxford English Dictionary (2008) Find word: Promotion. [Internet] Oxford, Oxford University Press. Available at: http://dictionary.oed.com/cgi/entry/50189923?single=1&query_type=word&queryword=promotion&first=1&max_to_show=10

chapter 16

Culturtainment

Stuart Moss

Entertainment that involves the demonstration, celebration or commemoration of the values, traditions or beliefs of a societal group.

According to the US Census Bureau (2009) the world population stands at 6.8 billion, and is composed of a plethora of races, religions, nations, sub-nations and physical environments. It is accepted by anthropologists that earliest human ancestors came from southern Africa around 200,000 years ago. Between then and now, humans decided to travel – at first on foot, and then thousands of years later by animal – eventually aided by wheeled carriages, and over water – using logs to make boats, and carve canoes.

Over thousands of years, humans spread, eventually adapting to the majority of the world's environments and establishing significant populations on all continents apart from Antarctica. From desert nomads, to rainforest tribes, humans learned to use the land to their advantage, growing edible plants, and hunting animals. Some human feats were truly spectacular, including conquering thousands of miles of ocean in boats to discover new lands such as Australian Aborigines travelling over sea from southern Asia; and in 12000 BC the ancestors of native Americans travelling from north-eastern Russia across the Bering land bridge (not the Bering Strait) to the North American continent, and from there walking south through what is now Alaska, Canada, the USA, Central America and to South America's very tip of Tierra Del Fuego.

Humankind's global journey took tens of thousands of years. During and since this time, Ice Ages came and went, and humans mastered not only fire, but they began to understand that metals could be extracted from the earth, and these could be moulded and shaped into tools to help everyday life, and weapons to protect and fight in a world that was becoming increasingly populous, and where progressively more complex societies, rituals and beliefs led to differences in opinions, which have resulted in conflict and war. Our planet has been (and continues to be) scarred by wars, the results of which are many of the accepted (and disputed) international boundaries and national territories that exist today. The United Nations (2009) comprises of 192 member states and there are approximately another 50 regions in the world where national sovereignty, border and identity are disputed. Within all of these, there are countless religions, races and languages that have evolved over thousands of years, and vocations and lifestyles that are more contemporary.

The word 'culture' first appeared in the English language in the 15th century, where its Anglo-Norman origins were associated with the tillage of the land – later to become known as agriculture (OED, 2008). There is a strong element of creativity within culture, crops are created from the sowing of seeds, meat products are created from the nurturing of animals, and wood products are created from the management of trees. Many of these (often ancient) creative agricultural techniques are still practised today, and are known as 'country crafts'. Today the word 'culture' has a number of meanings; apart from its agricultural origins, culture can relate to the values, norms and beliefs of societal segments; it can relate specifically to the performing and creative arts (Bennett, 2001 in O'Regan, 2001); and combining both of the above, in its broadest sense, culture can relate to the lives of past and present generations incorporating play, recreation, arts, sports, festivals, religion, gastronomy, architecture, health, language, traditions, travel and tourism.

Culturtainment is the provision of aspects of culture that can attract a recreation-seeking audience, who are typically curious or interested in witnessing or experiencing something that is different to what they are typically used to; normality is extraordinary through unfamiliar eyes and as such, novelty plays an important part in culturtainment due to the uniqueness of it. There are three main areas within the culturtainment sector, which are highlighted in Fig. 16.1.

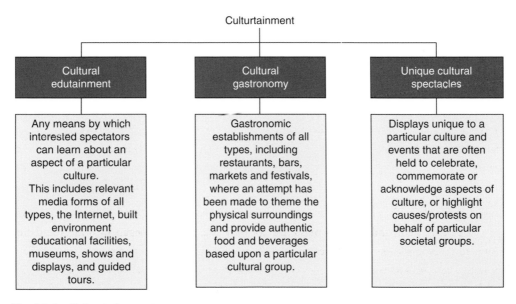

Fig. 16.1. Culturtainment sectors.

There is some commonality between these sub-sectors and other areas of the entertainment industry, for example everything within cultural edutainment could also be considered to be within the edutainment sector; there are linkages between cultural gastronomy and bars, pubs, and clubs (particularly themed bars), and some unique cultural spectacles may also be considered to be staged stories, an explanation of each of these sub-sectors now follows.

CULTURAL EDUTAINMENT

This is largely found within some culturally informative; media products (paper-based and electronic); web sites; educational shows, displays and demonstrations; built environment edutainment facilities; guided tours; and museums. Cultural edutainment is designed to educate audiences about specific aspects of culture (see Chapter 14 – Edutainment, this volume).

Political Factor: Cultural Policy, Education and Citizenship

Cultural policy now includes 'intellectual property, administrative and international law, political science, public policy, economics, sociology, art history, strategic management and international relations, gender studies, leisure sport and recreation studies, tourism and town planning' (O'Regan, 2001, p.30). Social conditioning and education through various forms of entertainment is nothing new. The recognition of particularly edutainment as a facilitator to a more informed, better educated, and more inclusive society is something which has and continues to be the concern of policy makers.

The protection of national identity has also been a determinant of cultural policy, particularly in terms of globalization and 'cultural erosion' by more dominant cultures 'from the West'. This has led to trade barriers in an effort to reduce West to East cultural flow, an example being the French 'cultural exception', where French culture was promoted by the French government and given tax breaks, while incoming (particularly US culture) was 'not encouraged'. So-called cultural imperialism, whereby populations are exposed to dominant 'popular' cultures, exacerbates the West to East cultural flow, so cultural edutainment remains important to policy makers who want their own populations as well as interested others to fully understand their origins, and what makes them unique (gives them an identity).

CULTURAL GASTRONOMY

A distinct characteristic of many cultures are the types of food and drinks that are associated with them. In this advanced age of globalization, many of these are now well travelled; emigration is largely responsible for the spread of food and drinks beyond their traditional cultural borders, which is why Mexican and Italian food are extremely popular in the USA, Indian food is popular in the UK, Japanese and Thai food is popular in Australia, and Chinese food is popular globally. In addition to this, tourists experiencing foreign holidays often partake in new gastronomic experiences, which they may subsequently want to take home, or experience again when they return home.

Global gastronomic spread has also been assisted by major corporations with international reach, brands such as Heinz, Pataks and Old El Paso have helped to raise awareness of food types in countries foreign to their origins, while Smirnoff, Bells and Moet et Chandon are now globally recognized alcoholic drink brands that have unique cultural origins. Television exposes potential audiences to a variety of types of food and drinks through cookery and travel shows, as well as films and dramas that are created in different countries from where they are being broadcast, which inadvertently expose regional food and drink to an international audience.

Demand for gastronomically exotic cultural experiences has fuelled a global rise in themed outlets, particularly restaurants and bars, which are themed around a specific culture. Globally, the largest spread of culturally themed restaurants are American, Chinese, French, Greek, Indian, Irish, Italian, Japanese, Mexican, Spanish, Thai and Vietnamese, although these are now being challenged by relative 'newcomers' such as Australian, Cuban, Lebanese, Polish, Turkish and Moroccan restaurants.

Many urban centres have significant established Chinese populations that occupy a specific area which may become known as a 'Chinatown'; examples of cities that have a 'Chinatown' include Manchester (UK), Nagasaki (Japan) and San Francisco (USA). In Chinatown, Chinese restaurants provide a culturally authentic experience to diners, by not only providing Chinese food, but also a suitable ambience that includes elements of decor, smells, textiles, utensils, language and music.

Participation in cultural gastronomy is about more than satisfying physiological needs through consumption. This is potentially a very rich and immersive entertainment experience as those in the audience can be stimulated in all five senses, which can trigger a variety of emotive responses among them, ranging from fear of the unknown, to delight at something that tastes good and satisfies. It is also very sociable, and commonly participated in by groups of individuals, who themselves become part of the 'cast' by partaking in such an entertainment–dining experience. The shared interaction of diners with their surroundings and food often provides entertainment for other members of the dining party (see Fig. 16.2).

In the UK, Indian restaurants have grown in popularity since an initial wave of immigration from Commonwealth countries including India, Pakistan and Bangladesh in the 1950s. Such restaurants were originally founded as social locations for Asian immigrants who wanted a taste of home. At the turn of the millennium it was widely reported in the British media that 'Britain's favourite dish' was Chicken Tikka Masala, which is a mild curried chicken dish in a creamy tomato sauce. Since then, a growing number of Asian entrepreneurs have transformed the Indian dining experience, and are now creating a contemporary ambience with enlarged menus based around traditional recipes, but surroundings that are very different from the

Fig. 16.2. Cultural gastronomy in The Gambia.

Indian restaurants of previous decades, which often included heavily patterned wallpaper and carpets, as well as 'piped in' Indian music. Today, shiny wooden floors and neutral colour schemes help to create a 'modern' decor, and flat-screen TVs playing the latest Indian music videos featuring well-known 'Bollywood' stars present an image of contemporary rather than traditional India. This helps to maintain interest in the Indian dining experience among younger diners, who may feel more comfortable in surroundings that they perceive to be 'cool', but at the same time, this is a slight step away from the authenticity of the cultural experience. In terms of growth, culturally themed restaurants in the UK have suffered 'from a certain amount of stagnation thanks largely to a distinct lack of innovation in the sector' (Mintel, 2008). However, this new generation of Asian entrepreneurs are at least making steps to combat this.

Culture is also utilized in order to theme pubs and bars around a particular national identity, common global examples include American-, British-, Irish- and Australian-themed pubs and bars. In such establishments, the surroundings are very often more authentic than the beverages being sold (most of these bars sell brands that are internationally recognizable and therefore less authentic culturally), although some specific brands are heavily promoted in these types of establishments. Common examples of draught products promoted in themed pubs and bars include: Budweiser (American), Fosters (Australian), Guinness (Irish) and John Smiths (British).

Case Study: Oktoberfest

Gastronomic markets and festivals are popular attractions that allow visitors to become immersed in a specific culture. In Germany, beer festivals are extremely popular among residents and tourists alike. Most notable on the cultural calendar is the Munich-based Oktoberfest, which is the world's largest event of its kind attracting six million visitors annually. Oktoberfest is a 16-day festival that begins in September and finishes in October. At Oktoberfest the main attraction is the beer on offer, all of which is supplied by German breweries, but traditional German dress, music, tankards (steins) and food – particularly meat (sausages, pork and chicken); potato (dumplings, pancakes and French fries); bread (soda bread, dark bread, malt bread and pretzels); as well as fish, cheese and sauerkraut. This all counts towards creating a uniquely German, culturally gastronomic experience.

Despite the global appeal of cultural gastronomy there are few major restaurant chains that have a near worldwide presence that can be considered to offer a culturally gastronomic dining experience. The largest restaurant chain in the world is McDonald's, which has over 30,000 restaurants in over 100 countries (McDonald's, 2008), but this 'fast food' outlet does not sufficiently qualify as offering a culturally gastronomic experience, as while the food is reasonably standardized around a 'burger' menu, there is little attempt at any cultural theming, which is relative to a particular societal segment. This is also the case with other predominantly 'fast food'-style restaurant chains, such as Pizza Hut, Subway and KFC that have operations in numerous countries, and do not theme their outlets around a particular cultural identity. Taco Bell is one restaurant chain that does make an attempt at theming around a Mexican-style fast-food dining experience, and does have international operations, although they have faced difficulties in some international locations where Mexican food is not popular.

Case Study: Nando's

Nando's is one of the few genuinely culturally themed restaurant chains that have significant international operations. They were founded in 1987 in South Africa, and offer a menu and decor that is loosely based around a Portuguese–African colonial-style dining experience. The Nando's logo features the Portuguese cockerel. The style of the dining experience is somewhere in-between a typical fast food outlet and a restaurant. Customers place their order at the counter like in a fast food outlet, but the rest of the experience is more restaurant-based, with food brought to tables by waiting staff.

Nando's menus are typically based around flame-grilled chicken dishes that are served with lemon, herb, or peri-peri-based marinades and sauces, there are also vegetarian and steak options, all of which can be accompanied by side orders including fries, rice, ratatouille and couscous. The restaurant chain has proved to be extremely popular, and

(Continued)

Case Study: Continued.

as of 2008 was represented on all continents apart from South America and Antarctica, with a high concentration in Europe, particularly the UK, many of which are franchised outlets. The popularity of Nando's has been its original approach to providing dishes that are strong in tastes and flavours, which are perceived as being a healthier option than many other 'chain' restaurants, and price wise they are also considerably cheaper than many other restaurants. The Nando's brand is now being used to sell foodstuffs including shake-on and cook-in sauces, as well as merchandise including clothing that carry the Nando's logo. Nando's merchandise can be purchased online, in Nando's outlets and in supermarkets.

The short- to mid-term future growth for cultural gastronomy is largely going to be dictated by wider economic factors. Forecast rises in the prices of food, fuel, gas and electricity do not bode well, and may ultimately lead to many in this sector struggling to maintain profitability, particularly in the face of falling tourist revenues, and supermarkets being able to provide a similar or the same product, albeit without the full cultural experience. The question from a consumer's perspective *might* be, 'What am I interested in, the food/drink, or the experience?' If the answer to this question is 'the food/drink', expect competitive price cuts and special offers in restaurants and bars, as well as a reduction in menu sizes in restaurants, as businesses themselves tighten their belts.

UNIQUE CULTURAL SPECTACLES

Society as we know it today is a gargantuan mix of individuals who can be divided up into numerous groupings and sub-groupings based upon a number of social factors. Nationality, race and religion are easy and obvious examples by which a population may be divided into subgroups, but there are many more also (too many for this text to cover); however, some common factors include vocation, education, type of dwelling lived in, sexuality, sports participation, wealth, health, age, hobbies and interests, disability, gender, political views, fashions worn, music tastes and dietary requirements. Commonly there are social groups or 'social–cultural identities' made up of a number of these. Unique cultural spectacles includes displays unique to a particular culture, and events that are often held to celebrate, commemorate or acknowledge aspects of culture, or highlight causes or protests on behalf of particular societal groups. Table 16.1 gives some examples of these.

Some cultural spectacles which often have quite historic or political origins (see Fig. 16.3) and have taken place for a number of years (sometimes centuries) have been capitalized upon by entrepreneurs, and as a result, while maintaining a historic significance can

Table 16.1. Some societal groups and their unique cultural celebrations and commemorations.

Societal group	Name of cultural event	Further information
The Irish	St Patrick's Day	This is a feast that is usually held on 17 March to celebrate St Patrick who is one of Ireland's patron saints. In Ireland this is a national holiday, but St Patrick's Day is also celebrated in other countries, most notably those that have had substantial immigration of Irish people, particularly the USA, where several cities hold St Patrick's Day parades, featuring kilt-wearing bagpipe players, and firefighters and police officers in ceremonial wear. In Chicago, the Chicago River is dyed green
Barnsley (UK) ex and current coal miners	Miners' Gala	The gala is a march and staged show with guest speakers that takes place in the town of Barnsley, to commemorate those lost in local coal mines; the role that the coal industry had in creating and shaping Barnsley and its borough; and to highlight the sufferance of miners and their families under the Thatcher government during the 1984–1985 Miners' Strike
Hindus, Sikhs and Jains	Diwali	Hindus celebrate this festival to mark the homecoming of Lord Rama of Ayodhya after his exile, and his subsequent victory over demon-king Ravana. To Sikhs the celebration centres on the freeing of Guru Har Gobind, the sixth Guru of Sikhism from imprisonment. Jains believe that Diwali marks the achievement of nirvana by Lord Mahavira. Diwali lasts over 5 days, during the festival clay pots filled with coconut oil are traditionally lit with string wicks, in recent times more elaborate illuminations and lights are lit, as well as fireworks set off to mark the event. Diwali is also known as 'the festival of lights'
London Afro-Caribbean Community	The Notting Hill Carnival	This is an annual street parade that takes place through the streets on Notting Hill in London on the last weekend in August (a public holiday is held in the UK on the Monday afterwards). It began as a public protest at the state of British race relations

(Continued)

Table 16.1. Some societal groups and their unique cultural celebrations and commemorations.

Societal group	Name of cultural event	Further information
		The carnival is held over both days of the weekend, with the main parade taking place on the Sunday. The parade is designed to highlight and celebrate Caribbean culture, and is one of the largest street festivals in the world. In the late 1970s and early 1980s the parade ended with clashes between drunken revellers and the police. Bad publicity threatened to put off potential carnival goers, which would have an economic impact. Since then a combination of highly visible stewards, community policing, political willpower and corporate ownership have turned the event into a largely peaceful celebration of London's multicultural diversity
Americans	Independence Day	The 4th of July is a national holiday, which is held to celebrate the independence of the USA from the rule of Great Britain. Celebrations that are held throughout the USA include galas, firework displays, picnics, street parties, barbecues, music concerts and sports games. In Columbus, Ohio, there is an annual firework display called Red, White & Boom. Other large-scale public firework displays are held in New York City and Boston

become largely commercial. This is an example of the commodification of culture. Social groups often partake in celebrations and displays that are unique to their own traditions and evolution. Some celebrations and displays attract spectators from the wider community, who are keen to witness something that may be considered a spectacle by them, while some people travel long distances solely to witness or experience these spectacles which may include events, traditions and ceremonies, and as such they become tourist attractions. In the EU alone cultural tourism's contribution to 'GDP is estimated to be around 11% and it provides employment to more than 12% of the labour force (24 million jobs)' (New Europe, 2008), there are numerous examples of cultural spectacles globally, including:

Fig. 16.3. Tourists view celebrations for the feast held in honour of Our Lady Stella Maris, in Sliema, Malta.

- 'Encierro' (the running of the bulls) in Pamplona, Spain, which is a part of the festival of San Fermin one of the regions Saints. In this spectacle, bulls and oxen are released on to city streets to 'chase' those brave enough to run in front of them from the Corral into the bullring.
- 'La Tomatina' (tomato fight) in Buñol, Spain, which takes place annually between 11 am and 1 pm on the last Wednesday in August in honour of the town's patron saint, San Luis Bertràn, and the Virgin Mary.
- The Haka, performed in New Zealand and Polynesia, is an aggressive-looking song and dance performed by groups (usually men) as a ceremonial greeting. Its origins lie in ancient tribal warfare. It is widely practised in New Zealand in tourist locations such as Rotorua (which as a close location to the recent *Lord of the Rings* trilogy has seen a rise in tourist numbers). In popular culture, it has become synonymous with the New Zealand 'All Blacks' (Rugby Union Team) who perform it before games.
- Thailand's 'long-necked women' are an example of a cultural spectacle that has taken place for centuries. Women in the border area of Burma and Thailand were instructed to wear brass rings around their necks to protect them from tigers. The number of rings gives the neck an elongated appearance, with the woman's head clearly further from her body than what is naturally possible.

Further examples of unique cultural spectacles can be found in Figs 16.4–16.6.

Fig. 16.4. A musician in authentic dress performs for tourists in The Gambia.

Fig. 16.5. Tourists watch authentic dancers at fiesta time in Rhonda, Spain.

Fig. 16.6. A display of themed Beethovens in Bonn, Germany.

Economic Factor: Sydney Mardi Gras and the Economic Impact of Culturtainment

An example of this in action is the Sydney Gay and Lesbian Mardi Gras, which despite its name is not held on or around Shrove Tuesday like many other Mardi Gras events in the world are. The Sydney Gay and Lesbian Mardi Gras began as a political demonstration in 1978 to highlight homosexuality (which was illegal in the Australian state of New South Wales at the time), and to protest against the persecution of those who were homosexual. Over the years the annual demonstration grew from being an organized march into a parade along a set route, with the addition of themes, costumes, music, theatre and dance. As the event became more elaborate, it began to attract non-gay spectators, as well as its traditional gay support. In 1998, Tourism New South Wales sponsored an economic impact statement of the event (Marsh and Levy, 1998) in recognition of the fact that the gay travel market was a lucrative one, with the average spend per capita being significantly higher than the average tourist spend (Waitt and Markwell, 2006). Economically, the Sydney Gay and Lesbian Mardi Gras benefited the region as a whole with accommodation and support services being in high demand during this period. By the mid-1990s, the Sydney Gay and Lesbian Mardi Gras was an established event on the cities entertainment calendar, and used by marketers to attract tourists to the city. Stories in local newspapers at the time told of entire 'plane loads' of gay tourists arriving in Sydney, including a chartered Boeing 747 arriving from San Francisco.

An international example of a cultural spectacle that has regional variations are the 'changing of the guard' or 'guard mounting' ceremonies that are held in many different nations globally. These are ceremonies that typically feature military personnel in decorative and ceremonial uniform relieving on-duty guards outside important governmental buildings and landmarks. In London, the changing of the guard outside Buckingham Palace and other London palaces and institutions draws in many visitors who wish to witness these novel ceremonies, which are a unique feature to London (unique in the sense of ceremony, uniform and regiments). A great many publications aimed at incoming tourists feature the dates and times of guard changes, which in terms of ceremony have changed very little over the years, although regiments, and displayed uniform and weaponry has. The origins and 'pomp' of ceremonial guard changes were certainly not connected with providing a spectacle for tourists; they were more so for royalty, government, and the respect of the state. Figure 16.7 demonstrates tourists watching such a guard-changing ceremony outside St James's Palace in London.

There are 44 remaining ruling monarchies in the world, nine of which are in Malaysia (Hassan, 2009). The novelty of witnessing the pomp and pageantry of royalty including palaces; gardens; the aforementioned guard-changing ceremonies; and other royal celebrations, festivities and ceremonies has led to the phenomenon of 'royal tourism'. Malaysia's large number of royal households, towns and connections make significant contributions in the development

Fig. 16.7. Tourists watching the guard changing ceremony outside St James's Palace, London.

of royal tourism in that particular country (Hassan, 2009). In the UK, major royal events (particularly weddings and funerals) attract huge live audiences, and television audiences, which are vastly greater. The funeral of Princess Diana on 6 September 1997 is estimated to have had a million people in attendance and a global television audience of 2.5 billion people (BBC, 2009).

Ethical Factor: Bullfighting – Should Animals Die for Entertainment?

In ancient Rome, animals were forced to battle man in amphitheatres, as a 'warm up' to gladiators taking the stage to do battle with one another. Animals used in such battles included many captured 'prizes' from throughout the Roman Empire including lions, giraffes, buffalo, bears, wolves, ostriches, elephants and rhinoceroses, as well as domestically bred animals such as dogs and bulls. Animals were also pitted against other animals in a seemingly wanton lust for bloody entertainment. The slaughtering of bulls was particularly revered by Roman soldiers, many of whom followed the Mithras religion (or cult), of which bull slaughter was depicted in related iconography as being something which would benefit humanity through the release of life force to aid agricultural growth (NUMA, 2008).

Centuries later, a descendent of these gruesome practices has developed into a bloody yet cultural art form, which is still practised throughout Spain, Portugal and Latin America – bullfighting. In this cultural spectacle, man still does battle 'to-the-death' with animal, and the vast majority of the time it is the animals' death, although there have been numerous human casualties. Bullfighting takes place in purposely built stadiums called 'bull rings', and these stone- and concrete-built structures are similar in design and shape to the amphitheatres of ancient Rome (see Fig. 16.8). It is estimated that globally 250,000 bulls die each year in bullfighting shows (PETA, 2008).

Bullfighting involves several human cast members, the most notable being toreadors (torero In Spanish). The toreador wears ceremonial dress, and his (they are almost always male) role is to tease the bull, stab it and then eventually deliver a deadly blow through sword or spear. There are different types of toreadors, including picadors who ride on horseback and attack the bull with a lance to begin the process of bloodletting so that the animal becomes weakened, while the horse on which the picador sits is usually attacked by the bull. Although horses are protected with padding and armour, they still commonly sustain injuries. There are also banderilleros, who stab the bull at the back of the shoulder with banderilleras, which are spears decorated with colourful material; this is itself considered to be an art form and banderilleras are judged by the audience on their technical merit. Finally there is the matador who is considered the 'star' of the show, as he stands against the bull and waves a red sheet for the bull to charge through, inciting chants of 'Olé' from the audience. It is the matador who has the 'honour' of delivering the final kill – usually with a ceremonial sword.

(Continued)

Ethical Factor: Continued.

Fig. 16.8. Tourists explore a bull ring in Spain.

Due to the suffering of bulls (and horses), bullfighting has caused a great deal of controversy among those who consider it an overly cruel and outdated form of entertainment. Animal rights groups such as the 'League Against Cruel Sports' (LACS) and 'People for the Ethical Treatment of Animals' (PETA) demonstrate against bullfighting through organized campaigns that include human demonstrations, the Internet, leaflets, T-shirts and posters that are designed to raise awareness of the cruelty to animals and the suffering caused. This does not go unnoticed by politicians in countries where bullfighting exists, who rely heavily on tourist income, and as such bullfighting imagery is now rare in promotional material aimed at tourists. The economic fear of tourists being dissuaded of visiting an area because of negative publicity associated with bullfighting is one factor that is causing a gradual decline of the practice. There are numerous other factors including a lack of interest in bullfighting among the new generation of Hispanic youth; relatively poor payments for toreadors in comparison to other sports and activities that are much less dangerous; a decline in televised bullfighting, leading to a drop in revenues; and bullrings running into disrepair, through costly maintenance which the practice can no longer pay for. Many old bullrings are now preserved for tourists as visitor attractions, but are no longer used for bullfighting, and as such have become museums; some have also been

(Continued)

Ethical Factor: Continued.

converted for other usage, including the bullring in the Portuguese city of Viana do Castelo, which is being converted into a science and education centre (PETA, 2008).

Those who are in favour of bullfighting argue that it is a deep part of their culture, and that banning it serves simply to enforce politically correct opinion upon them. Bullfighting advocates also state the following arguments in its favour: it brings economic benefits through increased visitor numbers; bulls are bred specifically for bullfighting and are not ones taken from agricultural use, therefore this is an industry in itself which people rely on for employment; and some monies raised from the sale of meat from the dead bull often go towards local good causes such as orphanages. Despite this, according to Gallup (2002) only 31% of Spaniards are in favour of bullfighting, with 68.8% having no interest, and 0.2% having no opinion, the same Gallup poll demonstrated that those most interested in bullfighting were the older generation, particularly over 65 (51% in favour), when compared to those aged under 24 (17% in favour). This cultural spectacle lacks appeal among young Spaniards and will most likely disappear in Europe altogether in the 21st century. With that stated, in Latin America, there is less resistance to bullfighting. In January 2009, 11-year-old Michelito Lagravere sparked controversy by slaying six calves in a Mexican bullfight, and in doing so he became the youngest matador to achieve so many kills (Attewill, 2009).

Social Factor: Youth Cultures and Culture Gaps

The term 'youth cultures' appeared from the 1950s onwards. In youth cultures, distinctive dress styles combined with particular tastes for creative and cultural products would help to carve identities for those who no longer wanted to have to wear the same clothes or listen to the same music as their parents. Typical examples of youth cultures that have emerged since the 1950s are teddy boys, skinheads, mods, punks, rockers, casuals, b-boys, ravers and chavs. Youth culture typically involves an element of rebellion; after all the 'youth' market, being predominantly teenagers and young adults, are all at a stage in their life when freedom, choice and decision making becomes something that they can exercise more liberally as they outgrow the constraints of parent and home, and become an age when legally they have more entitlements.

In youth cultures, artistic and cultural products are used by consumers to help shape identity, so the rebellious and 'non-conformist' element of particular art forms has been of concern to parents, authorities, governments and invariably policy makers for decades – especially as the current youth can and /will change the future of society as we currently know it. This is an example of a culture gap, which is 'a difference in values, behaviour, or customs between two cultures or groups of people, esp. as a hindrance to mutual understanding and communication' (OED, 2008).

THE FUTURE

The economic benefit of culturtainment makes it attractive to politicians and policy makers alike. A potential increase in inbound visitor numbers coupled with their demand for related goods and services (travel, accommodation, retail) is an incentive for those within governments and authorities to work with cultural groups in order to develop celebrations and commemorations into larger and more high-profile events. However, such commercialization risks culturtainment becoming homogeneous and losing its original 'message' that could lead to a dilution of audiences. This could also lead to smaller non-commercial independent events being set up that would only serve to fragment audiences further. This is something that planners and stakeholders will need to balance against potential financial gain. Changing political, social and religious landscapes will lead to the emergence of new cultures, and with them new culturtainment experiences. Overall this is a healthy growth sector of the entertainment industry, but one that by its very nature is fragile in the face of exploitation (see Fig. 16.9).

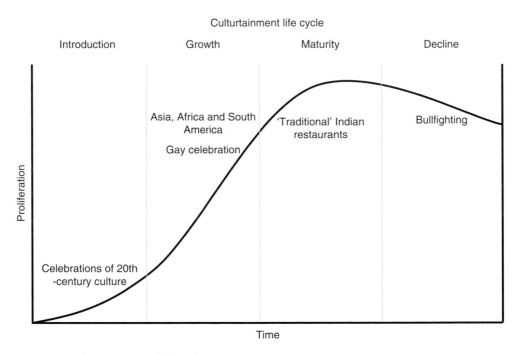

Fig. 16.9. Culturtainment life cycle.

Introduction

Celebrations of the twentieth century – there will be a growth in culturtainment attractions that are themed around the 20th century, popular culture and the celebration of celebrity. Many other recent and current aspects of modern life will be preserved for future generations to appreciate, in recognition of the importance and popularity of cultural heritage-based attractions.

Growth

Asia, Africa and South America – cheaper air fares combined with greater media exposure of destinations on these continents will lead to them growing rapidly as tourism destinations. A result of this will be increased cultural exploitation for the entertainment of tourists, with previously uncelebrated aspects of culture being revisited for the benefit of tourists, as well as fictitious culturtainment being used to create 'something from nothing'; an example of this can be found with 'Shangri-La', which is a fictional location from the 1933 novel *Lost Horizon* by James Hilton. Several destinations in East Asia have been marketed by tourist authorities as being 'Shangri-La' – even though it has never actually existed.

Gay celebration – gay pride parades have steadily grown in number and popularity throughout the latter half of the 20th and into the 21st century, and this trend will continue, with parades becoming larger more lavish events attracting increased mainstream corporate sponsorship.

Maturity

'Traditional' Indian restaurants – these are now being taken over by the children and sometimes grandchildren of those who established them. As this happens, they are being redecorated and rebranded in a modern contemporary style. What is currently considered to be a traditional Indian restaurant will eventually go into decline in the face of such re-imaging and competition from more contemporary counterparts.

Decline

Bullfighting – continued pressure from animal rights activists, revulsion from many tourists and disinterest from Hispanic youth will cause bullfighting to continue to decline.

REFERENCES

Annual Meeting of the Law and Society Association, 2007, Berlin (2007) Outsourcing culture: the role of the diaspora in the commodification. In: Long, D. (ed.). The Law and Society Association, Amherst, Massachusetts.

Attewill, F. (2009) Matador 11 is 'abuse victim'. *The Metro* 26th January 2009, p. 11.

British Broadcasting Corporation (BBC) (2009) 1997: Princess Diana dies in car crash. [Internet] London, BBC. URL available at: <http://news.bbc.co.uk/onthisday/hi/witness/august/31/newsid_3186000/3186299.stm>

Gallup (2002) Interes por las corridas de toros. [Internet] New York, Columbia University. URL available at: <http://www.columbia.edu/itc/spanish/cultura/texts/Gallup_CorridasToros_0702.htm>

Hassan, F. (2009) *Royal Tourism in Malaysia: Prospects and Challenges*. Lecture given at Leeds Metropolitan University, 16 April 2009.

Marsh, I. and Levy, S. (1998) *Sydney Gay and Lesbian Mardi Gras: Economic Impact Statement 1988*. Sydney Gay & Lesbian Mardi Gras Ltd, Sydney, Australia.

McDonald's (2008) About McDonald's. [Internet] Oakbrook, McDonald's. URL available at: <http://www.mcdonalds.com/corp/about.html>

MINTEL (2008) *Ethnic Restaurants and Takeaways – UK*. MINTEL International Group, London.

Newcastle University Museum of Antiquities (2008) Temple of Mithras. [Internet] Newcastle, Newcastle University. URL available at: <http://museums.ncl.ac.uk/archive/mithras/text.htm>

New Europe (2008) Employment up 11% thanks to cultural tourism. [Internet] Diegem, The Media Company. URL available at: <http://www.neurope.eu/articles/86857.php>

O'Regan, T. (2001) *Cultural Policy: Rejuvinate or Wither*. Professorial Lecture, Griffith University, Queensland, 26 July 2001.

Oxford English Dictionary (OED) (2008) Oxford English dictionary. [Internet] Oxford, Oxford University. URL available at: <http://www.oed.com/>

People for the Ethical Treatment of Animals (PETA) (2008) Portuguese city bans bullfighting. [Internet] London, PETA Europe Ltd. URL available at: <http://blog.peta.org.uk/tag/bullfighting>

US Census Bureau (2009) WorldPOPClock projection. [Internet] Washington, US Census Bureau. URL available at: <http://www.census.gov/ipc/www/popclockworld.html>

Waitt, G. and Markwell, K. (2006) *Gay Tourism Culture and Context*. Haworth Press, Philadelphia, Pennsylvania.

chapter 17

Spiritual Entertainment

Dr Nigel Morpeth

Entertainment that is based upon spirituality, religious belief and the supernatural.

Arguably, while spirituality, religion and entertainment might have intersecting meeting places for relationships to emerge between consumers and worshippers, to engage in and absorb spiritual and entertainment experiences, their associations might seem to be less than obvious. Historically, quasi-religious spiritualist and associated gatherings of this nature epitomized an unquantifiable but nevertheless significant nexus between spirituality and entertainment. For example, spiritualist meetings, seances and more latterly the ubiquitous ghost walk are perhaps evidence of the desire among consumers to connect either with spiritual authenticity, or to seek out supernatural entertainment. On a daily basis various ghost walks in York, UK, attract groups totalling several hundred people seeking this connection. This chapter explores the complex nature of the concepts of spirituality, religion and entertainment, considering the contemporary relationships that exist between all three elements both in individual and collective expression, identifying that in contemporary society spirituality, religion and entertainment enjoy the qualities of repetitive and ritualistic cultural practice (Beit-Hallahmi and Argyle, 1996).

While there is seemingly a paucity of academic literature on explicit connections between spirituality, religion and entertainment, there are arguably implicit connections on the role of visitor attractions with a religious theme, and indeed these have been given recognition as part of the 'entertainment industry'. In this respect, education and interpretation play an important role in enervating a diverse range of attractions, and education 'occurs' in entertainment settings, as well as formal educational institutions (see Chapter 14, this volume). Likewise, and apposite to the focus of this chapter, spiritual and religious experiences 'happen' in non-religious settings, and not least, locations which might be construed to be primarily entertainment settings.

RELIGION AND SPIRITUALITY

In offering an understanding of what constitutes religion, Raj and Morpeth (2007) noted the qualities of religion as an age old and dynamic concept, which incorporates both ancient and living belief systems and the emergence of new religious and quasi-religious faith-based organizations. The common elements are belief in supernatural and heavenly beings, transcendent deities, demons and divinations (Hinnells, 1984). They noted that the study of world religions requires an understanding of a diverse collection of practices, rituals and ideas and might incorporate polytheist beliefs in many gods and monotheist belief in one god.

Prior (2002) reminds us of the power of religion to be a conduit for societies' 'most cherished values' and perhaps an agency of social control and social order. Both religion and entertainment search for diverse audiences or customers, increasingly operating in competitive environments, in competition with other attractions and experiences and venues. Likewise, Bruce (1996) notes that the collective religious identity of a group can be resistant to pressures of cultural change (e.g. groups trying to adjust to changes such as migration), and that religious identity is about demarcating difference 'to others' (the sense of 'us and them').

The act of religious worship can be viewed as a metaphor for understanding and establishing an ordered world within the larger universe, perhaps increasingly competing with entertainment which can be viewed as 'a fitting metaphor for the mentality of the age' (Pearce, 1992, p. 93).

Within dynamic global cultural landscapes, religion continues to retain a significant place in society and together with a range of social, economic and political institutions epitomizes the complexity of structures and symbols that pervades diverse cultures and traditions. Yet, ironically the 'old certainties' have now been replaced by associated uncertainties of the enduring clarity of purpose and scope of religion within contemporary society. These uncertainties are partly predicated on the ability of religion to inform and inspire existing and new audiences. Perhaps audiences have become more receptive to the sensory perception honed on the messages in the medium of entertainment. While lexicographical definitions or at least characteristics pertaining to *the spiritual* might include references to the soul, god, sacred or religious things, it is far from obvious how linkages might be made between spirituality and entertainment.

Famously Karl Marx noted that religion was the opiate of the masses and likewise in popular parlance sport has also been dubbed in a similar vein. Similarly, while Ritzer (1992) in the 'MacDonaldization of Society' characterized shopping malls as the 'cathedrals of consumption', sports stadia have historically assumed the role of spiritual citadels, with 'congregations of fans' engaged in rituals which are akin to religious ceremony.

Magdalinski and Chandler (2002, p. 1) noted that 'sport and religion, while possessing disparate philosophical foundations appear to share a similar structure. Each offers its respective adherents a ritualistic tradition, a complement of suitable deities and a dedicated time and space for worship'. They cite the degree of complementary devotion from both sports fans and religious worshippers, together with the religious icons such as 'Touchdown Jesus' (behind the end zone of the University of Notre Dame's gridiron (Magdalinski and Chandler, p. 1) as evidence of structural similarities between sport and religion. While not wanting to overstress the similarities, they nevertheless categorize them as cultural institutions in which the 'social formation of collective groups' is worthy of investigation. Their central thesis is that sport (as an important element of the entertainment industry) can add to the identity and theological underpinnings of religious groups. Similarly, they also recognize that sport and religion both function as a form of escapism from 'the real world', with the sports arena as an entertainment facility as a place for fans to 'lose' themselves. Hughson identifies the emergence of neo-tribes which akin to religious evangelicals.

Spiritual entertainment is based upon the concept that 'supernatural', spiritual and religious forces have been and continue to be responsible for occurrences, including: renowned legends that are 'bought into' and shared by many, such as 'Noah's Ark'; phenomenon such as stigmata or the image of Christ appearing; quests around personal destiny; and the need to experience emotions brought about by the power of feeling associated with spiritual and religious practices and locations. The spiritual entertainment sector is structured as in Fig. 17.1.

SACRED SITES WITH SPIRITUAL ENGAGEMENT

Shackley's (2001) typology of sacred attractions (highlighted in Fig. 17.1) leads to questions of who should define sacred sites, what their core business is and the question of whether they should promote (perhaps simultaneously) opportunities for worship, education, reflection and entertainment. Shackley (2002) notes that the organization of such sites must be sympathetic to their core sacred function and in her words 'heterotopia' is maintained, that is, the removal from the world of time constraints and commerce and opportunity to engage in spiritual contemplation. What is construed to be a sacred site particularly in the advent of an experience economy is not without its contestations and controversies. Whitby in North Yorkshire in the north-east of the UK is synonymous with Captain Cook and 'Yorkshireness'. However, the emergence of a Dracula Society and associated Goth Culture is intended to pay homage to literary culture and the iconic Bram Stoker novel *Dracula*, which used in the literary narrative, used Whitby Abbey and St Mary's Parish Church as the backdrop to Dracula's arrival on the UK soil. Attempts by the Dracula Society to carry out 'commemorative ceremonies' in the graveyard of the parish church have led to opposition from the church, who feel such manifestations of *spectacle* are the stuff of counter-religious groups and an act of deliberate entertainment. Such acts of deliberate entertainment are yet another example of contested use of sacred spaces, a wider discussion which sees clashes and collisions of contemporary ephemeral fads and fashions, with the ancient girders of faith systems.

Pilgrimage and faith-based tourism

In April 2003, the European Association for Tourism and Leisure Education's 'Religious Tourism and Pilgrimage Special Interest Group' wanted to consider how those who manage religious spaces or sacred sites might respond to the complex needs of a range of visitors who

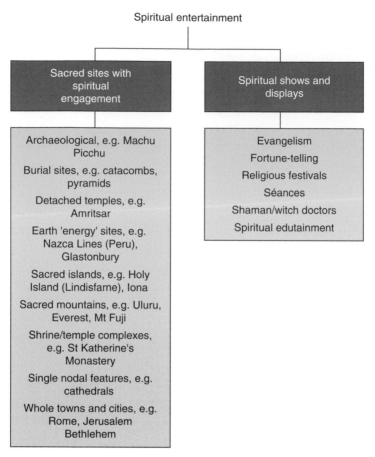

Fig. 17.1. Spiritual entertainment sub-sectors. (Based partially on the work of Shackley, 2001.)

might be exposed to elements of commercial development. The term religious space 'was taken to refer to both the confined space within a shrine, sanctuary, cathedral … as well as the religious space a pilgrim travels through' (2003, p. 175.) Tension was noted by Eade (1992) who highlighted the over-commercialization of the religious pilgrimage site of Lourdes, in the French Pyrenees and the associated 'tackiness' of the sale of religious trinkets (including a 'winking Christ', a Christ-like statue with flashing eyes) together with rowdiness between 'pilgrims,' with the excess consumption of alcohol. This could be contrasted with the work of Raj and Morpeth (2007) who expressed the distinctiveness of the Hajj to resist the tourist gaze. Figures 17.2 and 17.3 highlight two very different examples of sites that were not conceived, designed or created with the tourist gaze in mind, yet attract pilgrims and voyeurs from afar.

It is important to state that there is a well-established body of literature which explores the relationships between faith-based tourism and visitation. In particular the work of Nolan and

Fig. 17.2. The Lockerbie Memorial, Scotland, draws visitors from afar who wish to pay their respects.

Fig. 17.3. Tourists mingle among worshippers at the Frauenkirche in Dresden, Germany.

Nolan and Nolan (1992) expresses the complexity of the blurred conceptual boundaries, which might hamper the analysis of what constitutes a religious tourist, suggesting that 'if a tourist is half a pilgrim then a pilgrim is half a tourist'. Tourism literature also contains references to a religious visitor system, which reveals the significance of attractions and festivals as an important part of 'religious experience'. While discussion of a series of religious tourist attractions in a contemporary context inevitably focuses on the increasing pressures of visitation patterns stimulated by the emergence of an experience sector (Richards, 2001), it is important that the spaces for religious and spiritual devotion involve to a greater or lesser degree *spectacle* and *theatre*. Of course religious attractions systems also accommodate the serendipity voyeur, which is the visitor who stumbles across a Spanish religious festival, who will witness local community re-enactments of Christ's journey to the cross. Perhaps to the secular visitor this is perceived to be a moment of theatre, *performance* and *spectacle* (see also Chapter 16, this volume).

Ethical Factor: Religion and Entertainment in Conflict

There are acute pressures on religious venues trying to cater for both sacred and secular visitors, partly due to what purpose those venues have for visitors. Venues need to cater for spiritual needs, and increasingly an audience, which demands the trappings of deliberate entertainment. Conflicts of interest have occurred and continue to occur between worshippers and voyeuristic audiences at many religious sites, specific examples include York Minster (see the later case study), as well as on the Mediterranean island nation of Malta, which is a country with over 360 historic, ornate and highly decorated Catholic churches (see Fig. 17.4), and a predominantly devout Catholic population. Malta experiences peak inbound tourism during the summer months when temperatures can easily reach 30°C. A high proportion of tourists visiting Malta are from northern European countries including the UK. Maltese churches feature heavily in 'Visit Malta' marketing materials. Tourists on the island tend to dress casually including 'beach attire'; however, within churches the wearing of such clothing (which often bares significant amounts of flesh) is very much frowned upon by church authorities and worshippers. Of particular offence are bare shoulders and bikini tops which have been banned from most churches unless visitors cover up before entering. Some churches have compromised, and offer those who are inappropriately dressed shawls to cover up with, so that they may still enter, although many churches do not. Also of offence to some church authorities and worshippers is photography (particularly with flashes) and video filming within churches – two activities, which are of course synonymous with tourism. Being prevented from recording memories in this way can cause disquiet among tourists whom the island relies upon for its economy. Some churches have again reached compromises, allowing photography to take place without flashes or in specific areas only, or at particular times. Perhaps this suggests that an expanding entertainment and experience industry requires new styles of management and 'new' management strategies to respond to a new generation of consumer behaviour. Not least are the challenges of creating and managing visitor strategies that are sensitive to the impact of secularism on sacred and religious spaces.

Fig. 17.4. Mosta Dome, Malta.

The work of Arellano (2007) and Mulligan (2007) reveals the wider interpretations of faith-based travel, with less traditional elements of New Age philosophies, and indeed secular aspects moving quasi-religions towards the mainstream of what is considered to be spiritual worship and religion. Arellano identifies the emergence of the 'transformational pilgrimage' and 'religions of the self' with the 'mystic gaze' seeking out 'a global network of 'power places', where ancient and prehistoric civilizations and specific 'energy' spots (which) link up Stonehenge, Egypt's pyramids, Mount Everest, 'mystical' temples like the Taj Mahal and the like on a 'global' pagan path (Arellano, 2007, p. 91).

Festivals such as the Eavis family-inspired Glastonbury Festival have over many decades provided an 'outlet' in a UK context, for a 'power place', and an intersection of the entertainment industry and 'transformational pilgrimage'. Likewise, Mulligan (2007), with reference to the Caribbean, identifies the emergence of eclectic faith systems where 'destination managers treat culture like a new religion, transforming cultural places into sacred spaces and making cultural practices worthy of worship. By engaging in this process, destination managers are tapping into a niche market of New Age faith tourists seeking new types of pilgrimage' (2007, p. 113). This quest for faith-based experiences which have qualities of religious veneration are part of a wider transformation of consumers within an experience economy where consumers are increasingly seeking out opportunities for personal expression, and the confirmation of identity through new experiences. Such economies express the qualities of post-modernity, which is characterized by the blurring of boundaries between previously demarcated institutions and activities (Richards, 2001).

Part of the complex conundrum of how spirituality and religion fit within the entertainment industry requires a responsiveness to the powerful forces and patterns of globalization and the emergence of new social narratives. This undoubtedly poses complex challenges for 'managers' of religious and entertainment facilities, which attempt to respond to fragmented motivations for visitation. Practical issues of site management have to determine how existing facilities are able to combine different functions successfully, and incorporate forms of entertainment which reflect the mainstream, but also potentially offer a departure away from everyday rituals and 'centres of society'. Indeed, in this respect they reflect New Age philosophies of travel and pilgrimage to explore the emergence of new tourists or 'Esoteric tourists' being able to engage in processes of spirituality and enlightenment.

Case Study: York Minster

York Minster presents a site with both secular and sacred functions. York has been a magnet for visitors for many hundreds of years, and as tourism has grown in significance in the 20th century, it has created a base for excursion circuits (Holloway, 1987). Indeed it would appear that it became a main motivator for tourist trips and a core tourist product for visitation to York. In short, it can be argued that York Minster is a key part of selling York and indeed is central to York's marketing strapline of 'York Live the History'! This poses questions about the specific management and marketing challenge of religious buildings such as York Minster, and whether specifically there is pressure economically to promote the Minster to bring in revenue to both maintain the fabric of the Minster and to the wider tourist economy of York. There are potential problems for the sacred and religious integrity of a religious attraction, and the potential of such a site to compromise its religious and sacred core functions, in order to accommodate the wider needs of tourists. Ashworth (1996) noted the problems of interlinking tourism with heritage and the commodification and theming of the UK's history. This raises questions as to whether 'managers' and marketers have concerns about who is consuming the heritage product and whether the personal needs of consumers are being satisfied, describing the 'fortunate-by-product approach' of managers of heritage sites where products, which are used for one purpose can be consumed for another. York Minster encounters such pressures to accommodate a range of visitation functions. Ashworth (1996) reminds us that heritage dissonance occurs when there is a selective selling of the past, which can lead to a distorted or disinherited form of heritage. This places an additional responsibility of heritage (and interchangeably entertainment) managers to apply management and marketing strategies that faithfully adhere to the authenticity of the site. York Minster is pictured in Fig. 17.5.

Fig. 17.5. York Minster.

Secular pilgrimage: sacred or entertainment icon?

Another element of Shackley's typology of sacred sites is the notion of the site for secular pilgrimage. Rodman in his publication '*Elvis After Elvis: The Posthumous Career of a Living Legend* (1996, p. 1) emphasizes 'the importance of Graceland as a place of pilgrimage for Elvis fans and followers'. He observes the ubiquitous qualities of Elvis, stating:

> For a dead man, Elvis Presley is awful noisy ... sneaking out of songs, movies, television shows, advertisements, newspapers, magazines, comic strips, comic books, greetings cards, trading cards, T-shirts, poems, plays, short stories, novels, children's books, academic journals, university courses, art exhibits, home computer software, cookbooks, political campaigns, postage stamps, and innumerable other corners of the cultural terrain.

He notes how Elvis has assumed a Christ-like status as someone who, if not quite risen from the dead, is assumed by some fans and followers not to have died (Elvis's non-death), and is omnipresent in different parts of the globe with Elvis sightings on an annual basis since his death in 1977 (sometimes simultaneously in different parts of the globe). The Elvis Experience Industry is also enlivened by thousands of Elvis impersonators in the USA alone. Rodman extends this religious metaphor of Elvis as a religious (Christ-like) figure citing Allen Steele's novel *Clarke County, Space* (1990), where there is a mid-21st-century Elvis religion 'organized entirely around the life and teachings of Elvis' (p. 5). Likewise Elvis's followers are viewed as 'Elvis-worshipping cult' and Elvis as a holy figure (although conversely he states how the 1990s US band 'Living Colour' were at pains to press the same message through their music, 'Elvis is Dead').

However, it is Graceland that has been described by Rodman as a home for the 'community of Elvis fans', and he identifies 'the holiness of Graceland' and 'the all-night Candlelight Vigil that occurs at Graceland every year during "Tribute Week", is perhaps best understood in comparison to explicitly religious ceremonies' (1996, p. 117). He likens the fans and followers visiting Graceland as akin to 'Christian pilgrims of the first millennium' (Rodman, 1996, p. 117) with fans leaving graffiti in the form of prayers. Clearly, similar to a Christ-like venerated figure, the dead – but risen again, 'Elvis … Is Everywhere', a cultural icon, who through immortal ubiquity straddles the institutions of religion and entertainment.

SPIRITUAL SHOWS AND DISPLAYS

Taking a variety of guises, spiritual shows and displays are designed with one or more of the following purposes: to exploit the audiences belief in the supernatural (often the curing of illness or that 'destiny' can be influenced or predicted); to give respect to particular spiritual and religious practices; to 'sell' the fundamentals of spirituality and religion; and to educate audiences about issues relating to spirituality and religion. Common forms of spiritual shows and displays are listed in Table 17.1.

Table 17.1. Characteristics of spiritual shows and displays.

Type of spiritual show or display	Characteristics
Evangelism	The promotion of Christianity through evangelism is where spiritual entertainment meets sellertainment. The primary purpose of evangelism is to convert non-Christians into Christian believers in god. Evangelism is almost as old as the Bible itself, and has been practised by preachers for centuries. Today preachers can be seen and heard in churches, on city streets, on radio and television and on the Internet. Television evangelism is big business, particularly in North America where specialist television channels generate millions of dollars for churches annually, through viewers phoning premium-rate telephone numbers to leave messages or talk to a representative of the church, phoning to pledge cash donations and through the sale of memorabilia
Fortune-telling	This exploits the belief that the future can be foreseen, and often involves the use of techniques such as palmistry, or tools and accessories including tarot cards, crystal balls, tea leaves, rune

(Continued)

Table 17.1. Continued.

Type of spiritual show or display	Characteristics
	stones and bones. Fortune-telling often involves an audience of one, although there may be other onlookers. Fortune-tellers may claim to have an ethnic or family background that has practised in the fortune-telling field. 'Romany' fortune-tellers can often be found in tourist locations in the UK and Ireland, as featured in Fig. 17.6
Religious festivals	These are generally moderate- to large-scale events that are designed to celebrate or commemorate a religious occurrence from history. The novelty of religious festivals is their main attraction to audiences, particularly to tourists
Seances	These exploit the belief that the dead are still 'with us', albeit in spiritual form. Seances typically involve an audience of people being lead by a 'medium' who has the 'ability' to interact with the spirit world and convey messages to audience members from them. Seances have been exposed by many, including Derren Brown, as being no more than showmanship and the power of suggestion
Shaman/witch doctors	These are usually associated with cultures from less-industrialized areas of the world. Shows or displays are often staged for tourists that involve any of the following elements: communication with the spirits of the dead; theatrics such as going into trance-like states; fortune-telling; healing abilities – particularly casting out evil spirits that may cause illness; magic – particularly sleight of hand appearance–disappearance of items; chanting; elaborate costumes; and 'the unexpected' to maintain the attention, and respect of the audience
Spiritual edutainment	This takes place in a variety of guises, sometimes live with interpretation, and sometimes via media or the Internet. Spiritual edutainment is designed to inform audiences about aspects of spirituality and religion. This can also be in the form of a re-enactment of a recorded historic event that has spiritual or religious connotations, so that the watching audience learn 'what actually happened', this often takes place at religious sites in the form of guided tours, where the tour guide also becomes a 'storyteller'. Spiritual edutainment may also involve the promotion of religion through explaining 'what things mean' in a manner that is entertaining

Fig. 17.6. A Romany fortune-teller's booth, Great Yarmouth, UK.

Case Study: Oberammergau

This German village in the foothills of the Kofel mountains in Bavaria has a theatrical appearance to its buildings, which are decorated with fresco paintings, and the village spawned a religious icon industry with wooden carvings of crucifixes and saints being exported around the world. The village has gained notoriety for staging the performance of a *Passion* play every 10 years (supposedly an example of miracle plays which were popular throughout Europe between 13th to 16th centuries).

This miracle play is one of the earliest examples of the intersection between theatre and spirituality depicting the *Passion* week (the last few weeks of the life of Christ). This play was first staged in 1634, after the residents (in gratitude at the end of the Black Death), stated that they would stage the *Passion* play every 10 years. The play starts at 8 a.m., and runs for 8 h, containing 18 acts, staged by over 700 local residents (and orchestra and chorus) who are selected by a committee of key community members. The play attracts over 300,000 people each season. The play is testament of the theatricality of the *Passion* week and the capacity of religion to intersect with entertainment.

Political Factor: the Rise of the Religious Right

Arguably, the politically inspired intersections of entertainment, religion, spirituality and the media have become crystallized and are (or were) the embodiment of US society, and the role of the evangelical right as a guiding ideology of central government policy making. Former US President George Bush's proclamation that 'God had told him to end tyranny in Iraq' and that he had told the Palestinians that 'God had told him to bring peace to the Middle East', which emphasized the unapologetic approach of major political figures to connect political decision making with supernatural intervention. Martin (2008, p. 1) noted how '[t]he terms of engagement in America's "culture wars" have been subtly changing since the 1990s with the economic, intellectual, social and political coming of age of many Evangelicals in the Bible Belt', partially supported by TV evangelism.

THE FUTURE

The conundrum for the entertainment and religion industries is that perhaps they are chasing too few visitors, and trying too hard to 'fit' the product with consumer expectations and requirements. What emerges from this analysis is the dominant question as to what extent is the increasing entrepreneurial function of religion and spirituality eclipsing their other more 'traditional' functions? The dominant changes to spiritual and religious facilities and locations, as entertainment spaces creates a tension of trying to expand into new audiences as part of the commodities of mass culture and the experience industry. Taking this into account, Fig. 17.7 illustrates the immediate future for this entertainment industry sector.

Introduction

New religious pilgrimage – collections of artefacts and relics in locations connected with new and emergent religions (particularly religions that are 'celebrity-endorsed') will provide a setting or 'attraction' for pilgrims to visit.

Online pilgrimage – the growth in virtual worlds and 'second lives' will cause new online systems of worship to be developed that will lead to online gatherings and pilgrimage. Online pilgrimage to existing real-world sites will also emerge through interfaces such as second life.

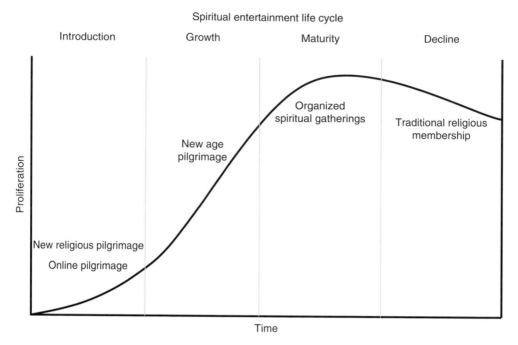

Fig. 17.7. Spiritual entertainment life cycle.

Growth

New Age pilgrimage – religions of the self and visitation to so-called power places will lead to growth in entertainment festivities to enable such expressions to take place.

Maturity

Organized spiritual gatherings – particularly travelling fairs with shamanistic interaction that are less attractive to younger audiences.

Decline

Traditional religious membership – a consequence of this will be the further blurring of boundaries of the use of spiritual locations for both worship and entertainment. This may also lead to the closure of some religious premises, the buildings of which may then be used for other purposes as in Fig. 17.8.

Fig. 17.8. Halo nightclub, Leeds, UK, in what used to be Trinity St David's Church. The DJ performs from what was the pulpit in front of the stained-glass window.

REFERENCES

Arellano, A. (2007) Religion, pilgramge, mobility and immobility. In: Raj, R. and Morpeth, N.D. (eds) (2007) *Religious Tourism and Pilgrimage Management: An International Perspective.* CAB International, Wallingford, UK, pp. 89–97.

Ashworth, G.J. (1996) Elements of planning and managing heritage sites. In: *Planning, Managing and Marketing Heritage, International Conference on Tourism and Heritage Management (ICCT),* Yogakarta, Indonesia.

Bruce, S. (1996) *Religion in the Modern World, from Cathedrals to Cults.* Oxford University, Oxford.

Durham, M. (2000) *The Christian Right, the Far Right and the Boundaries of American Conservatism.* Manchester University Press, Manchester, UK.

Beit-Hallahmi, B. and Argyle, M. (1996) *The Psychology of Religious Behaviour. Belief and Expression.* Routledge, London.

Eade, J. (1992) Pilgrimage and tourism at Lourdes, France. *Annals of Tourism Research* 19 (1), 18–32.

Hinnells, J.H. (ed.) (1984) *The Penguin Dictionary of Religions.* Penguin Books Ltd, London.

Holloway, C. (1987) *The Business of Tourism.* London, Pitman.

MacDonald, S. (1996) Theorising museums: an introduction. In: MacDonald, S. and Fyfe, G. (eds) *Theorising Museums.* Blackwell, Oxford, pp. 1–18.

Magdalinski, T. and Chandler, J.L. (2002) (eds) *With God on Their Side: Sport in the Service of Religion.* Routledge, London.

Mulligan, J. (2007) Centring the visitor: promoting a sense of spirituality in the caribbean. In: Raj, R. and Morpeth, N.D. (eds.) *Religious Tourism and Pilgrimage Management: An International Perspective.* CAB International, Wallingford, UK, pp. 113–126.

Nolan, M. and Nolan, S. (1992) Religious sites as tourism attractions in Europe. *Annals of Tourism Research* 19, 1–17.

Pearce, P. (1982) *The Social Psychology of Tourist Behaviour.* Pergamon Press, Oxford.

Prior, N. (2002) *Museums & Modernity: Art Galleries and the Making of Modern Culture.* Berg, Oxford.

Raj, R. and Morpeth, N.D. (2007) *Religious Tourism and Pilgrimage Management: An International Perspective.* CAB International, Wallingford, UK.

Richards, G. (ed.) (2001) *Cultural Attractions and European Tourism.* CAB International, Wallingford, UK.

Ritzer, G. (1992) The McDonaldization of society: an investigation into the changing character of contemporary social life. *Thousand Oaks*, Pine Forge Press.

Rodman, G.B. (1996) *Elvis After Elvis: The Posthumous Career of a Living Legend.* Routledge, London.

Shackley, M. (2001) *Managing Sacred Sites*, Thomson Learning, London.

Shackley, M. (2002) Space, sanctity and service: the english cathedral as a managed visitor attraction. *International Journal of Tourism Research* 4(5), pp. 345–352.

chapter 18

Health Entertainment

Volker Rundshagen

Entertainment that is designed to support positive physical and mental health.

To achieve and maintain a state of good health is one of humankind's most basic needs. Throughout history and across cultures the importance of good health has received much attention and provoked a wide range of health-related recreational activities, many of which are sports-related or are directly leisure activities, but some of which are health treatments aimed towards a recreational audience that through sensory stimulation are designed to provoke a positive emotional response, and as such these treatments are entertainment. The importance of good health is reflected by the existence of the World Health Organization (WHO) – a specialized health agency belonging to the United Nations (UN). Health is defined in this organization's constitution as 'a state of complete physical, mental and social well-being and not merely the absence of disease or infirmity'. Furthermore, it is stated that 'the enjoyment of the highest attainable standard of health is one of the fundamental rights of every human being without distinction of race, religion, political belief, economic or social condition' (World Health Organization, 1946). This definition of health extends beyond the traditional Western biomedical paradigm that tends to treat body, mind and society as separate entities.

Health entertainment is on the periphery of the entertainment industry, but the fundamental factor that makes this an entertainment industry sector is the nature by which health entertainment utilizes sensory stimulation in order to invoke an emotional response among the audience. Health entertainment typically involves stimulating all five senses in order to promote positive emotions and an improved state of health.

In today's society, patients are at the same time customers, consumers or even connoisseurs who are well informed about health issues and who celebrate their efforts to promote their own health and their well-being. As a consequence, entertaining methods of therapeutic delivery have entered the medical stage. Besides the medicine market, health entertainment encompasses the large and growing markets of travel and tourism, leisure and also nutrition. Health-related products and services mix with other offerings, and in many cases it is indeed difficult to differentiate between the health portion and the entertainment aspect.

HISTORY

Medical lore was passed down from generation to generation long before human beings settled in the first villages between the Tigris and Euphrates Rivers roughly 10,000 years ago. In those days, members of the priestly classes were keepers of most knowledge, including that related to the healing arts. The shaman was the first identifiable priest-physician, and can be considered a noble figure in history (Calvert, 2002). In ancient times, healing was associated with magic. Rituals and spirituality outweighed technical knowledge of the body or natural sciences. Medical historians have described medicine evolution from magic to religion to empiricism to science. The application of massage as a healing technique can be traced back to the earliest days when medicine was still in its magic stage. The first inferential evidence of massage was found in the Code of Hammurabi, carved in stone *c.*2350 BC by Babylonians living in the Mesopotamian region of the Near East (Calvert, 2002).

In 1663, Johann Andreas Eisenbarth was born in Oberviechtach, Germany. He learnt the profession of an oculist as well as that of a stonecutter. To date, his name is associated with medical treatments and crude therapies spectacularly performed on patients at markets or even fun fairs. Eventually, he worked as a self-employed surgeon practising in public. For marketing purposes, he was accompanied by an illustrious troop of jugglers, musicians and dancers. At some point his group comprised some 120 people (Doktor-Eisenbarth-Schule Oberviechtach, 2009). Besides the startling appearances he actually developed a number of innovative medical instruments, and he gained attention with remarkable successes. In this historic period, there were also less-gifted travelling surgeons and many swindlers on the road who harmed innumerable patients desperately looking for help. Science has proven that Dr Eisenbarth was not one of them, and is accepted as a dedicated medic of the late 17th and early 18th centuries. Furthermore, he represents an historical example of health and entertainment wisely combined.

The word 'spa', which is derived from the Belgian town of Spa located in the Ardennes, became the symbol for health resorts when British tourists started visiting the Belgian town in the 16th century. However, the concept of water-centred restoration and health promotion has been around much longer. Hippocrates proposed that all disease was the result of imbalances of bodily fluids (Klick and Stratmann, 2008). The ancient Romans knew about the healing effects of water, baths soon became popular locations of social life as much as health-promoting functional places. Spa therapies have existed since ancient times in many different forms. The culture of hot springs and thermal bathing draws from different traditions around the world such as the Japanese *onsen* (hot springs with Zen gardens), Finnish *saunas* (sweating rooms and ice plunges) and Ottoman *hammams* (steam rooms and private washing quarters) (Tabbachi, 2008). Figure 18.1 features a spa bath that has been created from natural spa mineral waters.

European spa culture escalated in the 1900s, when bathing locations appealed to the wealthy classes who were seeking relaxation away from their home surroundings. Spa physicians dealt with an array of injuries, allergies and other, mainly chronic, conditions. Besides the medical aspect, entertainment played a major role in this evolving spa culture integrating gambling, concerts and diverse events into the spa-stay experience. In Europe, mineral spring spas including natural hot springs with associated healing properties, and seawater or seaweed-based thalassotherapy spas were especially popular. European colonists emigrating to the Americas took the quest for health-promoting mineral springs to the USA, where the bathing culture also took off, generating many regular customers returning to benefit from the healing effects of the water.

Contemporary health entertainment is mostly associated with spas and wellness facilities, but also with health promotion, which is the educational aspect of health entertainment, as detailed in Fig. 18.2.

Fig. 18.1. A spa bath in Budapest, Hungary.

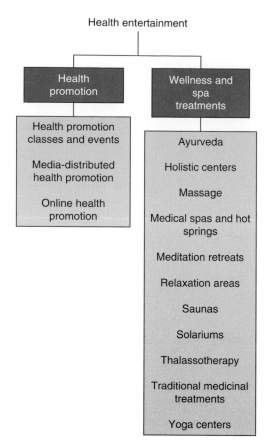

Fig. 18.2. Health entertainment sub-sectors.

HEALTH PROMOTION

Health promotion is 'the process of enabling people to exert control over the determinants of health and thereby improve their health' (Health Promotion Agency, 2009). It covers all aspects of health including physical, mental, nutritional, dietary, sexual and smoking cessation. Health promotion involves a combination of health education and the selling of ideals, and as such it shares traits with several entertainment industry sectors (as highlighted in Fig. 18.3).

Due to the similarity in nature of the components of the health promotion sub-sector (highlighted in Fig. 18.1) to other similar components and sub-sectors covered within Chapters 14 and 15, health promotion will not be covered in any further detail in this chapter.

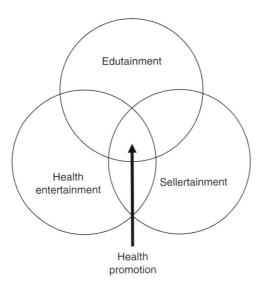

Fig. 18.3. Health promotion's positions within the entertainment industry.

WELLNESS AND SPA TREATMENTS

According to the *Oxford English Dictionary*, the term 'wellness' has been in use since the 17th century to express health and well-being. In the 1950s, the American physician and medical statistician Halbert L. Dunn promoted a paradigm shift in the US medical system by emphasizing self-management competencies and individual responsibility for health promotion. It was based on a methodological framework that was intended to maximize the individuals' potential, taking into account their given life settings (German Wellness Association, 2008). The notion of the individual taking on more responsibility in all areas of life with a particular emphasis on social insurance and health care issues reflects a change from public-fund health care systems towards private-fund ones, underlining the financial responsibility of the individual seeking health care, in the developed world as well as in emerging markets.

Systems based on public- or employer-based health care are reaching their limit, while the financial burden seems to rise into the indefinite. On a macroeconomic scale, it is roughly estimated that the US health industry's expenses will exceed GDP by 2025 (Pilzer, 2007), and it has been detected that health care costs have doubled from 1990 to 2001 and are projected to again double by 2012 (Clark, 2008).

Deterioration in levels of health globally, but particularly in 'Western' societies due to diet and lifestyle, combined with restructuring efforts of public health systems, inspire new ways of thinking about health and individual responsibility for a healthier lifestyle (Bodens, 2003). A combination of prevention-orientated lifestyle-driven health products and a financial regime redirecting means into products and services that prevent diseases, rather than just treating diseases and their symptoms, opens up new market segments with tremendous growth promises. As individuals assume the role of health care product consumers rather than that of a patient waiting for the service imposed by a public body, marketing aspects become pivotal in the conceiving of health entertainment offers. Being confronted with the obligation to spend their own money on health-related services instead of relying on the state, newly generated customers become more demanding, better informed and more self-conscious in selecting the product or service of their choice.

Wellness institutions promote a feel-good factor, often by providing a high-quality, stylish, encouraging and service-orientated setting, where atmosphere is of utmost importance. Whether the customer turns to the institution to spend a few relaxed hours, to prevent illness, to stay in good physical or mental shape, or to get relief from medical conditions, comfort is a necessity, particularly due to inseparability of body, mind and spirit. A crucial success factor of a health entertainment facility is its design. Spa designers face the challenge of a heightened level of expectation. As a consequence of growing, sophisticated technology and increasing international travel, the consumers have gained more experience with evermore refined and innovative design in general, which has raised expectations (Remedios, 2008). A common trend in Europe is towards historical references including Roman, Turkish and Asian bath cultures which are in keeping with the growing general trend towards authenticity. Therapy and relaxation elements are often combined to create a coherent flow of sensory emotional experiences, which are in keeping with the facility's theme.

Social Factor: Demographics and Health

Due to the ageing population in many Western countries, designers of commercial spas and wellness facilities need to ensure that their products remain relevant to the needs of their clientele. Europe is undergoing profound demographic change; the proportion of children and adolescents among the population is reducing, while at the same time the number of elderly people is growing (Hamm, 2008). In Germany, it is estimated that by 2050, the population aged 60 or older will make up 40.4% of the total population, and the population aged 80+ is expected to be 14.6% (Höhn *et al.*, 2008). With this ageing population, health issues increasingly gain importance and attention. Older people naturally have to cope with more health problems than younger people; however, there are a growing number of older people who enjoy good health. They actively contribute to that status by participating in prevention programmes and by leading a more health-conscious lifestyle in order to maximize their chances of a healthy and long-life expectancy.

This latter aspect gains even greater importance among the middle-aged population. Being aware of increasing costs for health care, especially once severe illnesses have occurred, and also acknowledging that the demanding world of work causes more and more cases of exhaustion, depression, burnout and physical wear, many look for options to prevent theses adverse effects. Healthier lifestyles are in vogue, and there is an increasing readiness to devote much time as well as an increasing portion of the discretionary income to health-related activities. Wellness-centred holidays and the membership in a local health club have become integral parts of society and even contemporary status symbols.

The predominant entertainment treatments and facilities offered at wellness centres and spas are detailed in Table 18.1.

Table 18.1. Wellness and spa entertainment treatments and facilities.

Name of treatment/ facility	Characteristics
Ayurveda	Ayurveda is a medical treatment and healing arts tradition from India. The word is derived from the Sanskrit words of *ayu*, meaning life, and *veda*, meaning knowledge. Ayurveda has been described as 'a complete and integrated life science' and 'a holistic, spiritual and philosophical system of medication that covers all the principles of allopathy, homoeopathy, and naturopathy' (Hannam, 2008, p. 343). The traditional concept of ayurveda implies an intrinsic order in the world, and any illness is a departure from that order. According to ayurvedic philosophy everyone possesses the three elements of wind/air, fire, and water/earth. Any disease is diagnosed as an imbalance of these elements within the human body. Consequently, the therapies aim at restoring the balance

A famous centre of traditional Indian health care attracting many Western tourists is Kerala, which is the first state of India to sell health tourism abroad by promoting Ayurveda |
| Holistic centres | Holism refers to the philosophy of viewing the universe and especially living nature as an entity made up of interacting wholes that are more than the mere sum of its elements. Relating to health care, this concept implies the treatment of body, mind and spirit together, as physical, mental and spiritual aspects of life are understood to be closely interconnected. A holistic centre could be defined as a purpose-built centre where guests engage in the learning or the improvement of body–mind–spirit activities (Smith and Puczkó, 2009, p. 199). Various programmes are offered, and many activities are organized in seminar group settings. Typical concepts involved include meditation, yoga, feng shui and aromatherapy |
| Massage | According to Calvert (2002, p. 11) massage is 'the manipulation of the body by kneading, stroking, friction, percussion, vibration … applied with the hands, feet, elbows, forearms, or with tools … and the use of water, herbs, salts and muds'. Massage stimulates physical sensations that are translated into feelings and emotions |

(Continued)

Table 18.1. Continued.

Name of treatment/ facility	Characteristics
	by the brain. Massage is generally used to physically heal damaged body areas or to promote a sense of mental well-being. It is extremely popular and constitutes the largest portion of many day and hotel spas (Tabbachi, 2008). Popular forms of massage include: aromatherapy, back, deep tissue, hot stone, pregnancy, reflexology, shiatsu, sports, Swedish and Thai. Massage has found its place in contemporary health entertainment settings, and ancient traditions are increasingly revived. Another increasing trend is the future of massage as an adjunct therapy to psychology (Calvert, 2002)
Medical spas and hot springs	The spa industry has recently emerged as a global phenomenon, which has become possible through the convergence of industries, traditions and therapeutic practices. It is estimated that spas are a US$40 billion global industry with over 50,000 spas around the globe and at least 16,000 spas in the USA (Spafinder, 2007, cited in Cohen, 2008, p. 4). There are several categories of spas, which are highlighted in Table 18.2
	Spas are a melting pot for a range of products and services that enhance health and well-being, drawing from a range of aligned industries including, among others, beauty, hospitality, tourism, architecture, property development, landscape design, fashion, fitness and leisure (Cohen, 2008)
Meditation retreats	The origin of this concept is derived form the Latin word *meditatio*, meaning to align towards, or to focus on, the centre. Meditation, sometimes also described as a devoted form of contemplation, is a spiritual practice deeply rooted in several religions, especially in East Asia. Within Buddhism, Hinduism and Taoism, meditation has a similar meaning as the prayer in Christianity. Increasingly, meditation retreats are part of wellness-themed tourism resorts
Relaxation areas	Relaxation areas can be designed for the purpose of mental relaxation or physical relaxation or both. In many cases these areas are an integral part of a spa or another health or wellness facility. Many treatments will have a lasting effect only if silence

(*Continued*)

Table 18.1. Continued.

Name of treatment/ facility	Characteristics
	is emphasized. At some locations, light music or even nature sounds such as waterfalls, singing birds or sizzling fireplaces are featured. Aromas distributed by vaporizers or burners could also play a crucial role. Smell has a fundamental relationship with memory – emotions are recalled through aromas triggering good or unpleasant recollections (Howard and Vincent, 2008), and refreshing or relaxing aromas will support to build up the desired emotion while staying at the facility
Saunas	The so-called *dry* or Finnish sauna is an enclosure accommodating several individuals. It is heated to the desired temperature, which is then maintained for the duration of the intended session. At the core of a sauna session there is the alternation of heating and cooling stimuli caused by staying inside the sauna and the cooling-off phase outside where cold-water pools and fresh air may be used. Effects of the heating phase include increase in metabolism in the skin, secretion of sweat, cleansing, and relaxation of muscles and the psyche. Effects of the cooling-off phase include saturation of the blood with oxygen, stimulation of the kidney functioning and feeling of freshness (Interwellness, 2009). Fig. 18.4 demonstrates a typical sauna scene
Solariums	Solariums are enclosed sunbeds built with light tubes emitting UV radiation. Based on the Latin word *sol*, meaning sun, this feature is intended to imitate or replace sunlight effects. Typically, people looking for a more intense-looking tan frequent solariums. Authorities and consumers' rights associations increasingly draw the attention of the public to the adverse effects of solariums, 'even small doses of UVA and UVB radiation damage the skin, contribute to the ageing process, and can even cause skin cancer (New South Wales Department of Health, 2009)
Thalassotherapy	The origin of this concept is derived from the Greek word *thalassa*, meaning the sea. It refers to a variety of treatments that use seawater and seaweed to revitalize the body and skin (Gray and Liguori, 1994; Smith and Puczkó, 2009). In the 16th century, the French King Henry III was advised by his doctor to take seawater treatments. In 1750, Richard Russell from England published a dissertation on seawater therapy. Following these early stages,

(Continued)

Table 18.1. Continued.

Name of treatment/ facility	Characteristics
	thalassotherapy became widely accepted as being beneficial. Nowadays, the most popular destinations are France, Spain, Ireland and increasingly North Africa as well as the Middle East; the latter place being famous for Dead Sea resorts (Smith and Puczkó, 2009)
Traditional medicinal treatments	The transfer of traditional Chinese medicines to North America and Europe began in the 1970s, and especially the practice of acupuncture has found its way into Western medicine. Although the actual health-promoting effects of therapies, e.g. acupuncture, or at least the reasons for such effects, are disputed within the scientific community, there are growing numbers of followers enjoying treatments at dedicated centres or wellness resorts
Yoga centres	Yoga is a combination of physical and mental actions that are designed to improve heath; its origins are in ancient India. Yoga centres today involve teaching yoga techniques as well as providing an environment that is conducive to yoga practice in its aesthetics, atmosphere and particular sensory stimulation

Fig. 18.4. A typical sauna.

(Continued)

Ethical Factor: Misleading Consumers, Health Risks

Bodens (2003) states that an inflated use of the term *wellness* by hotels, tour operators and tourist destinations has been noted. This holds certainly true for many industries beyond leisure and tourism, too. Businesses have picked up on the boom or even hype around wellness, and in order to increase sales or enhance profit margins, regular products might just be renamed. The question arises regarding the point at which the border between harmless marketing exaggerations and betrayal of the customer is crossed.

Health issues tend to be delicate in their nature, as individuals might be harmed and suffer, in the worst case, irreparable damages. In cases of products labelled as wellness or health-promoting that actually do not have any such effect, it is rather the absence of a positive outcome which has to be feared more than a negative, damaging result. However, in the case of therapeutic activity, there still is the danger that it is administered by inadequately trained staff, in an incomplete or inappropriate manner, or provided to individuals who actually have contraindications. Furthermore, in the case of facilities bearing certain risks such as sauna or solariums, guests should be advised or warned.

Even if a therapy is conducted correctly and has proven beneficial effects in general, another issue might arise: Due to the short duration of a typical wellness holiday stay, the medical effect of health promotion is limited to a short period of time in most cases (Bodens, 2003). The patient or customer should be informed accordingly. The suggestion to install an independent, neutral accreditation body establishing and enforcing clearly defined criteria has been brought forward. This would help promote the customers' confidence in wellness providers and products (Bodens, 2003).

Case Study: Keidel Mineral-Thermalbad Freiburg (KMTF), Germany

Thermal spas play a major role in the German health and wellness sector. There is a rich tradition of visiting baths and administering health resort treatments. Thermal spas have been at the heart of preventive and curative health regime programmes for decades, and they are a key asset of recreational health and wellness-oriented tourist destinations. Figure 18.5 denotes the KMTF spa bath.

KMTF is located in the Mooswald forest, just outside the city of Freiburg in southern Germany. The city has some 220,000 inhabitants, making it the fourth-largest city in the state of Baden-Württemberg, and the southernmost metropolis of Germany. Besides being a distinctive
(Continued)

Case Study: Continued

Fig. 18.5. One of the KMTF bathing areas.

place of higher education attracting many students, Freiburg is also the centre of Black Forest tourism, being situated at its base in the valley of the upper Rhine, also close to the French and Swiss borders.

Tourists as well as inhabitants represent the target groups of the regional spas. The average travel time to reach a thermal spa in Germany is just over 40 min. Eighty per cent of the KMTF visitors live within a travel time of 0–30 min, 11% travel 31–60 min, and 9% of the visitors travel more than 60 min. In this southern German area, there is a strong tradition of thermal spas. Within a range of some 130 miles, many mineral spas and also recreational bathing facilities compete to attract visitors.

KMTF represents a typical European recreation institution combining entertainment aspects with an underlying health motive. Furthermore, it illustrates the fundamental change German health-related facilities are undergoing, accompanying the shift from public-sector health insurance-based medical treatments towards entertainment-driven wellness products and services paid for by customers rather than patients. Its history and background is featured in Table 18.2.

KMTF is a mineral thermal spa. Its owners are *Freiburger Stadtbau GmbH*, a state-owned real estate administration corporation, and *Sparkasse Nördliches Breisgau*, a regional savings bank.

(Continued)

Case Study: Continued

In its early years, KMTF relied on bathing guests and the medical treatment section used by patients who were sent by their doctors prescribing therapies mostly paid for by the public health insurance systems. Following several health reforms only a few treatments are still fully covered nowadays, and only 15% of the visitors are patients. Therefore, opening the sauna centre in 1995 and introducing entertainment-oriented as well as supplemental therapy treatments (that both have to be paid for by the individual guest) have been vital for business.

KMTF offers a variety of health and wellness services, and consists of some $1800\,m^2$ of water areas. The temperature of the pools ranges between 25°C and 41°C. The thermal bathing area features two indoor pools and three outdoor pools. The therapy pools are equipped with massage jets and thermal mineral waterfalls. Outdoors the large swimming pool and an adventure pool with a stream channel are at the guests' disposal, including an overheated pool. In addition, an Irish-Roman steam bath is offered. The latter feature is reserved for ladies or gentlemen one afternoon per week, respectively. A fitness level offers exercise options and also solaria.

The sauna centre features four indoor saunas, one of which features relaxation music and light effects (for additional sensory stimulation); a Turkish steam bath; four outdoor log cabin saunas; relaxation zones with sunbathing areas; a *meditarium*; and a bar. On a regular basis, aromas are infused with the steam in the saunas, with the temperatures ranging from 60°C to 90°C. A pool and a natural lake are offered to cool off after sauna cabin sessions.

The medical treatment centre offers a variety of massages, including classical treatments, backrubs and soap-brush massage. Besides the entertainment-driven massage programmes, prescribed spa therapy treatments are offered.

To attract visitors, KMTF engages in a number of promotional activities. Advertisements are placed in local and regional media, and brochures are distributed via the local tourism information offices and hotels. To promote repeat business, reduced prices for multiple entries such as ten-ticket booklets are offered, and the membership cards, *SaunaClubCard* and *ThermalClubCard*, reduce the regular entrance fees. To address the considerably lower visitor numbers in the summer season, extended ticket validity is then offered. Furthermore, web site functions are enhanced, as the Internet is gaining importance as a direct sales channel. Customers order tickets online, and they are informed about special offers as well as the latest news online.

KMTF has numerous competitors, including an array of leisure offers in general and health entertainment facilities including other thermal spas and therapeutic options in the region. The opening of the sauna centre in 1995, and its enlargement with innovative outdoor facilities in 2001, were pivotal steps in securing a favourable position in the market. For spa-based health entertainment institutions, some kind of renewal or enhancement is required about every three to five years. KMTF is committed to innovation, and the next project in this regard is going to be a family hall. Besides these visions, major investments in the near future will focus on energy-efficiency improvement.

(Continued)

> ## Case Study: Continued
>
> KMTF has mastered the change from an institution living almost 100% on public-health system-financed patients into an innovative service provider, selling health and wellness entertainment to patrons, 95% of whom pay on their own. To cater to all patients and to delight fastidious entertainment-seekers remains a formidable challenge.
>
> Source: Keidel Mineral-Thermalbad Freiburg (2008a,b,c, 2009).

Table 18.2. History of Keidel Mineral-Thermalbad Freiburg.

Year	Occurrence
1977	KMTF construction began after exploratory limestone drilling revealed thermal waters at a temperature of 45.4°C
1979	Accreditation as *Heilquelle* (mineral spring spa) through the regional government office. KMTF opened
1980	The department of physical therapy and balneology was founded comprising KG, massage, lymph drainage, baths and kinesitherapy
1983	A second water source was explored where waters were found at 29°C
1984	A Roman-Irish themed steam bath opened
1991	Accreditation was awarded as a *Heilquellen Kurbetrieb* (enhanced legal mineral spring spa status)
1992	An outdoor pool with water temperature of 28°C opened
1994	The fitness level opened
1995	The sauna area opened with four indoor cabins, two outdoor saunas, one sauna pool, Turkish steam bath, solaria, relaxation and sunbathing areas
1996	A third water source was explored and found to be 30°C
1998	A hot water pool opened
2001	The sauna area was enlarged with a sauna building on the lake, natural bathing lake, and rock landscape
2004	An event pool with stream canal and integrated overheated pool at 41°C opened. This was the first KMTF project to be subsidized by the tourism infrastructure fund of the *Bundesland* (state) of Baden-Württemberg

THE FUTURE

The future for the health entertainment sector is largely positive. Good health remains an area of great importance, and the era of *psychosocial health* has only just begun. The global trend towards health and fitness is leading to increasing health awareness. Enabled by more sophisticated diagnostics, people will concentrate more on their susceptibilities (Ludwig, 2007), and it is likely that the convergence of health entertainment, healthy leisure activities, fitness, lifestyle, wellness and tourism will continue at a steady pace. The ageing population of most Western countries also contributes greatly to this sector's growth. Future-oriented philosophies such as the 'lifestyle of health and sustainability' (LOHAS) have inspired the creation of new holistic health entertainment offers. At the same time, the pressure on the working population is increasing, leading to a greater need for relaxation of body, mind and spirit during short, yet intense and fully focused leisure and entertainment breaks, as highlighted in Fig. 18.6.

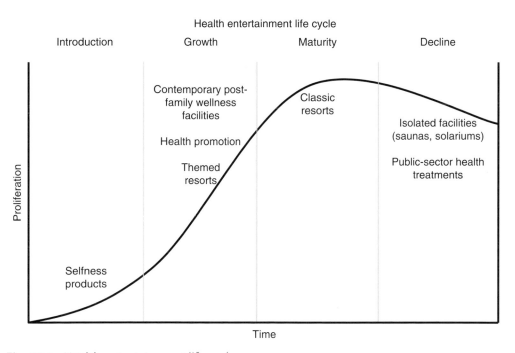

Fig. 18.6. Health entertainment life cycle.

Introduction

Selfness products – at the core of the wellness wave, we find the quest for redefining quality of life. In the future, the individual will strive for continuous individual development and change, rather than mere relaxation or temporary well-being (Horx and Wenzel, 2003). Selfness customers are no longer wellness consumers, but self-transformers assuming full responsibility for their own progress, and dedicated coaching services will evolve in this context.

Growth

Contemporary post-family wellness facilities – the ageing population will be a driver of changing health entertainment products and services. The challenge in this area is in marketing psychology – how to promote products designed for those aged 50+ and particularly senior citizens to a target group, which does not like to be associated with being old and of fragile health, and in the worst case, with feeling obsolete.

Health promotion – obesity awareness, addiction treatment and sexual health have gained media prominence over the past decade. As part of government strategies to educate people about prevention, there will be a rise in the number of health-related edutainment facilities as well as more participative and active health initiatives in place at existing facilities.

Themed resorts, authentic settings – venues with carefully selected materials, tasteful design of exterior and interior architecture, and well-trained or expert staff. Achieving the most authentic environment and atmosphere where great attention is paid to every detail and every aspect of the leading theme or concept. The biggest challenge for providers usually is the large investment required to open a dedicated, state-or-the-art facility. Moreover, the risk remains high that, and even if a particular theme is popular today, it might not be in vogue long enough to be profitable.

Maturity

Classic resorts – these include typical holiday destinations, such as seaside resorts or Alpine villages, with their resort hotels where traditional medical or old-fashioned wellness concepts still play the major role. While there are still regular customers, the competition of innovative, dedicated and different offers has grown strongly. A few traditional treatments, along with additional massage or sauna and bathing facilities, do not attract significant new patronage, endangering many resorts to reach the decline stage.

Decline

Public-sector health treatments – products that are financed by public-sector health insurance and dependant on patients being sent to them rather then self-paying. In the wake of an overwhelming private-sector competition, the 'patients-only' institutions will mostly vanish, unless they are reinvented.

Isolated facilities – old-fashioned, typically small facilities offering only one isolated product such as the simple sauna or solarium. Neither the atmosphere nor the scope of services is attractive any more to a broad customer base. In the case of solariums there is the additional issue of health risks. The awareness of adverse effects has already surpassed the vanity-driven aspect of a good-looking tan. While it is likely that a certain customer base will remain on board, the market is already shrinking.

REFERENCES

Bodens, C. (2003) *Kritische analyse der gesellschaftlichen hintergründe des wellnesstrends und die reaktionen des Deutschen tourismusmarktes*. Eigenverlag FTM e.V, Trier, Germany.
Calvert, R.N. (2002) *The History of Massage*. Healing Arts Press, Rochester, Vermont.

Clark, A.D. (2008) The new frontier of wellness. *Benefits Quarterly*. Second quarter, pp. 23–28.

Cohen, M. (2008) Spas, wellness and human evolution. In: Cohen, M. and Bodeker, G. (eds) *Understanding the Global Spa Industry: Spa Management*. Butterworth-Heinemann, Oxford, pp. 3–25.

Doktor-Eisenbarth-Schule Oberviechtach (2009) *Johann Andreas Eisenbarth*. [Internet] Oberviechtach, DESO. URL available at: <http://www.vsovi.de/eisbiogr.htm>.

German Wellness Association (2008) Deutscher wellness verband. [Internet] Düsseldorf, DWV. URL available at: <http://www.wellnessverband.de/medical/index.php>.

Gray, W.S. and Liguori, S.C. (1994) *Hotel and Motel Management and Operations*, 3rd edn. Prentice-Hall, Englewood Cliffs, New Jersey.

Hamm, I. (2008) Preface. In: Hamm, I., Seitz, H. and Werding, M. (eds) *Demographic Change in Germany*. Springer, Berlin, pp. V–VIII.

Hannam, K. (2008) Ayurvedic health tourism in Kerala, India. In: Smith, M. and Puczkó, L. (eds) *Health and Wellness Tourism*. Butterworth-Heinemann, Oxford, pp. 341–344.

Health Promotion Agency (2009) What is health promotion? [Internet] Northern Ireland, HPA. URL available at: <http://www.healthpromotionagency.org.uk/Healthpromotion/Health/section2.htm>.

Höhn, C., Mai, R. and Micheel, F. (2008) Demographic change in Germany. In: Hamm, I., Seitz, H. and Werding, M. (eds) *Demographic Change in Germany*. Springer, Berlin, pp. 9–33.

Horx, M. and Wenzel, E. (2003) Trend report – Die 11 wichtigsten driving forces des kommenden wandels. [Internet] Kelkheim, Zukunftsinstitut GmbH. URL available at: <http://www.zukunftsinstitut.de/verlag/zukunftsdatenbank_download.php?aktion=download&datei=tr2004_selfness.pdf>.

Howard, G. and Vincent, G. (2008) Product development. In: Cohen, M. and Bodeker, G. (eds) *Understanding the Global Spa Industry: Spa Management*. Butterworth-Heinemann, Oxford, pp. 221–236.

Interwellness (2009) Sauna. [Internet] Eckental, Interwellness GmbH. URL available at: <http://www.interwellness.de/gmbh/content/sauna/sauna_main.htm>.

Keidel Mineral-Thermalbad Freiburg (2008a) Daten MTF. Freiburg, KMTF management document.

Keidel Mineral-Thermalbad Freiburg (2008b) Besucherzahlen im Eugen Keidel Bad. Freiburg, KMTF management document.

Keidel Mineral-Thermalbad Freiburg (2008c) Bericht zur Aufsichtsratssitzung der Freiburger Kommunalbauten GmbH Baugesellschaft & Co. KG. Freiburg, KMTF management document.

Keidel Mineral-Thermalbad Freiburg (2009) Keidel Mineral-Thermalbad Freiburg. [Internet] Freiburg, KMTF. URL available at: <http://www.keidel-bad.de>.

Klick, J. and Stratmann, T. (2008) Do spa visits improve health: evidence from German micro data. *Eastern Economic Journal* 34, 364–374.

Ludwig, E. (2007) The future of leisure travel. In: Conrady, R. and Buck, M. (eds) *Trends and Issues in Global Tourism 2007*. Springer, Berlin, pp. 227–235.

New South Wales Department of Health (2009) NSW health factsheet: solarium safety. [Internet] Sydney, NSWDoH. URL available at: <http://www.health.nsw.gov.au/factsheets/general/solarium.html>.

Pilzer, P.Z. (2007) *The New Wellness Revolution*, 2nd edn. Wiley, Hoboken, New Jersey.

Remedios (2008) Built environment-spa design. In: Cohen, M. and Bodeker, G. (eds) *Understanding the Global Spa Industry: Spa Management*. Butterworth-Heinemann, Oxford, pp. 281–295.

Smith, M. and Puczkó, L. (2009) *Health and Wellness Tourism*. Butterworth-Heinemann, Oxford.

Tabbachi, M. (2008) American and European spa. In: Cohen, M. and Bodeker, G. (eds) *Understanding the Global Spa Industry: Spa Management*. Butterworth-Heinemann, Oxford, pp 26–40.

World Health Organization (1946) Constitution of the World Health Organization. [Internet] Geneva, WHO. URL available at: <http://www.searo.who.int/LinkFiles/About_SEARO_const.pdf>.

chapter 19

Adult Entertainment

Penelope Griffiths

Entertainment that is intended to arouse sexual desire amongst audience members.

Sex has been depicted from humankind's earliest times from cave drawings to the more recent written word, painting, sculpture, photography, theatre, film-making; but in the last decade digital formats and Internet distribution have catapulted adult entertainment into a global phenomenon, with 'sex' becoming the most searched for word on the Internet during the 1990s. The desire to know, see and hear more about sex has resulted in adult entertainment becoming very big business, according to Ropelato (2009) a new pornographic video is being produced in the USA every 39 min. China, South Korea, Japan and the USA generate between them 80% of global adult entertainment industry revenue.

Adult entertainment is not 'any' type of entertainment that is aimed at adults, it is solely entertainment that is intended to impart emotions related to arousal and sexual desire, including adoration, bliss, lust, love and infatuation. This is achieved predominantly via visual and touch stimulation, but can include stimulation via all five senses. This chapter will examine the various forms of adult entertainment and the limitations surrounding moral and cultural differences that these businesses face, with particular attention to historic, legal and technological changes that have occurred over the last century.

Adult entertainment is synonymous with prostitution, pornography and erotica. From the less salubrious, and socially accepted form of 'lighter' adult entertainment, which is enjoyed by singles, couples, hen parties, stag parties, by both sexes for both sexes, straight or gay, to the seemingly 'seedier' side of adult entertainment that addresses recreational sexual desire.

It is much mooted that prostitution is the oldest profession. This may have emulated from early traditional male activity such as hunting or food gathering as a means of survival, for which the female offered services such as the cooking of food found or sexual favours in return for a share of the food. This could have been the basis of human society and bartering, pre-dating formal marriage ceremonies. Prostitution was an acceptable and important service in many ancient societies including Greek and Roman, but it was not until the Victorian era when pornography was found on ancient artefacts by archaeologists that laws were put in place to protect the morals of society.

SEXUAL REVOLUTION OF THE 20TH AND 21ST CENTURIES

Socio-cultural change and sexual revolution occurred in 'Western' societies in the 20th century at a pace never seen before. Table 19.1 provides a timeline of historic significant events.

Table 19.1. Significant events in the 'sexual revolution' of the 20th and 21st centuries.

Decade	Significant events in the 'sexual revolution'
1900s	• Soft porn peep shows had already been around for up to 50 years, but now flickers and movies were being shown in private booths passed down from the previous century when viewing camera obscura was furtive male populist activity. This was observing images in isolation under a cover in a little box (Donlon, 2002). • First wave of feminism – fighting to vote.
1910s	• The First World War meant that there were more women working in 'men's jobs', and coping without having men around. • US troops suffered high levels of sexually transmitted diseases (STDs) due to prohibition in use of condoms. This was reversed, and use was actively encouraged over the next 2 decades. • Burlesque and striptease shows replaced vaudeville shows; French and American shows were the most popular (see Fig. 19.1).
1920s	• In 1920, women were granted the right to vote in the USA; from 1928 all women and working-class men were allowed to vote in the UK. • In 1921, Marie Stopes opened her first family planning clinic in London. • Music, dancing the Charleston, music halls and tea dances were very popular bringing young singles into close social contact.

(Continued)

Table 19.1. Continued.

Decade	Significant events in the 'sexual revolution'
1930s	• The Great Depression brought a need for lighter entertainment to escape the economic gloom. • The outbreak of the Second World War meant that men were taken away again and women went back out to work in 'men's' jobs. • The Big Band era played early jazz, while vaudeville shows and theatre gave way to cinema, and peep shows and burlesque's popularity began to wane with fewer male audiences around. • The 'red light district' in Soho, London, became very popular with artisans and creatives. • The Windmill Theatre sign declared 'we never close' and was the first stage in the UK to feature still nudity live on stage – but standing still because artists were not allowed to move. • Marie Stopes' women's clinics began distributing latex condoms with sex and health advice, all given out freely.
1940s	• The Second World War continued until 1945, meaning that there were more independent women. • Crooning male singers developed adoring female fanbases. • Poster pin-ups of glamour girls became popular, as did men's magazines featuring actresses like 'bad-girl' Marlene Dietrich. • In 1948, the UN said all women were to be given voting rights.
1950s	• Rock and roll and fashion-conscious rebellious youth culture arrived and has remained ever since. Elvis Presley made women faint, rhythm and blues and soul music was very sensual, and dancing became popular as the nearest thing to sex that people could do with their clothes on. Jiving often meant that skirts flew up displaying underwear to all. • *Playboy* magazine was launched with Marilyn Monroe on the front cover (see case study). • Television began to be commercially available in time to document the teenage uprising that was happening. • The successful saucy *Carry On* films began in 1958 and three were made in rapid succession.
1960s	• Another 15 *Carry On* films were made. • Here began the 'hippy' era of promiscuous 'free love' and sex out of marriage.

(Continued)

Table 19.1. Continued.

Decade	Significant events in the 'sexual revolution'
	• Miniskirts and hot pants were all the rage on the fashion scene, exposing more leg and thigh than females had ever shown before.
	• The contraceptive pill was made available to women free from doctors or family planning clinics, making promiscuity an option without having to wear prophylactic contraception, but this only fuelled the rise of sexually transmitted diseases.
	• There was a growth of sex shop chains, and bars with private peep show booths showing films that were paid for with tokens (each token would open the 'peep-hole' for a minute or two. Some had circular stages with booths around and the customer could request the live model to do some act, or even to fondle the model.
	• Drugs including acid and cannabis were not yet wholly illegal, and their usage was common. Drug-fuelled parties were held to the musical backdrop of Jimi Hendrix, The Rolling Stones, The Doors and The Beatles to name a few.
	• Second wave of feminism – fighting for equal rights and equal pay.
	• Jackie Collins's first novel *The World is Full of Married Men* was released in 1968, and subsequently banned in several countries including Australia and South Africa. Sales of it boomed in the UK and the USA.
	• In 1969, Denmark became the first country in the world to legalize hard-core pornography, and *The Sun* newspaper featured its first scantily clad 'Page 3' girl – Ulla Lindstrom.
1970s	• In 1970, *The Sun* featured its first fully nude 'Page 3' girl, Stephanie Rahn, who posed in a side profile with one exposed breast, this lead the way for 'topless' photo shoots to become the 'Page 3' norm in some tabloid newspapers.
	• Another 12 *Carry On* movies were released over the 1970s.
	• *Playboy* opened a string of clubs, and Hugh Hefner opened the Playboy Mansion.
	• Club 18–30 – a tour operator that targeted young British singles for holidays in the Mediterranean with a mantra of sun, sand, sea and sex was formed.
	• XXX-rated movie theatres began to open in the USA; famous releases included *Deep Throat* (1972) and *Debbie Does Dallas* (1978) as well as the French *Emmanuelle* films, starring Sylvia Kristel.
	• Literature-wise *The Joy of Sex* by Dr Alex Comfort was published in 1972 and took the world by storm, selling over 18 million copies.
	• Due to the tabloid press, celebrity sex antics become notorious; gay and straight.

(Continued)

Table 19.1. Continued.

Decade	Significant events in the 'sexual revolution'
1980s	• Pornographic 'video-nasties' and XXX films begin to appear for home viewing on video cassette recorders, a format perfect for porn due to the privacy enabled by viewing at home. While this proved to be a thriving industry in the USA as well as several European countries, in the UK censorship legislation lead to the illegalization of supplying XXX films, cutting the supply chain. The R18 certificate was later introduced to allow the supply of some pornographic films by licensed retailers.
	• Sales parties of sex products (typically underwear, costumes and marital aids) in the home of consumers began, with Ann Summers parties becoming popular among 'housewives'.
	• Samantha Fox, Linda Lusardi and Maria Whittaker – all 'Page 3' girls became household names in the UK and beyond.
	• 'Swingers' parties became reasonably commonplace in suburbia.
	• The commercially acceptable face of striptease 'kiss-o-grams' were booked for office and private parties.
	• The 'Chippendales' male strippers were founded in Los Angeles.
	• Premium rate 'phone sex' telephone lines began to appear.
	• The rise in cases of anti-immune deficiency syndrome (AIDS) came like a cold bucket of water over a very promiscuous society, and this was a decade to reconsider sexual practices. Condom companies attempted to make sex safer and more fun by diversifying their product range to include colours and flavours, and made available in vending machines in public toilets.
1990s	• Professional touring: strip and exotic dance troupes, attracted large audiences to mainstream venues.
	• The development of the rave scene, and its subsequent export to Ibiza, made the island a hedonistic resort for adult partygoers.
	• More risqué clubs opened for fetish nights including Torture Garden in London.
	• Implants of silicone or botox became the norm for porn stars and celebrities.
	• The popular television series *Sex and the City* began in 1998; it promoted sexual practices and promiscuity and female empowerment among its female cast members.
	• The Internet challenged all established rules and laws around pornography and censorship, allowing easy access to hard-core pornography to global audiences, either directly through web sites, or through peer-to-peer file-sharing networks. Sex became the most searched for word online.

(Continued)

Table 19.1. Continued.

Decade	Significant events in the 'sexual revolution'
2000s	• The dark side of the Internet is exposed as a trading ground for paedophilia and other illegal materials. Several international 'sting' operations convict thousands of paedophiles globally. • In 2000, the gay age of consent was brought in line with that of heterosexuals in the UK (16). • In 2003, the term 'dogging' entered the British language after a report by the BBC exposed a growing trend for people to have sex in public places (often cars) in a way that would provide impromptu adult entertainment for audiences. This term and craze has now become an international phenomenon thanks largely to the Internet. • In 2005, gay weddings became legal in the UK. • There was a revival of Burlesque, with Dita Von Tease becoming internationally renowned. • Mobile technologies with video cameras made amateur do-it-yourself (DIY) and homemade porn films and web sites popular. • The Internet dominates as the single largest source of pornography for audience consumption.

Fig. 19.1. The Moulin Rouge, Paris, France – a legendary adult entertainment showcase venue.

The three sub-sectors within the adult entertainment sector are erotica, pornography and prostitution; these are highlighted in Fig. 19.2. These terms are widely debated and often used with negative connotation as they are considered by many to be exploitative and derogatory, usually depicting women in demeaning sexual poses or scenarios. In order to legitimately explore what range of adult entertainment exists, an attempt to clarify key terminology is pertinent.

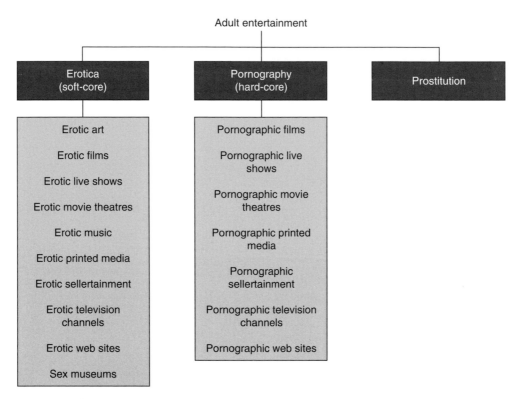

Fig. 19.2. Adult entertainment sub-sectors.

EROTICA

This is considered a 'soft' and a lesser offensive term than pornography or prostitution. Erotica can still involve sexually explicit material but often with higher artistic aspiration (see Table 19.2).

Table 19.2. Key areas of erotica and descriptions.

Erotic Entertainment	Description
Erotic art	Erotic art nude paintings and statues have been hidden and exposed over the centuries when various leaders argued about whether they were pornography or art. Today we are experiencing a much more liberal society that recognizes the right to being exposed to images of the naked body and sex is on National Curriculum in UK schools
Erotic films	Films with a high degree of nudity, and sexual scenes that do not graphically portray sex acts, rather leaving it to the imagination of the audience. These can be viewed on DVD, television, online and at erotic cinemas
Erotic live shows	Live erotic dance shows in clubs (see Fig. 19.3) have grown in popularity, particularly in the last 30 years, of particular popularity are traditional strip shows where the performer undresses and dances to music either as a staged show or a strip-o-gram; lap-dancing shows, where a dancer will provide a private dance in a booth for a fee; and pole dancing where performers (typically female) in various states of undress (or indeed nude) perform acts of strength, athleticism and agility on a metal pole akin to a fire station pole
Erotic movie theatres	Movie theatres that specialize in the showing of erotic films
Erotic music	Music that includes references to, or audio of, sexual activity. Examples include: '*Je t'aime…moi non plus*' by Serge Gainsbourg and Jane Birkin; '*Kiss Kiss Kiss*' by Yoko Ono; and '*She Swallowed It*' by NWA
Erotic printed media	The publishing of erotic printed media is a multimillion pound industry, featuring books, magazines, photographs, calendars, posters and leaflets (to name but a few), sold in sex shops, erotic boutiques, through mail order and on 'top shelves' in news agents Vatsyayana's *Kama Sutra* is one of the most well-known erotic publications, which was designed as an informative volume to young nobility, to seek pleasure and fulfilment at various stages of their lives, including a healthy sex life for singles and married people, to make a loving union stronger through skilful and varied love-making. D.H. Lawrence's 1928 novel *Lady Chatterley's Lover* is an example of a literary classic that divided opinion about whether it is erotica and/or pornography. The sexual encounters were fractional but central to the plot; the story

(Continued)

Table 19.2. Continued.

Erotic Entertainment	Description
	building a relationship between two unlikely partners, from different social classes was just as shocking
	Erotic magazines often contain a combination of erotic stories and photographs of nudity. Some magazines are almost wholly erotically themed, such as *Bizarre*, and some contain erotic articles and photographs among other content, particularly 'lads mags' such as *Nuts*, *Zoo* and *Loaded*, and *Cosmopolitan*, which is targeted towards a female audience
Erotic sellertainment	This typically involves trade shows and conferences such as 'Erotica', which is held at Olympia in London annually, and is attended by thousands of customers as well as industry delegates looking for new products or industry contacts. Similarly, the AVN Expo in Las Vegas is a major annual event for the sex industry in the USA, where over 250 exhibitors gather to show their latest films and sex products to over 30,000 visitors (AVN, 2009)
Erotic television channels	Specialist subscription-based channels, usually broadcast via satellite or cable, which show erotic films, often with semi-clad or nude presenters
Erotic web sites	There are thousands of pages of erotic literature online, some written by amateurs, and others on wholly erotic web sites with accompanying photographs and video. Erotic web sites are not as 'hard-core' as pornographic web sites, which concentrate more on a hard-core graphical and video content
Sex museums	Museums with an educational and informative content around sex, often with highly artistic and novel exhibits. The sex museum 'Venustemple' in Amsterdam has grown and welcomes more visitors than ever before. In 2008, the Amoura sex museum in London opened, a modern high-tech experience based upon learning about sex rather than just observing. The success of Amoura has lead to a travelling version of the museum going on tour around Britain from April 2009. Amongst the staff there are medical and academic experts on hand to give gravitas to the educational element of the museum.
	In Brighton, UK, a small sex art gallery called 'Impure Art' opened in 2008 to display erotic art, including the body castings of intimate genitalia in various forms of sexual arousal by Jamie McCartney (see Fig. 19.4), the most memorable piece being a clear glass like casting of the interior of a vagina – something one never sees

Fig. 19.3. Erotic dancers.

PORNOGRAPHY

Pornography comes from the Greek word *pornai*, which was a term used to describe in literature the 'lowest' form of ancient Greek prostitute. Pornography literally means to write about women selling sex. The written word being the earliest form of descriptive text which would only have been readable by the learned and elite, who then felt responsible to protect the poorer classes and more vulnerable. The usage of the term pornography is further removed from actual prostitution in modern times to more specifically mean sexually explicit material with the intention of causing sexual arousal for the audience, be they a viewer, consumer or reader.

The areas that make up the pornography sub-sector are pornographic films, pornographic live shows, pornographic movie theatres, pornographic printed media, pornographic sellertainment, pornographic television channels and pornographic web sites. They are the same as their erotic counterparts, except that their content is 'hard-core', sexually explicit and graphic in detail. It can portray (but is not limited to) explicit genital contact or penetration, sado-masochistic (S&M) scenes of bondage, various fetishes (unusual and kinky sex) and many more niche and risqué tastes.

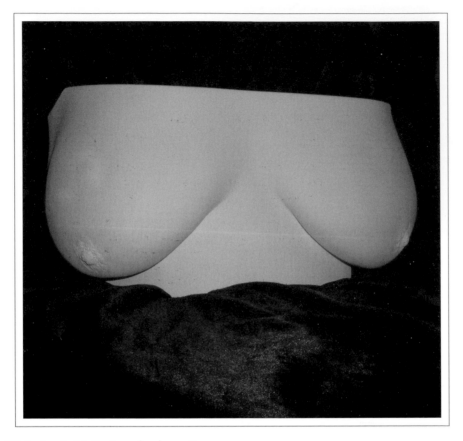

Fig. 19.4. Jamie McCartney body casting.

Case Study: Playboy Enterprises Inc. (PEI)

PEI originates from 1953 when Hugh Hefner founded *Playboy* magazine in 1953. The company was set up to fill a perceived gap in the porn publication industry with a glossy magazine to appeal to respectable businessmen. Hefner wished to demonstrate that 'nice girls had sex too' and aimed to remove the negative 'dirty mag' image that porn had previously had. Hefner's first edition featured a naked calendar pin-up of starlet Marilyn Monroe, taken in 1949 before she was famous, which made her the first 'Playboy Playmate'. Playboy has continued to introduce new stars as well as attract top models, singers and actresses to pose either scantily clad or tastefully nude – such is the kudos for appearing in the magazine. PEI is still the most recognized porn brand, with the *Playboy* rabbit (bunny) head image being the most recognized porn industry logo the world over. Some key dates in *Playboy*'s history are featured below.

The *Playboy* brand is responsible for a broad range of products and services, from magazines and merchandise to multimedia entertainment and technical facilities and

(Continued)

Case Study: Continued.

services. The product with most longevity and success is the magazine itself, which is the biggest-selling magazine in the world; although this is now seeing sales figures fall. This may be partially due to easier access online options, which PEI have themselves embraced so as to remain at the forefront of the global porn industry.

Today PEI has four divisions; these are as follows: Playboy Publishing Group – this oversees operations largely relating to *Playboy* printed media publications; Playboy Entertainment Group – this oversees operations relating to *Playboy* broadcast media and online operations; Playboy Licensing Group – this deals with the use of he *Playboy* logo and trademark on merchandise such as clothing, games and toys; and *Playboy* on-campus – a network of Playboy representatives on College Campuses across the USA who perform both marketing and market research activities among students.

Playboy has grown from one magazine title to an entertainment empire, almost bringing its brand into the mainstream through the use of the iconic *Playboy* logo. *Playboy* is set to further its entertainment operations by seeking to open up new clubs in a number of locations globally, including Macau. The significant events of Playboy Enterprises, Inc. are provided in Table 19.3.

Case study based upon Playboy Enterprises Inc. (2009) and *NYT* (2009).

Table 19.3. Significant events in the history of Playboy Enterprises, Inc.

Year	Event
1953	*Playboy* magazine was launched by Hugh Hefner's self-titled HMH Publishing Company. Hefner was editor and chief of the publication, including content sourcing, production and promotion. The first edition was not numbered in case there was not a second. It soon sold out with a cover price of US$0.50
1960	*Playboy* opened the first of what was to become 40 Playboy club premises featuring Playgirl Bunny waitresses
1965	The Playboy Foundation was formed to support and campaign for health and reproductive rights, sexual awareness, women's rights, children's rights and many other causes
1969	One in every four American college boys bought *Playboy* monthly
1971	Hefner bought a gothic mansion which he named Shangri-la, also known as the Playboy Mansion, an opulent and luxurious setting in which to live out the lifestyle his magazine promoted. He welcomed the rich and famous into the mansion to party in private with the resident Playmates
1972	*Playboy*'s circulation peaked at over 7.1 million copies worldwide The company published *Oui* magazine

(Continued)

Table 19.3. Continued.

Year	Event
1979	The Hugh M. Hefner First Amendment Award was established to honour those who have championed freedom of speech and freedom of the press in the USA
1981	*Oui* magazine was published for the last time
1982	The Playboy Channel for television was launched in the USA
1995	The Playboy channel was launched in Japan
1996	Cisneros formed a partnership with Playboy TV to launch adult TV to Latin America
1997	Playboy TV was launched in Scandinavia with ViaSat
	Playboy TV became available 24/7 in the USA
2000	Playboy TV was launched in Benelux
2001	A worldwide deal was struck with Playboy TV in conjunction with Indigo Entertainment offering the world's first interactive erotic full length feature film *Fast Lane To Malibu* to be available on TV-VOD (video on demand) and video/DVD for movies
2002	Playboy Radio first went on air via XM Satellite Radio
2004	Playboy TV was launched in Germany
2003	A 50th-anniversary special edition of *Playboy* was released
2006	'Flava Flav' of rap group 'Public Enemy' became Playboy's first ever celebrity photographer
	SIRIUS Satellite Radio re-launched Playboy Radio with more programmes than ever before
	The first Playboy Concept Boutique opened in Tokyo, Japan and was named as one of the world's Top 40 stores by Retail Leaders Association
2009	New club venture was opened in Las Vegas

PROSTITUTION

Prostitution is a service-based agreement involving offer and acceptance of money or goods in exchange for services of a sexual nature. The earliest use of the word 'prostitute' referred to a woman who was neither married nor a widow, and there was no other term available. Most references imply that the female is the provider of the service and the male is the receiver or consumer of the service. In more modern times, this sexual service could also occur if the gender roles were reversed as is increasingly prevalent in society today where women have more independence and increased disposable income, there is also a significant market in same-sex gay prostitution. In economic terms, prostitution is a result of supply and demand, addressing the needs and wants of both parties. The prostitute is earning a living and the service receiver is relieved of his or her sexual frustration and release, but ethically the selling or renting of a human body for sexual gratification is widely disputed.

Prostitutes can work alone, selling sexual services on the streets, from their homes or a hotel room. They control their client list, diary and keep all the proceeds, which is typically undeclared income in terms of tax-avoidance. Contact services are when there is a third party between the customer and the prostitute, e.g. an agency, pimp or 'madam'. There are darker types of prostitution where people are groomed for the role, and this is often the case when vulnerable young girls are desperate, e.g. homeless girls living 'rough' on the streets, or girls needing money to supplement a drug habit or alcohol dependency. Human trafficking and child prostitution are often run by organized criminals, where the girls are tricked into a situation, e.g. promise of legitimate work abroad, and are then enslaved with no choice other than to do as they are told or be punished. This exploitative illegal form of prostitution is not a part of the legitimate entertainment industry.

Escort agencies operate within the law by offering legitimate companionship, through escorts or dating services. These never openly advertise sexual services, and indeed there are many escorts who purport to just date, without hidden extras. The client books an escort by contacting the agency via telephone or online from advertisements in newspapers, magazines and web sites. The agency arranges for the escort to meet the client at an agreed destination. This can be to accompany the client to a specific business function, theatre trip, dinner or hotel room, but the hourly rate for company is paid directly to the agency in advance. 'Extra service' or time is to be agreed with the escort herself, by private agreement. The escort will negotiate terms and rates directly and keep the proceeds.

Premium rate chat lines also put clients in touch with men and women for phone flirting or phone sex, but the call costs are very high; agencies sometimes use these services for agreements to meet in between customer and worker. The Internet also serves as a marketplace whereby client and service provider can 'meet' either in typed 'chat' form or with the use of webcams, and customers can pay with credit cards to watch live performances tailored to their requirements.

Legal Factor: the Law and Prostitution

Laws concerning prostitution vary from country to country; some examples of these are contained below, but this is by no means a definitive list.

Australia

Prostitution is legal in Australia, although street prostitution is illegal in some states, and restricted to certain areas in others. Legalized brothels that are licensed and bound by state rules on their size and number of employees operate throughout Australia. Sex workers are also bound by rules making them take regular health checks.

(Continued)

Legal Factor: Continued

England and Wales

Paying for sex is in itself not a crime, but 'under the Sexual Offences Act 2003, it is an offence to cause or incite prostitution or control it for personal gain' (Casciani, 2008). Therefore, to advertise sexual services is illegal, which results in escort services or models placing adverts (that do not strictly state that sex is what is being offered) in newspapers, and shop windows in salubrious parts of towns, as well as placing 'tart cards' in telephone boxes, even though adverts placed in phone boxes have been banned since 2001 (Casciani, 2008). Laws soon to be introduced will also make kerb-crawling (driving slowly through 'red-light' districts) and buying sex from women who have been 'trafficked' illegal.

The Netherlands

The Netherlands has been known as a sex tourism destination for decades, attracting millions of visitors because of the relaxed cannabis laws and cafe culture. The notorious 54 windows in the canal lines streets and surrounding red light district house 20,000 legal prostitutes. However, recent decades have seen influxes of immigrants from Latin, Asian and Eastern European countries, which has brought tensions between organized crime gangs. Hostile violent incidents and atmospheres pervade the streets causing the Mayor of Amsterdam, Job Cohen, to set up a cleaning up campaign that will see half the coffee shops and windows closed by 2014 (Reed, 2009).

New Zealand

The Prostitution Reform Act 2003 made adult prostitution and brothels completely legal throughout New Zealand. There are tough rules on brothels, including restricting locations, restricting signage, and health and safety requirements include making sex workers use condoms.

Sweden

In Sweden, a decade ago the onus of the law changed. It became legal to sell sex but illegal to buy it. The intention was to reduce the demand for sexual services, combined with actually offering lifestyle alternatives via retraining opportunities to sexual workers, thereby reducing the supply and demand. There have been no official follow up reports or statistics yet but other nations including Finland are considering adopting this model.

The USA

Prostitution is illegal in every state apart from Nevada and Rhode Island. In Nevada, prostitution is legal only in licensed brothels in counties with less than 400,000 residents; this includes the 'Moonlite BunnyRanch', which opened in 1955, and has become famous through the HBO *Cathouse* television series. In Rhode Island, prostitution is only legal in the home of the prostitute.

> **Ethical and Legal Factor: Sex Tourism**
>
> Either independently or through arranged tours, people visit countries where the laws maybe more relaxed, or non-existent, in order to allow the tourist to observe the practice openly, or to indulge in their sexual preferences freely. This maybe as an observer of street culture; attending live shows; legally hiring sexual workers, e.g. Amsterdam; or for travelling to areas where the age of consent is lower than allowed in the tourists home country, enabling legal sex with someone who is technically a minor, e.g. Bulgaria and Estonia at 14 (Avert, 2009). The hosts of such countries often turn a blind eye to the sex trade due to the valuable economic impact that sex tourism brings.

THE FUTURE

As times change, so do cultural values and norms; what was wholly unacceptable and indeed illegal some years ago, may now be considered to be tolerable or even standard. With these changes, adult entertainment, and particularly pornography, has gradually become more accepted within some societies. There are, of course, wide-ranging variation in laws and rules upon this, and while globally adult entertainment is more accepted as a legitimate entertainment industry sector, it is still considered too taboo a subject in some societies for it to even be discussed from an analytical or academic perspective.

The impact of technology has made pornography available globally, and given it a level of exposure that it has never before seen, this in itself presents challenges to governments and policy makers, who may wish for a greater degree of regulation, but at the same time do not want to be seen as creating a 'nanny-state'. The immediate future for some areas of the adult entertainment sector is considered in Fig. 19.5.

Introduction

Streaming and live porn for mobile phones – advances in technology, coupled with demand will result in pornographic movies being compressed and streamed to mobile phones and other portable media devices. It is entirely probable that streaming media players will be developed specifically for the mobile porn market. Live 'video call' porn services that are either subscription-based or pay-per-minute via camera phones will also appear with advances in video call and display technology.

Growth

Amateur pornographic media hosting online – the rise in popularity of YouTube, where users' own video content can be uploaded for a global audiences appreciation, has caused a host of similar web sites to appear, some specializing only in pornographic content, an example

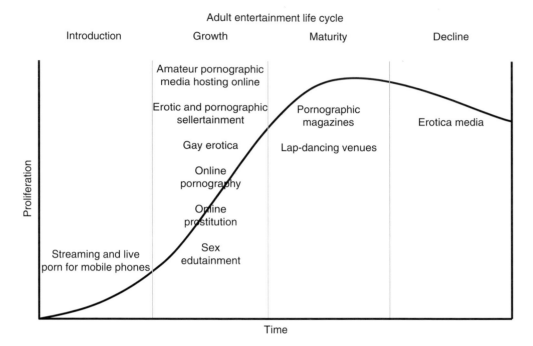

Fig. 19.5. The adult entertainment life cycle.

being YouPorn, with technology becoming increasingly accessible, these types of amateur porn hosting web site will increase in number. This may make those sites that charge to access their content reconsider how they do business.

Erotic and pornographic sellertainment – sex sells, and with an increasingly open attitude towards sex, its use in advertising will continue to grow. While this will predominantly be mild erotica, there will be a rise in professionally made hard-core porn adverts, predominantly for Web usage. Adult entertainment conventions, trade shows and conferences will continue to grow in popularity, and become more commonplace.

Gay erotica – changing attitudes towards homosexuality globally will lead to an increase in gay erotica in the media so that its integration into mainstream entertainment becomes more commonplace.

Online pornography – this will continue to grow in popularity for the foreseeable future, although the millions of hours of online pornographic content will make this a difficult marketplace to profit from.

Online prostitution – the use of the Internet to meet, vet and charge clients in advance will lead to an increase in online prostitution, as agencies go online, and prostitutes 'work from home'.

Sex edutainment – a combination of sex education from both a health and a voyeurs' perspective will lead to an increase in sex being a feature of public art works, and to institutions such as sex museums becoming much more commonplace. High-profile institutions such as 'The National Sex Museum' may be less than a decade away.

Maturity

Pornographic magazines – the continued growth of online pornography will make magazines peak, before going into decline, or being seen as 'high-end' luxury items.

Lap-dancing venues – these have grown rapidly in number, but in many cases beyond their demand, leading to saturation in many urban areas and the subsequent closure of venues. The current global financial situation also means that the disposable income to 'enjoy' such venues may not be as forthcoming among potential audience members; see Fig. 19.6.

Decline

Brothels and massage parlours – as physical entertainment venues these are already declining as more prostitutes utilize technology such as mobile phones and the Internet in order to manage themselves, their workloads and their financial gain.

Erotica media – the popularity of pornography has lead to audiences wanting to 'push' the boundaries, and for many, erotic media simply is not enough anymore.

Fig. 19.6. The outside of a lap-dancing venue.

REFERENCES

Adult Video News (AVN) (2008) AVN adult entertainment expo. [Internet] San Fernando Valley, AVN. URL available at: <http://show.adultentertainmentexpo.com/adult-expo/v42/index.cvn>.

Avert (2009) Worldwide ages of consent. Horsham, Avert. URL available at: <http://www.avert.org/aofconsent.htm>.

Casciani, D. (2008) Q&A UK prostitution laws. [Internet] London, BBC. URL available at: <http://news.bbc.co.uk/1/hi/uk/7736436.stm>.

Donlon, J.G. Dr (2002) Peep shows. [Internet] San Francisco, Bnet. URL available at: <http://findarticles.com/p/articles/mi_g1epc/is_tov/ai_2419100937>.

New York Times (*NYT*) (2009) Playboy Enterprises Inc. [Internet] New York, New York Times. URL available at: <http://topics.nytimes.com/top/news/business/companies/playboy-enterprises-inc/index.html>.

Playboy Enterprises Inc. (2009) Corporate overview. [Internet] Chicago, PEI. URL available at: <http://www.playboyenterprises.com/home/content.cfm?content = t_template&packet = 00077802-06C6-1C74-8FEA8304E50A010D&artTypeID = 000A2BE7-0596-1C74-8FEA8304E50A010D>.

Reid, J. (2009) Amsterdam plans 'cannabis clean up'. London, BBC. URL available at: <http://news.bbc.co.uk/newsbeat/hi/the_p_word/newsid_7857000/7857533.stm>.

Ropelato, J. (2009) Internet pornography statistics. [Internet] Top Tenreviews Inc. URL available at: <http://internet-filter-review.toptenreviews.com/internet-pornography-statistics.html>.

About the Authors

Having now reached this stage in the book, you will note how completely diverse the global entertainment industry is. It is doubtful that anybody could truly claim to be an expert in so many of these areas, which is why this book was put together with the help of a team of experts in their fields. Without their assistance and contributions this book would not be able to present such a thorough and in-depth view of so many diverse areas of the entertainment industry and I thank each and every one of them for their contributions.

My own personal and vocational background is extremely varied and includes hotel management, mobile telecommunications customer services, cable television human resources, theme park and museum marketing, music festival and event stewarding, nightclub doorman, nightclub promotion, Web design, bar manager, pub landlord, author, photographer and short-film maker. Prior to becoming an academic, I spent much of my life travelling, and have worked upon three continents. I am currently a Senior Lecturer and Teacher Fellow at Leeds Metropolitan University where I am also the course leader for the BA (Honours) Entertainment Management programme, upon which I champion innovative assessment, and develop employability skills and nurture entrepreneurship among my students. I keep a blog on entertainment industry developments, which is called 'Entertainment Planet'; it can be found at http://entplanet.blogspot.com. My own current research interests include: the impacts of technology upon all entertainment industry sectors; the relationship between music, politics and society throughout the 20th and into the 21st century, particularly in relation to youth cultures; and entrepreneurship in the cultural and creative industries.

Stuart Moss, editor and lead author
s.moss@leedsmet.ac.uk

Dr Ben Walmsley

Ben is a Senior Lecturer in Entertainment Management at Leeds Metropolitan University with a professional background in theatre producing. In 1997, he produced and directed Ionesco's *La Cantatrice Chauve* as part of the Edinburgh Fringe Festival, before moving to Paris, where he taught at the Sorbonne. He managed One World Actors Productions in Paris for two years and then moved back to the UK to manage the leading Scottish touring company Benchtours, before taking up a managerial post at the new National Theatre of Scotland. Ben is a modern languages graduate from Nottingham University and holds an MBA from the University of Surrey's School of Management. In 2000, he completed a PhD in French Theatre and Philosophy at the University of Glasgow, comparing the plays of Jean-Paul Sartre and Eugène Ionesco. His current research interests are related to the qualitative value and impact of theatre from the audience perspective. E-mail: **b.walmsley@ leedsmet.ac.uk**

Dr Stephen Henderson

Steven worked in the consulting and manufacturing sectors with blue-chip clients including Heinz, Britvic Soft Drinks, Gossard, KPMG and Yorkshire Chemical. He gained an MBA from Warwick Business School, a stepping stone to working on MBA courses for Business Schools at the Universities of Warwick, Durham, Bradford, The Open University and acting as Module Leader for International Marketing at The University of Liverpool.

A passion for music has led to Steven promoting concerts with artists such as Elvis Costello, The Clash, The Ramones, Tony Benn, Roy Bailey, Iggy Pop, Richard Thompson and Ian Dury (among others). Steven has worked for various music festivals in consultancy or director roles, and now uses this wide experience in his role as a Senior Lecturer with the UK Center for Events Management at Leeds Metropolitan University. His current research activities are around strategic or marketing issues of live performance. E-mail: **s.henderson@ leedsmet.ac.uk**

Rebekka Kill

Rebekka is a Senior Lecturer in Creativity, Enterprise and Engagement, as well as a Teacher Fellow and Enterprise Pioneer at Leeds Metropolitan University, where the majority of her teaching is in the School of Film, Television and Performing Arts. Rebekka's teaching develops a range of innovative pedagogic strategies that are student-led and focus on supporting creative, and subject-specific, outcomes and assessment strategies. Her publications span the fields of art, performance, creative enterprise, film and popular music and her writing can be found in books, journals, exhibition catalogues, on the Internet and in fanzines. Rebekka's current research foci are twofold; constructions of academic identity and interactive festival performance. E-mail: **r.kill@leedsmet.ac.uk**

Laura Taylor

Laura is currently the Course Leader for Foundation Degree Film and Television production at the Northern Film School, Leeds Metropolitan University. She teaches across the university, specializing in sound, professional practice and work-based learning. Her background is in location sound recording and she has numerous broadcast credits having worked for the BBC, Channel 5 (UK), ITV Yorkshire and The Discovery Channel, mainly on factual television programmes. She has also worked professionally in post-production sound and commercial and community radio, and has vast experience working within the educational and community sector. E-mail: **l.taylor@leedsmet.ac.uk**

James Roberts

James spent 12 years working in strategy consulting for international entertainment and media companies, latterly with Mercer Management Consulting covering television, film, music, online and packaged media sectors.

He undertook casework with a wide variety of firms including The Walt Disney Company, Warner Bros., Sony Corp, Vodafone, IBM and EMI. His television work included multiple cases for BBC, Channel 4 (UK), Rai (Italy), Canal+ (France), ABC and Viacom (USA) and Fremantle (Germany). During this time, he also advised major broadcasting regulators (e.g. Ofcom), and was called as an expert witness advising on entertainment market developments to the European Commission (2000). James has subsequently undertaken primary research into the product development activities of broadcasters and independent producers in the UK and the USA. He is currently completing his doctorate at the Institute of Communication Studies at the University of Leeds, where he also lectures on developments in the entertainment industries. E-mail: **jamesrobertshome@yahoo.co.uk**

Dr Erika Pearson

Erika is a lecturer at the Department of Media, Film and Communication at the University of Otago, New Zealand. She has a PhD in Internet Studies, and is currently working in the broad area of virtual identity, social networking, trust and mediated interpersonal networks, with a special focus on multimedia and networked identity construction. She has published a wide range of articles on Internet issues, yet still spends most of her free time lurking in cyberspace, updating her social networking profiles. E-mail: **erika.pearson@otago.ac.nz**

Dr Alexandra J. Kenyon

Alex worked in the advertising industry on both the client and agency sides. She was involved in media buying and promotional planning for accounts such as Sky TV, London Zoo and Beneficial Bank. Her interest in print and broadcasting media has continued with her research and teaching focusing on advertising and promotional activity on television, newspapers and magazines. Alexandra's professional experience of marketing and promotional activity in the entertainment, leisure and finance industry has led her to academic publications, including papers in the *Journal of Advertising Research* and *International Journal of Marketing Research*. She has written two books: *Ethics in the Alcohol Industry*; and *Services Marketing, Concepts, Strategies and Cases*. Alex is now a Senior Lecturer in the Center for Hospitality and Retailing at Leeds Metropolitan University. E-mail: **a.kenyon@ leedsmet.ac.uk**

Marc W. Etches

Marc graduated in Leisure Studies in 1983 and has spent 26 years in the UK leisure and tourism industry, with companies such as Granada Plc, First Leisure Corporation, Center Parcs (UK) Ltd and Leisure Parcs Ltd. He was managing director of Windsor Safari Park during the late 1980s, followed by 6 years with Center Parcs, a company that set new standards for domestic tourism in the UK during the 1990s. Marc turned down an offer to take up a senior position with the Walt Disney Company in Paris in 1998 to become managing director of Leisure Parcs Limited, owners of Blackpool Tower, and lead the campaign for resort casino development as a catalyst for the economic regeneration of Blackpool.

Marc is currently researching for a PhD in 'Public Policy and Gambling' at the Centre for the Study of Gambling at the University of Salford. E-mail: **marc@warrenenterprises.co.uk**

Phil Clements

Phil Clements is the Academic Director for Leeds Metropolitan University's Bhopal campus in India. Prior to this he was a Senior Lecturer in Sports Event Management at the UK Centre for Events Management (UKCEM). He has 20 years experience within the sports event industry sector in Australia. E-mail: **p.clements@leedsmetindia.in**

Nicola McCullough

Nicola is a Senior Lecturer in Sports Event Management at the UK Centre for Events Management at Leeds Metropolitan University. She has eight years experience within the sports event industry sector, including the logistics management of scheduling overseas sporting tournaments and the development of new public–private partnerships for sports clubs. She managed the development and promotion of new partnerships for several Super League rugby clubs between 2003 and 2007 alongside the Team Manager of the Great Britain Rugby League Team from 2006/07 onwards. She has vast experience of seeking sports funding opportunities and managing contracts and research projects within the public sector and alongside international sports governing bodies. She is currently working to sustain sports partnerships with the Winter Olympics in Vancouver 2010 and Sochi, Russia in 2014. E-mail: **n.l.mccullough@ leedsmet.ac.uk**

Dr Nigel D. Morpeth

Dr Nigel D. Morpeth is a Senior Lecturer in Tourism Management at Leeds Metropolitan University. He first started to research the relationship between tourism, religion and spirituality in 1996 with a conference paper delivered at the 'Tourism and Culture Conference' at Northumbria University, and more recently, in 2002 in Bonn, at an International Festivals and Events Conference. Furthermore, he co-edited a CAB International published book in 2007 entitled *Religious Tourism and Pilgrimage Management: An International Perspective*, which in part explored the blurring of boundaries between secularity and sacredness, and the range of religious spirituality globally and as an increasing dimension of tourism and the experience economy. Through his work with Entertainment Management students, he is keen through current research, to extend the linkages between entertainment, spirituality and religion as an expression of the experience economy. He has published widely in different aspects of cultural tourism and the application of sustainability to tourism. E-mail: **n.morpeth@leedsmet.ac.uk**

Volker Rundshagen

Volker worked as a travel agent in his early career before entering education in tourism management studies at Angell Academy and Business School Freiburg. He worked part-time for the Eugen-Keidel-Bad health spa in 1996/97, where he realized the importance of changing business models towards service-oriented units, catering to the needs of an entertainment-seeking clientele looking for enjoyment rather than just therapies. In 2001, he earned a Master of Arts in Tourism Management from the University of Brighton, completing a thesis on Change Management. As a lecturer at Cologne Business School, he has been teaching various health-related tourism subjects. His academic profile is completed by the part-time MBA of the University of Louisville, Kentucky, USA, awarded in 2007. E-mail: **vrundshagen@web.de**

Penelope Griffiths

Penelope Griffiths is a Senior Lecturer at Coventry University specializing in Creative Industries and Entertainment Management. Having been a pop/rock singer most of her life, she paused touring around Europe for childbirth, and to attain a BA (Honours) in Music Industry Management from Buckinghamshire New University in 2000. After five wonderful years in the Programming Department and as personal assistant to a succession of managing directors at The Stables, a 400-seater live music venue in rural Milton Keynes, she was lured out of nocturnal activity to set up the course in Creative Industries Management. Her research interests are in live music and adult entertainment. E-mail: **Penelope.griffiths@coventry.ac.uk**

INDEX